Discover Music

Discover Music

Jeremy Yudkin
Boston University

PEARSON
Prentice
Hall

Upper Saddle River, NJ 07458

Library of Congress Cataloging-in-Publication Data

Yudkin, Jeremy.
    Discover music / Jeremy Yudkin.—1st ed.
       p. cm.
    Includes bibliographical references (p.) and index.
    ISBN 0-13-091578-5
    1. Music appreciation—Textbooks. I. Title.
  MT6.Y86 D57 2003
  780—dc22

                                                   2003058015

Senior Acquisitions Editor: Christopher Johnson
Editorial Assistant: Evette Dickerson
Senior Marketing Manager: Chris Ruel
Marketing Assistant: Kimberly Daum
Managing Editor (Production): Joanne Riker
Production Editor: Randy Pettit
Permissions Supervisor: Ronald Fox
Manufacturing Buyer: Benjamin Smith
Creative Design Director: Leslie Osher
Interior Design: Laura Gardner
Cover Design: Carmen Di Bartolomeo
Cover Illustration/Photo: Tim Webb/Illustration Works
Photo Researcher: Kathy Ringrose
Image Permission Coordinator: Beth Brenzel
Manager, Print Production: Nick Sklitsis
Composition: Preparé
Printer/Binder: Courier-Westford

Credits and acknowledgments borrowed from other sources and reproduced,
with permission, in this textbook appear on page 335.

Pearson Prentice Hall™ is a trademark of Pearson Education, Inc.
Pearson® is a registered trademark of Pearson plc
Prentice Hall® is a registered trademark of Pearson Education, Inc.

Pearson Education LTD.
Pearson Education Australia PTY, Limited
Pearson Education Singapore, Pte. Ltd
Pearson Education North Asia Ltd

Pearson Education, Canada, Ltd
Pearson Educación de Mexico, S.A. de C.V.
Pearson Education–Japan
Pearson Education Malaysia, Pte. Ltd

10 9 8 7 6 5 4 3 2 1
ISBN 0-13-091578-5

To my wonderful family

CONTENTS

PREFACE

THE MAGIC OF MUSIC

We all know that music is special and has special powers. You don't need a textbook to tell you that. So what is the point of this book? It does two things. It introduces you to some wonderful music that you may not know, and it shows you how music works and *how* different pieces have the effect that they do.

Sometimes the effect of a piece of music will depend on a very simple idea, like just using a catchy rhythm; or it may depend on something a bit more sophisticated, like an unusual series of chords. We will first go through some of the basics of music so that you understand these effects. Knowing how something works helps you appreciate it more.

Then I'll share with you some of the great musical works that I have become familiar with from a lifetime of listening to music. Sharing music is something I do with my students all the time. Usually, of course, I am the one who tells them about pieces they don't know. But quite often they introduce me to some wonderful music that I hadn't known before. Sharing music is one of the great pleasures in life. When you find a piece of music in this book that you think has the *magic*, share it with someone.

Music is an ancient phenomenon: it is probably as old as language. It has even been suggested that singing developed before speech. Prehistoric humans also must have banged on hollow logs or rocks to make music. Flutes made of animal bone have been found from many thousands of years ago.

We are born with an innate sensitivity to music. Before we are born, we hear sounds and rhythms in the womb, and even the tiniest infants seem to express pleasure at the sound of music. At four months, an infant can distinguish between sounds that are consonant and those that are dissonant. And most of us have seen babies who can barely walk, rocking back and forth on their feet and clapping their hands to the sound of music.

Music is also a worldwide phenomenon. Music is an art or an activity that appears in all cultures around the world.

The greatest influence today on music around the world is that exerted by Western classical and popular music. It is this Western tradition that we shall be studying. This does not mean that other musical traditions are less valuable. There are other books that explain the fascinating music of other cultures. But our focus is on the music of Western culture. This culture is very ancient. Its roots are in the Jewish tradition, the tradition of ancient Greece and Rome, and early Christianity. More recently it has been influenced by non-religious concerns, like dancing, and expressions of love, sentiment, youthful rebellion, and sexual attraction.

So for most of this book, we will be examining music of the Western tradition, which has a rich and lengthy history. To do this, we will need a working vocabulary to describe music. We will need to learn how to listen to a piece of music intelligently. And we will need to learn about the different historical periods of Western music. For example, Gregorian chant sounds very different from a Beethoven symphony. There are historical reasons for this, which we shall examine.

But the very first part of this book is about listening and the elements of music. Listening is not the same as hearing. You can hear all kinds of sounds without listening to them. Really listening to music is an art. It takes time. And it takes commitment. You have to concentrate, just as you do when you are reading a good book.

The chapter on listening also introduces you to the elements of music. You can't read a book without knowing vocabulary and grammar. So as you learn about listening, you'll also learn about the grammar and vocabulary of music, such as what a scale is and how harmony works. After you have studied this chapter, you'll be able to hear all kinds of things in the music that you hadn't heard before, and you'll be able to describe them accurately. The rest of the book goes through all the main historical periods of Western music from the Middle Ages up to the present day and discusses some of the great musical works from those periods.

You'll end up knowing much more music than you did before. And you'll be able to talk (and think) about *all* music with more intelligence and insight. You'll have discovered the magic of music.

SPECIAL FEATURES OF *DISCOVER MUSIC*

Brief, Clear, and Accessible

Designed to be used in a semester- or quarter-long course, *Discover Music* is a lively and interesting companion for the student studying music for the first time. It is not meant to be a music encyclopedia, either in length or tone. The intent is to engage students in a meaningful discussion of music without overwhelming them with an avalanche of extraneous detail.

Focus on Listening

Discover Music stresses the importance of active listening as a vital activity. Chapter 1 introduces the basic elements of music (melody, rhythm, harmony) while simultaneously teaching the skill of active listening. Listening examples illuminate the theoretical concepts.

Listening guides to the "Overture" of Handel's *Water Music* are employed several times in the chapter to illustrate basic concepts. Students can focus on a small number of ideas at a time and can learn the art of active listening with a short, appealing work. This chapter lays a solid foundation for the students' listening activities throughout the remainder of the book. In addition, brief recorded examples called MusicNotes (listed in the text and available on the free CD that is bound into the book) immediately illustrate all the other musical phenomena discussed.

This focus on listening is maintained throughout the book. Concluding each chapter are "Listening to . . . " sections. These distill and summarize the most important stylistic characteristics of each musical era using the clear, accessible vocabulary introduced in Chapter 1. Students can *hear* the difference between Baroque and Classical music, Classical and Romantic music, etc.

Timed Listening Guides

The Listening Guides are very clear, easy to follow, and illuminating. Every important aspect of what is heard is explained, and special moments are highlighted. Each Listening Guide is supplied with exact timings and internal track numbers to identify important points within each work.

Cultural and Social Context

Throughout the book, music is presented in the context of its social and historical milieu. Parallel discussions of the other arts provide a cultural setting for the understanding of music.

Music as a Worldwide Phenomenon

The main focus of the book is on music of the European tradition, but this focus is both explained and put into context by a brief look at music as a global phenomenon. Chapter 2 a short chapter on "Music Around the World."

Contributions of Women

Throughout the book the contributions of women to the history of music, as composers, patrons, teachers, and performers, are carefully considered.

Popular Music

Popular music is treated not just as a token but as a cultural phenomenon in its own right. The history of popular music is surveyed from its beginning until the present, and due weight is given to musical, cultural, and commercial considerations.

SUPPLEMENTARY MATERIALS FOR INSTRUCTORS AND STUDENTS

Recordings and Recording Packages

Discover Music is supported by two important recording programs:

1. A *free* **Companion CD** is included with every copy of the book. This contains several of the most important pieces discussed in the text, along with all the brief illustrative MusicNotes from the opening chapters.
2. A **Complete Collection** of four CDs, available for separate purchase, contains all the remaining works analyzed in the text.

All CDs are tracked not just for the beginnings of works or movements but also at internal points, so that instructors and students can instantly find important moments within a piece.

In addition to these programs, a ***Custom Repertoire CD*** is available. With this program, instructors may design their own extra CD with repertoire that their own students will find helpful to the listening experience. (Instructors, please contact your local Prentice Hall representative for details.)

Companion Website (www.prenhall.com/yudkindiscover)

The *Discover Music* Companion Website greatly enhances students' experience. Through a variety of on-line multiple-choice and essay questions, critical listening exercises that use RealAudio™ to deliver sound and music, and links to pertinent Websites around the world, students are able to reinforce their comprehension of all important concepts in the book.

Other Resources

To facilitate the teaching and learning processes, *Discover Music* is also accompanied by an **Instructor's Resource Manual,** filled with helpful items, including chapter summaries, related readings, tests, suggested short essay topics, critical thinking exercises, and much more. Also available to the instructor are **computerized testing files,** available for both PC and Macintosh computers.

Discover Music

1
Listening: The Elements of Music

LISTENING TO MUSIC

The most important part of the musical experience is *listening*. There are many ways of listening to music. One of the most common ways is a passive kind of listening, the kind of listening we do when music is playing while we are doing something else: eating at a restaurant, talking at a party, reading a book. There is even a kind of unconscious listening, the kind we do in the supermarket or in a store, when the music creates a particular mood without our really thinking about it. These ways of listening to music should really just be called *hearing*.

In order to really *listen* to music you have to concentrate. This kind of listening is a conscious, active, *committed* kind of listening, in which we really concentrate on everything that is happening. This kind of listening takes a great deal of concentration. It also offers very special rewards.

You also have to listen to a work several *times* to appreciate what is in it. Imagine reading a Shakespeare play. The first time you read it, some of the meaning comes across, but a great deal is missed. Each new reading provides you with greater insight into the thoughts and feelings expressed, the rhythm and sound of the words, the interplay of form and meaning. The words remain the same, but your understanding of them deepens. The same is true of music. A great composition repays repeated listenings, and some of the greatest works reveal something new every time you listen to them.

This type of *active listening* is not easy at first. It takes practice. The secret of enjoying music, especially complicated and unfamiliar music, lies in two things: the quality of your concentration as you listen and your willingness to listen to a work more than once.

What Is Music?

What exactly is music? This sounds like an easy question. We all know music when we hear it. And yet, if you think about it, perhaps it's not so easy to define.

Here are various definitions of music from writers through the ages:

"Music gives soul to the universe."—Plato

"The food of love."—Shakespeare

"Heaven is music."—Thomas Campion

"Music is almost as dangerous as gunpowder."—Jeremy Collier

"Music is a strange thing. I would almost say it is a miracle."—Heinrich Heine

"Music is our myth of the inner life."—Susanne Langer

"There are only two kinds of music: good music and bad music."—Duke Ellington

"Music is a decoration of time."—Frank Zappa

There is a difference between music and sound. Not many of us would consider the unpleasant sounds of a jackhammer to be music. But we cannot simply say that unpleasant sounds are noise and pleasant sounds are music. Many of us enjoy listening to the pleasant sounds of nature, such as rain falling or the rustle of leaves, yet we would not call these sounds music.

It seems that we need to sense an element of human organization before we can call something music. In general, we define music as the deliberate organization of sounds by people for other people to hear.

THE ELEMENTS OF MUSIC

Composers rely on certain basic organizing principles to express their ideas in music. Indeed, each art has its own organizing principles. In literature, for example, we learn about vocabulary, grammar, and rhetoric. In music, the three basic elements are **melody**, **rhythm**, and **harmony**.

Melody

Memorable melodies are an integral part of our lives. Most people sing to themselves, as they are walking around, sitting at their desks, or showering. We hear melodies every day: on the radio, on television, at school, and at work. Melodies can be smooth and lyrical, short and jagged, simple or complex. Some melodies, like those in television ads or video games, stick in our heads even if we want to forget them. Popular melodies are an important element of all cultures.

A melody typically consists of different types of **melodic motion**. Melodic motion describes the way the melody moves from note to note in a melody. Most melodies contain a mixture of *steps* (movement to adjacent notes), *leaps* (movement to notes more than a step away), and *repeated notes*. The distinctive quality of a melody is determined by the combination of steps, leaps, and repeated notes.

MUSICNOTE 1

Companion CD, track 1 "Happy Birthday"

The melody of "Happy Birthday to You" (see example) contains a mixture of steps, leaps, and repeated notes. It is very simple in construction and can be divided into four sections: 1, 2, 3, and 4. Each of these sections is called a **phrase**. A musical phrase is marked off by a small break at its end, like a comma in a sentence. If you sing "Happy Birthday," you will notice that you naturally take a breath at the end of each phrase.

The first phrase starts out with repeated notes and steps on the words "Happy birthday." Then there is a leap between "-day" and "to." And then another step between "to" and "you." The second phrase is similar. The third phrase has a much bigger leap (on the words "happy birth-"). That leap is the most memorable part of the melody.

Another element of melody is **shape**. It is shape that makes melody interesting. You can see the shape of "Happy Birthday" just by drawing a line that connects the notes in each phrase. The shape of the first two phrases is very similar, rather like a small wave. The shape of the third phrase is quite different: it is more angular, like an inverted "V." The fourth phrase is more like a backwards wave. It is the only phrase that starts high and then descends.

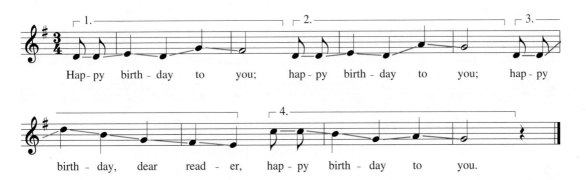

In other ways, the four phrases are very similar. Each is the same length. Each features almost the same rhythm. The difference between the phrases is in their melodic motion and shape.

MUSICNOTE 2

Companion CD, track 2 "America"

"America," also known as "My Country 'Tis of Thee" (see example), has a longer melody than "Happy Birthday," but it also contains phrases of equal length featuring similar rhythm. This melody, however, is made up almost entirely of steps. In fact, if you don't count the leaps that occur *between* phrases, there are only three leaps in the whole song. The first is a downward leap right at the beginning on "-try 'tis." The second, ascending, comes towards the end on "-'ry moun-." And the third, descending again, comes on the single word "let." These are all very small leaps, but they sound big since the rest of the melody is in stepwise motion. The word "let" also has the highest note. These two factors together create a strong climax for the words "let freedom ring!" The shape of the melody also stays very smooth until we get towards the climax at the end.

MUSICNOTE 3

Companion CD,
track 3
"Twinkle, Twinkle"

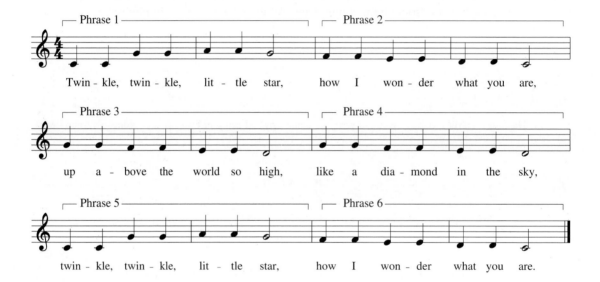

"Twinkle, Twinkle, Little Star" (see example) is an example of a melody that ends the same way it begins. Again, each phrase is the same length, and each phrase uses exactly the same rhythm. You will notice that the last two phrases (5 and 6) are identical to the first two (1 and 2). The middle two (3 and 4) provide contrast. The organizing structure of a composition, whether it is very simple (like this one) or very complex, is known as musical **form**.

The melody of "Twinkle, Twinkle, Little Star" is made up primarily of repeated notes and descending steps, though there is an upward leap at the beginning of the first phrase (and phrase 5). The shape of the melody is simple but very effective. The first two (and last two) phrases present an upward curve followed by a descending line, but the middle phrases are both descending lines. The simple shape and form, the repetitive rhythm, and the pattern of its melodic motion make this a favorite early song for children.

"Happy Birthday," "America," and "Twinkle, Twinkle, Little Star" are very simple melodies. Yet they all exhibit the most important aspects of melody: the mixture of steps, leaps, and repeated notes known as **melodic motion**, division of a melody into **phrases**, the concept of melodic **shape**, and the idea of organizational **form**.

PITCH   In any melody some notes are higher or lower than others. **Pitch** is the term used to describe the exact highness or lowness of a note. If you sing the first two words of "Twinkle, Twinkle Little Star," you will hear that the notes on the second "twinkle" are higher in pitch than those on the first.

Sound is created through vibrations. When an object vibrates, the vibrations are picked up by our ears and transmitted to our brain as sound. The rate (or "frequency") at which the object vibrates determines the pitch that we hear. The faster the vibrations, the higher the pitch. For example, the high note at the top end of a piano has a frequency of 4,186 (that is, it vibrates 4,186 times per second), whereas the low note at the bottom end has a frequency of 27.5.

Most differences in pitch are not so extreme. Two adjacent notes on the piano may only have a difference of about 10 vibrations, but there is still a clear difference in pitch. Most of us can hear differences in pitch much smaller than this (for example on an out-of-tune guitar), and some trained musicians can detect a difference in pitch of only one vibration per second.

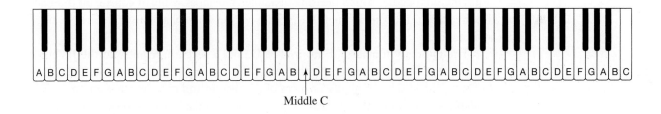

Middle C

NOTE NAMES   We use the first seven letters of the alphabet to indicate notes: A, B, C, D, E, F, and G. The seven letter names are repeated again and again. For example, find "middle C" on the piano keyboard. There are lots of other "C"s on the piano, both higher and lower. Similarly there are lots of other "D"s and "E"s and so on. All notes with the same name are closely related. The "C" above middle C, for example, has exactly twice the number of vibrations as middle C. The C below it has half the number of vibrations. So these notes are very closely related in pitch. That is why they have the same name.

INTERVALS   The distance between any two pitches is called an **interval**. The closest possible interval is a **unison**. A unison is made up of two notes on the same pitch. You would hear a unison when two different people sing the same note at the same time. But most intervals are made up of combinations of half steps and whole steps. A **half step** is the distance between a white note on the piano and the adjacent black note. A **whole step** is the distance between one white note and the next, if there is a black note in between. (Some of the white notes do not have black notes between them. That is because they are only a half step apart.) In the first phrase of "Happy Birthday," the two notes on the syllables "-py" and "birth-" are a whole step apart.

After the unison, the other intervals are the *second, third, fourth, fifth, sixth, seventh,* and *octave.* You determine the name by counting the distance from one note to the next. (In music, you always count the first note as 1.) The interval from C to F, for example, is a fourth: count C as 1, D as 2, E as 3, and F as 4. The interval from C to A is a sixth. If you count up to 8, you'll get to another note of the same name (C up to C,

MUSICNOTE 4

Companion CD, track 4
Unison, Whole Step

for example). The name for this interval is an **octave**. In the third phrase of "Happy Birthday," the interval between "-py" and "birth-" is an octave.

We use the word *sharp* to indicate a note that is just a half step up from a particular note. For example, the black note just above C is called "C-sharp." We use the word *flat* to indicate a note that is just a half step *down* from a particular note. For example, find E on the piano. The black note just below it is called "E-flat."

The clever ones amongst you (and that's all of you, right?) will have noticed something interesting. Look at the C-sharp again. Now find D-flat. YES, Einstein, *it's the same note*! And the same applies to all the notes. On the piano, D-sharp is the same as E-flat; G-sharp is the same as A-flat; F-sharp is the same as G-flat; and so on.

Just one more thing: Look again at those white notes that don't have black notes between them. There is no black note between E and F, and there is no black note between B and C. So, for example, E-sharp is the same as F, and C-flat is the same as B.

The quality of sound of each of the intervals can be described in terms of *consonance* and *dissonance*. Generally speaking, an interval is **consonant** when the two notes played together sound pleasing or stable. The most stable or consonant intervals are the unison, the fourth, the fifth, and the octave; somewhat consonant are the third and the sixth.

The intervals of a second, from C to D, and a seventh, from C to the B above, sound harsh. These intervals are **dissonant**. To our ears, dissonances sound unstable or "unfinished." The harsh dissonances of the second and the seventh seem to require *resolution* to a consonance. We can "resolve" the dissonance of the seventh by playing an octave C–C after it. And the interval of the second can be resolved either up to a third or down to a unison. (Unisons are rather hard to play on one piano!)

DYNAMICS   Loudness and softness, or **dynamics**, are an intrinsic part of the character of most music. A melody can surge and ebb in volume; and there is no quicker way to get an audience's attention than with a sudden change in dynamics.

Dynamics are mostly indicated by a simple system of three letters: *p, m*, and *f,* which represent the Italian words ***piano*** (soft), ***mezzo*** (medium), and ***forte*** (loud). The letters are combined to create a wide variety of dynamic markings.

p	piano	*soft*
mp	mezzo piano	*medium soft*
pp	pianissimo	*very soft*
f	forte	*loud*
mf	mezzo forte	*medium loud*
ff	fortissimo	*very loud*

When composers want to indicate a *gradual* change in volume, they use the term **crescendo** for a gradual increase in volume and **decrescendo** or **diminuendo** for a gradual decrease.

LISTENING EXAMPLE

GEORGE FRIDERIC HANDEL (1685–1759)

From the *Water Music*

Date of Composition: 1717
Two trumpets, two horns, oboes, bassoons,
  and strings.
Allegro
D Major
4/4
Duration: 1:48

Companion CD, Track 62

Let us take a break from this discussion to listen to a wonderful piece of music. It is from Handel's *Water Music*. In the summer of 1717, an English newspaper reported the following about a trip taken by King George I along the river Thames in London:

> On Wednesday evening, at about 8, the King went up the river in an open barge. Many other barges with persons of quality attended. A barge was employed for the orchestra, wherein were 50 instruments of all sorts, which played the whole way the finest music, composed expressly for this occasion by Mr. Handel, which His Majesty liked so much that he caused it to be played over three times.

Listen to some of the music the king heard. Listen first without thinking too much. Just concentrate on the sound and the energy. Now listen again, and think about this music in the context of what you have learned. It presents lots of melodies, which have motion and shape, are divided into phrases, and create form. We'll also listen for pitch, intervals, consonance and dissonance, and dynamics. Let's listen to one section at a time.

Portrait of Handel in his middle years.
Anonymous. Portrait of G. F Handel, Civico Museo Bibliografico Musicale Rossini, Bologna, Italy. Giraudon/Art Resource, NY.

0:00 TO 0:09

The piece starts with a single chord. Then we hear two trumpets ringing out. The accompaniment to the trumpets (played on oboes and stringed instruments) has descending runs, which add to the excitement. The **melodic motion** is of repeated notes that go ever higher and then are rounded off. The **shape** of the melody is upward with a slight fall at the end. The melody is divided into short **phrases,** the first three of which are very similar but at different **pitches**.

The music is repeated, but there are significant differences. Can you hear what they are? The differences are these: 1) the instruments playing the melody are two horns instead of two trumpets, and 2) the accompanying runs are played an **octave** lower (actually one octave lower the first time and two octaves lower the second time). These differences are very effective, because they make the whole passage sound like an echo of the trumpet music.

0:18 TO 0:21

Very short two-note phrases (down–up) alternating between trumpets and horns. A change of **dynamics** here: the second alternation is played more quietly.

0:22 TO 0:29

Short repeated notes in small descending waves. Notice the accompaniment is in the same rhythm. Again the melody is echoed in the horns. You might notice that the accompaniment to the horns has a tinkling instrument playing along; this is a harpsichord.

0:30 TO 0:45

More military phrases here, like a fanfare. The accompaniment is in a different rhythm. Again echoed in the horns, and again the accompaniment is an octave lower, in the bass. Throughout the piece the trumpets and the horns play in pairs. Different **intervals** are used between them, but the most common interval is a third.

0:45 TO 0:49

Short phrases staying around the same pitch.

0:49 TO 0:57

Now this is clever: The last part of the short phrases is repeated a couple of times to make a new phrase. But this is played by only one of the instruments (trumpet/horn). The other holds a high note, which then gets louder (**crescendo**) and rounds off the section.

0:58 TO 1:13

Now Handel intensifies the music by introducing much shorter notes that go back and forth and reach a long, high note before rounding off.

1:13 TO 1:29

Handel saves his most brilliant idea for the last section of the piece. All along, as we have seen, every phrase has been played first by the trumpets and then echoed by the horns. Now the composer *combines* the trumpets and horns to get the fullest possible sound. He also brings back the accompanying descending runs from the very beginning of the piece. The melody is played in longer notes that gradually descend. Since every phrase in the whole piece so far has been repeated, this time he also repeats the phrase, but just to get a little variety and final intensity, he divides each of the longer notes into two (*de-de de-de* **daa** instead of *da da* **daa**).

1:30 TO 1:36

Four short chords end the whole piece.

This is wonderful music. No wonder the king wanted to hear it three times! Later in this chapter we'll analyze it again. Here, we have seen how the music can be analyzed in terms of melodic motion and shape, how it is divided very clearly into phrases, and how these phrases give the piece its form. We also heard differences in pitch and noticed some intervals. We can hear that the music is almost entirely consonant throughout. We should also note that the dynamics are mostly *forte* (loud) with occasional crescendos to *fortissimo* (very loud). Remember, the sound had to carry across water!

Rhythm

When we analyzed simple melodies ("Happy Birthday," "America," and "Twinkle, Twinkle, Little Star") and when we listened to Handel's *Water Music*, I had to sneak in an occasional reference to the second main organizing principle of music: rhythm. Rhythm is a fundamental component of all music.

If a melody is sung without its rhythm, it immediately loses much of its essence. Rhythm is as fundamental to music as pitch, possibly even more so. Rhythm is built into our bodies as heartbeats and the motion of our limbs in walking. Rhythm is one of the most important distinguishing features in music.

BEAT   If you are listening to music and find yourself tapping your finger on the table or your foot on the floor, then you are following the **beat**. You are responding to the regular pulse of the music. If you tap a steady, even rhythm while singing "Happy Birthday," the rhythm that you tap is the beat. Try it a couple of times.

You will notice that on the syllable "-py" of "Happy," you are singing a note, but there is no accompanying beat. This is because the two notes of "Happy" are contained in the same beat. On the other hand, when you sing "you," the note is held for two beats. All the other syllables receive one beat each.

In the case of "Happy Birthday," the beat corresponds to one **quarter note**. It's called a quarter note because *usually* there are four of them in a unit, and the unit is called a whole note. We'll get into this more in a minute. In a lot of music the quarter note is the usual "unit of beat."

A quarter note is written like this: ♩. A half note (worth two quarter notes) looks like this: ♩. A whole note (worth four quarter notes) looks like this: o . But there are smaller note values than a quarter note, too. An eighth note has a small flag on the stem: ♪. There are two eighth notes in a quarter note. A sixteenth note has two flags on the stem: ♬. There are four sixteenth notes in a quarter note. And the smallest usual note value is a thirty-second note. This has three flags on the stem, and there are eight of them in a quarter note: ♬. Thirty-second notes are quite rare. Corresponding to all these note values are **rests**, which indicate units of pause or silence.

If the beat is steady, each row of this chart would take the same amount of time to play. You can see just how fast thirty-second notes might be!

MUSICNOTE 5

Companion CD,
track 5
"Happy Birthday"
with beat

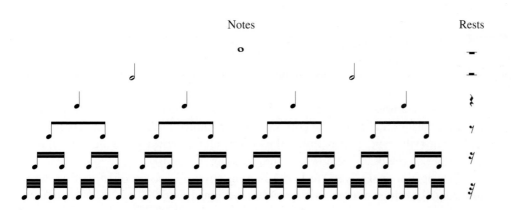

| | Notes | | | | Rests |

MEASURE AND METER   When musicians say that a certain melody or theme is in two-four- or six-eight "time," they are referring to the number of beats in a **measure**. A measure is a grouping of beats. In most music, every measure in the piece has the same number of beats. The measures are marked off by **bar lines** (small vertical lines). **Meter** describes the *number* and the *length* of the beats in each measure. For example, if the measures each contain three quarter-note beats, then we say that the meter is $\frac{3}{4}$: the upper number (3) indicates that there are three beats in a measure; the lower number (4) indicates that the length of each beat is a quarter note. If there are four quarter-note beats in a measure, the meter is $\frac{4}{4}$. And $\frac{3}{8}$ means three eighth-note beats in a measure.

Duple meters are those, such as $\frac{2}{4}$ or $\frac{4}{4}$, whose upper number (the number of beats) is divisible by 2. Duple meters sound firm and solid. Marches, for example, are always in duple meter. **Triple** meters, such as $\frac{3}{8}$ or $\frac{3}{4}$, tend to be graceful or flowing. Waltzes are in $\frac{3}{4}$ meter.

There is one other meter you are likely to come across fairly frequently, and that is $\frac{6}{8}$ (six eighth notes to a measure). The eighth notes are divided into two groups of three ♪♪♪ ♪♪♪. A $\frac{6}{8}$ meter has a very special feel to it. Melodies in $\frac{6}{8}$, such as "Row, Row, Row Your Boat" or "Greensleeves," often have a gentle, lilting, slightly swinging quality. Other well-known melodies in $\frac{6}{8}$ include the lullaby "Rock-A-Bye Baby" and "Take Me Out to the Ball Game."

The meter of a piece of music is always printed at the beginning. This indication is sometimes called the **time signature**. The chart below shows some of the most common time signatures with examples of songs that use them. Before you look at it, try to figure out the time signatures of "Twinkle, Twinkle, Little Star" and "Happy Birthday."

MUSICNOTE 6

Companion CD,
track 6
"Happy Birthday"
with meter

METER	EXPLANATION	EXAMPLE
$\frac{4}{4}$	Four quarter notes in a measure	"When the Saints Go Marching In"
$\frac{2}{4}$	Two quarter notes in a measure	"Yankee Doodle"
$\frac{3}{4}$	Three quarter notes in a measure	"Happy Birthday to You"
$\frac{6}{8}$	Six eighth notes in a measure	"Row, Row, Row Your Boat"

MUSICNOTE 7

Companion CD,
track 7
"Camptown Races"

SYNCOPATION   Sometimes a melody contains notes that seem to come ahead of the beat. When this happens, the rhythm is said to be **syncopated**. Tap your foot or your finger lightly as you sing through the first lines of Stephen Foster's "Camptown Races," paying special attention to the rhythm on the words "doo-dah, doo-dah."

Camp - town   la - dies   sing   this   song,   doo - dah,   doo - dah

These measures are syncopated. Instead of placing "dah" directly on the beat, the composer placed it ahead of the beat, making for a much livelier rhythm. Try it again, and see how the syncopation pushes the melody along. Now try singing "dah" a little later, right on the beat. See how dull and plodding it sounds?

Syncopation makes you "feel" the rhythm physically, so it's often used in dance music and jazz. It gives the music a special rhythmic drive.

TEMPO   A composer usually indicates the speed, or **tempo**, at which a piece should be played. This can be done in two different ways. Sometimes composers use both in the same piece.

The first way is to use a general indication in words at the beginning of a piece. These indications often appear in Italian, and the most common are listed below. You'll notice that some of them indicate the character or *spirit* in which the piece is to be played as well as the speed.

Largo	Broad
Adagio	Easy
Andante	At a walking pace
Moderato	Moderate
Allegro	Fast
Vivace	Lively
Presto	Very fast

The second way to indicate tempo is by means of a **metronome marking**. A metronome is a machine that can be set to click regularly at a specified tempo. The composer might indicate, for example, ♩ = 60, or ♩ = 96. This means that the quarter notes should be played at the rate of 60 per minute (one every second) or 96 per minute. Performers often check their metronomes before practicing a piece, to get a clearer idea of what tempo the composer intended.

Musicians realize, however, that music is a living, breathing thing and not a machine. A metronome speed is rarely maintained exactly throughout a piece. It is usually used only as a guide.

LISTENING EXAMPLE

GEORGE FRIDERIC HANDEL (1685–1759)

From the *Water Music*

Date of Composition: 1717
Two trumpets, two horns, oboes, bassoons, and strings.
Allegro
D Major
4/4
Duration: 1:48

Companion CD, Track 62

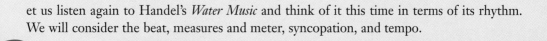

L et us listen again to Handel's *Water Music* and think of it this time in terms of its rhythm. We will consider the beat, measures and meter, syncopation, and tempo.

In this section, the **beat** is firmly established. It's the beat that you tap your foot to. You'll find yourself tapping to the first chord and to the three repeated notes of each trumpet phrase. These are all **quarter notes**. The **tempo** is quite fast (*Allegro*).

Keep tapping your foot as the horns play.

In this section each note is on the beat.

Two notes to a beat here (*de-de, de-de …*). These are eighth notes.

This is the military, bouncy, fanfare-like rhythm. The accompaniment, however, has even eighth notes.

Short phrases staying around the same pitch, mostly eighth notes.

The very short notes in these phrases are sixteenth notes.

Most of the notes now are sixteenth notes (four to a beat: *diddlediddle*).

Now let's start concentrating on **measure** and **meter**. You have probably noticed that there is a heavier accent every four beats of the music. If you tap your foot and count *one* on the heavier accent and *two, three, four* on the lighter ones, you'll see that there are four beats to every measure. This means that the meter is $\frac{4}{4}$: four beats (each a quarter note) to every measure.

Four quarter-note chords end the whole piece. These chords have quarter-note **rests** between them, which make them particularly effective. Rests are used before this point, of course, when some of the instruments aren't playing, but here, when all the instruments are silent, we can really *hear* the rests.

We've figured out that the meter in this piece is 4/4, that the beat is very steady, that the tempo is *Allegro*. There doesn't seem to be any **syncopation** (off-beat accents) in this piece, which makes the rhythm very straightforward. To make sure that this is all clear to you, listen to the music again and follow the outline above. Remember, I said at the beginning of the chapter that the two most important things about listening to music are concentrating carefully and listening several times.

Harmony

The third basic element of music is harmony.

KEYNOTE   The melodies we have studied ("Happy Birthday," "America," and "Twinkle, Twinkle, Little Star") have one other feature in common, one that is shared by almost every memorable tune: Each is dominated by a **keynote**. If you sing "Twinkle, Twinkle, Little Star" and stop at the end of phrase 4 ("like a diamond in the sky"), the melody will sound incomplete. This happens because the phrase does not end on the keynote of the melody. The keynote of "Twinkle, Twinkle" comes at the end of the last phrase. Only when you reach that note does the melody sound finished. In "Twinkle, Twinkle" the last note is C. We call that note the keynote (or **tonic**) of the piece.

Because C is the keynote, "Twinkle, Twinkle, Little Star" can be said to be *in the key* of C.

KEYS AND SCALES   The key in music is like the predominant color in a painting. It has an effect on the overall feel of the work. Most musical compositions begin and end in the same key, and this provides a sense of stability to the music. Key is a bit like gravity: it keeps everything in place.

Since the keynote of "Twinkle, Twinkle" is C, the song uses notes from the *scale* of C to form its melody. A **scale** is a group of notes arranged in an ascending or descending order. If you play all the white notes on the piano going up from middle C to the C an octave above it, you've just created a scale—the scale of C Major.

The C-Major scale is made up of a series of half steps and whole steps. Play the scale of C Major again, or look at it on the diagram. Between C and D there is a whole step. Between D and E there is a whole step. Between E and F there is a *half* step. F to G: whole step. G to A: whole step. A to B: whole step. B to C: another half step. So the pattern of intervals in this scale is whole, whole, half, whole, whole, whole, half. *All major scales use this same pattern: whole, whole, half, whole, whole, whole, half.* So you can actually create any major scale by starting on any note and reproducing exactly that pattern of intervals.

MUSICNOTE 8
Companion CD, track 8
C-Major Scale

Try the scale of G Major. All you do is start on G and go up, keeping the same pattern of intervals. The pattern again is: whole, whole, half, whole, whole, whole, half. Start on G. Then go to A (a whole step from G), then B (a whole step from A), then C (a half step from B), then D (a whole step from C), then E (a whole step from D), then F-sharp (a whole step from E), and finally G (a half step from F-sharp). You'll see that to keep the pattern, you have to use an F-sharp instead of a plain F. So the scale of G Major looks like this:

MUSICNOTE 9
Companion CD, track 9
G-Major Scale

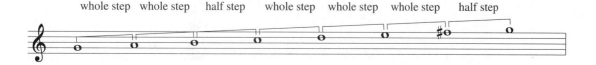

The same applies to any major scale: Just start on the keynote and keep the interval pattern exact. You'll see that some major scales need quite a few sharps or flats.

When a composer writes a piece *in the key of C*, he or she mostly uses notes from the C-Major scale. Now let's look back at the melody of "Happy Birthday" (see page 4). The melody ends on G, so the keynote is probably G. (Most melodies end on their keynote.) The notes used for this melody are from the G-Major scale (G, A, B, C, D, E, F-sharp, G), so "Happy Birthday" is in the key of G.

MAJOR AND MINOR SCALES There are two main types of scale: major and minor. Pieces that use a **major scale** are said to be in the major *mode*; pieces using a **minor scale**, in the minor mode. As we will see below, there is a difference in sound between the two modes: Many people say that pieces written in major keys sound positive or optimistic and that pieces written in minor keys sound a little sad or thoughtful. That difference is created by *differences in the pattern of the intervals*.

The minor scale still uses whole and half steps, but the arrangement is different. The pattern in the minor scale is this: whole step, half step, whole step, whole step, half step, whole step, whole step. The easiest minor scale is A minor, because it has no sharps or flats. So if you play the white notes on the piano starting on A, you get the minor-mode pattern. But just like a major scale, a minor scale can be built on any note. Start on D and keep the pattern: *whole step, half step, whole step, whole step, half step, whole step, whole step*. Here's D minor, with the same pattern of intervals: D, E, F, G, A, B-flat, C, D.

whole step   half step   whole step   whole step   half step   whole step   whole step

As you can see, D minor needs one flat. Try building other minor scales. For example, try building C minor. You'll see that C minor needs *three* flats: B-flat, E-flat, and A-flat.

Major-key pieces *sound* different from minor-key pieces. Pieces in a major key usually sound bright, positive, or cheerful, whereas pieces in a minor key sound more serious, even a little sad. Notice the difference in the sound of "Twinkle, Twinkle, Little Star" if we change it from C Major to C minor.

A well-known song in the minor mode is "All the Pretty Little Horses." This beautiful song is in D minor.

Twin - kle, twin - kle,   lit - tle star,   how   I   won - der   what you are.

There are many other kinds of scales. For example, a scale that is made up entirely of half steps (all the adjacent black and white notes on the piano) is called the **chromatic scale**. There is also a scale called the **pentatonic scale**, which has only five notes in it. Some Asian music uses the pentatonic scale.

RELATED KEYS When we constructed the G-Major scale above, we needed an F-sharp to keep to the pattern. But there is another key that always has an F-sharp, and that is the key of E minor. If you construct the minor scale on E, following the correct

---

MUSICNOTE 10
Companion CD, track 10
Major and Minor

MUSICNOTE 11
Companion CD, track 11
D-Minor Scale

MUSICNOTE 12
Companion CD, track 12
"Twinkle, Twinkle" in C Minor

MUSICNOTE 13
Companion CD, track 13
"All the Pretty Little Horses"

MUSICNOTE 14
Companion CD, track 14
Chromatic Scale

interval pattern, you get: E, F-sharp, G, A, B, C, D, E. E minor and G Major are therefore said to be *related*, or *relatives*, of each other. Each major key has a relative minor and vice versa. The relative minor of C Major, for example, is A minor. (Both have no sharps or flats.) And the relative major of D minor is F Major. (Each has one flat.)

When a composition is in a particular key, then most of the notes in it are taken from the scale of that key, including both the melody and the accompaniment. If a piece is quite long, then it is likely to wander into other keys before returning to the home key at the end. The process of moving from one key to another in music is called **modulation**. Modulation adds interest to music. It is another tool that composers use to vary the mood, like changes in tempo or dynamics.

CHORDS   Although melodies can be sung unaccompanied, most of them have accompaniment. Accompaniment adds depth and richness to a melody. **Harmony** is the combination of a melody and its accompaniment. A composer can create different moods and feelings by changing the harmony in a piece of music.

A **chord** is formed when three or more different notes are played together. The intervals among these notes determine whether the chord is consonant or dissonant. The most common consonant chord is the **triad**, which consists of one primary note (called the "root") and two other notes, one a third above it and the other a fifth above it. This is the most frequently used of all chords. Let's build a triad on the root C. A third above C is E, and a fifth above C is G. So a triad on C would consist of the chord C-E-G.

Both of the notes above the root are consonant with it, creating a very stable overall sound. If the notes are played one after another, rather than all at once, the result is called an **arpeggio**. An arpeggio contains the notes of a chord played consecutively rather than simultaneously.

Sometimes composers will write a triad with the notes rearranged, so that the third or the fifth, or both, lie *below* the root. So you could have the chords E-C-G, or E-G-C, or G-E-C, or G-C-E. All these chords sound slightly different, but the root in each case remains C, because that is the primary note of the triad.

Triads can be built on any root. Let's build a triad on F. A third above F is A, a fifth above F is C. So a triad on F is F-A-C.

Like scales, triads can be either major or minor. The difference depends on whether you count up the major or minor scale to find your chord notes.

Each key has a series of chords associated with it. The chords are formed by constructing triads on each of the seven notes in the scale. You can make a triad on any one of the notes in the scale. The most important of all these chords is the **tonic** chord, built on the keynote. This chord is sometimes called the I chord, because the keynote is the first note of the scale. (In music we use Roman numerals to designate chords.) More often than not, a piece will begin and end with the tonic chord, thereby establishing the key at the beginning of the piece and reaffirming it at the end.

The **dominant** chord (chord V) in a key is second in importance to the tonic chord. It is built on the fifth note of the scale, so, for example, the dominant chord in C Major is built on G. This chord has the notes G-B-D (root + third + fifth). The dominant chord in any key always sounds as though it requires resolution back to the tonic chord.

MUSICNOTE 15
Companion CD,
track 15
Pentatonic Scale

MUSICNOTE 16
Companion CD,
track 16
Simple Melody Using
Pentatonic Scale
"Amazing Grace"

MUSICNOTE 17
Companion CD,
track 17
C-Major Triad

MUSICNOTE 18
Companion CD,
track 18
C-Major Arpeggio

MUSICNOTE 19
Companion CD,
track 19
C-Major Triads

MUSICNOTE 20
Companion CD,
track 20
Chord Progression I-V-I

The effect of the chord progression I-V-I is the same whether it is played in C Major or in any other key.

There are dozens of other possible chords, of course. And many of them have more than three notes in them. Some chords imply movement to another chord. And this provides a sense of direction to the music. Music moves along as a result of this sense of direction. The move from one chord to the next and the next is called a **chord progression**.

CADENCES **Cadences** in music are like punctuation in grammar. They provide stopping points in the flow of the discourse. Stopping points in grammar have varying degrees of strength. A period marks the end of a sentence. A comma marks off a phrase. A semicolon provides both closure and continuity.

There are three main types of musical cadence: the authentic (or full) cadence, the plagal cadence, and the half cadence. Each consists of a different progression of two chords.

An **authentic** or **full cadence** consists of a V chord followed by a I chord. It is used to mark the ends of phrases or sections in a composition and to mark the end of the entire piece. You heard several authentic cadences in the *Water Music*.

The **plagal cadence**, on the other hand, features a IV chord (known as the **subdominant** chord) followed by a I chord. If you play these two chords consecutively, you will notice that the cadence is not as definitive or forthright as the authentic cadence. The plagal cadence is often called the "Amen" cadence, because it is frequently used to close hymns or liturgical pieces.

Both the authentic and plagal cadences end on a tonic chords (I). The **half cadence** ends on the dominant (V) chord, so it lacks the finality of the authentic and plagal cadences. It may be preceded by a IV chord or a I chord; in either case, it provides a pause at the end of a musical phrase, but not an actual ending. It leaves the listener with the sense that there is more music to come.

TEXTURE An important aspect of harmony is what is known as the **texture** of music. Texture describes the way in which different musical sounds are combined. One kind of texture, for example, is known as **monophony**. Monophony is a texture that involves melody with *no* accompaniment. (This can be produced by one or more people.) A single person in the shower or a family in a car are usually singing monophony. Monophonic texture means solo singing or singing in unison.

Homophony is music that moves by chords. The most common form of homophony, sometimes called **song texture**, involves a solo voice with chordal accompaniment, such as a folk singer accompanying herself on the guitar. Song texture can also be used to describe instrumental music, for example a solo instrument playing a melody with an accompaniment.

Polyphony, on the other hand, is music in which you can hear two or more distinct musical lines at once. This kind of texture is obviously more complex. Much Western classical music—a Beethoven symphony, for example—is at least partly polyphonic. If you listen carefully, you can hear several different musical lines at the same time.

MUSICNOTE 21

Companion CD,
track 21
Full Cadence

MUSICNOTE 22

Companion CD,
track 22
Plagal Cadence

MUSICNOTE 23

Companion CD,
track 23
Half Cadence

MUSICNOTE 24

Companion CD,
track 24
Homophony

MUSICNOTE 25

Companion CD,
track 25
Polyphony

The musical texture in which the separate musical lines are particularly clear and stay independent more or less throughout a piece is called **counterpoint**. A special kind of counterpoint is a **round** ("Row, Row, Row Your Boat"), in which one musical line is sung at staggered intervals to produce interweaving lines.

These textures may be easier to remember if you consider them visually. In the diagram, a single melody is depicted in the various textures.

MUSICNOTE 26

Companion CD, track 26 Counterpoint

MUSICNOTE 27

Companion CD, track 27 Round

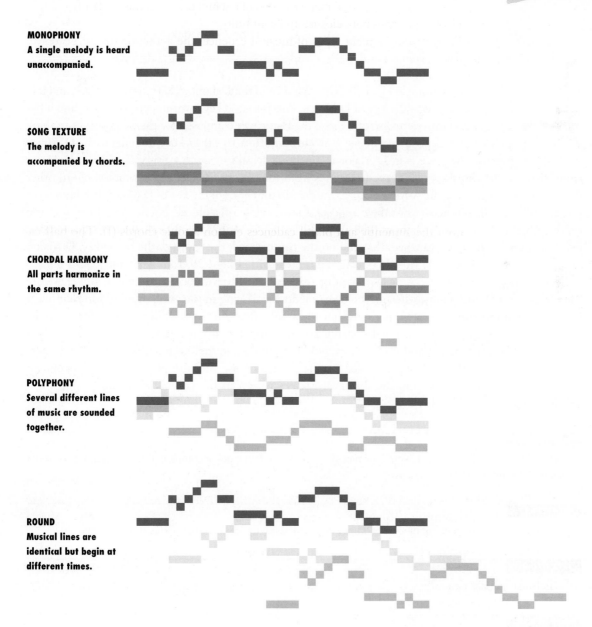

MONOPHONY
A single melody is heard unaccompanied.

SONG TEXTURE
The melody is accompanied by chords.

CHORDAL HARMONY
All parts harmonize in the same rhythm.

POLYPHONY
Several different lines of music are sounded together.

ROUND
Musical lines are identical but begin at different times.

LISTENING GUIDE

GEORGE FRIDERIC HANDEL (1685–1759)

From the *Water Music*

Date of Composition: 1717
Two trumpets, two horns, oboes, bassoons,
  and strings.
Allegro
D Major
4/4
Duration: 1:48

Companion CD, Track 62

L et's listen once more to Handel's *Water Music*, and think about its harmony, cadences, and texture. The piece is in the **key** of D Major. This is a good key for trumpets to play in, and it has a bright and extroverted sound. Since the music was composed for the outdoors, everything about it is cheerful and positive. There is no **modulation** to other keys; it remains in D Major throughout. Because the piece is in D Major throughout doesn't mean that every **chord** is a D-Major chord. Rather, the chords are all formed on notes from the *scale* of D. The most common chord other than the D-Major chord is the A-Major chord, the **dominant** chord of the key of D Major. It is used most prominently in **half cadences**, when the composer wants to close off a phrase, but not halt the music. You can hear half cadences on A Major at 0:08–0:09, 0:15–0:17, 0:24–0:25, 0:28–0:29, 0:52–0:53, and 0:56–0:57. **Authentic cadences**, cadences that end on the **tonic** chord, the chord of the home key, D Major, occur at 0:35–0:37, 0:44–0:45, 1:04–1:05, 1:12–1:13, 1:20–1:21, 1:28–1:29, 1:30–1:31, and 1:32–1:34.

The **texture** of the music is primarily **song texture**: melody with accompaniment. But there are some passages of homophony, when all the instruments are playing in the same rhythm, for example at 0:18–0:29. **Counterpoint** is used sparingly, but to telling effect. In the opening section, for example, 0:00–0:17, the rushing downward scales in the accompaniment can be clearly heard as independent lines. When the top trumpet and the top horn hold long notes and then round off the phrase (at 0:49–0:53 and 0:53–0:57), this can also be called counterpoint because they are playing lines independent from the other instruments. And the downward scales return in the combined trumpets-and-horns section before the end (1:14–1:29).

0:00 TO 0:09

Opening chord of D Major. Rising four-measure phrase on trumpets accompanied by descending D-Major scales in sixteenth notes. Half cadence.

0:09 TO 0:17

Repeat ("echo") of opening measures on horns. Accompanying descending scales in lower octaves.

0:18 TO 0:21

Half-measure phrases.

0:22 TO 0:29

Two-measure phrases, homophonic in eighth notes. Half cadences.

0:30 TO 0:45

Fanfare-like rhythm. Authentic cadences.

0:45 TO 0:49

Phrases of one measure. Mostly homophonic. Half cadences.

0:49 TO 0:57

Continuing closing gesture of previous phrases. Two-measure phrases. Solo instruments in counterpoint. Half cadences.

0:58 TO 1:13

Four-measure phrases using sixteenth notes. Authentic cadences.

1:13 TO 1:29

Trumpets *and* horns and whole orchestra combine for closing passages. Four-measure phrases in descending pattern match the opening. Descending scales return as accompaniment. "Echo" repetition breaks quarter notes into eighths. Authentic cadences.

1:30 TO 1:36

Four quarter-note chords separated by rests. Authentic cadences. End of movement.

We have discussed melody, rhythm, and harmony, the main elements of music. Now let us complete the picture by looking at aspects of form, sound, performance, and musical style

MUSICAL FORM

All art needs form. A book is written in words that are made up of letters and arranged into sentences; sentences are organized into paragraphs; and the whole book is divided into sections or chapters. Similarly, musical flow is carefully organized: into notes, melodies, chords, phrases, sections, **movements** (long, self-contained sections of a larger work), and entire works. Structure is vital to music. It enables us to make sense of what we hear.

The organizing structure of a piece of music is known as its **form**. We can look at form in music in quite short pieces. Let us look again at "Twinkle, Twinkle, Little Star." We already noticed that the first four measures are repeated in measures 9–12 (see page 6). We can label both of these parts "A." (Using letters makes musical analysis much simpler.) Measures 5–8, however, are different from measures 1–4, so we can label that section "B."

This melody may therefore be described as being in ABA form, otherwise known as **ternary form**. This is the most frequent form in small units such as melodies and themes. But ternary form is also quite common on a far larger scale in music. It is one of the forms that can be used for a whole movement. Occasionally, composers even use a type of ABA form for an entire composition. People seem to find the idea of

21

departure-and-return musically very satisfying. Sometimes the A section returns slightly modified; the form is then indicated as ABA′.

Binary form focuses on the idea of contrast. There are two sections, A and B, each of which is usually repeated to make the pattern AABB.

Sonata form, employed as the structure for many large movements, uses both the idea of contrast and the idea of departure-and-return. There is a large opening section, which contains two contrasting smaller units. Then there is a middle section, that itself contrasts with the opening in harmony, tonality, atmosphere, and presentation of thematic material, after which the entire opening section recurs, modified.

Theme and variations form also involves the idea of contrast. A theme is presented and then played several more times, but each time it recurs, it is varied in some way: in melody, rhythm, dynamics, tempo, or harmony. On each occasion, the theme is recognizably different and yet recognizably the same.

MUSICNOTE 28

Companion CD,
track 28
Theme and Variation

Jazz and Rock Forms

Two forms basic to jazz and rock are the **12-bar blues** and **32-bar AABA form**. Both of these depend on repeated patterns of chord progressions. The 12-bar blues has three lines of verse, with the second line being a repeat of the first. For example, let's make up a blues song. The first line might go something like:

> I'm bored to death with all this music stuff.

Then the second line is an almost exact repetition of the first:

> Yeah, I'm just bored to death with all this music stuff.

And the third line would rhyme with the first two:

> Gotta tell my teacher that I've really had enough.

So now you have the three lines of verse, and each line gets four measures of music.

> I'm bored to death with all this music stuff. (4 measures)
> Yeah, I'm just bored to death with all this music stuff. (4 measures)
> Gotta tell my teacher that I've really had enough. (4 measures)

That gives you twelve measures, or bars, of music—hence, the 12-bar blues form.

The harmony in the 12-bar blues is fairly simple. The first four measures are sung with the I chord. Measures 5 and 6 use the IV chord, then back to I for measures 7 and 8. Measure 9 uses V, measure 10 uses IV, then measures 11 and 12 go back to I. So the whole pattern looks like this:

I	I	I	I	(Measures 1–4)
IV	IV	I	I	(Measures 5–8)
V	IV	I	I	(Measures 9–12)

MUSICNOTE 29

Companion CD,
track 29
12-Bar Blues Song in C

If you can play three notes on the piano, you can play the blues. Let's try it in C. The I chord is C-E-G. The IV chord is F-A-C. And the V chord is G-B-D. Go for it!

Now go and make up your own blues. Do you expect me to do all the work around here?

The **32-bar AABA form** sounds complicated, but it's not. Many, many songs use this form, especially older ones. Here the upper-case letters stand for eight measures of music. So you start with an eight-measure phrase. Let's sing:

> Somewhere over the rainbow, way up high, there's a land that I heard of, once in a lullaby.

That's the first A. And it's set to eight measures of music. Now comes the second A. Different words, of course, but exactly the same music:

> Somewhere over the rainbow skies are blue, and the dreams that you dare to dream really do come true.

Now the B section. Another eight bars, but different music, designed to be a contrast:

> Someday I'll wish upon a star and wake up where the clouds are far behind me, Where troubles melt like lemon drops, away above the chimney tops, that's where you'll find me.

And the final eight bars of the A music again:

> Somewhere over the rainbow, bluebirds fly. Birds fly over the rainbow, why then, oh why, can't I?

That's 32-bar form. Do you know how many thousands of songs use this form? Neither do I.

SOUND

The first thing that strikes you when you first hear a piece of music is the **sound**. Who or what is making the music? Is it a rock band? A church choir? A symphony orchestra? The kind of sound you hear will greatly influence the way you experience the music.

Making Music: Voices

Singing is one of the most widespread ways of making music. Almost all people sing, whether they can carry a tune or not. People sing in the shower, walking along the street, driving their car, or just lying in bed. Others whistle or hum all the time.

Singing can be done alone or in groups. Manual workers around the world have devised ways of singing together that help them work, lighten their loads, and create a sense of togetherness. Songs can also create a sense of national identity. Every country has its own national anthem. On a smaller level, songs can confirm a sense of belonging to a recognizable group, such as when people sing their school song or the latest pop hit.

Songs can also evoke a strong sense of nostalgia. People often have only to hear a tune to recapture the entire atmosphere of an event or period in their lives.

Some music allows quite informal standards of singing. Family singalongs, folk songs, and most rock songs are like this. Jazz singing, however, is quite specialized. Jazz singers use their voices in very special ways, with "slides" between notes and with

The group *Manhattan Transfer*.

"bent" or "blue" notes. They also perfect a kind of singing that uses nonverbal syllables like "boo-dee-ba-doo-bah" (this is called "scat" singing), in which the voice is used as a kind of very flexible instrument.

Singing classical music also takes a great deal of training. The voice must be carefully controlled for pitch and dynamics. Breathing has to be developed so that long phrases can be sung. And singers have to learn how to sing clearly in several different languages.

In folk, rock, and jazz, singers are simply divided into men's and women's voices. In classical music, however, there are several voice classifications, depending on the range of the voice. The high women's range is known as *soprano*; the low women's range is called *alto* or *contralto*. The high men's range is called *tenor*, the low men's range *bass*. There are two intermediate voice ranges as well. A voice between soprano and alto is known as *mezzo-soprano*; a voice between tenor and bass is known as *baritone*.

	WOMEN	MEN
High:	Soprano	Tenor
Medium:	Mezzo-Soprano	Baritone
Low:	Alto	Bass

MUSICNOTE 30

Companion CD, track 30 Falsetto Singing

It is possible for men and women to make their voices go higher artificially. This type of singing, called *falsetto*, is hard to control precisely, but it can be perfected with practice.

Making Music: Instruments

Playing instruments also has a very long history. Some of the oldest surviving instruments are thousands of years old.

Around the world, people have devised many ways of creating musical instruments. In the Caribbean, instruments called steel drums are made from used oil barrels. In Africa, a musical bow is made from a stick, a string, and a gourd. In the Middle East, a type of double reed pipe is made from unequal lengths of narrow bamboo cane.

Apart from the way they are made, what most distinguishes one instrument from another is the tone color, or

Steel drums being played in the Caribbean.

timbre, of the sound it makes. A flute playing a certain pitch sounds very different from a guitar playing exactly the same pitch.

Instruments can play alone or together in small or large groups. Examples of small groups include a rock band, a jazz combo, or a chamber group. **Chamber music** is classical music played by a small group of instruments. This can range from a single violin and a piano, to a **string quartet** (two violins, one viola, and one cello), up to eight or ten instruments. Examples of large groups include a marching band and a classical orchestra.

The Orchestra

The term *orchestra* is used loosely to describe any large group of instrumental musicians playing together at one time. It generally refers to a classical group, though some jazz bands call themselves orchestras. The size of a classical orchestra can vary considerably, depending on the work being played.

The instruments of the modern classical orchestra are divided into four groups: strings, woodwinds, brass, and percussion.

Musical bow from Africa.

MUSICNOTE 31

Companion CD, track 31
Flute and Then Guitar
Playing Same Pitch

A modern symphony orchestra.

STRINGS Four stringed instruments are permanent members of the classical orchestra: violin, viola, violoncello (cello), and double bass. The violin is the smallest and the highest in pitch; the viola is slightly larger than the violin and consequently lower in pitch; the cello plays in the tenor and baritone ranges; and the double bass is the largest and the lowest in pitch of all the string instruments.

All four instruments are related, and their appearance and construction are similar. The handcrafting of string instruments is a demanding and time-consuming art. Some of the most beautiful, in sound and appearance, are quite old. The most famous (and most valuable) string instruments come from the seventeenth and eighteenth centuries.

The *violin* is small enough to be held under the chin by the performer as it is played. It is one of the most versatile instruments of the orchestra. It has a wide range and is very expressive. For these reasons, a great deal of music is written for solo violin. But the most recognizable violin sound is that of many violins playing together in an orchestra. An orchestra usually has two groups of violins, which play different notes. The instruments, of course, are the same in each group.

The *viola* is played in the same manner as the violin, but it is slightly larger, deeper in pitch, and mellower in sound. The viola does not usually play as many solo melodies as the violin, yet its dark tone quality is an essential component of the string section of an orchestra. The viola usually plays in the middle range, filling in harmonies and enriching the sound.

The rich, romantic sound of the *cello* is very special. It was explored extensively by great nineteenth-century composers such as Beethoven, Tchaikovsky, and Brahms. The cello is quite large, so it is held between the knees rather than under the chin. A spike protruding from the bottom of the instrument helps to support the weight.

The largest and deepest member of the string family is the *double bass*. Whereas a cellist always plays sitting down, the double bass player either stands in place or sits on a high stool. Although the double bass cannot be played with as much agility as the cello, it provides a firm harmonic bass for the string section and for the entire orchestra. When many double basses play together, the sound is strong, deep, and rich.

MUSICNOTE 32
Companion CD,
track 32
Violin

MUSICNOTE 33
Companion CD,
track 33
Viola

MUSICNOTE 34
Companion CD,
track 34
Cello

MUSICNOTE 35
Companion CD,
track 35
Double Bass

All four stringed instruments are usually played with a bow made of horsehairs stretched on a stick. The hairs are drawn across the strings, producing the sustained, intense sound that is characteristic of string instruments. The player's right hand holds the bow, and the way he or she draws the bow across the strings determines the character of the sound. The fingers of the left hand control the pitch of the sound. There are four strings, each tuned to a different note, and the player can change the pitch on any of the strings by pressing it down on the fingerboard at a certain point ("stopping" the string). It is extremely difficult to find the exact position on the string for each note while at the same time controlling the speed and pressure of the bow. Stringed instruments are among the hardest to learn.

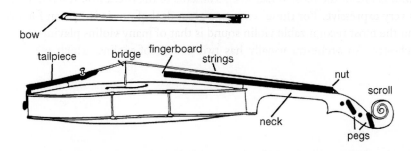

Other techniques have been developed to increase the sound possibilities of string instruments. They can be played **pizzicato**—that is, by plucking the strings with the fingers instead of using the bow. Sometimes a small device is placed on the bridge to dampen the sound slightly: This is called a *mute*. A technique called **vibrato** is used to make the playing more expressive. The fingers that are stopping the strings are often rocked back and forth against the fingerboard to make the pitch waver slightly.

There are other instruments that must be classified as string instruments because they have strings, but these are always played by plucking and never by bowing. They include the harp and the guitar.

The *harp* is often seen in expanded orchestras. Some very big pieces call for two or more harps. The instrument has forty-two strings that are graduated in size, and sharp and flat notes are obtained by pressing down pedals. The many strings allow the harpist to play **glissando**, a technique whereby the player runs his or her fingers across the strings in quick succession, creating an evocative, ethereal sound.

The *guitar* has six strings, and the sound is delicate and light. The guitar is strongly associated with music of Spain and Latin America, but it is widely used around the world, mostly for solo playing or to accompany singing. You will almost never see a guitar in an orchestra, but there are some guitar **concertos**, in which the guitar has the main solo part and is accompanied by the orchestra.

The string section is the largest of the four principal groups of the orchestra. The instruments complement each other perfectly. Many composers, such as Mozart and Tchaikovsky, have written pieces for strings alone (*Eine kleine Nachtmusik* and *Serenade for Strings*). The *Adagio for Strings*, by the American composer Samuel Barber, is also a most beautiful and moving piece.

WOODWINDS The flute, oboe, clarinet, and bassoon are the standard **woodwind** instruments in the modern orchestra. All are played by blowing past a reed (one or two thin slivers of bamboo that vibrate) or through a mouthpiece

MUSICNOTE 36

Companion CD, track 36
Pizzicato, Muted, No Vibrato, Vibrato

MUSICNOTE 37

Companion CD, track 37
Harp

Left to right: piccolo, flute, clarinet, bass clarinet, oboe, English horn, bassoon, contrabassoon.

attached to the main body of the instrument. An orchestra usually has only two or three of each kind of woodwind.

The *flute* was originally made of wood and is therefore classified as a woodwind instrument. Nowadays, however, it is usually metal. Most flutes are made of silver, but some famous flute soloists play gold or even platinum flutes. The instrument is held sideways, and sounds are produced by blowing across a hole in the mouthpiece, according to the same principle used in blowing across the top of a bottle. Different pitches are produced by moving the fingers on holes and keys.

MUSICNOTE 38
Companion CD,
track 38
Flute

The flute is famous for its bright, liquid upper notes and its haunting lower notes. It has a wide range and can be played very fast. The *piccolo*, a small version of the flute played in exactly the same way, is an octave higher than the flute and sounds very brilliant, even shrill.

The *oboe* and the *bassoon* are played by blowing through a double reed made of cane. Two small pieces of cane are tied together, and they vibrate against each other. The suave, yet edgy, quality of the oboe made it a favorite among eighteenth- and nineteenth-century composers. Two oboes playing together (with a bassoon playing the bass) are often used to contrast with the much smoother strings. Because the oboe varies little in pitch, the other instruments usually tune to it. Just at the beginning of a classical concert, you can listen carefully and hear the pitch being given first by the principal oboist.

MUSICNOTE 39
Companion CD,
track 39
Oboe

Whereas the oboe and the flute are among the highest-sounding instruments of the orchestra, the bassoon is one of the lowest. It is a large instrument and uses much larger double reeds than the oboe. Its length is disguised, because it is made of a tube doubled back on itself. If it were straight, it would be more than nine feet long. The bassoon has a full, rounded, vibrant sound in its low **register** (area of sound) and a strange, rather haunting sound in its high register. The most famous example of a bassoon playing high is at the opening of Stravinsky's *The Rite of Spring*, which is the music that accompanies the creation-of-the-world sequence in the movie *Fantasia*.

MUSICNOTE 40
Companion CD,
track 40
Bassoon

The *English horn* is neither English nor a horn. It is really a low oboe, pitched a fifth lower than the standard oboe. The English horn has a rich, evocative sound. It is one of the most distinctive instruments of the orchestra. Perhaps for that reason, it is used quite rarely. Its most well-known appearance is in the slow movement of Dvořák's *New World* Symphony.

The *contrabassoon* is the lowest woodwind instrument of all. It plays an octave lower than the bassoon and is a very large instrument. It is made of a tube doubled back on itself twice. Unwound, it would stretch to eighteen feet!

The *clarinet* is the most versatile of all the woodwinds. For this reason, perhaps, it is the only orchestral woodwind instrument that has been successful in jazz. Mozart was said to have

Bassoonist

MUSICNOTE 41
Companion CD, track 41
English Horn

adored the sound of the clarinet. It is played with a single reed, also made of cane, which is attached to the mouthpiece. The clarinet has a very wide range (nearly four octaves) and three distinct registers. In the low register, it sounds rich and melancholy; in the middle register, it is singing and warm; in the high register, it is piercing and shrill.

The *bass clarinet* plays an octave lower than the standard clarinet; it has a wonderfully rich, buttery sound. You can hear it in the famous "Dance of the Sugar-Plum Fairy" in Tchaikovsky's *Nutcracker* ballet. The *E-flat clarinet* is smaller and higher than the standard clarinet. It is bright and piercing and often used in bands.

Other woodwind instruments that are used mostly outside an orchestra are the saxophone and the recorder. The *saxophone* is, like the flute, made of metal, and like the clarinet, it has a single reed. Saxophones come in many sizes. The most common are the alto and tenor, though soprano, baritone, and bass saxophones have also had their proponents. The saxophone was invented in the mid nineteenth century, and it has not yet found a permanent niche in the classical orchestra. The saxophone is used mostly in jazz, where its smooth, flexible, melodious quality works particularly well.

The *recorder* was a favorite instrument in the sixteenth, seventeenth, and eighteenth centuries. It also comes in different sizes, the most common being the soprano and alto recorders. Because the recorder's sound is quite soft, its place in the orchestra was taken over in the eighteenth century by the more versatile flute. Recorders are fine instruments for children, because they are fairly easy to play at a basic level. Advanced recorder playing, however, is not at all easy.

BRASS INSTRUMENTS   The French horn, trumpet, trombone, and tuba are brass instruments. All four require the player to blow through a mouthpiece, which can be detached from the main body of the instrument. What sets up the sound in brass instruments is the vibration of the player's lips. Composers tend to use brass instruments

MUSICNOTE 42
Companion CD, track 42
Clarinet

MUSICNOTE 43
Companion CD, track 43
Bass Clarinet
(with Celesta)

MUSICNOTE 44
Companion CD, track 44
Saxophone

MUSICNOTE 45
Companion CD, track 45
Recorder

sparingly, because they produce considerable volume and can overwhelm all the other instruments in the orchestra. Yet the strident, extroverted character of brass instruments is balanced by a warm, mellow quality when they are played softly.

Different notes are obtained on brass instruments by tightening or slackening the lips in the mouthpiece and also by changing the length of the tube that has air going through it. On the French horn, trumpet, and tuba, this is done by using the fingers to press down valves. On the trombone, however, the length of the tube is changed by means of a slide: One length of tubing is slid over another, varying the length.

Left to right, clockwise from top left: French horn, tuba, trombone, trumpet.

Each of the brass instruments has its own distinctive sound. The *French horn*, often known simply as the horn, is often associated with "outdoor" sounds like hunting calls, though it also has a warm, rich quality. The *trumpet* is the highest-pitched brass instrument. Composers often take advantage of its bold, strident quality in fanfare-like passages. The *trombone* sounds very powerful and grand, sometimes even frightening. As with the horn, however, it has the potential to produce a rich, smooth, and mellow sound. Both the trumpet and the trombone are favored in jazz ensembles. The *tuba* is to the brass section what the double bass is to the string section—the lowest-pitched instrument and the supporting bass. Its sound is deep and round.

Tuba player.

When a whole choir of brass instruments is playing together, the sound is like no other. It can range from introspective and religious to utterly overwhelming.

PERCUSSION INSTRUMENTS   **Percussion** instruments are those that involve hitting or shaking. They can be divided into two categories: those that produce pitched (tuned) sounds and those that produce unpitched sounds. Pitched percussion include timpani, xylophone, glockenspiel, and celesta.

The *timpani* have been an important feature of the symphony orchestra since the late eighteenth century. Two, three, or sometimes four of these large drums are arranged in a semicircle around the player. They are sometimes called kettledrums because they are made of copper. Timpani have a skin stretched across the top (this used to be animal skin but is now usually made of plastic), and each drum is tuned to a different (low) pitch. They are played either with soft padded sticks or with hard wooden ones. Timpani can sound like distant thunder, or they can sound powerful and stirring (as in the main theme of the movie *2001: A Space Odyssey*). Often, however, they are used simply to reinforce the beat and the bass.

Timpani player.

The *xylophone* and the *glockenspiel* are very similar to each other. Each has two sets of bars—like the black and white keys of a piano—played with two hard sticks. The glockenspiel bars are made of metal and therefore produce a bright, luminous sound. The xylophone's bars are made of wood, so the sound is more mellow.

The *celesta* is based on the same principle as the previous two

MUSICNOTE 46
Companion CD, track 46
French Horn

MUSICNOTE 47
Companion CD, track 47
Trumpet

MUSICNOTE 48
Companion CD, track 48
Trombone

MUSICNOTE 49
Companion CD, track 49
Tuba

MUSICNOTE 50
Companion CD, track 50
Full Brass Choir

MUSICNOTE 51
Companion CD, track 51
Timpani

MUSICNOTE 52
Companion CD,
track 52
Xylophone

MUSICNOTE 53
Companion CD,
track 53
Glockenspiel

MUSICNOTE 54
Companion CD,
track 54
Celesta

MUSICNOTE 55
Companion CD,
track 55
Bass Drum

MUSICNOTE 56
Companion CD,
track 56
Snare Drum

MUSICNOTE 57
Companion CD,
track 57
Orchestral Cymbals

MUSICNOTE 58
Companion CD,
track 58
Jazz Drum Set

instruments, but it looks like a tiny upright piano. The hammers that strike the metal bars are controlled from a small keyboard. The sound of the celesta is tinkling, delicate, and sweet. You can hear it used most effectively (together with the bass clarinet) in the "Dance of the Sugar-Plum Fairy" in Tchaikovsky's ballet *The Nutcracker.*

Untuned percussion instruments include snare drum, bass drum, triangle, and cymbals. The *snare drum* has strings, attached to its underside, which sizzle or rattle when the drum is struck. The sound is dry and crisp. The *bass drum* is large and is suspended on its side. It gives a deep thump. The snare drum and the bass drum are prominently featured in jazz combos and marching bands and occasionally in classical music as well. The snare drum is the most conspicuous instrument in Ravel's *Bolero.*

The *triangle* is made of metal and is played with a metal beater. Its high, hard noise can be heard above a full symphony orchestra.

Cymbals come in many different sizes. Orchestral cymbals are usually a pair about fifteen inches in diameter. When they are struck together, the crashing sound can last for several seconds. A jazz drum set often has several cymbals, either hanging singly or set up in pairs. In jazz combos, the drum set is the heartbeat of the music.

KEYBOARD INSTRUMENTS   The most important keyboard instruments are the piano, the harpsichord, the organ, and the synthesizer. The *piano* is the best-known solo instrument, but it can also appear with an orchestra. This happens in one of two ways. In a *piano concerto,* the piano takes a starring role in front of the orchestra. But occasionally the piano appears as just another orchestral instrument.

A modern concert grand piano.

A superb sixteenth-century organ in a French cathedral.

The piano can claim to be both a stringed instrument and a percussion instrument. Each key on the keyboard activates its own hammer. The hammer strikes the piano's strings inside the instrument, and a note is sounded. The harder the pianist strikes a key, the louder the sound. This ability to control dynamics so directly gave the piano its original name, *piano e forte*, which is Italian for "soft and loud."

The most important predecessor of the piano was the *harpsichord*. The harpsichord was the fundamental instrument of the seventeenth and eighteenth centuries. It was used in symphonies, in operas, in chamber music, and as a solo instrument. Although the harpsichord may look quite similar to the piano from the outside, its internal mechanism is quite different. Pressing a key causes the string to be *plucked*. Regardless of how hard the key is pressed, the string is plucked in the same manner and produces the same dynamics. The sound of the harpsichord is delicate and dry, though full chords can be quite loud.

The *organ* is sometimes called the "king of instruments." Organs range in size from tiny, portable models to the enormous instruments found in large halls or churches. Air is propelled through pipes, and the route the air takes is controlled from a keyboard. Large organs can have hundreds of pipes and even two or three keyboards ("manuals"). They usually have a pedal keyboard for the lowest notes, which is operated by the player's feet. For this, the player wears special shoes.

The pipes of an organ may be made of a variety of materials, in a variety of shapes, and with or without reeds. Big organs have many different sets of pipes. Each set has a different quality of sound and is made accessible from the keyboard by special control buttons known as stops. This is where we get the expression "pulling out all the stops." As a result of this array of stops, the sound of the organ is very rich.

An instrument that can imitate the sounds of other instruments is the *synthesizer*. This is an electronic instrument, usually with a keyboard, that can be programmed to imitate the sound of almost any other instrument. The synthesizer can also modify sounds or create completely new ones. The synthesizer has revolutionized the recording and film industries. It can be made to sound very much like a full orchestra or like a single electric guitar. Synthesized film soundtracks are very common. It is far less expensive to use one synthesizer than to hire a conductor and an orchestra for several days!

MUSICNOTE 59
Companion CD, track 59
Organ

Contemporary musical instruments, synthesizer, and computer.

MUSICAL PERFORMANCE

Rehearsal

The amount of rehearsal time that goes into music differs greatly according to the type of music involved. Jazz, for example, depends a great deal on **improvisation**: people making up the music as they go along. Nonetheless, creative improvisation takes a great deal of practice. You have to know your instrument very well, and you have to be able to hear harmonies and listen carefully to what the other members of the group are doing.

Rock music takes quite a bit of studio time, but much of the work in making a recording nowadays is done by the engineers. Most recorded rock is "manufactured" in the studio by engineers mixing different tape tracks, adding synthesized sounds, and manipulating the overall result.

Classical concert music takes an enormous amount of rehearsal. Much more time is spent rehearsing for a concert than actually presenting it. A typical orchestral musician will work for nine two-and-one-half-hour periods a week, of which two-thirds are devoted to rehearsals. In addition, of course, the musician is expected to practice his or her instrument and learn new music.

During rehearsals, the conductor and orchestra will rehearse the pieces to be featured on that week's program, deciding questions of tempo, tuning, dynamics, balance among the instrumental groups, and interpretation. This last factor is what distinguishes one performance of a piece of music from another: whether to slow down a little here, speed up a little there, pause for a moment between sections, allow the brass section to let rip in the last movement, and thousands of other tiny details. There is much more to a conductor's job than just "beating time!"

Attending a rehearsal is one of the most fascinating ways of learning about orchestral music. You hear the music several times; you see which ways the conductor decides to shape the music; and you learn what these changes can do to the overall effect. Most orchestra rehearsals are private, but many orchestras have taken to offering inexpensive seats for occasional "open rehearsals."

Attending a Concert

When you go to a concert, there are certain conventions that everyone follows. First, most people get dressed a little more formally than usual. Tee shirts and jeans aren't really appropriate for a concert. Then it's a good idea to get to the concert hall fifteen or twenty minutes early. There is a lot to see and do during that time.

In fact, a lot of people start preparing for a concert a day or two beforehand. They find out exactly what pieces are on the program. They might listen to recordings of the pieces and read a bit about them. If there are vocal works on the program, it is really helpful to look at the texts (and, if necessary, translations of the texts) beforehand.

Different types of concerts generally have different kinds of programs. Again, there are conventions about this. An orchestral concert usually has three works on the program, and usually they are all by different composers. The first piece is usually fairly short and somewhat lighter than the others. This piece is often an overture (a short introductory orchestral work). The second piece is sometimes a concerto: a work for orchestra that features a soloist. Then comes the intermission. The second half of the concert is often taken up by one longer and more serious work, like a full-length symphony.

In your fifteen minutes before the concert begins, take a careful look at the program. In addition to the name of the orchestra and the conductor, it will tell you the titles and the order of the pieces, the titles of the movements, and the names and dates of the composers. Take a look at the sample program.

The Greater Kakofony Orchestra
Heffing von Togeza
Conductor

Overture to **La Gazza Ladra**   **Gioacchino Rossini**
                                                  (1792-1868)

Concerto in C Major for Piano   **Wolfgang Amadeus Mozart**
and Orchestra, K. 503   (1756-1791)

Allegro maestoso
Andante
Allegretto

Ticklin Dee Ivories
Piano

Intermission

Symphony No. 4 in E minor   **Johannes Brahms**
                                                  (1833-1897)

Allegro non troppo
Andante moderato
Allegro giocoso
Allegro energico e passionato

The first piece, by Rossini, is an overture that he wrote for one of his operas, *La Gazza Ladra*. That is why it says overture "to" *La Gazza Ladra*. You don't need to know the opera. You just need to know that an overture is a short, generally quite light, orchestral work. The second piece is in three movements (remember: a movement is a self-contained section of a larger work), and each one of them has a tempo marking. You learned some of these already. (See page 13.) But there are still some words you may not know. You learned that *Allegro* means fast. *Maestoso* means "majestic," so the first movement is marked "Fast and majestic." *Andante* means "at a walking pace" (see your list). And the last movement is an *Allegretto*, which means a "little allegro," therefore a rather lighter fast movement. The name of the solo pianist is also given, because she will have a starring role in this concerto.

In the second half of the program, the orchestra will be playing a Brahms symphony. *Non troppo* means "not too much," so the first movement is marked "Not too fast." The second movement will be at a moderate walking pace. *Giocoso* means "light-hearted" or "joky," so the third movement will be fast and lighthearted; and the last movement is marked "fast, energetic, and passionate."

By the time you have absorbed all this, most of the players will have arrived and taken their places on the stage. Most of them will be warming up or practicing difficult passages, so there will be a general hubbub. This is a good time to see where all the instrumentalists sit and see if you can recognize some of the instruments you have learned about. We are now about five minutes before the concert starts, so this is the perfect time to make sure that your cell phone (if you brought one with you) and the beeper on your watch are turned OFF. (You will get very nasty looks indeed from your neighbors if you forget this and your machines sound off during the music!) You should also know that you cannot get up during the concert and go to the bathroom, that you shouldn't talk during the concert, or unwrap noisy candies, or rustle your program, or do anything that might spoil other people's enjoyment of the music.

Orchestra and audience in a beautiful concert hall.

Now the musicians are starting to settle down, and a single long pitch is sounded. This is called "concert A," the pitch to which all the instruments tune. Sometimes it is sounded by a single oboe; sometimes it is just an electronic pitch. The instrumental groups tune to it in turn, and then everyone falls silent. There is an expectant hush, and then the conductor comes in from the wings, takes a bow, and the music starts. (Some orchestras also give a separate bow to the concertmaster or concertmistress, the person who plays at the head of the violins and sits immediately to the conductor's left.) For the second work on the program, the piano concerto, the solo pianist will also get a separate entrance and special applause after the piece.

Concerts nowadays normally last about two hours. But this includes a twenty-minute intermission, during which time you can go to the bathroom, get a drink of water or a soda, and relax to get ready for the second half of the concert.

This description has followed the order of events at an orchestral concert. Things are a little different for chamber-music (small-group) concerts or for other types of concert, such as a voice recital. At voice recitals, there are usually more shorter pieces, even though the concert as a whole may still be one and one-half or two hours long.

Emotion in Music

Music involves communication and the expression of feelings. The composer communicates by means of the written notes, and the performer communicates by interpreting those written notes for an audience. Performers often get deeply involved with the feelings they are trying to convey.

Conductors grunt and moan, violinists often close their eyes and sway, rock guitarists thrash at their guitars. Sometimes these emotions can seem theatrical, but a great performer can seem genuinely in touch with the deepest impulses of the soul and convey those feelings directly to the audience.

Yo-Yo Ma is immersed in the music he's making.

A conductor coaxes expression out of his orchestra.

Sonny Rollins plays at the 1993 Newport Jazz Festival.

Live Performances

Live performances have an air of excitement about them that can never be matched by a recording. Whether it is a rock concert, a jazz performance, or a full-dress classical concert, there is something special about hearing people create music on the spot. Music *needs* performance to bring it alive.

Many rock concerts are as much stage shows as they are musical performances. Makeup, clothes, dancing, and often elaborate stage machinery help create the special atmosphere.

Orchestra concerts are more formal affairs. The musicians wear formal dress, and members of the audience are often decently dressed, too. The audience is expected to be quiet during the performance, and appreciation is usually expressed as polite applause. Opera performances are even more formal. Members of the audience sometimes wear full evening dress. Opera fans can be as passionate about their favorite singers as rock fans are. At the end of a performance, some opera stars are showered with roses or presented with bouquets of flowers.

Jazz concerts are usually much less formal. Often they are held in a club, where the audience may be eating and drinking during the performance, and where music is a *part* of the experience, rather than the *focus* of the experience. Since the forties, though, jazz has also been presented in concert halls and festivals, where audiences are more likely to give the artists their undivided attention.

The rock band U2 playing at a concert.

In many countries around the world, music is integrated into the life of society, and the concept of a concert is quite alien. Music just appears in many aspects of life. But in every culture of the world, in whatever format or environment it is performed, music is regarded as special magic.

HISTORICAL PERIODS AND INDIVIDUAL STYLE

History is a strange affair. If we contemplate the present, we don't really consider it history. And yet after a while, of course, it turns into history. Similarly, people one hundred years ago didn't think of themselves as living in a historical period. They were just living.

Time simply continues. It is an artificial construct to organize time into years and centuries and especially into historical periods. But it is useful. It gives us a sense of clarity and perspective to know the eras of Shakespeare or Jesus or John F. Kennedy, or to be able to discuss "The Middle Ages" or "Romanticism."

Of course, people in the eleventh century didn't think they were living in the Middle Ages. And in the nineteenth century, nobody said, "Okay, time for Romanticism to begin!" It's only in retrospect that we can distinguish different historical periods because certain characteristics set them apart.

When we study literature or the arts, these period labels are useful because we feel that a book or a painting actually *reflects* the historical period in which it was created. A painting of the Virgin Mary from the Middle Ages has very different aims and expresses very different things from a painting of a nude in 1830.

The history of Western music is much shorter than the history of art or literature. The great epics of Homer, the *Iliad* and the *Odyssey*, appear to date from nearly 3,000 years ago. And cave paintings have been discovered in France and Spain that are more than 20,000 years old. We can imagine that people must have sung and played music that long ago, but unfortunately we have absolutely no trace of it. If music is not written down, it tends to disappear, for it is a *sounding* art.

There are a few fragments of written music from ancient Greece and Rome, but not enough to be able to reconstruct whole pieces. The earliest manuscripts of whole pieces date from the Middle Ages, starting about the ninth century, though they contain music that seems to have been around for a few hundred years already.

The main historical periods in music of the European tradition are given here, with approximate dates for each.

Middle Ages	400–1400
Renaissance	1400–1600
Baroque	1600–1750
Classic	1750–1800
Romantic	1800–1900
Twentieth century	1900–2000

The word *style* in music is used in two senses. First, it is used to describe those characteristics that set apart the music of one historical period from another. We speak about the style of Baroque music or the style of Classic music. It is also used to describe the individual style of one particular composer. No composer works in a vacuum: his or her music will be recognizably of the period in which he or she lived. And yet, especially for a great composer, the music will also have some special features that set it apart from the music of other composers of the time. Mozart, for instance, used the language of mid- to late eighteenth-century Classicism. And yet there are things about the works of Mozart that mark them as unmistakably his. And, try as they might, nobody else sounds like Louis Armstrong. Throughout this book, I will try very carefully to balance these two aspects of style: the historical and the individual.

But to end this chapter, I return to the point I made at the very beginning. The only way to understand great music is to listen to it *very* carefully.

LISTENING GUIDE

GEORGE FRIDERIC HANDEL (1685–1759)

From the *Water Music*

Date of Composition: 1717
Two trumpets, two horns, oboes, bassoons, and strings.
Allegro
D Major
4/4
Duration: 1:48

Companion CD, Track 62

Let's listen one more time to Handel's *Water Music*, and think about it in terms of its form, instruments, historical period, and composer's individual style.

In terms of **form**, the piece is quite simple. The form is provided by the simple device of the "echo" technique. Every phrase of the melody is played twice, usually by the trumpets first and then by the horns. This tight organization provides so much structure for the short piece that Handel did not seem to feel the need for any more.

The choice of instruments adds to the bright and extroverted effect of the music. Trumpets and horns are designed for outdoor use. There is also a full complement of stringed instruments (two groups of violins, and violas, cellos, and double basses). A harpsichord plays along with the cellos and basses, as was traditional in the eighteenth century. And, although they are hard to hear, a pair of oboes plays along with the violins. If you listen very carefully, you might hear the extra edge they give to the violin **timbre**. Even harder to hear are a pair of bassoons that play along with the basses. Again, the difference is one of tone color or timbre more than anything else.

As mentioned above, the style of a piece of music can be thought about in two ways: historical and individual. The *Water Music* of Handel was composed in the first part of the eighteenth century and therefore belongs in the **Baroque** period (1600–1750). This was a period of clear-cut music, in which the mood of a piece stays constant from beginning to end, the harmonic structure is strong, and the bass line is firm and direct. All these things are true of our piece.

What makes the music typical of Handel, however, is a different and more subtle matter. Handel's music is always clear and accessible. Even when he writes counterpoint, it is easy to follow. But there is always something interesting and subtly unconventional about his music, even if it sounds extremely simple and straightforward. The special features to notice in this piece are the following:

1) The variable phrase lengths. In the first section the opening trumpet melody and the answering horn melody are exactly four measures long. But this is followed by two-note phrases (half a measure!). Then the homophonic section has two-measure phrases. This kind of variety of phrase length is typical of Handel and makes his music much more intriguing than it would otherwise be.

2) Very careful planning of ideas. For example, listen again to the very first chord. You might think this chord is unnecessary. (In fact, I thought so for a while.) The piece could just start with the trumpets. So why did Handel put in this first chord? Well, one can never really *know* the answer to a question like that, but a couple of ideas come to mind. First, it makes the trumpets sound more ringing when they enter right after it, since the chord uses neither the trumpets nor the horns. In fact, it's the only moment in the whole piece in which both the trumpets and the horns are silent. Second, that opening chord balances the four chords at the end of the piece and makes them sound more "correct."

As another example, think of the way Handel *combines* the trumpets and horns at the end, after having alternated them throughout. He must have planned this from the beginning. Think too of how the downward scales come back at the end, rounding off the piece perfectly with a subtle reference to the opening. Even more subtle is the fact that the *rhythm* of the trumpets' and horns' melody in this combined ending section is the same as the rhythm at the opening of the piece, but the instruments move down instead of up. (Down feels more right for an ending, up for a beginning.)

Handel may have thought of all these things consciously or unconsciously. It doesn't really matter. What matters is that they are there, that they are strokes of genius, and that you have already learned enough to be able to hear them!

Here is a final Listening Guide that summarizes these points about form, instruments, historical period, and the composer's individual style.

0:00 TO 0:09

Opening chord on strings, oboes, and bassoons. Rising four-measure phrase on trumpets accompanied by descending scales on strings and oboes.

0:09 TO 0:17

Repeat ("echo") of opening measures on horns. Accompanying descending scales in lower octaves.

0:18 TO 0:21

Half-measure phrases.

0:22 TO 0:29

Two-measure phrases

Fanfare-like rhythm.

One-measure phrases.

Continuing closing gesture of previous phrases. Two-measure phrases.

Four-measure phrases.

Trumpets *and* horns and whole orchestra combine for closing passages. Four-measure phrases in descending pattern match the opening. Descending scales from opening return as accompaniment. "Echo" repetition breaks quarter notes into eighths.

Four final chords also remind us of opening. End of movement.

KEY TERMS

metronome marking
(p. 13)
pentatonic scale **(p. 16)**
cadences **(p. 18)**
polyphony **(p. 18)**

movement **(p. 21)**
binary form **(p. 22)**
theme and variations
  form **(p. 22)**
sonata form **(p. 22)**

32-bar AABA form
(p. 23)
string quartet **(p. 25)**
concerto **(p. 27)**

2
Music Around the World

INTRODUCTION

We saw in Chapter 1 that music is made up of the basic elements: melody, rhythm, and harmony. We also saw how one composer, Handel, combined these elements to produce an impressive composition. Music is an art or an activity that appears in all cultures around the world. Each nation, each ethnic group, each tribe develops its own music and preserves its own musical traditions.

Our study of the rich and ancient store of European music is made possible by written descriptions and notated music that stretch back over a thousand years. But in most of the rest of the world, musical traditions are oral. Music is not written down, but transferred from one person to another, and from one generation to the next, simply by "word of mouth." One person learns the music by hearing someone else perform it; an older person teaches it to a younger person.

In many cultures around the world, it is very difficult to determine how old a musical tradition may be. There is also no way of knowing how the music of an **oral tradition** may have changed over the generations. We have a tendency nowadays to think that the music of an unfamiliar small tribe or society is "purer" or more "natural" than our own. This is wrong for two reasons. First, the music of the European tradition also began as an orally transmitted art. Second, there is very little music in the world that has not undergone change and influence from outside forces. People are always adapting their music to sounds they hear from elsewhere.

The greatest influence today on music around the world is that exerted by Western classical and popular music. In Japan and China and India and Korea and Singapore, orchestras play symphonic music of the European tradition, and young musicians are trained in the styles and techniques of Western classical music. Music in

A Chinese girl practicing the violin.

A cajun practice session in Louisiana.

West Africa borrows influences from American country music, soul, reggae, and disco. In France, cafés and restaurants in the smallest villages are filled with the sounds of English and American rock. In the Middle East, popular songs are an amalgam of American pop with native rhythms and singing styles.

It has often been said that music is a universal language, that it transcends boundaries of nation and race. This is true, but only in a very specific sense. The fact that there is music seems to be universal: Every known human group has music. But for each culture, music has a slightly different meaning. It takes different forms in different cultural groups.

Music reflects the society that creates it, and each society creates the music that it wants. This sounds obvious, yet it is important, because it reminds us that in order to understand a culture's music, we need to understand the culture itself. And this is as true of the music of Europe and the United States as it is of ancient Japan or modern-day Indonesia or Zimbabwe.

Zulu boys dancing in South Africa.

MUSIC AS A REFLECTION OF SOCIETY

The United States: A Test Case

Let's take a look at music in the United States today as a reflection of its culture. We'll describe the situation as though we were anthropologists looking at an unfamiliar tribe. This will help us focus on the kinds of questions we might ask about music from other cultures and other times.

Let us start with classical music. In the United States, we note that classical music is treated as something of an elitist activity. Performances are formal: Members of the audience sit listening quietly until the end of each piece. The society treats the music of the past with reverence. In addition to classical music, people in the United States listen to many other types of music. There seems to be a distinction by class and age among these different types. Most young people listen to rock or pop music, although some of them may also be interested in classical music. Classical music seems to be re-garded as more of a "high-class," intellec-tual form of music than rock, which is far simpler and less formal. Young people lis-ten to rock mostly in a convenient recorded format, either in their own rooms or as they walk about. Often they listen to the same pieces over and over again. Many of the songs are about love or sex. Concerts of rock music are very informal, but famous performers make huge sums of money. Popular music in the United States is a multibillion-dollar industry. (We will con-sider twentieth-century popular music in the last chapter of this book).

Our anthropological survey would also note that there is another type of in-formal music making called jazz. Perform-ers don't play from written music and often seem to make up what they play during a performance. Audiences for this type of music tend to be small. Many famous jazz performers are of African ancestry. (We will study jazz in detail in Chapter 10.)

Many other types of music occur in the United States. Each ethnic group has a dis-tinctive traditional music that helps to fos-ter its separate identity. Religious groups are often distinguished by their music. Some large public events are marked by the singing of nationally known songs.

Since music mirrors the way a culture works, what does this "anthropological" description tell us about American society?

The audience at a rock concert.

Singing of the national anthem at a baseball game.

It tells us that culture in the United States is extremely diverse. We learn that a very ancient musical tradition has been carefully preserved, and new music is constantly being produced. It is clear that the society is undergoing rapid change, as the production of music has become a highly profitable business. Music is regarded primarily as an entertainment, and despite the existence of a repertory of great masterworks, there is a commercial schism between popular and classical music. Some other cultures are different, as we shall see.

World Music: View From a Satellite

For the purposes of our discussion, it is possible to divide the world into two large areas. The first of these areas is made up of the Americas, Europe, and the entire portion of Africa that lies beneath the Sahara desert (often called sub-Saharan Africa). Music from this area has profoundly influenced the development of Western culture, and in turn, for the last several hundred years, Western culture has exercised a strong influence throughout these regions. The second area is made up of North Africa, the Middle East, the Far East, central and southern Asia, the Pacific Islands, New Zealand, and Australia. Broadly speaking, this area has been influenced by the religions and civilizations of Asia and the Middle East.

These two large areas, although broadly different, have some things in common. Both contain cultures that have developed a sophisticated, "classical" repertory of music, played primarily by professional musicians. And both contain nonliterate cultures whose music is not written down but is generally performed by most of the members of the society. Music of the second type is sometimes known as tribal music.

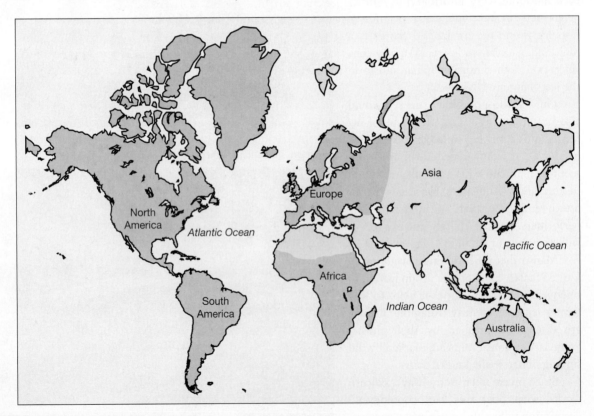

The two broad musical areas of the world.

A scene from a Chinese opera.

In both areas, there are also two types of music that lie somewhere between these two extremes. These we may call folk and popular music. Folk music exists alongside classical music and continues to be performed in rural areas. It is often several generations old. In addition to folk music, most cultures also have a flourishing popular music industry. This music tends to be ephemeral (a hit may last only a few weeks), commercial (designed to sell), and aimed at a broad, generally urban, audience. This is as true in India, for example, as it is in Finland or Argentina or any number of other countries.

WHAT TO LISTEN FOR IN MUSIC AROUND THE WORLD

Some of the general characteristics of world music have been discussed above, but let us summarize them here.

1. Much of the music around the world is part of an oral tradition. It is not written down, but is passed along the generations by memory.
2. All cultures use both voices and instruments.
3. Music is a reflection of a culture. To understand the music, we need to understand the role it plays in that culture.

There are some more-detailed observations we can make about music that lies outside the European-American classical tradition, and we shall consider them now. We shall take the music of the European-American tradition as a point of comparison, not to make value judgments, but simply because for many of us it is the most familiar.

Attitude Toward Music of the Past

We have already noted that in the United States, much of the music played in concerts dates from hundreds of years ago. Because most music in other cultures around the world is not written down, a different attitude exists with regard to music of the past.

A *jali* from Gambia.

In some cultures, for example, works from the past serve as a basis for improvisation. In India and Japan, for instance, some traditional pieces serve as the framework for learned improvisations by highly trained master musicians. In other countries, music is regarded as a living, flexible artifact, constantly open to change. In these cultures, the music is constantly being reinvented, so that, in a sense, music of the past doesn't really exist: It is constantly turning into music of the present.

Texture

The texture of most music around the world is very different from that of European classical music. The works composed in Europe and the United States over the last several hundred years are highly organized, very sophisticated complexes of sound. These works often involve large numbers of people playing different musical lines on different instruments, all of which blend into a dense, unified whole.

Music of other cultures has focused on different aspects of musical style, and as a result the texture is very different. With significant exceptions, particularly in Africa, most other music has only one melody sounding at a time, often with a rhythmic accompaniment of considerable interest. The essence of this music is therefore very different, and our way of listening to it must therefore be consciously modified. In some cultures, several different performers play the same melody, but each in his own way. The result is simultaneous, slightly varying, interweaving strands of a single tune.

A violinist and singer in India.

Melody

Although a great deal of European-American classical music contains beautiful melodies, we could not say that melody is the central focus of the music or that the music explores melody to the fullest. In many musical styles around the world, melody is of paramount interest. The prevailing musical texture, with its focus on a single line, helps in this regard. The *essence* of the music is in the melody.

Rhythm

Many musical styles are highly complex in rhythm. Rhythmically, it has to be said, Western music—classical and popular alike—is rather dull. Most pieces use the same beat or meter throughout. By contrast, many musical styles around the world use extremely intricate rhythms. African drummers frequently produce several complex rhythms simultaneously. In India, rhythm is raised to the level of a special art, and rhythmic patterns are established in Indian music theory. There are hundreds of these patterns, and an Indian drummer has to study for years to learn them all.

na ga dhet   ta   ka ra dha ti ra ki ta dha ti ra ki ta ta ka ta   ti ra ki ta ta ka

ti   ra ki ta ta ka dha tit   dha   ta   ka ta dha tit   dha ta ka ta dha tit   dha

Excerpt from a *majara*, a type of North Indian drumming pattern that often occurs at the close of a phrase or entire work. The syllables below the notes refer to specific drumstrokes.

Tone Color: Voices and Instruments

European-American classical music encompasses a wide range of instrumental and vocal sounds. A symphony orchestra boasts dozens of different instruments, and these can play singly or in large numbers of different combinations. Music of other cultures, however, often displays **tone colors**, vocal and instrumental, that are very different from anything heard in Western classical music.

An Indian master of the *tabla* or drums.

In many cultures, the ideal vocal sound is not smooth, flowing, and relaxed, as it is in the cultivated European tradition. Singers often use a very tense, strained technique (Native Americans). Or they may be able to produce two tones at once (in Tibet, Mongolia, Siberia), or sing in an extremely florid manner, with incredibly fast, clean runs and trills and ornaments (in Morocco, Saudi Arabia, Pakistan). The singers of some areas practice a yodeling technique, in which the voice moves rapidly between a regular singing voice and a high, artificial voice. This technique is practiced by the Swiss, the Pygmies of central Africa, and the Berbers of the Sahara.

Instruments around the world produce a wide variety of tone colors. The instruments a culture develops often depend on the raw materials available. In Africa, instruments are made of wood, animal skins, and animal horns, sometimes even of ivory. In China, Laos, Cambodia, Vietnam, and Indonesia, bronze instruments, such as gongs and chimes, are favored.

Four alphorn players in Switzerland.

Musical instruments around the world can be classified into four groups: stringed instruments, including those that are plucked and those that are bowed; wind instruments, which are blown; and two types of percussion instruments, those whose sound is produced by hitting some material stretched over a hollow object (drums) and those whose sound is made by hitting, shaking, or waving a solid object (gongs, chimes, rattles, scrapers, etc.).

Each of these categories includes an enormous variety of instruments. Stringed instruments can be long or short, have one or many strings, and range in sound from

Tiny clay *ocarina*.

Dancers in Zaire.

very loud to exceedingly soft and delicate. Wind instruments range from the gigantic alphorn, designed to be heard over mountain ranges, to the dovelike tones of the small clay ocarina.

Percussion instruments represent the largest number of instruments around the world. They can often produce a definite note rather than just a bonk or a clunk. In many cultures, percussion is produced *without* instruments. Rhythmic sounds and complex rhythmic patterns are made by clapping hands, slapping thighs, and stamping feet.

In some cultures an instrument that seems familiar to us may produce a very different sound. The *hardingfele*, or Norwegian fiddle, is a violin that has been adapted to folk culture. It has extra strings that are not bowed but vibrate when the fiddle is played. The sound is highly resonant and penetrating.

Many instruments have no Western equivalent, and their tone color is distinctive. An instrument in widespread use in Africa is the *mbira* (pronounced "mmm-beera"),

MUSICNOTE 60

Companion CD, track 60 Mbira

The African *mbira* or thumb piano.

often translated as "thumb piano." The *mbira* has thin metal strips fastened to a small wooden box or gourd and is held in both hands while the thumbs pluck the strips. The sound is soft, buzzy, watery, plunky. The buzz is often enhanced by means of metal bottle tops loosely attached to the wood.

The most dramatic illustration of the importance of tone color in instrumental playing is given by the *didjeridoo* of the Australian aboriginal people. This is a long, wet, hollowed-out eucalyptus branch, played like a trumpet. The *didjeridoo* can produce only two pitches, but the subtlety of the instrument lies in its tonal qualities. A skilled player can produce upwards of nine or ten different tone colors on his instrument.

Musical Context

In many regions of the world, music is part of a ceremony or a group activity. Music most commonly occurs in combination with dance. But there are many other group contexts in which music plays a role. In Africa, rhythmic group songs are widely used to facilitate work. Native American tribes use music to accompany gambling games, contact guardian spirits, conduct the medicine bundle ceremony, cure illnesses, and distinguish among age and sex groups.

Australian Aboriginal playing the *didjeridoo*.

Attitudes Toward the Participation of Women

The place of women is closely defined, and often severely restricted, in most cultures around the globe. In many communities, women do not take part in musical activities, these being reserved for men. In Japanese Kabuki theater and Chinese traditional opera, for example, female roles are sung by men.

In other communities, women participate as singers or dancers, but instruments are seen as inappropriate for them. (This is not very different from jazz in North America: There have been many female jazz singers, but most of the instrumentalists have traditionally been men.) In Islamic countries, where most music is regarded with suspicion, and women's roles are strictly defined, women traditionally sing only wedding songs.

MUSICNOTE 61

Companion CD, track 61 Didjeridoo

Time

One final facet of music that differs greatly among cultures is time. In twentieth-century European and American society, the length of a musical performance is highly conventionalized. A classical music concert is designed to take almost exactly two hours, including a twenty-minute intermission. Rock concerts can run longer, but more or less the same limits apply.

But in other cultures, ideas about the length of a musical event can be very different. The Peyote ceremony of many Native American tribes consists of an entire night of singing. The religious Hako ceremony of the Pawnee lasts for several days. And the Navajo curing ceremony continues over a period of nine days and nights and includes hundreds of different songs. The Pygmies of central Africa, who enjoy a deep and spiritual relationship with the forest in which they live, have developed a ceremony in which they sing to the forest every night over a period of several months.

In almost every facet of its existence, then, music is regarded in different ways among the various peoples of the world: in the melody, rhythm, tone color, and texture of the music itself; in the context in which music is performed; and in attitudes toward music of the past, the participation of women, and the duration of a musical event. As human beings, we vary widely in our understanding of the meaning of music and the role it plays in our lives. Yet music is one of the great human accomplishments that we all share.

MUSIC FROM AROUND THE WORLD

By now, you have some basis for listening to some examples of music from around the world. These will be chosen primarily to illustrate the enormous variety of kinds of music and attitudes toward music that exist on our planet. In all cases, we shall consider cultural context as well as musical content. The first two examples come from the Eastern half of our world, the third from the Western half. We shall listen first to solo music for the Japanese *shakuhachi*, then to the sounds of the Indonesian *gamelan* orchestra, and finally to *mbira* music from Africa.

Japanese *Shakuhachi* Music

Ancient Japanese music dates back at least to the early Middle Ages and continues to the sixteenth century. In this feudal period, rival warlords established their own courts and fought for power, and the indigenous Shinto religion was joined by Buddhism, imported from China. The music includes religious chant for the Buddhist liturgy, choral singing for the Shinto religion, medieval courtly orchestral music known as *gagaku* ("elegant music"), and music for the **Noh** theater, which combines singing, dancing, and instrumental playing.

In addition to this ancient repertoire, there is a body of "classical" music from Japan's Edo period, which lasted from 1615 to 1868. It is called "Edo" because the ruling clan at that time moved the capital of the country to Edo (modern-day Tokyo). This was a period of relative peace and prosperity after the military strife of the samurai era, and a prosperous middle class developed in the cities. The colorful music of this period is a reflection of this new audience.

Scene from Japanese Noh theater.

There is a large repertory of theatrical music as well as music for instruments. The purely instrumental music of the Edo period includes both small-group music and solo music. The traditional small ensemble is made up of a singer and three instruments: a *shamisen*, which is a three-stringed, long-necked lute; a *koto*, which is a delicate, thirteen-stringed plucked zither; and the *shakuhachi* bamboo flute. But there also exist repertories of exquisite solo music for *koto* or *shakuhachi* alone. These repertories have been passed down the generations by means of oral tradition. Many, many years of dedicated learning, careful listening, and self-discipline are required to become a master of the *koto* or the *shakuhachi*. **(See Listening Guide on p. 55.)**

Popular music in Japan is highly varied, ranging from folk-inspired melodies to Western pop and rock styles. Indeed, much popular music played now in Japan is imported from the United States and England, reflecting the current Japanese fascination with the West. Many young musicians today are also trained in Western classical music, and Japanese composers write symphonic music that is a blend of the Western symphonic idiom and traditional Japanese elements.

Let us summarize the ways in which Japanese music has responded to the changing nature of its society over time.

1. *The feudal period:* Music from this period includes both Buddhist chant and Shinto songs and prayers, together with courtly instrumental music and Noh theater.

2. *The Edo period:* Music becomes more urban and middle-class, involving entertaining stage works as well as instrumental compositions for master musicians.

3. *The modern period:* Music becomes more focused on popular song and begins to show Western popular and classical influences.

LISTENING GUIDE

Koku-Reibo (A Bell Ringing in the Empty Sky)   Duration: 4:27

Complete CD Collection: 1, Track 1

The *shakuhachi* is a bamboo flute with five finger holes and is blown from one end. Its name means "one and eight-tenths," because in Japanese measurement the *shakuhachi* has the length of one and eight-tenths *shaku* (a shaku is roughly a foot).

Music for the *shakuhachi* has a profound, mystical quality. The instrument was used as part of religious ceremony by Zen Buddhist monks in the seventeenth century, and it has been said that a single note of the *shakuhachi* can bring one to the state of nirvana (perfect blessedness).

The piece that we shall hear is one of the oldest in the repertory, dating back to the seventeenth century. It is called **Koku-Reibo (*A Bell Ringing in the Empty Sky*).** The title refers to the death of Zen monk Fuke-Zenji, who used to walk around ringing a small handbell. On his death, the sound of his bell could be heard getting fainter and fainter as it ascended into the clear blue sky. Playing the *shakuhachi* takes great skill, requiring an enormous amount of control and subtlety of expression. The musician performing here, Nyogetsu Seldin, has studied the

A Shakuhachi flute player.

traditional art of the *shakuhachi* for thirty years. He studied with Kurahashi Yodo Sensei in Kyoto and is now a Grand Master of the instrument.

The music is riveting. It demands all of your attention, because it depends on such minute details. There are only a few notes, but the variety of sounds is amazing. The player uses slides between notes, shadings of color and sound, variations of intensity, and carefully controlled gradations of volume to produce an atmosphere that is truly mystical. Our excerpt ends after only a few minutes, but the entire composition lasts more than fifteen minutes. Listen to the excerpt very carefully, and listen to it several times. Each time you will hear something new. The music will capture your imagination in an entirely new way.

Gamelan Music from the Indonesian Island of Java

In Indonesia, traditional music is played on a group of instruments made up primarily of metal percussion. This small orchestra is known as a **gamelan** (an Indonesian word meaning "musical ensemble"). A *gamelan* includes a wide variety of instruments. Among them are metal xylophones of three different sizes. There are two sizes of bronze bowls, which produce different tone qualities. *Gamelans* also include a series of gongs (*gong* is another Indonesian word), one approximately three feet in diameter, with a very powerful sound, and several sizes of smaller ones. There are also skin drums, wooden percussion instruments, and sometimes flutes, a bowed two-string fiddle, and a plucked string instrument. The sound of the *gamelan* is unique, with its highly varied metallic sounds, its wide range from the deep gong to the highest xylophone, and its complex of interlocking parts. **(See Listening Guide on p. 57.)**

When you see a *gamelan* in performance, you will notice something very ceremonial about it. The players sit cross-legged on the floor, as do players in much Eastern

An Indonesian *gamelan*.

music. The instruments, with their elaborately carved and painted cases, are spaced about the floor in a carefully organized manner. And the performers treat their instruments with great respect. *Gamelan* orchestras are often owned by wealthy patrons, and some of the ensembles have names (such as "Dark Cloud" or "Thunder of Honey").

The *gamelan* in Indonesia is regarded with reverence. This derives partly from its association with ancient religious ritual, partly from its representation of royalty. Shoes must not be worn when playing the *gamelan*, and it is considered disrespectful to step over an instrument. Some ancient *gamelans* are regarded as possessing special spirituality and are presented with ritual offerings of food, flowers, and incense.

Gamelan compositions must be played with the appropriate reverent attitude, and the music should not be reproduced casually.

Gamelan music requires the cooperation of a large number of people, all of whom submerge their own personalities into the power of a unified whole. In this, perhaps more than in any other aspect, the Indonesian *gamelan* displays its link to a courtly, as well as to a spiritual, past. An author has written: "Javanese *gamelan* is comparable to only two things: moonlight and flowing water. It is pure and mysterious like moonlight; it is always the same and always changing like flowing water. It is not a song. It is a state of being."

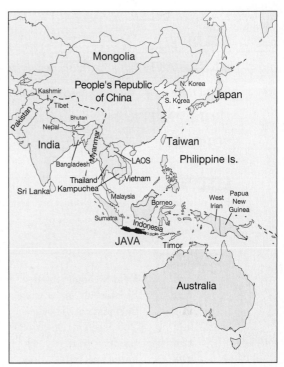

The island of Java in Indonesia.

LISTENING GUIDE

JAVANESE *GAMELAN* MUSIC
Gangsaran–Bima Kurda–Gangsaran

Duration: 6:21

Complete CD Collection: 1, Track 2

*G*amelan music usually has picturesque or philosophical titles. In Javanese, **Gangsaran** means "achieving one's purpose," and **Bima Kurda** means "angry hero."

This composition mostly features metallic instruments—xylophones, bronze bowls, and gongs—but you will also hear at least two sizes of drum: a large bass drum and a medium-sized drum. Soon after the beginning, the music slows down for the main central section; it speeds up again toward the end. While the music is being played, a stylized dance is performed by two men: a drillmaster and a soldier. They utter occasional shouts and laughter, and twice they speak a ritual dialogue. The dialogue is as follows:

DRILLMASTER:	*ORANG DUA-DUA!*	Hey you!
SOLDIER:	*Yaaah!*	Yes sir!
DRILLMASTER:	*Apa kita berani temen?*	Are you really brave?
SOLDIER:	*Yaaah, berani temen!*	Yes sir, I am!
DRILLMASTER:	*Haah, serobah!*	Then carry on!
SOLDIER:	*Inggih djadhaaaak, sendika!*	Yes, teacher, I obey! (laughs)

GANGSARAN

2	0:00	Regular rhythms, same note repeated.
	0:26	Music slows down.

BIMA KURDA

3	0:40	Melody gathers interest, more notes are heard.
	0:55	Rhythm and melody become steady. Long section.
	2:35	Beginning of dialogue.
	2:57	Quiet section. Occasional shouts and laughter.
	4:20	Louder.
	4:36	Music gets faster again.
	5:18	Repeat of dialogue.

GANGSARAN

4	5:32	Return of music from the opening section.
	6:15	Abrupt ending.

African Drumming and *Mbira* Music

Some people in the United States and Europe think of Africa as a single entity. This is, of course, an oversimplification. The continent contains several hundred distinct ethnic groups, whose peoples are scattered widely across the national boundaries that were mostly established in colonial days. This diversity of social organization, language, ethnicity, race, and religion is mirrored in a great diversity of musical practices. Yet it is possible to make some generalizations that hold true.

First, there is a broad cultural division between North Africa and sub-Saharan Africa, which is mirrored in their musics. Music in North Africa (primarily Morocco, Algeria, Tunisia, Libya, and Egypt) is very similar in style to that of the Middle East. Music from sub-Saharan Africa is more like what we think of as "African" music.

Second, it is possible to discover certain general characteristics within the music of sub-Saharan Africa, despite its enormous size and diversity. These include the following elements:

1. Music is strongly associated with dance.

2. Instruments are numerous and widespread.

3. Sounds of percussion are heavily favored; these include drums as well as other percussion instruments.

4. Polyphonic (multiple) sounds predominate. These may involve several rhythms produced simultaneously or two or more melodies interwoven.

5. Melodies are made up of repetition, variation, and improvisation on short melodic fragments.

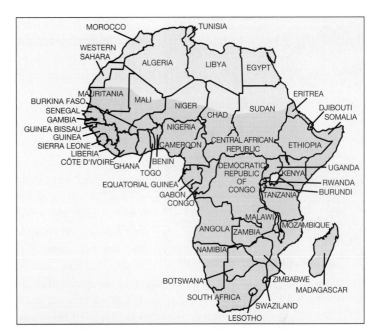

Map of present-day Africa.

The two most widespread instruments in sub-Saharan Africa are the drum and the **mbira**. Drums come in many different sizes and forms. They include tall, single-headed drums, closed at the lower end; large, open-ended drums; small drums in an hourglass shape; two-headed drums with even-sized heads or with one small and one large head; and even a two-headed drum whose pitches can be changed by tightening or loosening the tension on the heads while the drum is being played.

African drumming is often extremely complex. A single drummer can produce an array of rhythms, as well as different notes and tone colors. Drumming ensembles are common: Several players of different-sized drums produce a dense, interlocking texture of multiple, simultaneous rhythms and notes.

Mbira music is no less complex. **(See Listening Guide on p. 60.)** As mentioned previously, an *mbira* is an instrument made of a small wooden box or gourd with a row of thin metal strips attached to it. The strips are plucked by the thumbs of both hands. The *mbira* also comes in many different types, depending on the material of the resonating body, the size and number of the strips, and the objects (beads, shells, bottle tops) that are sometimes attached to the instrument to enrich the sound. The *mbira* is regarded as sacred by certain tribes. The Shona of Zimbabwe, for example, use it to summon the spirits of their ancestors.

Mbira music, like drum music, illustrates a very African view of music, which itself derives from a special sense of time. *Mbira* music and drum music are not frozen into "pieces" that can be reproduced more or less identically on any given occasion. Each performance involves a lengthy combination of repetition and very gradual variation, so that the music may be seen as a *process* rather than as a piece. (Modern composers in the West have been heavily influenced by this African aesthetic.)

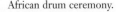

African drum ceremony.

The Zimbabwean musician
Forward Kwenda with
his mbira.

Mbira instrumentalists play a short melodic pattern over and over again. As time passes, they gradually weave slight changes into the melodic pattern, creating a variation. Each slightly different variation is also played over and over again before a new change is introduced. Change thus takes place over a long period of time.

This special conception of time may derive from the closeness to nature with which Africans have lived for so long. The world of the plains, the forests, and the jungle unfolds at its own pace, which is different from the frenetic pace of modern urban life. Perhaps the music of African peoples is a reflection of this slow unfolding.

Like drum music, *mbira* music displays the African fascination with complex, multiple sounds. Because of the resonance of the instrument, each note played continues to sound for a while during the next few notes. Also, the attachment to the body of the instrument of beads or bottle tops, which vibrate or buzz slightly when the instrument is played, gives each note a rich, slightly hazy quality, like the moon on a misty night. An *mbira* melody, even on one instrument, is made up of the interlocking of two parts, one played by the right thumb, the other by the left. Often, however, *mbiras* are played in pairs or in groups, producing an even more complex web of sound.

LISTENING GUIDE

Mandarendare (A Place Full of Energy)

Duration: 5:32
Complete CD Collection: 1, Track 5

For the Shona, a people who make up most of the population of Zimbabwe and extend also into Mozambique, *mbira* music is mystical music that is used to communicate with the spirits of ancestors and guardians of the tribe. *Mandarendare* (A Place Full of Energy) is usually played at a dawn ceremony. The performer on this recording, Forward Kwenda, has been involved in keeping alive the musical traditions of the Shona people since he was a young boy. He says, "When I pick up my *mbira*, I don't know what is going to happen. The music goes by itself. It is so much greater than a human being can understand."

Although it sounds as though more than one person is playing on this piece, there is only one performer. Three distinct layers of sound can be detected: a deep, regular pattern in the bass and two interlocking lines above it. Although there seems at first to be constant repetition, careful listening will reveal slow, but constant, change. The tone quality is unusual; the notes are surrounded with a hiss or buzz that sounds to our ears like a sonic distortion. This hiss, which adds depth and complexity to the sound, is considered an essential element in *mbira* playing.

CONCLUSION

In this chapter, we have taken only a glance at several different cultures around the world, and we have seen how very different the music is in each of them. And yet we can make a few general observations. The first is that music is a reflection of the society that creates it. In order to understand the music, we need to understand something about that society.

Looking at the Japanese, Indonesian, and African cultures as briefly as we have, we begin to see how daunting a task it is to get a full picture of the meaning and significance of music in a particular cultural context. To understand even one type of music, in one corner of the world, requires a wide range of knowledge: historical and cultural background, specific listening skills, and a method for putting musical observations into words. Each type of music could fill a book on its own.

For most of this book, we will be examining music of the Western tradition, which has an extremely long and rich history. To do this, we will need to work on a greater understandin of the culture surrounding the different historical periods of Western music and apply the skills of listening and terminology we learned in the previous chapters.

Listening to...

MUSIC FROM AROUND THE WORLD

For each kind of music you hear, you need some background on the society that produced it.

- The example of Japanese *shakuhachi* (bamboo flute) music that we heard (p. 55) dates from the Edo period (early seventeenth to late nineteenth century). The music is elegant, sophisticated, and colored by the introspective and perceptive nature of Zen Buddhism. Every slight shading of the sound has meaning.

- Indonesian *gamelan* music (p. 57) utilizes a complex orchestra made up of many varied sounds, dominated by metal percussion instruments. It comes from a courtly as well as a spiritual society. "It is always the same and always changing."

- *Mbira* music of the Shona people from southeastern Africa (p. 60) is a fabric of separate lines woven together, often produced on just one instrument. The music seems to undergo a very gradual process of change and has a mystical, trancelike quality.

KEY TERMS

oral tradition **(p. 45)**   mbira **(p. 52)**   noh **(p. 54)**
tone color **(p. 51)**   gamelan **(p. 54)**   shakuhachi **(p. 54)**

3
The Middle Ages: 400–1400

INTRODUCTION

As we saw in Chapter 1, historians generally divide European history into convenient periods. The first period from which any substantial amount of music survives is the Middle Ages. Why is it called the Middle Ages? The name arose because the period is *between* the end of the Roman Empire (about 400 A.D.) and the beginning of the Renaissance (1400).

For the sake of convenience, historians today usually divide the Middle Ages into two periods: an early period, from 400 to 1000, and a later period, from 1000 to 1400. In the early Middle Ages, most of Europe was covered with forests. Most of the countries we know today did not exist. A small number of noble families controlled much of the land, and most of the rest of the population worked in near slavery. A highly organized system of power, called the feudal system, held everyone in its grip. The serfs owed their allegiance to the landowners, the landowners to the local lords, the lords to the king.

As time went on, the land was gradually cleared, and small villages were established. By the later Middle Ages, some of these villages had grown into towns. The towns were magnets for trade and commerce and for many of the people from the countryside. The streets were filled with peddlers and beggars, children playing, and wagons rumbling through. Shopkeepers set up tables to display their wares and tried to attract the attention of wealthy merchants as they passed.

In Europe as a whole, some of the noble families became particularly powerful, and gradually the boundaries of many of the European countries were established more or less as we know them today. The rise of a middle class—represented by bankers and traders,

Peasants working in the late Middle Ages.

400

500

Pope Gregory 540–604

600

700

Charlemagne crowned
Emperor 800
First use of numeral zero 814

800

900

Most of Catholic liturgy
composed by 1000
Invention of solfege and
four-line staff 1025

1000

1100

Beatriz de Dia
c. 1150–c. 1200

Perotinus c. 1170–c. 1236
Consecration of the Cathedral
of Notre Dame 1182

1200

Thomas Aquinas 1225–1274

Marco Polo journeys
to China 1271
Invention of eyeglasses 1290
Guillaume de Machaut
c. 1300–1377

1300

The Black Death devastates
Europe 1348

1400

An illustration from a fifteenth-century French manuscript.

The medieval cathedral of Chartres in France.

Photography by Jean Bernard, "Univers de Chartres," copyright Bordas, Paris, 1988.

merchants and shippers—helped to break down the feudal system.

Most people were serfs and spent their lives working in miserable conditions. Wars were frequent, and whenever one occurred, all the serfs controlled by the local lords were forced to take part. Most of the population was illiterate, and scientific and medical knowledge was rudimentary. There were no vaccines or antibiotics, so most diseases and infections that we regard today as minor inconveniences were fatal. The average life expectancy was in the forties.

But the image that people have nowadays of the Middle Ages as the "Dark Ages" is incomplete. Technological innovations were enormously influential. In the early Middle Ages, three important inventions led to increased food production and a significant growth in the population. These were the heavy wheeled plough, the padded horse collar, and the horseshoe. In the later Middle Ages, the rate of innovation increased. Trade routes were established because of naval improvements in the compass and mapmaking and the invention of double pulleys and cargo ships. Entire economies were changed by the utilization of water power to drive flour mills and the invention of the spinning wheel, the mechanical clock, and the immensely efficient, humble, wheelbarrow. Eyeglasses became widely available; gunpowder transformed warfare; and the adoption of paper and the invention of printing transformed the spread of education.

Learning and literacy were kept alive by Jews and Christians and Muslims all over Europe. Gradually, education became more widespread, and universities were established in towns all the way from England to Hungary. As well as being centers of trade and commerce, the new towns were centers of cultural exchange. The arts flourished: Music, painting, poetry, sculpture and architecture all brought forth remarkable achievements.

In the Middle Ages, most artistic endeavor was inspired, encouraged, and paid for by the Church. And in each important town, the place where all the medieval arts were concentrated was the cathedral. Medieval cathedrals are marvels of architecture; their doorways and outer walls were graced by superb sculptures; paintings and tapestries adorned their inner walls; and every day the cathedrals were filled with music.

GENERAL CHARACTERISTICS OF MEDIEVAL MUSIC

A huge quantity of music has survived from the Middle Ages. The earliest *written* examples come from the eighth or ninth century, but much of the music dates from even earlier. This earlier music must have passed from generation to generation by means of an oral tradition. By the year 1000, an enormous amount of medieval music had been composed and was being performed throughout Europe.

Because Christianity was the dominant religion as well as the principal unifying feature of much of Europe, most of the surviving music from the medieval period was for use in Christian religious services. This music is known as **liturgical music** (music of formal religious ritual). The music is vocal music and is known generically as **plainchant** (unison singing of the medieval liturgy).

By the later medieval period, two innovations were emerging. One was the rise of written **secular music** ("secular" means "non-religious"), and the other was the rise of **polyphony**—music with more than one musical line sounding at a time. Both of these innovations had vital consequences for the entire later history of Western music. The idea that composers could devote their attention to topics outside religion—such as love—broadened the scope of music immensely. And polyphony gave rise to harmony, which is one of the main features that distinguish most Western music from that of other cultures.

Our survey of medieval music is therefore divided into two parts. First, we will discuss early medieval liturgical chant. Then we turn to music of the later Middle Ages—especially polyphony and love songs.

A medieval depiction of Pope Gregory VII. The Holy Spirit (in the form of a dove) is whispering chants in his ear; Pope Gregory, in turn, is dictating the chants to a scribe.

Pope Gregory VII (1073–1085), previously Hildebrandt, c. 1021 – Salerno 25.5.1085. Gregory VII and a scribe. Book illustration, contemporary, Leipzig, University Library. Photo: AKG London.

THE MUSIC OF THE MIDDLE AGES

Plainchant

Many people call plainchant "Gregorian chant" after the famous Pope Gregory I, who lived from about 540 to 604. During the early Middle Ages, thousands of chants were composed.

Plainchant is **monophonic**—that is, it has only one line of music sounding at a time. Several people may be singing that one line in unison, but there is no accompaniment and no harmony. It may seem very limiting to have music restricted to just one line, but in fact plainchant is extremely varied. It ranges from very simple melodies, centered primarily on a single pitch, to highly elaborate ones, with long, flowing lines.

The most important element of variety in plainchant comes from the melodic system in which it is written. Plainchant is not written in modern scales or keys. It uses a system of **modes**. Each mode has a unique pattern of intervals and therefore its own special sound and feeling. In the medieval system, there are four main modes, which end, respectively, on D, E, F, and G.

Interestingly, many folk songs, perhaps because of their antiquity, are **modal**. You can hear the special evocative quality of the D, or Dorian, mode in a song such as "Scarborough Fair" (better known by the words of its refrain, "Parsley, sage, rosemary, and thyme"), or others, such as "Donna, Donna" and "Greensleeves."

The pattern of intervals in E-mode pieces is different. So chants composed in that mode sound different from those composed in the D mode. And the same is true for F-mode and G-mode pieces, because each has its own characteristic pattern of intervals.

The chart gives the names and some of the characteristic patterns of these four main medieval modes. This system of modes is very important. It is the basis upon which over a thousand years of Western music is built, and it is this system that makes the world of medieval plainchant so colorful, so rich, and so appealing.

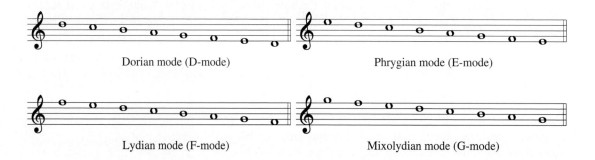

Dorian mode (D-mode)

Phrygian mode (E-mode)

Lydian mode (F-mode)

Mixolydian mode (G-mode)

Why does plainchant sound the way it does, with its serene, otherworldly character? The first reason has to do with the rhythm. The music flows along without a clearly defined rhythm and, unlike later music, it has no meter and no regular pattern of strong or weak beats. The second reason for the special sound of plainchant is the nature of the modes. They are very subtle. They are like pastel colors used in painting. They lack the intense drive of modern scales or keys. Finally, because there is only one musical line, the listener can concentrate entirely on the shape and direction of the melody. Indeed, plainchant is the greatest repository of pure melody in the whole history of Western music.

A medieval manuscript from the fifteenth century, showing the music for a Kyrie, with an illumination of monks and a choirboy singing.

Kyriale, Italy (Cremona), third quarter 15th c. M685, f.1. The Pierpont Morgan Library, New York, NY. Art Resource, NY.

LISTENING GUIDE

KYRIE (PLAINCHANT)

Performers: Men's choir singing in unison
Mode: G
Duration: 2:06

Companion CD, Track 63

This is a chant from a medieval Catholic Mass. It is one of many settings of this text. Although most of the Mass was in Latin, the words to the Kyrie are in Greek. There are three statements in the text: "Kyrie eleison—Christe eleison—Kyrie eleison" ("Lord, have mercy—Christ, have mercy—Lord, have mercy"). And each of these three statements is sung three times. There is great symbolism in this repetition scheme: The number three represented the Trinity, and three times three was considered absolute perfection.

Corresponding to the three statements of the text, there are three phrases of music. The whole piece begins and ends on G, so it is in the G mode. As in a painting, however, a composition may have a mixture of colors, and there are hints of the E mode in the first phrase, which ends on E. The shape of the melody is very carefully designed. The first phrase is the shortest and moves in waves. The second phrase starts high, and the motion is mostly descending. The last phrase is in the form of an arch and starts and ends on the same note (G). At the top of the arch, the music reaches up to the highest note in the whole piece. The last time the third statement of the text is sung, the music changes slightly, with the addition of three notes to the beginning of the phrase.

Kyrie eleison.	*Lord have mercy.*
Kyrie eleison.	*Lord have mercy.*
Kyrie eleison.	*Lord have mercy.*
Christe eleison.	*Christ have mercy.*
Christe eleison.	*Christ have mercy.*
Christe eleison.	*Christ have mercy.*
Kyrie eleison.	*Lord have mercy.*
Kyrie eleison.	*Lord have mercy.*
Kyrie eleison.	*Lord have mercy.*

Polyphony

The idea of composing music with two or more simultaneous musical lines took hold strongly about 1200, when there was a sudden explosion of polyphonic liturgical composition. The polyphony of this time is striking in its power and grandeur. Compositions of two, three, and even four voices were written to celebrate the major feasts of the church year. At a time when the cycle of life revolved around the church calendar,

The magnificent Cathedral of Notre Dame in Paris.

feasts such as Christmas and Easter must have been spectacular and vivid occasions. People spent days or even weeks preparing for the special celebrations that surrounded the feast days. In the clothes that were worn, in the meals that were prepared, in the brief escape from the constant burden of work, these days must have had special significance for the majority of medieval society. It is not surprising, therefore, that such days were marked by very special music.

Paris was the place where the most significant amount of polyphony was composed in the twelfth and thirteenth centuries. Paris was one of the primary centers of the late medieval world. The kings of France had their palaces in Paris; the first university in the Middle Ages was established in Paris; and Paris was a hub of commercial activity for the whole of Europe.

In the center of Paris, on an island in the middle of the river Seine, stood a huge cathedral, newly built around 1200. It was a magnificent sight. Indeed, it still is. Visitors to Paris still visit Notre Dame Cathedral, for it remains one of the great architectural marvels of Europe.

To match the splendor and beauty of this cathedral, and to celebrate the main feasts of the church year, two composers created the first great collection of polyphony in the history of Western music. Their names were Leonius and Perotinus, and we know little about either of them. They probably were officials at the cathedral in some capacity.

The collection of compositions by these two men is known as the *Magnus Liber Organi* (*Great Book of Polyphony*). This book contains a series of elaborate polyphonic compositions for the main feasts of the church year. These compositions are based directly on the ancient plainchants for those feasts. The music may contain several independent musical lines, but one of them is always the original chant melody. Among the most famous of the pieces written for the Cathedral of Notre Dame is the four-voice *Viderunt Omnes* by Perotinus, based on the plainchant of the same name. This chant is sung right in the middle of the Mass on Christmas.

Perotinus set some portions of the chant polyphonically for solo singers. The rest of the chant, sung by the choir, stays monophonic. So the piece has an alternation of performing forces (soloists–choir), but it also has an alternation of polyphonic and monophonic textures.

But there is even more to it than that. First, the textural contrast is reinforced by a rhythmic contrast. The monophonic (choir) sections are sung in the traditional way, in a free, smooth, essentially rhythmless style. The polyphonic (soloist) sections, however, are marked by very clear-cut rhythms. In addition, there are contrasts within the polyphonic sections themselves. Parts of these sections have extremely long, sustained notes underpinning them; other parts have faster notes in the lower voice, which move almost as quickly as those in the upper voices.

Below is a sample of this kind of polyphony, showing some of these elements: a bottom voice starting with a sustained tone but turning more rhythmic, a somewhat more complex middle voice, and an extremely elaborate upper voice. Even if you cannot read music, you can see plainly in the example that the top voice sings more notes than the middle voice, which in turn has more notes than the bottom voice.

Di ——   xit   Do-   mi-   nus

The remarkable thing about this music is the fact that, despite its variety and density, it retains the whole of the original plainchant embedded in it. All the words are still there, and all the original notes are retained in the lower voice. The composition is a complex and sophisticated work, but it is built entirely on the foundation of an ancient structure. This is entirely appropriate, for the music was designed for a cathedral that was one of the glories of the new Gothic age but was erected on the site of a Paris church many centuries old.

LISTENING GUIDE

PEROTINUS (c.1170–c.1236)

Viderunt Omnes (four-voice polyphony for the Cathedral of Notre Dame)

Date of composition: 1199
Solo singers and choir
Duration: 4:42

Complete CD Collection: 1, Track 6

The listening guide brings together all the elements of the preceding discussion. The text is given, with indications specifying whether it is sung in chant or in polyphony. In the polyphonic section, the contrast between sustained-tone and rhythmic accompaniment is marked. Note also the intricate intertwining of the three upper voices over the two different styles of the lower voice. The rich harmonies, the unrelenting rhythmic drive, and the sheer scope of the piece show how magnificent and awe inspiring a piece of music from 800 years ago can be. (Here, only a portion of the overall work is given; the entire piece lasts for nearly twelve minutes.)

POLYPHONY				
6	0:00	(soloists)	*Vi-* (sustained tone)	[rhythmic upper voices throughout]
	0:57	(soloists)	*de-* (sustained tone)	
	1:25	(soloists)	*runt* (sustained tone)	[dissonant opening; brief cadence for end of word]
	2:29	(soloists)	*om-* (rhythmic/sustained tone)	
	3:40	(soloists)	*nes* (sustained tone)	[strong dissonance just before cadence]
		[cadence]		

MONOPHONY				
7	3:46	(choir)	*fines terrae salutare Dei nostri. Jubilate Deo omnis terra.*	[smooth plainchant]
		[cadence]		

Viderunt omnes fines terrae salutare Dei nostri. Jubilate Deo omnis terra.

All the ends of the earth have seen the salvation of our God. Praise God all the earth.

The original medieval manuscript of Viderunt Omnes.

Love Songs

Medieval composers did not invent the idea of love songs; in Western culture the idea goes back to ancient Greek and Latin poets. But the renewed interest in the love song can be dated to the twelfth century, when the **troubadours** were active. Troubadours were poets who composed songs for performance in the many small aristocratic courts of southern France. They wrote their own poetry and music, and the subjects they favored were love, duty, friendship, and poetry itself. But the primary topic was love. The poems address an idealized vision of a woman, who is remote and usually unattainable. (Most of the troubadours were men.) The lover pines away and pleads for some sign of favor. There are also a few songs by women troubadours about men, written in the same manner.

This topic is sometimes called **courtly love**, because it flourished in the aristocratic courts. It influenced the whole history of Western love poetry. Eight centuries of love songs, up to and including pop songs of the twenty-first century, have been influenced by the conventions and vocabulary of courtly love.

Troubadours wrote mostly monophonic love songs, though they might have been sung with instrumental accompaniment. Instruments became much more numerous in the later Middle Ages. There were many different kinds: bowed, plucked, wind instruments (both of wood and brass), keyboard and percussion instruments.

Later composers, such as **Guillaume de Machaut** (c. 1300–1377), and **Francesco Landini** (c. 1325–1397) wrote songs on themes similar to those of the troubadours, but with sophisticated polyphonic settings that included both voices and instruments.

GUILLAUME DE MACHAUT AND THE LOVE SONG IN FRANCE

Machaut is one of the first composers about whom we know quite a few biographical details. He was educated at Rheims, an important town in northeastern France. He became an administrator, a poet, and a composer. He held positions at the courts of some of the most prominent members of the French ruling aristocracy. Machaut also was an administrator of the cathedral at Rheims. He died in his late seventies after a busy and productive life.

Machaut's musical style is both subtle and intense. The music is full of little rhythmic and melodic motives that tie the composition together and form beautiful melodies. The rhythm is very fluid and depends on a constant interplay between duple and triple meters (groupings of two beats and groupings of three beats). Machaut often uses **chromatic** notes (unexpected sharps and flats) to make the sound more colorful.

LISTENING GUIDE

GUILLAUME DE MACHAUT (c. 1300–1377)

Love song *Doulz Viaire Gracieus*

Date of composition: Mid fourteenth century
Voice, lute, and recorder
Duration: 2:00

Companion CD, Track 64

This short piece is a good example of Machaut's style. It is a setting of a poem that has a two-line **refrain** (printed in italics). The refrain comes at the beginning and the end, and its first line comes in the middle of the poem too. This kind of poem is known as a **rondeau**.

The music sounds very simple but is actually quite subtle. There are only two sections of music, which alternate in setting each line of the poetry. (I have marked the two sections of the music A and B.) The first section is five measures long, the second seven. This contrasts with later music, where the number of measures in each phrase or section tends to be more even. A short descending passage on the lute joins the sections together.

There are other aspects of this music that seem unusual to a listener of today. Although the prevailing meter of the piece is triple, there are several places where the music moves in duple meter. Bar lines were not used in medieval music, so the meter could be much more flexible than it is today. Also, many of the notes are chromatic: Even the opening chord contains two sharps. And although the first section ends on G, which leads you to expect that the whole piece will end on G, the final cadence is on B-flat.

The voice is accompanied by two instruments: a recorder below the voice and a **lute** above. (A lute is a plucked instrument similar to a guitar.) Although the accompanying parts are fairly independent, all three lines together create interesting harmonies, and there is a brief echo among them at the beginning of the second section.

This kind of carefully constructed polyphony, as well as the overall gentle beauty of the piece, are typical of Machaut's music and of the love song in late medieval France.

(Remember the *music* has only two sections: A and B.)

0:00	(A)	*Doulz viaire gracieus,*	*Sweet, gracious countenance,*
0:12	(B)	*De fin cuer vous ay servy.*	*I have served you with a faithful heart.*
0:30	(A)	Weillies moy estre piteus,	Take pity on me,
0:42	(A)	*Doulz viaire gracieus;*	*Sweet, gracious countenance;*
0:55	(A)	*Se je sui un po honteus,*	If I am a little shy,
1:07	(B)	Ne me mettes en oubli.	Do not forget me.
1:25	(A)	*Doulz viaire gracieus,*	*Sweet, gracious countenance,*
1:38	(B)	*De fin cuer vous ay servy.*	*I have served you with a faithful heart.*

FRANCESCO LANDINI AND THE LOVE SONG IN ITALY In Italy, late medieval musical style was rather different from that in France. Italian music tended to concentrate on florid vocal display or on beauty of vocal sound. The Italian language is so musical, even when spoken, that it has always seemed to lend itself well to song.

Landini was a musician, a poet, singer, organist, and composer. He spent his whole life in the beautiful Italian town of Florence. His playing and singing were described as so sweet that listeners were transported, and birds stopped singing to listen.

LISTENING GUIDE

FRANCESCO LANDINI (c. 1325–1397)
Love Song *Gram Piant' Agli Ochi*

Date of composition: Late fourteenth century
Two singers and lute
Duration: XXX

Complete CD Collection: 1, Track 8

This song is composed for two voices and one instrument. The lute binds the two voices together as they sing in harmony. The melodic curves of the upper voice are beautifully shaped. Again the music is in two sections (which I have labeled A and B), though the pattern of repetition is different. In this song, too, there is a refrain (printed in italics). The two lines of the refrain are sung at the beginning and repeated at the end. Each section of the music has the same very peaceful ending, which adds to the feeling of unity and repose.

The single stanza of the poem laments the pain of love. The despair of the refrain is contrasted with the image later in the poem of the "brightest star and sweetest love." And the music of the whole song is poignant, beautiful, and expressive.

0:00	(A)	*Gram piant' agli ochi, greve dogli' al core,* *Abonda senpre l'anima, si more.*	The eyes full of tears, the heart full of grievous pain, The soul is filled to overflowing, and dies.
0:12	(B)	*Per quest' amar' ed aspra dipartita* *Chiamo la mort'e non mi vol udire.*	For this cruel and bitter departure I call on Death, but he will not hear me.
0:30	(B)	*Chontra mia voglia dura questa vita,* *Che mille morti mi convien sentire,*	Against my will this life endures, Which would rather undergo a thousand deaths.
0:42	(A)	*Ma bench'i' viva, ma non vo'seguire* *Se non vo', chiara stella et dolce amore.*	But although I live, I would never follow This brightest star and sweetest love, if I did not wish to.
0:55	(A)	*Gram piant' agli ochi, greve dogli' al core,* *Abonda sempre l'anima, si more.*	The eyes full of tears, the heart full of grievous pain, The soul is filled to overflowing, and dies.

THE END OF THE MIDDLE AGES

At the end of the fourteenth century, the musical styles of France and Italy began to merge. There were political reasons for this. There was more commerce between the two areas, and political alliances were formed. In some of the Italian city-states, French was spoken at court, and French was also used for official documents and scholarly writings. The most important place where French and Italian artists and musicians met was at the papal palace in the south of France, in Avignon.

For centuries, the popes had lived in Rome. But popes were not always Italian by birth, any more than they are today. And when a Frenchman was elected pope at the beginning of the fourteenth century, he decided to set up his papal residence in Avignon. The papal court at Avignon was immensely wealthy. A great deal of money was spent on clothes, furniture, paintings—and music. Both French and Italian composers lived there and were able to learn from one another.

The result of this intermingling of composers in a place of such influence and prestige was a fusing of the French and Italian styles in music. This new international style was the basis for a new period of musical history—a period known as the Renaissance.

Listening to...

MEDIEVAL MUSIC

- The music is based on modes, not modern scales (*Kyrie* and MusicNotes 73 and 74).
- Plainchant is sung in unison, with neither harmony nor accompaniment (*Kyrie*).
- Polyphony was invented (Perotinus, *Viderunt Omnes*).
- Courtly love songs became popular (Machaut, *Doulz Viaire Gracieus* and Landini, *Gram Piant' Agli Ochi*).
- Instruments began to be used as accompaniment (Machaut, *Doulz Viaire Gracieus* and Landini, *Gram Piant' Agli Ochi*).

KEY TERMS

chromatic **(p. 71)**

courtly love **(p. 70)**

liturgical music **(p. 65)**

lute **(p. 72)**

modal **(p. 66)**

mode **(p. 65)**

monophonic **(p. 65)**

plainchant **(p. 65)**

polyphony **(p. 65)**

refrain **(p. 71)**

rondeau **(p. 71)**

secular music **(p. 65)**

troubadour **(p. 70)**

4
The Renaissance: 1400—1600

LIFE AND TIMES IN THE RENAISSANCE

"Renaissance" means "rebirth." The term is used to show that during this period, the values of classical Greece and Rome were revived. People in the Renaissance adopted some of the ideas of the ancient Greeks and Romans—their feeling of individual responsibility, their focus on education, and their sense of the importance of the arts. As a result, the Renaissance was a time of remarkable artistic accomplishments.

There were three notable changes from the climate of the Middle Ages. First, there was more stress on individual achievements as the rigid feudal system began to break down. Second, people began to show more interest in the real world than in spirituality. And third, the spread of printed books and the growing ease of travel led to a widespread mingling of cultures.

These were dynamic, fast-changing times. The French and the English exchanged large tracts of land on the Continent as they won and lost battles such as those at Agincourt (dramatized by Shakespeare in his play *Henry V*) and at Orleans (where the French army was led by Joan of Arc). Trade flourished. The Eastern Church agreed to be united with the West under a single pope. A German craftsman, Johann Gutenberg, invented the art of printing from metal type. After centuries of living in Spain, the entire Jewish community was expelled in a forced mass emigration reminiscent of the Biblical exodus. In three little ships, an Italian explorer, Christopher Columbus, discovered the New World and proved that the world was round. The first African slaves were shipped to the Spanish colony in Cuba. A thirty-four-year-old university professor, named Martin Luther, exposed the corruption in the Catholic Church and established a new branch of Christianity. A Portuguese navigator, Ferdinand Magellan, made history by sailing around the world. The first English translation of the New Testament appeared in print. A Swiss doctor was the first to suggest that disease was caused by outside agents and might be cured by medicines. A German astronomer, Copernicus, suggested that the sun, not the Earth, was

1400
1410
Battle of Agincourt 1415
1420
1430
Death of Joan of Arc 1431
1440
1450
Invention of printing 1453
1460
1470
1480
1490
Christopher Columbus discovers the New World 1492
First university degrees in music (at Oxford) 1499
1500
1510
Beginning of Reformation movement 1517
Leonardo da Vinci 1452–1519
Josquin Desprez c. 1440–1521
1520
First book on surgery 1528
Church of England splits from Rome 1531
1530
1540
Copernicus 1473–1543
1550
Michelangelo 1475–1564
1560
1570
1580
1590
Palestrina 1525–1594
1600
Thomas Morley 1557–1602

A copy of the Gutenberg Bible, the first book printed from movable type.

the center of the universe. A major church council was held in Italy in the small town of Trent to discuss Catholic doctrine and practice in the face of the challenges from the Reformation. Henry VIII died at the age of fifty-six after establishing yet a third branch of Christianity, in England. The decimal system was invented.

A sense of the expanding possibilities of life in the Renaissance is reflected in the artistic accomplishments of the time. Artists and sculptors concentrated on the dignity of the individual human figure. And painters developed the techniques of perspective, three-dimensional representation, and working with oil paints, with which the most detailed effects of light and shade could be rendered naturally. The works of Renaissance painters such as Michelangelo and Leonardo da Vinci are still famous 500 years later.

Christopher Columbus in an engraving.

Leonardo da Vinci in a self-portrait.
Courtesy of the Library of Congress.

Renaissance architects throughout Europe used buildings from antiquity as models for their new buildings. Florence Cathedral, St. Peter's Basilica in Rome, Fontainebleau castle in France, and the palace of Charles V in Spain show how the Renaissance style became an international style. Columns and rounded roofs replaced the soaring, spiky look of medieval architecture.

St. Peter's Basilica in Rome.

Literary masters of the age included Petrarch of Italy, Cervantes of Spain, Rabelais of France, and Shakespeare of England. In the works of these writers, there is new emphasis on self-expression and on the worth of the individual.

The world of science became a major focus of the European Renaissance. Inventions and scientific discoveries were impressive in quantity and scope. The most important of these was the invention of printing (1453)—a development as revolutionary in its time as the computer has been in ours. The rapid increase in the number of available books had an enormous effect on education, as well as on the spread of scientific knowledge. Toward the end of the Renaissance, the invention of the telescope and the microscope changed forever the way people looked at the world.

Scholars pursued both scientific and literary studies. Many of the great figures of the Renaissance were highly educated and knowledgeable in all known fields—hence our modern phrase "Renaissance man (or woman)." The perfect example of the true Renaissance man was Leonardo da Vinci, who was a brilliant painter, sculptor, musician, engineer, and scientist.

In many ways, the Renaissance must have been an exciting time in which to live. New lands were discovered and explored, including much of the Far East, the coast of Africa, and North and South America. By the sixteenth century, there was enormous economic and commercial expansion throughout Europe, and a larger middle class was formed. Members of the middle class were also interested in learning and culture, and the growth of education and the new availability of books helped them to achieve their goals.

A couple from the Renaissance.

Music played an important role in Renaissance society. Most educated people could either play an instrument or sing written music. People were not considered socially accomplished if they did not have some

Instruments from the
Renaissance.

musical training. And an evening's entertainment usually included some kind of musical performance.

Music printing, which became widespread in the sixteenth century, greatly increased the amount of available music. Amateur music making became more and more common.

The professional musicians included composers and performers. Many more individual musicians found jobs at court, and many towns supported musicians as public employees. Although very few women achieved careers as composers, some women began to be included in the ranks of performing musicians, and some of them were highly paid and became internationally known.

As with the other cultural achievements of the Renaissance, music reached great heights. Some of the most beautiful compositions in the history of Western music were composed during this period, and the greatest musical works of the Renaissance match the finest works of literature, painting, and architecture in their depth and beauty.

GENERAL CHARACTERISTICS OF RENAISSANCE MUSIC

Renaissance music is distinguished from medieval music in one important way: The overall sound is much smoother and more homogeneous, with less contrast. This change in sound is the result of a change in compositional technique. The highly contrasting and independent lines of late medieval polyphony were replaced by a new polyphonic style based on **imitation**.

Imitation is a form of polyphony in which all the musical lines present the same musical phrase, one after the other. As each line enters, the previous ones continue, so there is a constant sense of overlapping. This technique can be much more varied than it sounds. The strictest kind of imitation is a round, in which all the voices sing exactly the same thing in turn (see MusicNote 27 in Chapter 1). But often, imitation is much freer than that. In free imitation, only the first few notes of a melodic phrase are sung by each entering voice; the voices then continue freely.

Even though the *style* of music in the Renaissance was very different from that in the Middle Ages, the predominant types of composition were the same. They were these: (1) **liturgical music** (music for church services, usually **Mass settings**), (2) **motets** (settings of Latin texts, usually from the Bible), and (3) **secular songs**.

THE RENAISSANCE MASS

A Roman Catholic Mass as it was celebrated in the 1400s was a long service, with many different readings and prayers, ceremonies and processions, and a large amount of music. Through most of the Middle Ages, all of this music had been sung in plainchant. In the twelfth and thirteenth centuries, some parts of the Mass began to be sung polyphonically. Gradually, composers began to concentrate on those sections of the Mass that remained the same, regardless of the day, feast, or season. There are five of these sections—the Kyrie, Gloria, Credo, Sanctus, and Agnus Dei—and they are known collectively as the **Ordinary of the Mass**. The tradition of setting these five sections to music began in the fourteenth century and has continued to the present day.

The principal musical characteristic of a Renaissance Mass is polyphony, usually imitation. Composers in the fifteenth and sixteenth centuries used this one compositional technique with great flexibility and variety.

Composers also experimented with ways of linking the five different sections of the Ordinary by drawing the *musical* material for them from a single source: a piece of plainchant or even a popular song of the day. The borrowed melody usually appears in the tenor voice (the third musical line from the top in a four-voice piece), but the other voices are often derived from it as well.

Josquin Desprez (c. 1440–1521)

Josquin Desprez was the most versatile and gifted composer of the mid-Renaissance. He was from northern France and spent much of his career there, as well as at some of the cathedrals and courts of Italy. During his lifetime he became quite famous, and rich noblemen were eager to hire him for their households.

Josquin composed prolifically in the three main genres of Renaissance music: Masses, motets, and secular songs. He brought the Renaissance technique of musical imitation to new heights of clarity and flexibility.

As an example of Josquin's style, we shall study one of his Mass settings: the *Pange Lingua* Mass, composed toward the end of his life. This composition is known as the *Pange Lingua* Mass because all five movements of the Mass are based on the plainchant hymn *Pange Lingua Gloriosi*. Before examining Josquin's polyphonic Mass setting, let us look at the plainchant that provided the basis for it.

LISTENING GUIDE

THOMAS AQUINAS (1225–1274)

Plainchant hymn, *Pange Lingua*

Date of composition: Thirteenth century
Duration: 2:24

Complete CD Collection: 1, Track 9

Pan - ge lin - gua __ glo - ri - o - si

Cor - po - ris my - ste - ri - um, ____

San - gui - nis - que pre - ti - o - si,

Quem in mun - di - pre - ti - um ____

Fruc - tus ven - tris ge - ne - ro - si

Rex ef - fu - dit __ gen - ti - um.

The *Pange Lingua* hymn was written by Thomas Aquinas, one of the foremost scholars and theologians of the late Middle Ages. The hymn is **strophic**, which means that all four stanzas are sung to the same music. Each stanza has six lines, and they seem to fall into pairs. The chant is in the E (Phrygian) mode, but the only line to end on the E is the last one. This gives the music a sense of continuity until the end. The chant is almost entirely syllabic, and the text urges praise for the miracle of Christ's birth and death.

We shall listen to all four stanzas, but what is important here is the *music*; therefore, the text is not given in its entirety. Remember: All four stanzas have exactly the same music.

9	0:00	Stanza 1	("*Pange lingua ...*")
	0:33	Stanza 2	("*Nobis datus ...*")
	1:04	Stanza 3	("*In supremae ...*")
	1:39	Stanza 4	("*Verbum caro ...*")
	2:12	"Amen"	

Josquin's Mass

In his Mass based on the *Pange Lingua* hymn, Josquin took almost all of his *musical* ideas from the plainchant. Remarkably, each vocal line in every section of the Mass is derived from the chant. The way in which he uses the musical material demonstrates Josquin's talent and enabled him to create a completely new composition from the ancient chant.

In the first place, of course, Josquin's Mass is polyphonic. It is written for four voice lines: sopranos, altos, tenors, and basses. Second, the Mass—unlike the chant—has rhythm (plainchant is usually sung with all the notes equal in length). Every musical phrase has a rhythm especially created by Josquin to fit the words. Josquin also molds and varies his phrases by adding notes to or modifying the chant melody.

The Mass is by no means a lesser piece because of its dependence on earlier melodic material. Indeed, it is precisely in the molding of a well-known original that Josquin shows his ingenuity. The *Pange Lingua* Mass not only stands alone as a new composition. It also is colored throughout with the presence of an ancient tradition, in the music of the hymn—a hymn that would have been very familiar to Josquin's audience. The words of the original hymn are not sung in Josquin's Mass, but they would have been called to mind by his audience when they heard the strands of the hymn's melody woven into the polyphony.

Three characteristics of Josquin's special musical style can be heard clearly in this work:

1. Josquin has given each short segment of the music its own **point of imitation**, a musical passage that presents a single tiny musical phrase that is then imitated among the voices.
2. The music is controlled by **overlapping cadences**: The next group of voices begins just as the first group comes to a cadence, thus allowing the forward motion to continue.
3. The imitation is usually **paired imitation**: One pair of voices begins the imitation and another pair answers.

LISTENING GUIDE

JOSQUIN DESPREZ (c. 1440–1521)
Kyrie from the *Pange Lingua* Mass

Date of composition: c. 1520
Sopranos, altos, tenors, basses
Duration: 2:51

Companion CD, Track 65

ll three of the characteristics listed previously may be heard in the opening Kyrie of Josquin's *Pange Lingua* Mass. The movement as a whole has three main sections:

1. Kyrie eleison.
2. Christe eleison.
3. Kyrie eleison.

Each section begins with a new point of imitation, and all are derived from the original hymn. The first section is based on the music of the first and second line of the hymn, the "Christe" section is based on the third and fourth lines of the hymn, the final "Kyrie" section on the fifth and sixth lines.

Let us look at the first phrase from the original plainchant hymn and see how Josquin has adapted it for his Mass.

First, Josquin has applied an interesting rhythm to the phrase. He starts out with long notes and increases in motion until just before the end. Second, he has added a nice curving passage of his own invention to provide intensity and drive towards the cadence. As you listen, notice that the rhythm of the music is very fluid and flexible. That is because composers of this era did not use measures or bar lines (look at the facsimile of the original manuscript shown here).

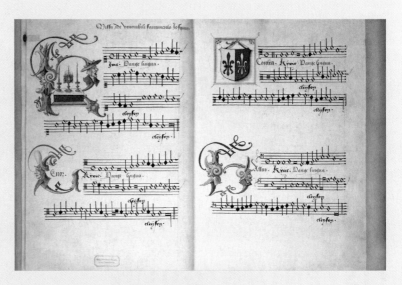

65	0:00	*Kyrie eleison*	(Based on opening of hymn melody.) Tenors and basses; cadence overlaps with entry of altos. Sopranos enter before final cadence.
	0:45	*Christe eleison*	(Based on lines 3 and 4 of hymn melody.) Paired imitation, overlapping entries.
	2:02	*Kyrie eleison*	(Based on lines 5 and 6 of hymn melody.) Sopranos, altos, tenors, basses enter in turn; activity increases before final cadence.

THE RENAISSANCE MOTET

During the Renaissance, composers became ever more interested in giving expressive emphasis to the words they set. Since the texts of the Mass were fixed and could not be changed, this interest focused on motets and secular songs. The Renaissance motet usually has four voice parts. It is entirely vocal and is usually sung by a small choir. The text is usually from the Bible or the Psalms and is usually in Latin. Finally, the music is usually a mixture of two textures: imitative and homophonic.

The Counter-Reformation and the Music of Palestrina

Composers flourished throughout Europe during the Renaissance: in France and Germany, the Netherlands, Spain, Poland, and England. But the main center of musical activity in the sixteenth century was Italy.

Italy was the focal point of the Counter-Reformation, which was a movement to reform the Catholic Church from within and came about as a reaction to Martin Luther's establishment of Protestantism. The Counter-Reformation was not primarily concerned with music, but music played a role in the deliberations of the church reformers. They wanted to make sure that music used in church services was pure and spiritual. At first, they considered allowing only plainchant. In the end, however, the cardinals agreed that, in addition to the traditional chants, polyphonic music could be used in church, provided that the words could be heard clearly and the style was not too elaborate.

The composer whose music most clearly represents these ideals is Giovanni Pierluigi da Palestrina (c. 1525–1594). Like many people during the Middle Ages and the Renaissance, this man took his name from his hometown. He was born in Palestrina, forty miles from Rome, and was sent to Rome as a choirboy to study and sing. He spent most of his life there at some of the city's greatest musical institutions, including the Sistine Chapel (the private chapel of the pope).

The purity, serenity, and perfection of Palestrina's music have made him the most highly regarded composer of late Renaissance choral music. The principal characteristics of his style are balance, control, evenness, clarity, and perfect text setting.

It might be thought that such a highly disciplined approach to composition would lead to dull, constricted music. On the contrary, Palestrina was a superbly gifted and resourceful composer, and he found many ways to introduce variety into his music. In the first place, there is a constant interplay between **counterpoint** and **homophony**. In the counterpoint sections, you hear several independent musical lines interweaving. In the homophonic sections, the voices all move more or less together. And within the sections of counterpoint, Palestrina draws on an almost limitless variety of methods. The melodic phrases used and their distribution among the voices are extremely varied. Different points of imitation can even be introduced at the same time—something that never happened in Josquin's music. And through it all, the text sounds clearly, with its natural rhythm perfectly conveyed.

Palestrina wrote more than 100 settings of the Mass and several volumes of secular songs, but perhaps his most impressive achievement is the composition of 250 motets. Motets could be written on almost any sacred text, but composers usually chose expressive texts with elements of drama or mystery, and they matched them with music of remarkable intensity or poignancy.

LISTENING GUIDE

GIOVANNI PIERLUIGI DA PALESTRINA
(c. 1525–1594)

Motet, *Exsultate Deo*

Date of composition: 1584
Sopranos, altos I, altos II, tenors, basses
Duration: 2:24

Complete CD Collection: 1, Track 10

he motet *Exsultate Deo* was first published in Palestrina's fifth book of motets in 1584. This book contains twenty-one motets written for five voices. The text is from Psalm 81. Palestrina uses only the first three lines of the psalm, the text of which is given here.

Exsultate Deo adiutori nostro,	Exult in God our refuge,
iubilate Deo Iacob.	acclaim the God of Jacob.
Sumite psalmum et date tympanum,	Raise a melody; beat the drum,
psalterium iucundum cum cithara.	play the tuneful lyre and harp.
Buccinate in neomenia tuba,	Blow the trumpet on the new moon,
insigni die sollemnitatis vestrae.	and on the day of your solemn feast.

In his setting, Palestrina concentrates only on these exuberant opening verses of the psalm. The music is bright and joyful, filled with fanfare-like rhythms and running eighth-note patterns, which help to enliven the work. In addition, the composer uses some word painting, such as on the opening word "Exsultate," where the musical line rises triumphantly.

With five independent musical lines, the number of possible combinations is large, and Palestrina constantly varies the texture of his music. The clearest examples of this variation are when the sopranos drop out briefly, leaving only the lower voices, or when only three voices are sounding (on the words "psalterium iucundum"—"tuneful lyre"). The motet is full of imitation, but Palestrina points up the entrance of new lines of text by having them sung homophonically by a pair of voices, which adds an underlying structure to the work as a whole. Cleverly, he departs from this technique towards the end of the motet on the words "Buccinate" ("blow") and "tuba" ("trumpet"), where there is very close imitation, suggesting the echoing of the trumpet blasts.

This performance is by the choir of Christ Church Cathedral, Oxford, England. The choir, which has been in continuous existence since the early sixteenth century, is made up of the same distribution of voices as it was originally: sixteen boys and twelve men. So all the high voices you hear are those of boys.

Christ Church Cathedral choir.

10	0:00	*Exsultate Deo adiutori nostro,*	Exult in God our refuge,	[Imitation in pair of upper voices alone; rising line on "Exsultate."]
	0:11			[Pair of lower voices. Cadence in all five voices; overlaps with:]
	0:28	*iubilate Deo Iacob.*	acclaim the God of Jacob.	[Many entries, suggesting a crowd "acclaiming."]
	0:37			[Lower voices.]
	0:49	*Sumite psalmum et date tympanum,*	Raise a melody; beat the drum,	[Quite homophonic, becoming more imitative. Note the march-like rhythm on "tympanum."]
	1:04	*psalterium iucundum cum cithara.*	play the tuneful lyre and harp.	[Elaborate flowering of the voices on "iucundum" ("tuneful").]
11	0:00	*Buccinate in neomenia tuba,*	Blow the trumpet on the new moon,	[Multiple echoes on "Buccinate"; homophonic climax on "neomenia."]
	0:13			[Running echoes on "tuba."]
	0:23	*insigni die solemnitatis vestrae.*	and on the day of your solemn feast.	[Slower, lower, more "solemn."]

THE RENAISSANCE SECULAR SONG

The Renaissance secular song (song with a nonreligious text) evolved in two phases. In the fifteenth century, secular songs were not very different from those of the late Middle Ages. And they were international in style. But in the sixteenth century, several European countries developed their own distinct national styles for secular songs.

The most influential of all these countries was Italy, and the distinctive type of secular song that developed there was the **madrigal**. Madrigals are secular vocal pieces for a small group of singers, usually unaccompanied. The favorite topics are love, nature, and sometimes war or battles. The music for madrigals mingles homophonic and imitative textures and sensitively reflects the meaning of the text. The Italian madrigal became so influential in the sixteenth century that composers of many other nationalities wrote madrigals in Italian, and some composers in England copied the style and wrote madrigals in English.

The Madrigal

As we have seen, expressing the meaning of words in music was a primary concern of late Renaissance composers. The madrigal is the musical genre that demonstrates this most colorfully.

Composers used a variety of techniques to bring out the meaning of the words they set. In general, the same mixture of chordal textures and imitative polyphony is used in madrigals as in motets, but composers went much farther in their search for direct expression. If the text had words such as "rising," "flying," or "soaring," then the music would have fast upward scales. "Peace" and "happiness" might be set to sweet major chords, "agony" and "despair" to wrenching dissonances. In fact, contrasts of this kind—between happiness and despair, for example—often appeared in madrigal texts within the same poem. This contrast is known as *antithesis*, and it presented ideal musical opportunities for madrigal composers.

The madrigal became immensely popular during the sixteenth century and survived well into the seventeenth. Composers strove for ever greater intensity of expression, and the late madrigalists managed to wring every ounce of feeling from the text. The technique of depicting the meaning of words through music is known as **word painting**.

Toward the end of the sixteenth century, a fascination with madrigals took hold in England. Italian madrigals sometimes appeared in English translation. One set was published in 1590 under the title *Italian Madrigalls Englished*. But English composers also wrote their own madrigals with English texts. These were often lighter in tone and more cheerful than their Italian counterparts.

The guiding force for the development of English madrigals was Thomas Morley (1557–1602). Morley published more madrigals than any other English composer and established a style that was followed by most other English madrigalists.

We shall listen to a pair of extremely short madrigals by Thomas Morley from a collection he published in 1595. Both are for two voices rather than the conventional four. The first (*Sweet Nymph Come to Thy Lover*) is for two women; the second (*Fire and Lightning*) is sung by two men. They make a wonderfully pleasing and contrasting pair.

LISTENING GUIDE

THOMAS MORLEY (1557–1602)

Two English Madrigals

Date of composition: 1595

Two sopranos (*Sweet Nymph Come to Thy Lover*); two baritones (*Fire and Lightning*)

Duration: 2:31

Companion CD, Track 66 and 67

The texts for these short pieces were probably written by Morley himself. Each one contains picturesque images, which the music captures beautifully. The first madrigal, *Sweet Nymph*, presents a nightingale. The second, *Fire and Lightning*, is lively and frenetic, with a kicker at the end. Both are primarily imitative, with very close imitation in some sections to liven up the proceedings or intensify the sound. The very last line of *Fire and Lightning* is suddenly homophonic to draw attention to the sting at the end. This last line also exploits antithesis ("fair"/"spiteful") to make its effect.

Both madrigals have such short texts that there are many repetitions of each phrase, and you will hear many instances of word painting. The fine performances here are by students Sarah Pelletier and Suzanne Ehly, sopranos, and faculty members William Sharp and Mark Aliapoulios, baritones, of the Boston University School of Music.

66	0:00	Sweet nymph come to thy lover,	Imitation.
	0:12	Lo here alone our loves we may discover,	Touches of homophony on "Lo here alone."
	0:20	(*Repeat of first two lines*)	
	0:39	Where the sweet nightingale with wanton gloses,	Imitation; high notes and close harmony on "gloses" [trills].
	0:49	Hark, her love too discloses.	High notes, very close imitation, especially last time through.
	1:03	(*Repeat of last two lines*)	
67	0:00	Fire and lightning from heaven fall	Lively; very close imitation.
	0:08	And sweetly enflame that heart with love arightful,	Smooth descending scales on "sweetly."
	0:16	(*Repeat of first two lines*)	
	0:31	Of Flora my delightful,	Scales in opposite direction on "delightful."
	0:45	So fair but yet so spiteful.	Last time through: homophonic, close pungent harmony, dissonance on "spite-," incomplete sound on "ful."
	0:47	(*Repeat of last two lines*)	

After the heyday of the Italian and English madrigals, the Renaissance polyphonic style had run its course. It had produced works of great beauty and variety, but new composers had new ideas. Their interest in text expression remained paramount, but they felt that new ways had to be found to allow the words to dominate the music. These new ways were the foundation of the new musical style of the seventeenth century, the Baroque style, in which instrumental music also became more and more prominent. But before we turn to the next chapter, let us examine the origins of the Baroque style in the rise of instrumental music in the Renaissance.

THE RISE OF INSTRUMENTAL MUSIC

During the Renaissance, instrumental music became more and more popular. A wide range of instruments was in use, from the loud, extrovert trumpets to soft, delicate strings and recorders. Compositions ranged from serious contrapuntal works to light-hearted dances.

One form of contrapuntal instrumental music was the **canzona**, and the master of the canzona was Giovanni Gabrieli (c. 1555–1612), an organist and composer at St. Mark's Church in Venice. St. Mark's had two choir lofts facing each other, and Gabrieli took advantage of this to place contrasting groups of instruments in the two lofts, creating an early version of stereo sound. Gabrieli was also one of the first composers to indicate "loud" and "soft" in his music, which adds to the echo effect.

LISTENING GUIDE

GIOVANNI GABRIELI (c. 1555–1612)

Canzona Duodecimi Toni

Date of composition: 1597
Two groups of brass instruments
Duration: 3:53

Complete CD Collection: 1, Track 12

This work by Giovanni Gabrieli is divided into several sections and contrasts two groups of brass instruments, which are heard in dialogue. As in Josquin's *Pange Lingua* Mass, the music is pushed forward by overlapping cadences, one group beginning as the previous one ends. Sometimes the two groups play together. The piece features dynamic contrasts of loud and soft, which are characteristic of late Renaissance and early Baroque music. A special effect involving dynamic contrast is "echo," in which the exact repetition of a phrase at a lower volume suggests distance.

The canzona is full of varied rhythmic patterns, but the most pervasive is the "canzona rhythm," LONG-short-short ♩♪♪ which you will hear throughout the piece, in fast and slow tempos.

INTRO		
12	0:00	Fairly slow, medium loud, both brass groups; canzona rhythm is prominent.

SECTION 1		
	0:15	Faster tempo, same musical motive and rhythm, faster tempo, homophonic, Group I.
	0:20	Group II, growing louder.
	0:27	Both groups, loud, featuring flourishes by trumpets in imitation; cadence.

SECTION 2		
	0:43	Second motive, quieter, mostly homophonic, echoes, passages of imitation between groups, lively rhythms; cadence.

SECTION 3		
	1:26	Third motive, loud, mostly homophonic, echoes, both groups.
	1:43	Trumpet flourishes, cadence.
	1:49	Canzona rhythm; close imitation, cadence.

SECTION 4		
	2:10	Fourth motive, quiet, canzona rhythm, lots of imitation between groups, cadence.
	2:35	Multiple echoes, from loud to soft, between groups; crescendo …
	3:02	Final motive, both groups loud, leading to big climax.

Dance Music

The largest category of instrumental music during the Renaissance was dance music, since dancing was one of the favorite forms of entertainment. The music was usually binary in form (AABB) and followed the characteristic tempos and rhythms of each dance type. Dances were frequently performed in pairs, contrasting slow with fast, or duple meter with triple meter.

Dancing was important to Renaissance society as more than a mere diversion, as the following extract makes clear. Taken from a dance treatise published in 1589, the excerpt is cast as a dialogue between student and teacher:

Student: "Without knowledge of dancing, I could not please the damsels, upon whom, it seems to me, the entire reputation of an eligible young man depends."
Teacher: "You are quite right, as naturally the male and female seek one another, and nothing does more to stimulate a man to acts of courtesy, honor, and generosity than love. And if you desire to marry, you must realize that a mistress is won by the good temper and grace displayed while dancing. And there is more to it than this, for dancing is practiced to reveal whether lovers are in good health and sound of limb, after which they are permitted to kiss and touch and savor one another, thus to ascertain if they are shapely or emit an unpleasant odor as of bad meat. Therefore, apart from the many other advantages to be derived from dancing, it becomes essential to a well-ordered society."

LISTENING GUIDE

TIELMAN SUSATO (fl. 1543–1561)

Ronde and Saltarelle

Date of composition: 1551
Recorders and percussion

Duration: 1:52
Complete CD Collection: 1, Track 13

This example is a dance pair written by the Flemish composer Tielman Susato. Both dances are binary (AABB) in form. On the repeats, the melody is occasionally ornamented with trills and decorative figures.

The two dances contain the same melody, but the ronde has duple meter, whereas the saltarelle is triple. The effect is very different in each case.

RONDE

[duple meter: recorders and drum]

13   0:00   First phrase (A):

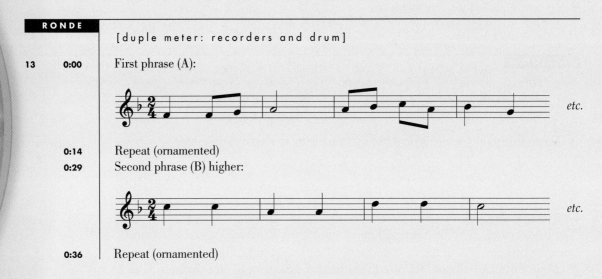

0:14   Repeat (ornamented)
0:29   Second phrase (B) higher:

0:36   Repeat (ornamented)

SALTARELLE

[triple meter: recorders and tambourine]

0:43   First phrase (A):

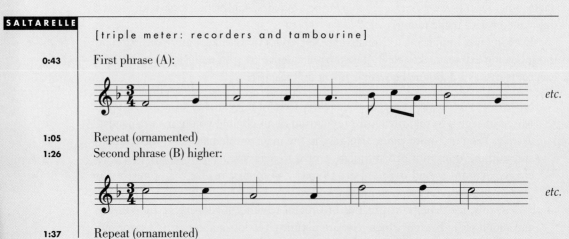

1:05   Repeat (ornamented)
1:26   Second phrase (B) higher:

1:37   Repeat (ornamented)

In the Renaissance, musical style changed dramatically. In place of the stark or subtle sounds of medieval music, Renaissance compositions present smoothly contoured and carefully woven textures. The three main genres of Renaissance music are vocal: Mass settings, Latin motets, and secular songs. Interestingly, musical styles seem to shift back and forth from one era to the next. In the next musical period, the Baroque era, it was instrumental music that came to the fore.

Listening to...

RENAISSANCE MUSIC

- The music is mostly vocal.
- There are three main genres: Mass settings (musical settings of the five main items in the Catholic Mass—example: Josquin, *Kyrie*), motets (Latin Biblical texts—example: Palestrina, *Exsultate Deo*), and secular songs (example: Morley, *Two Madrigals*). Remember: Masses are *liturgical*, motets are *sacred*, songs are *secular*.
- The principal element to listen for is the texture. The most common textures are imitation (example: Josquin, *Kyrie*) and homophony (example: passages in Palestrina motet, Morley madrigals, and Gabrieli canzona). But there are many different kinds of imitation, so listen carefully to see if you can hear exactly what the composer is doing. And notice how the passages of homophony occur as contrast.
- Word painting is a special technique—mirroring in the music the meaning of the words (example: Morley, *Two Madrigals*).
- You can also hear different styles of instrumental music—either serious and imitative (example: Gabrieli, *Canzona*) or light and dancelike (example: Susato, *Ronde and Saltarelle*).

KEY TERMS

canzona **(p. 90)**

counterpoint **(p. 85)**

homophony **(p. 85)**

imitation **(p. 80)**

liturgical music **(p. 81)**

madrigal **(p. 88)**

Mass setting **(p. 81)**

motet **(p. 81)**

Ordinary of the
  Mass **(p. 81)**

overlapping cadences
  (p. 83)

paired imitation **(p. 83)**

point of imitation **(p. 83)**

secular song **(p. 81)**

word painting **(p. 88)**

5
The Baroque Era: 1600—1750

1600

1610

1620

1630

1640

1650

1660

1670

1680

1690

1700

1710

1720

1730

1740

1750

CHAPTER OUTLINE

Life in the Baroque Era

General Characteristics of Baroque Music

The Early Baroque (1600–1700)
Monteverdi and the First Great Opera
Opera in the Seventeenth Century
Henry Purcell and the English Opera
Sonata and Concerto
French Music

The Late Baroque (1700–1750)
Late Baroque Opera
The Late Baroque Concerto
Antonio Vivaldi (1678–1741)
Johann Sebastian Bach (1685–1750)
Bach's Music
George Frideric Handel (1685–1759)
Handel's Music

Listening to Baroque Music

The word "baroque" began as a term of disapproval. In the seventeenth century, it was used by philosophers to describe tortuous forms of argument, and by jewelers to describe oddly colored or misshapen pearls. The word was first applied to music in the eighteenth century. In 1768, the French philosopher Rousseau defined Baroque music as that in which the harmony is confused, and the melody is harsh and unnatural—not a flattering definition!

Nowadays the term is not used disapprovingly. The creative works of the seventeenth and early eighteenth centuries are now recognized for their grandeur, depth, and technical mastery. The Baroque period, after all, is the age of the writers Milton, Racine, and Molière; the artists Rembrandt and Velázquez; and the composers Bach, Handel, and Vivaldi.

LIFE IN THE BAROQUE ERA

The Baroque era was a period of absolute monarchs, rulers who had total control over every aspect of their realms: the economy, the content of books, the style of art, and even life and death. The model for absolute monarchy was set by Louis XIV of France, who raised the power of the king to unparalleled heights. He regarded himself as synonymous with the whole nation of France. "I am the state," he said.

Louis XIV himself!

Hyacinthe Rigaud (1659–1743). Louis XIV, King of France (1638–1715). Portrait in royal costume (the head was painted on a separate canvas and later added). Oil on canvas, 277 × 194 cm. Louvre, Dpt. des Peintures, Paris, France. © Photograph by Erich Lessing. Erich Lessing/Art Resource, NY.

Dutch first use Manhattan for trade 1612

First African slaves brought to Virginia 1619

Monteverdi 1567–1643

René Descartes 1596–1650
Founding of Harvard College 1650

Rembrandt 1606–1669

Molière 1622–1673
John Milton 1608–1674

Purcell 1659–1695

Founding of St. Petersburg, Russia 1703

Corelli 1653–1713
Louis XIV 1643–1715

Isaac Newton 1642–1727

Antonio Stradivari 1644–1737
Vivaldi 1678–1741
Invention of centigrade thermometer 1742
Jonathan Swift 1667–1745
Bach 1685–1750
Handel 1685–1759
Thomas Gainsborough 1727–1788

Louis XIV's palace at
Versailles.

Self-portrait by Rembrandt
as an old man.

Rembrandt Hamensz van Rin
(1606–1669). Rembrandt, self-
portrait at old age. Oil on canvas.
National Gallery, London, Great
Britain. © Photograph by Erich
Lessing. Erich Lessing/Art Resource, NY.

In many parts of Europe, life was characterized by a strict social hierarchy, rigid laws, and elaborate codes of dress and manners. The political instability and wars that had dominated Europe for so many years gave way to a period of peace and economic expansion. There may have been political repression and terrible social inequities, but there were no major wars, and rulers supported the arts as expressions of their cultivation and learning.

During the seventeenth and eighteenth centuries, a radical change took place in philosophical and scientific thinking. Aided by new technological developments, scientists began to test their ideas by measurement and analysis rather than by relying on preconceived notions. The foremost scientist of the age was Sir Isaac Newton, who developed calculus, discovered the principle of gravity, and explained the laws of motion.

The discoveries of Newton and other scientists had a profound effect on philosophers, who began to apply the same principles of orderly thought to human life and society. Order and organization were valued above all else in society and in the arts. Baroque artists thought that the emotions could be objectively classified and that art could be designed to arouse specific emotions in its audience. Baroque art displays a fascination with states of emotion: grief, joy, despair. Baroque works of art evoke intense reactions. They involve the viewer immediately. Portraits stress the grandeur and personality of their subjects; sculptures depict fleeting moments of emotional intensity; buildings radiate wealth and strength.

The most impressive building of the Baroque period is surely the palace of Versailles, built by Louis XIV in the mid 1600s. It is breathtakingly grand and symmetrical, with more than a thousand rooms, including one hall lined entirely with mirrors. The effect of grandeur continues outside, where the geometrically organized landscape extends for miles.

In all Baroque art, contrast and illusion are the dominant forces. Painters discovered the dramatic possibilities of strong contrasts between light and shade. In Rembrandt's portraits, light falls generously on the subject's face, while the background falls away in the gloom.

Illusion was a favorite device. Paper was decorated to resemble dense marble; paintings of doors and windows were put onto walls; scenes of outdoor vistas were drawn inside false window frames. Painted ceilings offered special opportunities for spectacular effects: The ceilings seem to open up to the heavens, with whirling clouds and cherubs leaping out of the sky.

Comparable characteristics are found in Baroque music. Baroque composers set out to portray specific states of emotion, and they created contrast and illusion through the use of dynamics and contrasting groups of musicians.

The emphasis on contrast can be heard most clearly in the **concerto**. Concertos are built on the idea of contrast—between a whole orchestra and a small group of instruments, or between the orchestra and a single instrument.

Dynamic contrasts also achieve illusion. In Baroque instrumental music, the same phrase is often played first loud and then soft. This echo effect gives the illusion of space and distance.

GENERAL CHARACTERISTICS OF BAROQUE MUSIC

The Baroque era lasted only 150 years, somewhat shorter than the Renaissance and a fraction of the length of the Middle Ages. In spite of this, only the last fifty years of the Baroque era, the period of the famous composers Bach, Handel, and Vivaldi, are generally represented in today's concert halls. It is logical, then, to divide our examination of Baroque music into two parts: the early Baroque (1600–1700) and the late Baroque (1700–1750). In fact, this division corresponds to actual musical events, because the early Baroque was the period in which stylistic trends were established, while the late Baroque was the time of the well-known masters and of fixed musical forms.

The greatest invention of the early Baroque was opera, which displayed the best of all contemporary arts. It featured elaborate stage machinery, gorgeous costumes, and beautiful stage sets. All this was combined with exciting stories, expressive acting, and dramatic music.

Early Baroque music was designed to be emotional. There was also a tendency toward more rigid formal design. Composers began to use bar lines to organize their music into regular metric groupings. And modern tonality (the major and minor key system) began to evolve. The growth of tonality, with its carefully organized sequence of keys, may also be seen as a mirror of the Baroque social order.

The main vocal forms of the early Baroque were the **opera** and the **cantata**. Operas were large-scale productions, expressive and elaborate. They immediately became extremely popular. Great rulers and aristocratic families built their own private theaters for the performance of opera, and opera houses sprang up across Europe.

Cantatas were, in effect, short unstaged operas: They were written for only one or two characters and portrayed a single scene or situation. They told stories of love lost and found, of nymphs and shepherds. Later cantatas were written for the church and were based on religious themes.

During the Baroque period, instrumental music gained greatly in importance. Instruments began to take on the shape and sound of their modern counterparts, and instrumental technique began to rival the brilliant speed, expressiveness, and control of the famous opera singers of the day. The most important instrumental forms of the Baroque era were the **concerto**, the **sonata**, and the **dance suite**.

Concertos are based on contrast. They feature interplay between a small group of players (or a single soloist) and a large group. This interplay allowed Baroque composers to create considerable drama in a purely instrumental form.

Sonatas are chamber works (works written for a very small number of instruments), smaller in scale than concertos and less dependent on contrast. Numbers could range from two or three instruments to a small handful, but a sonata was always designed for a small group.

Dance suites were originally designed exclusively to accompany dancing. An evening's entertainment often consisted of a series, or "suite," of contrasting dances. Later, the dance suite became one of the most popular independent instrumental genres of the late Baroque.

The spread of the Protestant movement had an important influence on music. The most distinctive musical feature of a Protestant service was the **chorale**, a hymn with an even rhythm and simple tune, usually sung in unison by the whole congregation. Chorale tunes found their way into many types of Baroque music, including organ pieces and church cantatas. Another form of sacred music was the **oratorio**. This is a large-scale work like an opera, but it is based on a sacred story, and it is not staged. Instead, a narrator sings the story, and other singers sing the words of people in the story. Similar to the oratorio is the **Passion**, a composition based on the gospel account of the last days of Jesus.

Stylistically, all Baroque music has one very notable characteristic: a strong instrumental bass line. This line not only forms the harmonic underpinning for Baroque music but also provides a strong foundation for the rhythmic momentum. But whether the upper parts of a Baroque composition have strong rhythmic drive or extended expressive melodies, the bass line is always the driving force, both harmonically and rhythmically. Since the bass line is almost never silent in a Baroque composition, it is known as the *basso continuo* ("continuous bass"). The basso continuo part is usually played by a combination of a keyboard instrument, such as a harpsichord, and a low melody instrument, such as a cello. Whatever the genre, you can recognize a Baroque piece by the strength and powerful sense of direction of its bass line.

A Baroque instrumental concert. Notice the central position of the basso continuo players.

"Court concert at Prince Bishop of Luettich at Seraing Palace" (with violoncello of Prince Bishop Cardinal Johann Theodor of Bavaria). Painting, 1753, by Paul Joseph Decloche (1716–1759). Oil on canvas, 186 × 240.5 cm. Munich, Bayersiches Nationalmuseum. Photo: AKG London.

THE EARLY BAROQUE (1600–1700)

Monteverdi and the First Great Opera

The first great opera in the history of Western music was Monteverdi's *Orfeo*, written in 1607. The opera is based on the ancient Greek myth of Orpheus and Euridice.

THE STORY OF THE OPERA   Orpheus ("Orfeo" in Italian) and Euridice are in love. Shepherds and nymphs sing and dance together. Suddenly the revelries are interrupted by a messenger who announces that Euridice has been bitten by a snake and is dead. Orpheus, a musician, is grief-stricken and decides to travel to the underworld to bring Euridice back to life. The king of the underworld is moved by Orpheus's plea and allows Euridice to return, but on one condition: that Orpheus not turn back and look at her. On their journey, Orpheus becomes anxious and steals a glance at his beloved. She disappears forever.

Monteverdi sets this story with a wide variety of music. There are madrigal-like choruses, dances, and instrumental interludes. But the most striking style of all is called **recitative**. Recitative is designed to imitate as closely as possible the freedom and expressiveness of speech.

Recitative is always sung by one singer with accompanying basso continuo. It is very flexible, for it follows the changing meanings of the text, with the bass line supporting the voice and providing punctuation. It can be very simple or quite elaborate and songlike. It is designed to mirror, moment by moment, the emotional state of the singer. In all of his music, but especially in his recitatives, Monteverdi displays the talent that all great opera composers have in common: the ability to capture and reflect the feelings of the human soul.

LISTENING GUIDE

CLAUDIO MONTEVERDI (1567–1643)

Orfeo's recitative, Euridice's recitative, chorus of nymphs and shepherds, and instrumental ritornello from the opera *Orfeo*

Date of composition: 1607
Tenor and soprano solo, chorus, instrumental ensemble and basso continuo
Duration: 3:55

Complete CD Collection: 1, Tracks 15–17

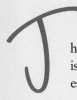

he following scene comes from the first act of the opera, in which the love of Orfeo and Euridice is celebrated. In his lyrical recitative "Rosa del Ciel ..." ("Rose of Heaven ..."), Orfeo expresses his passion for Euridice and his happiness. Euridice, responding to Orfeo's proclamation of love, affectionately pledges her heart to him in a declamatory passage ("Io non dirò …"—"I shall not say …"). A chorus of nymphs and shepherds follows with a celebratory dance ("Lasciate i monti …"—"Leave the hills …"), and the scene is closed by an instrumental **ritornello**, a musical passage that returns.

Monteverdi uses a variety of forms and musical means to depict this pastoral setting. Both Orfeo and Euridice sing in a free, expressive recitative. The melody imitates the rhythms of speech and mirrors the meaning of the text. In Orfeo's part, for instance, Monteverdi accentuates significant words such as "fortunato amante" ("happy lover") or "Mio ben" ("My love") and matches the musical rhythm to the rhythm of the words:

"fe-li-cís-si-mo" ("happiest")[♪♪♪♪♪]

"sos-pi-rá-i" ("I sighed"); "sos-pi-rás-ti" ("you sighed") [♪♪♩♩]

In Euridice's recitative, the composer uses lively motives for the words "gioir," "gioia," and "gioisca" ("rejoicing," "rejoice," "enjoys"); employs wide leaps to represent "Quanto" ("How much"); and provides the words "core" ("heart") and "Amore" ("Love") with soothing cadences.

The choral dance consists of two sections: The first, in duple meter, is based on imitative phrases that evoke the movement of dancers; the second provides a distinct contrast, since it is set in triple meter and its texture is completely homophonic. The instrumental ritornello that ensues is a faster dance, which adds variety and brings closure to this short and happy scene.

ORFEO			
		[soft arpeggiated chords in continuo]	
15	0:00	*Rosa del Ciel, vita del mondo, e degna*	O Rose of Heaven, life of the world,
		Prole di lui che l'Universo affrena,	And worthy offspring of him who rules the universe,
		[voice becoming more animated]	
	0:25	*Sol, ch'il tutto circondi e'l tutto miri*	Sun, you who surround and watch everything
		Da gli stellanti giri,	From the starry skies,
		[rising melody]	
	0:34	*Dimmi, vedesti mai*	Tell me, have you ever seen
		Di me più lieto e fortunato amante?	A happier or more fortunate lover than I?
		[gentle cadence]	
	0:45	*Fu ben felice il giorno,*	Blessed was the day,
		Mio ben, [loving phrase] *che pria ti vidi,*	My love, when first I saw you,
	0:56	*E più felice l'ora*	And more blessed yet the hour
		Che per te sospirai,	When first I sighed for you,
		Poich'al mio sospirar tu sospirasti.	Since you returned my sighs.
		[sighing phrases]	
	1:15	*Felicissimo il punto*	Most blessed of all the moment
		Che la candida mano,	When you offered me your white hand,
		Pegno di pura fede, a me porgesti.	As pledge of your pure love.
		[many notes]	
	1:34	*Se tanti cori avessi*	If I had as many hearts
		Quant'occh'il Ciel eterno, e quante chiome	As the eternal sky has eyes, and as many as these hills
		Han questi colli ameni il verde maggio,	Have leaves in the verdant month of May,
		[one "full" note]	
	1:45	*Tutti colmi sarieno e traboccanti*	They would all be full and overflowing
		Di quel piacer ch'oggi mi fa contento.	With the joy that now makes me happy.
		[soft cadence]	

EURIDICE

		[soft lute chords]	
16	2:09	*Io non dirò qual sia*	I shall not say how much
		[happy phrases]	
	2:15	*Nel tuo gioir, Orfeo, la gioia mia,*	I rejoice, Orfeo, in your rejoicing,
	2:21	*Che non ho meco il core,*	For my heart is no longer my own
	2:27	*Ma teco stassi in compagnia d'Amore;*	But stands with you in the company of Love;
		["lui" emphasized]	
	2:35	*Chiedilo dunque a lui, s'intender brami,*	Ask of *it* then, if you wish to know,
	2:42	*Quanto lieto gioisca, e quanto t'ami.*	How much happiness it enjoys, and how much it loves you.
		[soft cadence]	

CHORUS

		[happy imitation, duple meter]	
17	2:59	*Lasciate i monti,*	Leave the hills,
		Lasciate i fonti,	Leave the streams,
		Ninfe vezzose e liete,	You charming and happy nymphs,
		[same music]	
	3:09	*E in questi prati*	Practiced in dancing,
		Ai balli usati	And in these meadows
		Vago il bel pie rendete.	Move your pretty legs.
		[change of key, homophony, triple meter]	
	3:18	*Qui miri il Sole*	Here the Sun
		Vostre carole	Sees your dances,
		Più vaghe assai di quelle,	More beautiful yet than those
		[same music]	
	3:26	*Ond'a la Luna*	Which the stars dance
		La notte bruna	To the light of the moon
		Danzano in Ciel le stelle.	In dusky night.

INSTRUMENTAL RITORNELLO

3:33		Faster, recorders, strings, basso continuo

Opera in the Seventeenth Century

In Baroque opera, a distinction gradually arose between those portions of the recitative that were lyrical and songlike and those portions that were more straightforward and conversational. The lyrical part came to be known as **aria** ("air," or song), and the conversational part kept the old name of recitative. Arias were usually written in set forms, with a fixed pattern of repetition, whereas recitatives were freer in form and quite short. The sparse accompaniment and flexible style of recitative made it ideal for setting dialogue, while arias were reserved for contemplative or passionate moments when the composer wanted to explore the full emotional content of a situation. Recitative usually had simple basso continuo accompaniment; the arias were usually accompanied by full orchestra. The most common forms for arias were ABA form (the B section providing a contrast) and **ground bass** form, in which a single phrase in the bass is repeated over and over again while the voice sings an extended melody above it.

Henry Purcell and English Opera

While music flourished in Italy, the state of music in England was highly fragmented because of an unstable political situation and civil war. In 1660, the son of Charles I returned from exile in France and assumed the throne as Charles II. His return, known as the Restoration, brought with it a rebirth of musical life in England.

The most talented English composer of the late seventeenth century was Henry Purcell, who lived from 1659 to 1695. He held the important position of organist at Westminster Abbey in London and was one of the most prolific composers of his day. In his short life, Purcell wrote a large amount of vocal and instrumental music. His best-known work is a short opera called *Dido and Aeneas*, written in 1689.

Henry Purcell at the age of 36 (the year he died).

Dido and Aeneas is a miniature masterpiece. It is based on an episode of the great epic poem from antiquity, the *Aeneid* of Virgil. It tells the story of the love affair between Dido, Queen of Carthage, and Aeneas, a mythological Trojan warrior, and it ends with Aeneas's departure and Dido's death. There are three acts—with arias, recitatives, choruses, dances, and instrumental interludes—but only four main singers are required, together with a very small orchestra of strings and harpsichord. The whole opera takes only an hour.

The most famous aria from *Dido and Aeneas* is Dido's lament. Dido has been abandoned by Aeneas and has decided to kill herself. She expresses her determination, her grief, and the pathos of her situation in a deeply moving musical framework. The lament is a ground bass aria—that is, the entire aria is set over a constantly repeating phrase in the bass.

LISTENING GUIDE

Henry Purcell (1659–1695)

Dido's lament from the opera *Dido and Aeneas*

Date of composition: 1689

Voice, strings, and harpsichord
Duration: 4:07

Complete CD Collection: 1, Tracks 18–20

Dido's aria is introduced by a short recitative ("Thy hand, Belinda …") that sets the stage for the emotional intensity of the aria. The recitative has a sparse accompaniment that moves steadily downward, reflecting Dido's grief.

Immediately after this recitative, the ground bass for the aria is heard alone. It is worth looking closely at this phrase, not only because it occurs so many times in the aria (eleven times in all), but also because it is very carefully constructed, and the overall effect of the aria depends on it.

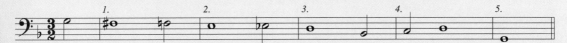

The first important element of this phrase is the fact that it descends chromatically (that is, by half steps). This chromatic descent immediately establishes a sad mood, which continues throughout the piece.

The next thing to notice is the rhythmic shift in the third and fourth measures of the phrase. (In the first three measures, a whole note is followed by a half note. In the fourth measure, the rhythmic pattern is reversed.) This is a very subtle shift, but it is very important: it gives the bass line extra interest.

Finally, the ground bass pattern that Purcell establishes for this aria is five measures long, which is quite unusual. Most musical phrases are made up of four or eight measures. But Purcell chose this irregular length deliberately. It sets up a tension in the music, which contributes to the overall sense of strain and grief. It also enables Purcell to allow the vocal line more freedom as it floats over the ground bass. During the aria, the endings of the ground bass pattern and the endings of the vocal phrases sometimes coincide and sometimes are independent. As the intensity increases, the vocal line becomes freer and freer from the constraint of the bass pattern. At the end of the aria, the voice and the ground bass come to a cadence together, and the orchestra provides a short conclusion that is in keeping with the overall mood of the piece.

There are only a few words in this aria, but, as in most opera arias, they are repeated for dramatic effect. Arias are designed not to convey information or to further the plot but to explore an emotional state. The aria lasts much longer than the opening recitative. It is worth listening to this piece several times to appreciate the skill with which Purcell created it.

RECITATIVE			
18	0:00	Thy hand, Belinda, darkness shades me,	[slowly descending voice throughout the recitative]
	0:19	On thy bosom let me rest.	
	0:29	More I would, but Death invades me:	
	0:40	Death is now a welcome guest.	[minor chord on "Death"; dissonance on "welcome guest"]
	0:54	[beginning of ground bass: quiet, slow, descending chromatic line heard throughout aria]	

ARIA			
19	1:08 (1:43)	When I am laid in earth,	[ground bass pattern begins again on "am"]
	1:20 (1:55)	May my wrongs create	[no pause between these two lines]
	1:27	No trouble in thy breast.	[voice falls on the word "trouble"]
	(2:02)	[repeat]	
20	2:17	Remember me, but ah! forget my fate.	[much repetition; highly expressive rising lines; last "ah" is particularly lyrical]
	2:42	[several repeats]	
	3:30	[cadences of voice and ground bass coincide]	
	3:32	[quiet orchestral closing; conclusion of chromatic descent]	
	4:02	[final cadence with trill]	

Sonata and Concerto

Along with the invention of opera, the other major development in the early Baroque was the rise of instrumental music. And the most important instruments were those of the violin family.

The favorite genres of violin music in the last part of the seventeenth century were the sonata and the concerto. A sonata was a chamber piece of several contrasting movements, written for a small number of instruments. It could be a **solo sonata**, for a single instrument with basso continuo, or a **trio sonata**, for two instruments and basso continuo. The basso continuo was usually made up of a harpsichord and a low string instrument, such as a cello. As in all Baroque music, a strong bass line was a characteristic feature of Baroque chamber music.

Both the solo sonata and the trio sonata had several contrasting movements. If the movements were based on dance rhythms, the sonata was known as a *sonata da camera* ("chamber sonata"). The movements of a *sonata da chiesa* ("church sonata") were more serious in character.

Apart from the sonata, the favorite form of instrumental music in the Baroque era was the concerto. This was a larger composition, meant for performance in public halls, and it involved solo players and an orchestra.

The Italian word "concertare" has two opposite meanings. It means to struggle or fight; it also means to cooperate. Both of these contrary meanings are present in a concerto, in which a solo player or a group of solo players is contrasted with an entire orchestra. Sometimes soloists and orchestra all play together, sometimes separately. Sometimes they play contrasting music, sometimes the same music. This dramatic balance and contrast of opposing forces is the essence of the concerto.

The earliest concertos had a small group of soloists contrasting with the whole orchestra. This type of concerto is known as a **concerto grosso** ("large concerto"). The usual solo group was made up of two violins with basso continuo, but other instrumental groups were possible. The orchestra consisted of violins, violas, cellos, and basso continuo.

The **solo concerto** developed later. In a solo concerto a single soloist is contrasted with the whole orchestra, and the element of drama becomes particularly striking. It was the rise of the solo concerto that led to an increase in technically demanding playing and the virtuoso or "showoff" element that has been a characteristic of concertos ever since.

The composer who first brought Italian violin music to international prominence was Arcangelo Corelli (1653–1713). In his compositions, Corelli expanded the technique of violin playing, using repeated notes, fast scales, and double stops (playing more than one string at a time). He once wrote that the aim of his compositions was to "show off the violin." He concentrated entirely on violin music, writing only sonatas and concertos. Corelli was one of the first composers to become famous exclusively from instrumental music, and his compositions were highly influential throughout the remainder of the Baroque era and beyond.

LISTENING GUIDE

ARCANGELO CORELLI (1653–1713)

Last movement of Trio Sonata, Op. 3, No. 7, for two violins and basso continuo

Date of composition: 1689
Key: E minor
Tempo: *Allegro*
Duration: 1:15

Complete CD Collection: 1, Track 21

*C*orelli composed two types of trio sonatas. Chamber (da camera) sonatas featured a series of dances. Church (da chiesa) sonatas were simply divided into four movements distinguished by tempo: slow–fast–slow–fast. The sonata featured here is of the church type, and the movement we will hear is the last movement: fast. It is written for two violins and basso continuo (chamber organ with cello). The basso continuo group is always present, supporting the two violins as well as supplying a third independent voice.

Notice how Corelli introduces a slight change in the second half of this movement, and yet the musical ideas remain very much the same. In this way, the movement is unified, yet continually evolving. This is a very lively movement, highly imitative, in two sections, both repeated.

21	0:00	First brief section with violins in dialogue.
	0:13	Section repeated.
	0:26	Second section. Slight change to create new motive; dialogue continues in lively exchange.
	0:49	Second section repeated. Quiet ending.

A grand ball at the French court.

French Music

During the seventeenth century, while England was still racked by civil war, France was ruled by one of the most powerful monarchs in European history. Louis XIV reigned for an unusually long time, from 1643 to 1715, and his tastes governed French life for the entire second half of the seventeenth century and well into the eighteenth. Fortunately, Louis XIV was an avid supporter of the arts, and French music flourished under his patronage.

Louis XIV loved to dance, and one of the most important influences on French music was dance. It was featured prominently in French opera and French instrumental music throughout the seventeenth century. By the 1700s, French dances, which were elegant and dignified in their steps, had influenced instrumental music across the whole of Europe. One of the most popular French dances, the minuet, a stately dance in triple meter, even became established as one of the standard movements of the eighteenth-century Classic symphony.

Dance influenced music in France in two ways. First, French opera included a great deal of ballet. Seventeenth-century French operas were splendid affairs, with elaborate scenery, large choruses, and frequent interludes for dancing. The most important composer of French opera was Jean-Baptiste Lully (1632–1687), the king's music director. Lully's ballet scenes were so popular that the dances from his operas were often played as independent suites. This popularity gave impetus to another trend that had begun late in the Renaissance: the use of dance forms purely as independent instrumental music.

There were many different kinds of French dance in the seventeenth century, each with its own meter, rhythm, and characteristic melodic style. The most important is the minuet, but there are many more. Each has its own special character.

A series of dances for instrumental performance is known as a **dance suite**. Usually, all the dances in the suite are in the same key. Composers of instrumental suites included François Couperin (1668–1733), known as le grand ("the great"), and Elisabeth-Claude Jacquet de la Guerre (1667–1729), who enjoyed the patronage of Louis XIV himself and was one of the first women to publish widely in French music.

THE MAIN FRENCH BAROQUE DANCES

Dance	Meter	Tempo	Description
Allemande	Duple	Moderate	Continuous motion
Bourrée	Duple	Moderate to fast	Short, distinct phrases
Courante	Triple	Moderate to fast	Motion often in running scales
Gavotte	Duple	Moderate to fast	"Bouncy" sound
Gigue	Usually 6/8	Fast	Lively, often imitative
Minuet	Triple	Moderate	Elegant
Sarabande	Triple	Slow	Stately; accent often on second beat

THE LATE BAROQUE (1700–1750)

We mentioned before that the Baroque period as a whole can be divided into two phases: the early Baroque (1600–1700) and the late Baroque (1700–1750). In the early Baroque period, the main styles and genres were established; in the late Baroque, the fixed musical forms flourished in the hands of the Baroque masters who have become so popular today: Vivaldi, Bach, and Handel.

Late Baroque Opera

Opera continued to flourish in the late Baroque period. Other countries developed their own operatic traditions, but the favorite type of opera throughout Europe was Italian opera, and the main form of Italian opera was *opera seria* ("serious opera"). This had become quite stylized by the late Baroque period. The plots were often standard. There were always three acts, and the music was built around a constant alternation between recitatives and arias.

Recitatives were still used for carrying the plot forward. They were simple, fast, speechlike, and accompanied only by basso continuo.

Arias were the main reason people went to the opera. They provided the opportunity for the great singers of the time to display their talents. Every opera contained three or four arias for each of the main characters. At these moments, the action would stop, and the aria would explore the emotion created by the story: grief, rage, love, despair, and so on.

The standard form for opera arias continued to be ABA form. The mood was established in the first A section. Then the B section was sung as a contrast, usually in a different key or tempo. After the B section, the A section was repeated, with the same words and the same music but considerably ornamented with improvised figures, runs and scales, high notes, dramatic pauses, and the like. It was here that a singer could really show off his or her talent, vocal agility, and taste (or sometimes lack of it!).

The Late Baroque Concerto

By the beginning of the eighteenth century, the concerto had also become fixed in form. Composers continued to write both concerti grossi (for small group and orchestra) and solo concertos (for soloist and orchestra), but the solo concerto became more and more popular. Instruments such as the flute, the oboe, and the trumpet began to be featured in addition to the violin in solo concertos. Composers even began to write concertos for keyboard instruments. This was quite revolutionary, because the role of the keyboard instrument in a concerto had previously been restricted to the basso continuo.

There were many concerto composers active at this time, but the undisputed master of the concerto in the late Baroque period was Antonio Vivaldi.

Formalized Baroque depictions of Hope and Fear. Opera singers were trained to depict emotion in highly stylized facial expressions and body gestures.

Two heads, Hope and Fear, from Charles Le Brun's "Conférence sur l'expression," 1698. Musée du Louvre, Paris. Réunion des Musées Nationaux/Art Resource, NY.

Portrait of Vivaldi in his
mid-forties.

Antonio Vivaldi (1678–1741)

Vivaldi's father was a violinist at St. Mark's in Venice, where Gabrieli and Monteverdi had made their careers, and Antonio learned music at an early age. Like many young men in the Baroque era, Vivaldi trained for the priesthood as well. Because of his red hair, he earned the nickname "The Red Priest." Illness prevented him from continuing his priestly duties, however, and he soon began the job that would carry him through the remainder of his career: He was appointed director of music at the Ospedale della Pietà in Venice. This was a residential school for orphaned girls and young women, which combined basic education with religious training and placed a strong emphasis on music.

Vivaldi wrote a large amount of music for the Ospedale. The girls gave frequent concerts, and people traveled from all over Europe to hear them play. Among the composer's works are nearly 600 concertos! Vivaldi wrote so much music that some of it has still not been published, and many of his pieces have not been heard since he first wrote them.

Vivaldi must have been inspired by the special talents of the young women in his school, because several of his concertos are for instruments that at the time were not normally thought of as solo instruments: small recorder, clarinet, bassoon, viola, and even mandolin. But most of his concertos are for one or more violins.

By the time of Vivaldi and the late Baroque period, concerto form had become clearly established. There are usually three movements, in the pattern fast–slow–fast. The first movement is usually an *Allegro*. The second movement usually has an expressive, slow melody that sounds like an opera aria. The third movement is a little faster and livelier than the first.

The first and third movements of a Baroque concerto are in **ritornello** form, which exploits the contrast between the solo instrument(s) and the orchestra in a highly organized way. *Ritornello* is the Italian word for something that returns. A ritornello in a concerto is an orchestral passage that constantly returns. Between appearances of the ritornello, the solo instrument plays passages of contrasting material, which are known as episodes.

At the beginning of a movement in ritornello form, the orchestra plays the entire ritornello in the tonic, or home key. During the body of the movement, the ritornello often will appear only in partial form and will be in different keys, but at the end it will return in its entirety in the tonic key. The solo episodes occur between these appearances. (See diagram.)

COMPLETE RITORNELLO	EPISODE 1	PARTIAL RITORNELLO	EPISODE 2	PARTIAL RITORNELLO	EPISODE 3	COMPLETE RITORNELLO

TONIC	OTHER KEYS	TONIC

Perhaps the most famous of Vivaldi's concertos today are a group of four concertos known as *The Four Seasons*. They were published in 1725, when Vivaldi was forty-seven years old. They show Vivaldi's wonderful sense of invention in the concerto medium and his extraordinary flexibility within this seemingly rigid form.

These are solo violin concertos; but in several of the solo episodes, other instruments from the orchestra join in, so that the sound sometimes approaches that of a concerto grosso. There is also constant variety in the handling of the ritornello form, both in the keys employed for the partial returns and in the choice of the part of the ritornello to be used. Finally, the *Four Seasons* concertos are an early instance of **program music**—music that is designed to tell a story.

Each of the concertos describes one season of the year. At the head of each concerto, Vivaldi printed a poem describing the season. Also, Vivaldi actually wrote lines from the poem directly into the musical score, so that the musical phrases are directly tied to the poetic descriptions. For example, there are passages for thunder and lightning, for a dog barking, for birds singing. But even apart from the poetic texts, the concertos are wonderful examples of the late Baroque violin concerto in their own right.

The Baroque concerto may seem rather rigid, with its set pattern of movements and its strict ritornello form, but, as pieces such as Vivaldi's *Four Seasons* show, it could be handled with great flexibility to produce music of variety, color, and contrast.

Vivaldi's music was heard and his influence felt not only in his native Italy but throughout Europe. Vivaldi's concertos were studied in great detail and closely imitated by another of the great masters of the late Baroque era: Johann Sebastian Bach.

LISTENING GUIDE

ANTONIO VIVALDI (1678–1741)

First Movement from Violin Concerto, Op. 8, No. 1, *La Primavera* ("Spring"), from *The Four Seasons*

Date of composition: 1725

Solo violin, strings, and harpsichord

Duration: 3:34

Companion CD, Track 68

Like most late Baroque concertos, Vivaldi's "Spring" concerto has three movements: fast–slow–fast. Both of the fast movements are in ritornello form and are in a major key (E Major). The slow movement has a long, lyrical melody and is in the minor. In both of the outer movements, instruments from the orchestra join the soloist in some of the solo episodes, giving the impression of a concerto grosso. Both movements are also full of echo effects. The orchestra is made up of first and second violins, violas, cellos, basses, and harpsichord.

Like all the Seasons, "Spring" is headed by a poem in the form of a sonnet. A sonnet has eight lines of poetry followed by six lines. The six lines are divided into two groups of three. Vivaldi uses the first eight lines for the first movement and the two groups of three for the next two movements.

First movement
(First eight lines of the poem):

Spring has arrived, and full of joy
The birds greet it with their happy song.
The streams, swept by gentle breezes,
Flow along with a sweet murmur.
Covering the sky with a black cloak,
Thunder and lightning come to announce the season.
When all is quiet again, the little birds
Return to their lovely song.

The first movement is written in the key of E Major. The ritornello is made up of two phrases, both of which occur at the beginning of the movement; all the other times, only the second half of the ritornello is played. Between these appearances, the solo violin plays brilliant passages, imitating birdsong and flashes of lightning. Sometimes it plays alone, and sometimes it is joined by two violins from the orchestra.

ALLEGRO			
		[fast]	
68	0:00	"Spring has arrived, and full of joy"	[First half of ritornello, loud and then soft]
	0:15		[Second half of ritornello, loud and then soft]
	0:32	"The birds greet it with their happy song."	[Trills; three solo violins alone, no basso continuo]
	1:08		[Second half of ritornello, once only, loud]
	1:16	"The streams, swept by gentle breezes, Flow along with a sweet murmur."	[Quiet and murmuring]
	1:41		[Second half of ritornello in dominant key, once only, loud]
	1:49	"Covering the sky with a black cloak, Thunder and lightning come to announce the season."	[Fast repeated notes; flashing runs and darting passages]
	2:17		[Ritornello in new key, second half, once only, loud]
	2:25	"When all is quiet again, the little birds Return to their lovely song."	[Long, sustained, single note in bass; rising solo phrases, trills again]
	2:43		[Buildup to:
	3:10		Second half of ritornello in home key, twice, first loud and then soft]

Plate 1: A modern symphony orchestra.

Plate 2: The rock band *U2* playing at a concert.

Plate 3: An Indonesian *gamelan*.

Plate 4:
Medieval manuscript
for a Kyrie with monks
and choirboys singing.
SOURCE: The Pierpont Morgan
Library/Art Resource, NY.

Plate 5:
Sixteenth-century
painting showing full
modeling of the face
and figure and
detailed texture
of the clothing.
SOURCE: "Maria de Medici."
Painting, Renaissance,
16th c. Bronzino, Agnolo
(Agnolo di Cosimo).
(1503 – 1572). Oil on
poplar wood.
Kunsthistorisches Museum,
Gemaeldegalerie,
Vienna, Austria.
Art Resource.

Plate 6:
Christ Church
Cathedral choir.

Plate 7:
Louis XIV's palace
at Versailles.
SOURCE: Reunion des
Musees Nationaux/
Art Resource, NY.

Plate 8:
A Baroque instru-
mental concert.
Notice the central
position of the basso
continuo players.
SOURCE: "Court concert
at Prince Bishop of Luettich
at Seraing Palace" (with
violoncello of Prince Bishop
Cardinal Johann Theodor
of Bavaria). Painting, 1753,
by Paul Joseph Decloche
(1716 – 1759).
Oil on canvas, 186 x 240.5
cm. Munich, Bayersiches
Nationalmuseum.
Photo: AKG London.

Johann Sebastian Bach (1685–1750)

One of the most influential musicians of all time, and certainly one of the greatest composers in the history of music, was Johann Sebastian Bach. His mastery of musical composition is so universally acknowledged that the date of his death is used to mark the end of the entire Baroque era.

Bach's whole career was spent in one region of Germany. He moved from one small town to another as job opportunities arose. The last part of his life was spent in the somewhat larger town of Leipzig.

Bach did not see himself as an artistic genius, but rather as a hard-working craftsman. He wrote most of his music to order, or to fulfill the requirements of a job. During his life, he was not widely known outside the relatively small circle of his family and acquaintances, and he traveled very little. He never wrote an opera, although that was the most popular musical genre of the time, because his jobs never required it.

The first jobs Bach held were as church organist in the small towns of Arnstadt and Mühlhausen near his birthplace. At the age of twenty-three, he married and found a better position at the court of the Duke of Weimar, first as organist and later as leader of the orchestra. He stayed there for nine years (until 1717), finally leaving when he was turned down for the position of music director. The Duke of Weimar was so angry at Bach's decision to leave that he had him put in jail for a month!

But Bach got the position he wanted at the court of a nearby prince. The Prince of Cöthen was young, unmarried, and an enthusiastic amateur musician. He kept a small orchestra of his own and made Bach music director. Here, Bach was very happy. He was well paid, he could write a range of varied music, and he was highly regarded by the prince.

In 1720, when Bach was thirty-five, his wife Barbara died. He was married again the following year to a young singer, Anna Magdalena, who, like Bach, was employed at the court of the Prince of Cöthen. Over the years, Bach and his wives had twenty children. Eleven of them died in childhood, as was common in those days, but nine grew to adulthood, and four became famous composers in their own right.

Bach might have stayed at Cöthen for the rest of his life, but the prince also married at this time, and his new wife did not like music. The prince's support for Bach and his activities diminished, the orchestra was dismissed, and Bach started looking for a new job.

At this time, the town of Leipzig—a relatively large town with a university, two theaters, and a population of 30,000—was looking for a music director for its St. Thomas's Church. This position involved responsibility for all the town's church music, including that of St. Thomas's and three other churches.

The town council interviewed several musicians and finally settled on Bach as its third choice! Bach happily accepted the position and moved with his growing family to Leipzig in 1723, when he was thirty-eight years old. He was to remain there for the rest of his life.

Bach was extremely busy in Leipzig. There were several aspects to his job, all of which he fulfilled cheerfully and efficiently. He was required to compose, rehearse, and direct a new church cantata for every Sunday and feast day of the year. He was also head of the music school attached to St. Thomas's and was responsible

The sole surviving portrait of Johann Sebastian Bach.
Stadtgeschichtliches Museum, Leipzig.

View of Leipzig in Bach's time. St. Thomas's Church is at the center, and the school to the left.

Frederick the Great playing the flute at a concert in his palace. Bach's son, C.P.E. Bach, is seated at the harpsichord.

for teaching Latin and composition, playing the organ, maintaining all the instruments, and preparing the choirs for the services at the three other main churches in Leipzig.

In 1747, Bach was asked to visit Frederick the Great, the powerful and autocratic King of Prussia. Like Louis XIV of France, Frederick loved music and employed several well-known musicians at his court. He also played the flute and composed a little flute music. One of Johann Sebastian Bach's sons, C. P. E. Bach, was the harpsichordist at Frederick's court. It was the younger Bach who was considered the more up-to-date composer. Johann Sebastian was known affectionately, but not very respectfully, as "Old Bach." By the middle of the eighteenth century, his music was regarded as old-fashioned and too complicated.

Bach died in 1750, leaving an unparalleled legacy to the musical world. Audiences ever since have been attracted to Bach's music for its careful organization, clear tonal direction, expressive nature, and intellectual brilliance. Bach himself saw his music as a means of supporting his family, instructing his fellow human beings, and glorifying God. For his sons and for his second wife, Anna Magdalena, he wrote books of short keyboard pieces. One book of organ pieces was written "for the instruction of my fellow men." And at the end of many of his compositions, he wrote the letters "S. D. G.," which stand for "Soli Deo Gloria" ("For the Glory of God Alone").

Bach was also exceedingly modest. Toward the end of his life, he said, "I was obliged to work hard. But anyone who is equally industrious will succeed just as well." Family man, teacher, good citizen, humble and pious spirit, Johann Sebastian Bach was also one of the musicians in history on whom we can unhesitatingly bestow the title "genius."

Bach's Music

Bach wrote in all the Baroque era's major musical genres, with the exception of opera. His works range from the monumental to the miniature, and they include both sacred and secular music. Every piece is marked by the same careful and faultless construction, the same unerring sense of direction and timing. The Baroque values of rhythmic drive and emotional intensity are vividly present in his compositions. His simple chorale harmonizations are magisterial models for students of harmony. Bach was also an unparalleled master of counterpoint, and composers ever since have studied his works to learn how to combine independent musical lines with conviction and clarity.

The types of music Bach wrote at different periods in his life depended on the kind of job he held at the time. In his early years, he primarily wrote organ music. At the court of the Prince of Cöthen, Bach mostly wrote for keyboard, or for orchestra and other instrumental groups. During the Leipzig years, he produced a large amount of church music, as well as more instrumental compositions.

BACH'S ORGAN MUSIC   Bach's organ music is extremely varied. It includes settings of Lutheran chorales, organ trio sonatas, and preludes and fugues. The chorales are either set in harmony for organ or used as the basis for a series of variations. In the organ trio sonatas, the right hand plays one line, the left hand plays another, and the pedals of the organ are used for the basso continuo.

The prelude and fugue contrast a free type of music with a very strict type. The prelude (sometimes called "toccata" or "fantasia") is a rambling, improvisatory piece of the kind that organists play to fill in time before, during, or after a church service. The fugue is a carefully worked-out polyphonic composition, that uses a theme (or "subject") that occurs in all the voices, or musical lines, in turn. It begins with a single voice playing the subject unaccompanied. As the second voice brings in the fugue subject, the first one continues playing—and so on, until all the voices are sounding independently. A fugue may have two, three, or four voices. After visiting Frederick the Great, Bach wrote one fugue that has six voices.

Bach was a master of counterpoint, and the fugue is the most demanding type of counterpoint to write. We shall listen to one of Bach's Preludes and Fugues for organ.

LISTENING GUIDE

JOHANN SEBASTIAN BACH (1685–1750)

Prelude and Fugue in E minor

Date of composition: before 1708
Solo organ
Duration: 4:13

Complete CD Collection: 1, Tracks 22–23

Bach, both an accomplished organist and an accomplished composer, makes full use of the organ in his organ works. In the Prelude and Fugue in E minor, Bach displays the capabilities of both the foot-operated pedal keyboard (which plays the lowest-sounding notes) and the hand-operated keyboard (known as a "manual"). Organs usually have more than one keyboard on which the performer can play different sounds. Changes in timbre can also be produced by pulling and pushing on knobs (known as "stops"). These stops may be used not only to change timbre but also to add an additional line in parallel octaves to the notes (particularly in the pedal keyboard). The phrase "to pull out all the stops" comes from organ playing.

Changes in timbre are quite evident in this recording. In the Prelude, the first long pedal low note is pure, simple, and flutey. Then the organist pulls out a stop to make the subsequent pedal notes richer and fuller. In the fugue, the organist uses the stops to set up what seem like two different instruments, one with an oboe-like sound and one with a clarinet-like sound. These instruments then compete with each other throughout the piece.

The theme or subject in the fugue is characterized by a special rhythm (dit diddle-DEE, dit diddle-DEE) that makes it easily recognizable.

PRELUDE		
22	0:00	Free-flowing music over sustained, soft, low pedal
	0:23	Timbre change; fanfare-like music with flourishes
	0:46	Pedal line alternating with keyboards
	0:55	Switches to top line answered by other voices
	1:10	Music gets "chunky," almost like a slow polka
	1:27	"Chunks" separated by climbing pedal line
	1:44	Pedals and manuals combine for full ending of Prelude

FUGUE		
23	2:08	First entry of fugue subject (dit diddle-DEE, dit diddle-DEE); instrumental effects created by different stops
	2:14	Second entry of subject (slightly lower)
	2:25	Third entry (high); the other lines are still playing
	2:34	Fourth entry
	2:45	Fifth entry (!) on pedals (in octaves)
	2:54	Change of texture; intervening passage with sixteenth notes
	3:07	Low entry; pedals return to accompany
	3:24	High section with entries spaced out
	3:37	Light section; no pedals
	3:58	Final entry on pedals; the big finale

BACH'S KEYBOARD, INSTRUMENTAL, AND ORCHESTRAL MUSIC

During his years at the Cöthen court, Bach produced a large amount of music for solo keyboard, other solo instruments, and small orchestra. In this music particularly, Bach melded the characteristics of Italian, French, and German styles. Italian music had rhythmic drive and brilliance. French music favored dance forms and ornament. German music was serious and contrapuntal. Bach drew on all these elements to produce an individual style that was the high point of the Baroque era.

Bach wrote much solo music, perhaps inspired by the fine players at the prince's court. There are suites and sonatas for solo violin and solo harpsichord, suites for solo cello, and a suite for solo flute. He also composed several sonatas and trio sonatas.

From the Cöthen years come a large number of orchestral compositions. These include some suites for orchestra, as well as several concertos, including the famous six Brandenburg Concertos, which present a fascinating mixture of solo concertos and examples of the concerto grosso, featuring violin, flute, oboe, and even the trumpet.

LISTENING GUIDE

JOHANN SEBASTIAN BACH (1685–1750)

First Movement from Brandenburg
  Concerto No. 2 in F Major

Date of composition: 1721
Instruments: Solo recorder, oboe, horn, and
violin; with strings and continuo
Tempo: *Allegro*
Key: F Major

Duration: 5:12
Complete CD Collection: 1, Tracks 24–27

Bach completed the six Brandenburg Concertos for the Margrave of Brandenburg in 1721 (a Margrave is a nobleman). They show a fusion of national styles, as well as Bach's brilliant mixture of melody and counterpoint.

The Brandenburg Concerto No. 2 is in three movements (fast–slow–fast), contrasting solo and ripieno (full ensemble) groups. Bach also explores coloristic possibilities within the solo group (recorder, oboe, horn, and violin) in various combinations of solos, duets, trios, and quartets throughout. Although this piece is often played with flute and trumpet, the word "flute" usually meant recorder in Bach's time, and an early manuscript copy of the score calls for "either trumpet or horn."

The first movement features three rhythmic motives, which combine to form the ritornello:

a. mixture of eighth notes and sixteenth notes:

Recorder, Oboe, Violins

etc.

b. eighth notes, triadic:

Horn

etc.

c. sixteenth notes, running:

Continuo

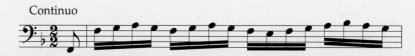

The ways in which these ideas are re-combined, sorted and re-sorted, and moved from one instrument to another, and the ways in which Bach organizes his harmonies and textures are nothing short of astounding.

	I		[opening section]
24		0:00	Ritornello (Tonic: F Major), motives "a," "b," and "c" together
		0:20	Violin solo
		0:25	Ritornello
		0:31	Duet (violin and oboe)
		0:37	Horn solo
		0:41	Duet (recorder and oboe), followed by horn
		0:51	Duet (horn and recorder)
		0:57	Continuation
	II		[second section]
25		1:12	Solo quartet, accompanied by continuo, based on "c"
		1:22	Sequences (fragment of "b"), horn answered by oboe; harmonic modulation
		1:40	Dynamic "echoes" (loud sections followed by soft); based on "a" and "c"
	III		[episode]
26		2:07	Continuing to modulate, steady eighth notes in bass, reaching:
		2:22	Ritornello in B-flat Major
		2:32	Duet (recorder and violin), joined by oboe and horn
(20)		2:53	Ritornello, C minor; motive "c" now prominent on top
		3:03	Another harmonically unstable section
		3:16	More sequences between horn and oboe, modulating to:
		3:24	G minor, ritornello
		3:35	Constant changes of texture and harmony (basses get motive "a"!); cadence

IV		[closing section]
27	4:24	Surprise! Everyone in unison on motive "a"; back to home key of F Major
	4:35	Another surprise! One last harmonic excursion
	5:02	Return to original texture
	5:07	Return to original key and ritornello

BACH'S VOCAL CHURCH MUSIC   During Bach's stay in Leipzig, he wrote hundreds of cantatas for church services, as well as several other important sacred vocal pieces. These include motets, Passions, and the *Mass in B minor*, which is regarded as one of the greatest traditional Mass settings ever composed.

Bach wrote two Passions for the Lutheran churches of Leipzig. (A third is rumored to exist, but has never been found.) A **Passion** is a musical setting of the story from the Gospels of the death and resurrection of Jesus. Bach based one setting on the account in the Gospel of St. John, and the other setting on the account in the Gospel of St. Matthew. Although Bach's musical legacy is full of masterpieces, the *St. Matthew Passion* is universally regarded as one of the most monumental musical masterpieces of all time. It is a huge composition, lasting some three hours, for solo singers, two choruses, one boys' choir, two orchestras, and two organs, and it runs the gamut of human emotion, from grief to awe to despair to spiritual transcendence. With this work alone, Bach shows us how music can reflect and deepen the meaning of human existence. We shall listen to a brief excerpt from this remarkable composition.

LISTENING GUIDE

JOHANN SEBASTIAN BACH (1685–1750)

St. Matthew Passion (excerpt)

Date of composition: c. 1727
Soprano, tenor, and bass voices, chorus, orchestra, and basso continuo
Duration: 8:07

Complete CD Collection: 1, Tracks 28–32

This excerpt from Bach's *St. Matthew Passion* shows the composer's mastery at achieving a fusion of seriousness and expressiveness suitable to the biblical text. The role of narrator for the Gospel story is performed by the "Evangelist" (tenor), who sings in recitative with a simple continuo accompaniment. The words of Jesus (bass) are "haloed" by lush string accompaniment. The chorus portrays the responses of the twelve disciples. This is most effective when Jesus predicts that one of them will betray him, and they ask, "Lord, is it I?" (If you listen very carefully, you will hear eleven questions. The voice of the twelfth disciple—Judas—is missing.)

A soprano soloist begins this excerpt in an aria that beautifully reflects the situation (Jesus as the sacrifice for all) that is ultimately the focus of the entire work. And the whole section is rounded off in peace and contemplation by the plain but moving harmonies of the final chorale.

28	0:00	[orchestral introduction]	

SOPRANO			
		[aria, A section]	
	0:31	*Blute nur, blute nur*	Only bleed, only bleed,
		Blute nur, du liebes Herz,	Only bleed, you dearest heart.
		[repeat text four times; answering phrases on flutes and violins; motion throughout in orchestra]	
	1:19	[orchestral interlude]	
29	1:51	[B section, change of key, similar accompanying figures as A section]	
		Ach! ein Kind das du erzogen,	Ah! a child that you raised
		das an deiner Brust gesogen,	and nursed at your breast
		droht den Pfleger zu ermorder,	has become a snake
		denn es ist zur Schlange worden;	and bites the one who cared for it;
	2:21	[repeat, varied]	
	3:00	[orchestral passage from beginning]	
30	3:32	*Blute nur, du liebes Herz ...*	Only bleed, you dearest heart.
		[A section, repeated exactly as beginning]	
	4:20	[orchestral closing passage]	

EVANGELIST			
		[recitative, simple basso continuo accompaniment]	
31	5:00	*Aber am ersten Tage der süssen Brot*	Now on the first day of the feast of unleavened bread
		traten die Jünger zu Jesu	the disciples came to Jesus
		und sprachen zu ihm:	and said to him:

CHORUS			
		[noble, serious tone]	
	5:10	*Wo, wo, wo willst du, dass wir dir bereiten, das Osterlamm zu essen?*	Where, where, where will you have us prepare for you to eat the Passover?
		Wo willst du, dass wir dir bereiten das Osterlamm zu essen?	Where will you have us prepare for you to eat the Passover?

EVANGELIST			
		[recitative]	
	5:36	*Er sprach:*	He said:

JESUS

[accompanied recitative—violins form a "halo" around the words of Jesus]

5:39
Gehet hin in die Stadt zu	Go to the city to a certain
einem und sprecht zu ihm:	man and say to him:
Der Meister lässt dir sagen:	The Master says to you:
Meine Zeit is hier,	My time is here,
ich will bei dir die Ostern halten	I will keep the Passover at your house
mit meinen Jüngern.	with my disciples.

EVANGELIST

[recitative—simple basso continuo accompaniment]

6:08
Und die Jüngern täten, wie	And the disciples did as
ihnen Jesus befohlen hatte,	Jesus had commanded,
und bereiteten das Osterlamm.	and prepared the Passover.
Und am Abend satzte er sich	And at evening he sat at the
zu Tische mit den Zwölfen,	table with the twelve,
Und da sie assen, sprach er:	and as they ate, he said:

JESUS

[accompanied recitative]

6:32
Warlich, ich sage euch:	Truly, I say to you:
Eines unter euch wird mich verraten.	One of you will betray me.

["halo"; dissonance and intensity
   on "betray"]

EVANGELIST

[recitative]

6:50
Und sie wurden sehr betrübt	And they became very troubled
Und huben an, ein jeglicher	and they spoke, each one
unter ihnen, und sagten zu ihm:	of them, and said to Him:

CHORUS

[fast, panicky music]

32   6:59
Herr, bin ichs? bin ichs?	Lord, is it I? Is it I? Is it I? Is it I?
bin ichs? bin ichs?	Lord, is it I? Is it I? Is it I? Is it I?
Herr, bin ichs? bin ichs?	Lord, is it I? Is it I? Is it I?
bin ichs? bin ichs?	
Herr, bin ichs? bin ichs? bin ichs?	

CHORALE

[calm setting of final chorale]

7:11
Ich bins, ich sollte büssen,	I should bear all of it,
an Händen und an Füssen	my hands and feet tethered
gebunden in her Höll;	in the bonds of Hell;
Die Geiseln und die Banden	the scourges and shackles
und was du ausgestanden,	that You endured
das hat verdienet meine Seel'.	so that my soul might be delivered.

George Frideric Handel (1685–1759)

Although Handel's life overlapped Bach's almost exactly, their careers were remarkably different. As we have seen, Bach lived a quiet, busy life in one small region of Germany. By contrast, Handel traveled extensively and became an international celebrity. Although the central musical genre of the Baroque era was opera, Bach wrote no operas. Handel's career was built on the nearly forty operas he wrote, mostly for the London stage. Bach was a family man; Handel never married.

Handel was born in Halle, a small town in Germany. His family was not musical, and his father wanted him to study law. He was so obviously gifted in music, however, that he was allowed to study with the music director and organist of the local church. He learned to play the organ, the harpsichord, and the violin, and he studied counterpoint and composition. Handel studied law at the University of Halle for only a year and then left for Hamburg, which was the main center of opera in Germany. He joined the opera orchestra there as a violinist and harpsichordist. At the age of nineteen, Handel composed his first opera, which was performed at the Hamburg opera house.

Because most operas at this time were Italian operas, Handel decided to travel to Italy, to the center of operatic activity. At twenty-one, he was still only a young man, but he scored a phenomenal success there.

After three years in Italy, Handel was appointed music director to the Elector of Hanover, back in Germany. This was a well-paid position, but Handel was rest-

The monument to Handel in Westminster Abbey in London.
Copyright: Dean & Chapter of Westminster, London.

less. He kept requesting leaves of absence to travel to London, which was fast becoming one of the most important musical centers in the world. In 1712, Handel was granted a short leave to London, which he greatly overstayed, ultimately turning it into a lifelong visit.

He made important contacts in London and soon became the favorite of Queen Anne. An embarrassing situation arose two years later, when the queen died, and the Elector of Hanover, Handel's former employer, whose generosity he had exploited, became George I of England. It is said that Handel won his way back into favor by composing his famous *Water Music* suite for a party King George was having on the river Thames (remember our analysis of the first movement of this work in Chapter 1?). Anyway, the king employed Handel again, as he had in Hanover; he was given a sizable salary and was soon composing, conducting at court, and teaching the king's granddaughters. Certainly the king and Handel had much in common. They were both foreigners in England, and they both spoke English with a strong German accent. A contemporary writer made fun of Handel's accent by reporting that one day when there was only a small turnout for one of his concerts, Handel said to the musicians, "Nevre moind; de moosic vil sound de petter."

Handel spent the remainder of his career in London. He was an amazingly prolific composer, a clever politician, and a tough businessman. He made and lost a great deal of money, loved food and drink, and had a quick temper and a broad sense of humor. A contemporary said that "no man ever told a story with more humor than Handel." He was at the center of English musical developments (and rivalries) for forty years. And in the end, he became an institution. The British people today still regard Handel as an English composer. He is buried in Westminster Abbey—an honor reserved for great English notables such as Chaucer, Queen Elizabeth I, and Charles Dickens.

During his London years (from 1712 until his death in 1759), Handel was involved mainly with opera and oratorio, though he wrote a great deal of other music as well. Italian opera was very fashionable in London until the 1730s, when public taste began to change. It was at this time that Handel turned his attention to **oratorio**.

The idea of a musical Bible story sung in English appealed to the English audience. Oratorio was also much less expensive to produce than opera. It was sung on the concert stage and required no costumes, no complicated machinery or lights, and no scenery. Handel's first oratorio was *Saul*, produced in 1739. But his first real success came with *Messiah* in 1741. This soon became his most popular work and remains one of his most frequently performed compositions today. After this, Handel's oratorios became the mainstay of the London concert scene. They were performed during Lent, when opera was not allowed anyway, and they attracted large audiences, especially from the prosperous middle class, which had always regarded Italian opera with suspicion or disdain. A special feature of Handel's oratorio performances was the appearance of the composer himself playing organ concertos during the intermission.

Toward the end of his life, Handel became blind, but he continued to perform on the organ and to compose by dictation. When he died, 3,000 people turned out for his funeral. He had become a British citizen many years earlier, and the British people had taken him completely into their hearts.

Handel's Music

Handel's music is attractive and easy to listen to. It appeals to a wide range of people because it sounds simple and tuneful. Handel's is the "art that hides art." As we saw in Chapter 1, the skill and brilliant craftsmanship of his music are hidden under an attractive exterior.

Curiously, most people today do not know the compositions on which Handel spent most of his time and for which he was best known in his own day: his Italian operas. These portray events of dramatic and emotional intensity. The main musical forms are the standard ones of opera seria: recitative and aria.

As you read earlier, Baroque arias are usually built in ABA form, with ornaments on the return of the A section. This kind of aria is known as a da capo ("from the beginning") aria, because after the B section, the composer simply has to write the words "da capo" in the score, and the singer can improvise the embellishments for the repeat of the A section.

Handel's opera *Giulio Cesare* (Julius Caesar) was written in 1724 at the height of his involvement with opera. It is based on the story of Caesar and Cleopatra in Egypt. In the opera, Caesar falls in love with Cleopatra and joins forces with her against Ptolemy, King of Egypt. (Baroque operas are full of women controlling men by means of their sexual attractiveness.) In the end, Ptolemy is defeated and Cleopatra is crowned Queen of Egypt.

The excerpt we shall study comes from the third act of the opera, during a temporary setback for Caesar. After a shipwreck, he is cast up on the shore where his army has been defeated in a battle. He laments his defeat, the loss of his troops, and his separation from Cleopatra.

Handel here deliberately manipulates the conventions of opera seria in order to inject more drama and realism into the situation. What the audience would expect at this point in the opera is a recitative followed by an aria. What Handel does, is to begin the scene with "breezy" music—wafting figures on the strings that are appropriate to Caesar's words later in the scene when he calls upon the breezes to soothe him. Then comes recitative *accompagnato*, recitative that is accompanied by the orchestra to

LISTENING GUIDE

GEORGE FRIDERIC HANDEL (1685–1759)
Giulio Cesare, Act III, Scene 4

Date of composition: 1724
Voice, strings, and continuo
Tempo: Andante
Key: F Major
Duration: 9:29

Complete CD Collection: 1, Tracks 33–36

| 33 | 0:00 | [Orchestral introduction] | "Breezy" music |

RECITATIVE

	0:46	*Dall' ondoso periglio salvo mi porta al lido il mio propizio fato.*	From the dangerous sea my lucky destiny safely takes me to the beach.	
		Qui la celeste parca non tronca ancor lo stame a la mia vita!	Here heavenly fate has not yet cut the thread of my life!	
	1:11	*Ma dove andrò e chi mi porge aita?*	But where shall I go and who will bring me help?	[Recitative becomes louder and more pronounced (martial rhythms)]
		Ove son le mie schiere?	Where are my armies?	
		Ove son le legione,	Where are my legions,	
		Che a tante mie vittorie il varco apriro?	that opened the way to so many victories?	

	1:31	*Solo in queste erme arene*	On these solitary sands	[Suddenly quiet]
		al monarca del mondo errar	only the King of the World is	[Loud again]
		conviene.	at home.	

ARIA

34	1:54	*Aure, aure, deh per pietà*	Breezes, breezes out of pity,	["Breezy" music
		Spirate al petto mio,	Blow on my body,	returns]
		Per dar conforto, O Dio!	To comfort me, O God!	
		Al mio dolor.	In my pain.	[Many repetitions]
	3:11	[Entire text repeated]		
	3:59	[Brief orchestral		[Minor key; contrast-
		interlude]		ing musical figures
				for B section]
35	4:11	*Dite, dite dov'è*	Tell me: where is she,	
		Che fà l'idolo del mio sen?	Where is the idol of my life?	
		L'amato e dolce ben di questo	Beloved and sweet object of	
		cor.	this heart.	

RECITATIVE

	4:52	*Ma d'ogni intorno i' veggio*	But all around me I see,	[Interruption: faster
		Sparse d'arme e d'estint,	Strewn with weapons and	and agitated]
			corpses,	
		L'infortunate arene,	These unfortunate beaches,	
		Segno d'infausto annunzio al	An ill omen of my end.	
		fin sarà.		

ARIA

36	5:12	*Aure, aure, deh per pietà*	Breezes, breezes out of pity,	[Return of "breezy"
		Spirate al petto mio,	Blow on my body,	music for repeat of
		Per dar conforto, O Dio!	To comfort me, O God!	A section]
		Al mio dolor.	In my pain.	
	7:08	[Orchestral conclusion]		

create a more dramatic effect. Finally, the aria starts, with its "breezy" music. All goes conventionally for a while; the A section of the aria continues. Then comes the B section ("Dite, dite dov'è,"—"Tell me, tell me where she is"). But at the point where everyone in the audience would expect the return of the A section (remember, the standard format is ABA), Handel interposes another accompanied recitative ("Mà, d'ogni intorno,"—"But all around me"), which dramatically reflects Caesar's state of mind at his unfortunate situation. It is as though Caesar's reflections are suddenly interrupted by the terrible sight of his surroundings. Handel breaks through the operatic conventions of his time to make his music correspond naturally to the psychological realism of the story.

Today, Handel's popularity rests mainly on his oratorios (musical settings of a Bible story sung in English). And even in his own time, the oratorios appealed to a very wide public. Why have they always been so popular? First, and most important, the words are in English. Even in the eighteenth century, much of the audience for Italian operas couldn't understand most of the words. Second, the stories are from the Bible (mostly the Old Testament), which was familiar to everyone in those days. Behind the stories, there were political implications as well: references, for example, to the military triumphs and prosperity of Georgian England. Finally, oratorios were less of an aristocratic, snobbish, social event than operas and thus had wider appeal.

The music of Handel's oratorios is vigorous and appealing. It is not so different from the music of his operas. There are recitatives and arias, just as there are in operas. But the main difference is in the choral writing.

Choruses are very rare in late Baroque opera, but they are central to Handel's oratorios. Some of the greatest moments in the oratorios come in the choral pieces, when the chorus comments on the action or summarizes the feelings of the people. Perhaps the best known of Handel's choruses is the "Halleluyah" chorus from *Messiah*.

Messiah was composed in 1741 and soon became the composer's most famous work. It was written in the unbelievably short time of just over three weeks. As he was composing it, Handel said, "I did think I did see all Heaven before me and the great God himself."

Messiah is in three parts, which last some two and one-half hours altogether. The music is made up throughout of recitatives, arias, and choruses. The famous "Halleluyah" chorus closes Part II.

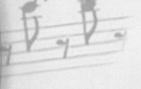

LISTENING GUIDE

GEORGE FRIDERIC HANDEL (1685–1759)

"Halleluyah" Chorus from *Messiah*

Date of composition: 1741
Chorus and orchestra
Duration: 3:49

Complete CD Collection: 1, Tracks 37–40

The "Halleluyah" chorus comes as the climax of Part II of *Messiah*. In it, Handel displays extraordinary ingenuity in combining and contrasting all the possible textures available to him: unison, homophonic, polyphonic, and imitative. In setting the word "Halleluyah" itself, he also uses a tremendous variety of different rhythms. Finally, much of the strength of the movement comes from its block alternation of simple tonic and dominant harmonies, as well as its triumphant use of trumpets and drums. The jubilant feeling is immediately evident and is a direct reflection of the text: "Halleluyah" is a Hebrew word that means "Praise God."

The text itself is treated in two ways:

1. Declamatory statements (e.g., "For the Lord God omnipotent reigneth") characterized by longer note values and occasional unison singing.

2. Contrapuntal responses (e.g., "forever and ever, halleluyah, halleluyah"), characterized by faster notes, and offering musical and textual commentary on the declamatory statements.

The "Halleluyah" chorus falls into nine relatively symmetrical sections, each featuring a single texture or combination of textures.

37	**0:00**	Instrumental opening ("pre-echo").

HOMOPHONIC		[Two phrases, each with five statements of "Halleluyah." Notice the changing rhythms.]
	0:07	First phrase, tonic.
	0:16	Second phrase, dominant.

UNISON		[With homophonic "halleluyah" responses: "For the Lord God omnipotent reigneth."]
	0:25	First phrase, dominant.
	0:37	Second phrase, tonic.

POLYPHONIC		
38	**0:49**	Statement by sopranos, tonic.
	0:56	Statement by tenors and basses, dominant.
	1:05	Statement by tenors and altos, tonic.
	1:14	Short instrumental interlude.

HOMOPHONIC		[With noticeable change in dynamics: two phrases, one soft (piano), one loud (forte).]
	1:16	piano: "The kingdom of this world is become …"
	1:27	*forte*: " …the kingdom of our God and of His Christ."

IMITATION		[Four entries, "And He shall reign forever and ever."]
39	**1:38**	Basses, tonic.
	1:43	Tenors in counterpoint with basses, dominant.
	1:49	Altos in counterpoint with basses and tenors, tonic.
	1:55	Sopranos in counterpoint with all other voices, dominant.

UNISON		[Three declamatory statements ("King of Kings and Lord of Lords") against homophonic responses ("forever and ever, halleluyah, halleluyah"), each at a different pitch, moving higher and higher.]
40	**2:01**	Sopranos and altos, answered by other voices.

UNISON/HOMOPHONIC	
	[Combination of unison and homophonic textures — "King of Kings" ... ("forever and ever") "and Lord of Lords" ... ("halleluyah, halleluyah").]
2:54	Tenors, answered by other voices.

HOMOPHONIC	
	[Statements by all voices.]
3:03	"And He shall reign forever and ever."
3:10	"King of Kings and Lord of Lords" (twice).
3:19	"And he shall reign forever and ever."
	[Final statement of "King of Kings and Lord of Lords."]
3:26	Tenors and sopranos, answered by other voices.
3:34	Pause; one final drawn-out homophonic statement: plagal cadence (IV–I).

Handel was also an accomplished composer of instrumental music. His two most famous instrumental suites are the *Water Music* (see Chapter 1) and *Music for the Royal Fireworks*.

Handel's music is less complex than that of Bach, with more focus on melody than on counterpoint, and he deliberately appealed to a wider audience than had been traditional. Music was becoming less the preserve of the wealthy and more the delight of everyone who cared to listen.

Listening to...

BAROQUE MUSIC

- Instrumental music reaches equal status to vocal music. The principal instrumental genres you will hear are sonatas (Corelli's Trio Sonata), suites, and concertos (Vivaldi's *The Four Seasons*; Bach's *Brandenburg Concerto*).

- The principal vocal genres are operas (Monteverdi's *Orfeo*; Purcell's *Dido and Aeneas*; Handel's *Giulio Cesare*), cantatas, and oratorios (Handel's *Messiah*).

- Baroque music is enormously expressive, colorful, and varied.

- With all of its variety, Baroque music has one unifying stylistic trait: the basso continuo. A Baroque piece is instantly recognizable from the power and momentum of its bass line.

- In opera, the main topics are stories from Greek and Roman myths (Monteverdi's *Orfeo*) or history (Handel's *Giulio Cesare*). The principal musical forms are recitative and aria. Recitatives are relatively simple, with sparse accompaniment. Arias are lyrical and expressive and usually in ABA form.

- Concertos exploit the Baroque love of contrast. The most important contrast is between the sound of solo playing and that of the whole orchestra. There may be a small group of solo players or just a single soloist.

- You can start to hear clear national differences in musical style. Instrumental music for strings is usually Italian. Music influenced by dance is mostly French. German music often incorporates two important elements: the Lutheran chorale and a love of counterpoint. A very English genre is the oratorio. Oratorios are sung in concert performances with English text.

KEY TERMS

aria **(p. 102)**

chorale **(p. 98)**

concerto **(p. 97)**

sonata **(p. 97)**

concerto grosso **(p. 104)**

dance suite **(p. 97)**

ground bass **(p. 102)**

opera **(p. 97)**

oratorio **(p. 98)**

Passion **(p. 98)**

program music **(p. 109)**

recitative **(p. 99)**

ritornello **(p. 100)**

solo concerto **(p. 105)**

solo sonata **(p. 104)**

trio sonata **(p. 104)**

6
The Classic Era: 1750—1800

CHAPTER OUTLINE

The Enlightenment: A Time of Change The Musical Public **General Characteristics of Classic Music** Genres of Classic Music Convention in Classic Music Forms of Classic Music	**The Classic Masters** Franz Joseph Haydn (1732–1809) Haydn's Music Wolfgang Amadeus Mozart (1756–1791) Mozart's Music **Listening to Classic Music**

The term "classic" is usually used to describe something that has an appeal that is both broad and long-lasting. A novel may be described as a classic, and so may a movie or a car. This means that the novel, the movie, and the car continue to attract enthusiasts long after they first appeared. It also means that they appeal to a wide range of people.

Both of these things are true of Classic music. The music of the greatest composers of the Classic era has been popular with audiences ever since it was written. What is it about Classic music that has given it such enduring appeal? To help answer that question, we need to consider the social and political climate of Europe in the middle of the eighteenth century.

THE ENLIGHTENMENT: A TIME OF CHANGE

The eighteenth century was a time of profound change, both social and political. It began with the death, in 1715, of Louis XIV of France, the most powerful ruler in Europe, and it ended with two of the most significant revolutions in modern history: the American War of Independence (1775–83) and the French Revolution (1789–94).

Voltaire in 1718.

The whole period was colored by the philosophical movement known as the Enlightenment. This movement, led by the great French philosophers Voltaire and Rousseau, attempted to apply the principles of scientific objectivity to social issues. Enlightenment thinkers favored simplicity over complexity. They tried to improve education, eliminate prejudice, and break down the rigid class structure that separated people from one another.

Declaration of American Independence 1776
Jean-Jacques Rousseau 1712–1778
Samuel Johnson 1709–1784
Frederick the Great 1740–1786
French Revolution 1789
Emperor Joseph II 1765–1790
Mozart 1756–1791
First copper pennies minted (in England) 1797

Jean-Jacques Rousseau.

Vienna in 1783.

Some of the rulers of the time were influenced by the ideas of the Enlightenment. Emperor Joseph II of Austria, for example, was regarded as an "enlightened" monarch. He was a strong supporter of the arts. In Vienna, which was the capital of the Holy Roman Empire and the place where Joseph held court, all the arts flourished. With names such as Haydn, Mozart, and Beethoven in the list of its citizens, Vienna was, by the end of the century, the musical center of Europe.

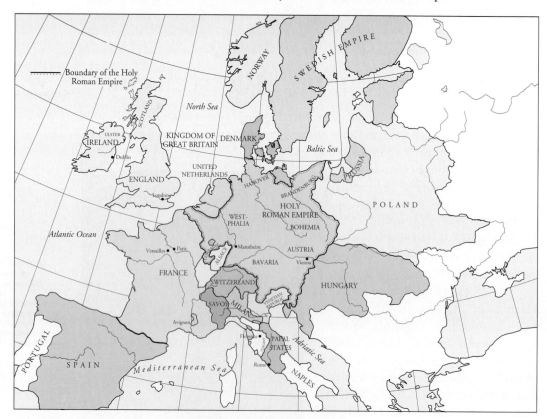

The Holy Roman Empire and its capital, Vienna.

Enlightenment ideals reached their high point in Vienna in the 1780s and 1790s, but many other parts of Europe were affected as well. In France, the reign of Louis XIV was succeeded by those of Louis XV and Louis XVI. The reign of Louis XVI ended in the turmoil of the French Revolution, which had as its slogan the rallying cry of the Enlightenment: "Liberty, Equality, Brotherhood!" Louis XVI was guillotined by his own people in Paris on January 21, 1793.

Emperor Joseph II of Austria.

Brotherhood was the concept behind many new organizations founded in the eighteenth century. Chief among these was Freemasonry, founded in England in 1717. Famous Freemasons of the eighteenth century were Joseph II, the great German poet Goethe, Mozart, and George Washington.

The idea of brotherhood did not include women, however. And because their roles were narrowly defined by society, few women became monarchs, well-known writers, or famous composers. Important exceptions were Maria Theresa, ruler of Austria from 1740 to 1780, and Catherine II ("Catherine the Great") of Russia, who ruled from 1762 to 1796. One of the greatest novelists of the period was Jane Austen (1775–1817), whose masterpieces include *Pride and Prejudice* and *Emma*. But the author's name did not appear on the title pages of her books when they were published, and she received very little public recognition during her own lifetime. Similarly, there were women who composed music but did not have their works published. Anna Amalie, the Duchess of Saxe-Weimar, wrote German operas and chamber music and was highly influential in bringing together intellectuals, poets, and musicians at her court, but her own music was never published.

The execution of Louis XVI.

Women's influence in all other areas of musical life was, however, great. They were accomplished music teachers, singers, instrumentalists, authors of instruction manuals, patrons, and organizers of musical life. A great deal more research, publishing, and performance work remains to be done to restore women's music in the Classic era to its rightful place.

The Musical Public

Changes in class structure in the eighteenth century had far-reaching effects on music. The flourishing economy created a large and prosperous middle class, whose members began to feel they were entitled to the same privileges as the aristocracy. The eighteenth century saw the rise of the public concert—a new idea at the time, because until then music had usually been performed in private courts or salons. By the end of the century, public concerts were the primary musical forum in cities and towns across Europe.

Women making music at home.

Pietro Longhi (1702–1785). The House Concert, Around 1760. Oil on canvas. 50 × 62 cm. Pinacoteca di Brera, Milan, Italy. © Photograph by Erich Lessing. Erich Lessing/Art Resource, NY.

The vast increase in the number of musical consumers affected other areas of music, too. Music publishing became a profitable business, and music publishers sprang up in many cities. Middle-class men and women wanted to learn to play music themselves. They arranged lessons for themselves and their children and bought musical instruments to play at home.

The social changes of the eighteenth century also affected the status of performers and composers. Although many musicians were still supported by powerful rulers or wealthy aristocrats, some could begin to make a living on their own. This gradual change is exemplified by the life of the composer Joseph Haydn. He spent most of his career in the employ of a wealthy prince, but toward the end of his life he became independent.

Even the type of music composed in the Classic era was affected by the new musical public. The intensity of Baroque music was no longer in fashion. Music was now designed to appeal to a broader public. It had to be lighter, clearer, and more accessible. It had to be easier to listen to and easier to play. A common musical language developed, one that could be understood by a broad range of society. Within this language—the "classic" language—enormous amounts of music were composed. All of it is pleasant and accessible. Geniuses like Haydn and Mozart used this same language to produce masterpieces of enduring significance.

GENERAL CHARACTERISTICS OF CLASSIC MUSIC

The primary features of Classic music are balance and proportion, clarity and accessibility. It is designed to be "easy on the ear." Yet that does not mean it cannot also be very beautiful, very moving, and very profound.

Classic music was a reaction to the complexity of Baroque music. Classic music usually has just a melody and an accompaniment, and the accompaniment is light and simple. Imitative counterpoint is used only rarely, and then only for special effect. The melodies are pleasing and tuneful—the kind you can hum or whistle as you go through the day.

Three technical aspects to the special sound of Classic music are short balanced phrases, simple harmony, and light accompaniment. Classic music is usually made up of two- or four-bar phrases, rather than the long lines common in Baroque music. This makes the music clear and balanced. These phrases are usually arranged into patterns of opening and closing phrases. A two- or four-bar opening phrase is immediately followed by a two- or four-bar closing phrase, creating a symmetrical pattern.

This pattern makes the music easy to follow and establishes a sense of regularity in the mind of the listener.

The second technical aspect of Classic music is its harmony. The harmony of Classic music is generally simple, logical, and clear. Classic composers do not usually go very far afield in their harmonies. They tend to stick to relatively straightforward keys, and they do not often use strange or dissonant chords.

Finally, the effect of Classic music depends a great deal on its accompaniment. Gone is the powerful basso continuo of the Baroque. In its place, we find a simple "walking bass" (in which the bass line moves mostly by step, in even notes and with a regular rhythm) or little bustling accompanying figures that keep the rhythm lively. (A special development of the Classic era was the "Alberti bass." This is an accompaniment in which the chords are broken up into separate notes played one after the other, instead of simultaneously, to keep the texture light and lively.)

These three features—the balanced phrases, the simple harmony, the light accompaniment—help to give Classic music its special sound and provide a framework for its tuneful, pleasing melodies.

Genres of Classic Music

Several musical genres were popular in the Classic era. The most important of these were opera, symphony, string quartet, and sonata. Some composers wrote in other genres, too. Mozart, for example, composed many beautiful piano concertos and some string *quintets* (pieces written for string quartet and one additional viola). But on the whole, composers stayed within the conventional genres. Notice that all these genres are secular. Although composers still occasionally wrote sacred works such as Masses and oratorios, these forms are far less common in the Classic era, reflecting a shift in society's makeup and interests.

Operas were staged in the palaces of a few very wealthy aristocrats or in the public opera houses of big cities such as Prague, Paris, or Vienna. Symphonies also were performed in aristocratic courts or at the public concerts springing up all over Europe. String quartets and sonatas, with their smaller ensembles and more intimate sound, were designed for private gatherings—in an aristocratic salon or in the living rooms of middle-class music lovers.

Let us look briefly at how the opera, the symphony, the string quartet, and the sonata developed in the Classic era.

OPERA   We have seen that opera was the Baroque art form *par excellence*. It combined a story with artwork, costumes, illusion, and best of all, superb singing. But during the late Baroque period, some people began to criticize Baroque opera as artificial. They complained that the plots were always about mythological or historical figures rather than real people; that the music was too heavy and complex; and that the stage sets, with their elaborate scenery and complicated machines for simulating battles and shipwrecks, were too involved. The arias were criticized for unnecessary length and embellishment. This attack on Baroque opera was another sign of the changing social structure of the eighteenth century. Baroque opera was the province of the aristocracy; what was demanded was a style of opera that would appeal to everyone. It should be about real people in everyday situations.

The result of these attitudes was the development of a new type of opera called *comic opera*. Comic opera became very popular in the Classic era. It featured simpler music, down-to-earth characters, and an amusing plot.

The most famous early example of Italian comic opera is Pergolesi's *La Serva Padrona* (1733). Even the title is meant to be comical: It really means "The Servant Girl Who Became Mistress of the House." The opera is about a clever servant girl who tricks her master, a rich old bachelor, into marrying her. The story was designed to appeal to an age in which rigid class barriers were being called into question.

LISTENING GUIDE

GIOVANNI PERGOLESI (1710–1736)
Opera, *La Serva Padrona* (Duet from Act I)

Date of composition: 1733
Orchestration: 2 singers, harpsichord, and strings
Duration: 4:23

Complete CD Collection: 2, Tracks 1–3

La Serva Padrona (*The Maid as Mistress*) is often referred to as the first example of comic opera. It is divided into two acts and features only two principal roles: Serpina (literally "little snake"), a maidservant, and Uberto, a bachelor, Serpina's master.

The plot is a simple one: Through various deceptions, Uberto is tricked into marrying Serpina, and she becomes the mistress of the house.

The following excerpt is a duet that comes at the end of the first act and features amusing exchanges between Serpina and Uberto. She insists that he must marry her, and he is equally adamant that he will not.

The musical language is appropriately simple, with many repeats, and it is easy to follow. Notice the comic interchange between the principals: "no, no–si, si," etc. Notice, too, how the music reflects the meaning of some of the words: "graceful," "spirited," "dignified," etc. Toward the end of the scene, the dialogue is repeated from the beginning, but the text is broken up to suggest an even more lively exchange.

1	0:00	[lively orchestral introduction, strings and harpsichord; dynamic contrasts, short repeated phrases.]	

SERPINA

0:17	*Lo conosco, lo conosco a quegli occhietti, a quegli occhietti Furbi, ladri, ladri, malignetti.*	I can see it, I can see it in your eyes, in your eyes: You're a cunning, scheming, naughty old man.
0:27	*Che sebben voi dite "no, no, no" Pur m'accennano di "si, si, si, si, si."*	You keep saying "no, no, no," but you really mean "yes, yes, yes, yes, yes."

UBERTO

	[same melody]	
0:38	*Signorina, signorina, v'ingannate, v'ingannate! Troppo, troppo, troppo, troppo in alto vi volate!*	Miss, miss, you're wrong, you're wrong! Too high, too high, too high Your ambitions fly! [loud, "flying"]
0:49	*Gli occhi ed io vi dicon "no, no, no" Ed è un sogno questo "si, si, si, si, si."*	Both my eyes and I say "no, no, no" and you're dreaming if you hear "yes, yes, yes, yes, yes."

SERPINA

	[new key]		
1:00	*Ma perché, ma perché? Non son graziosa? Non son bella e spiritosa?*	But why, but why? Am I not graceful? Am I not beautiful and spirited?	[expressive] [graceful] [spirited]
	Su, mirate leggiadria, leggiadria.	Just look how elegant, how elegant!	[elegant]
	Ve' che brio, che maesta, che maesta!	What panache! What dignity! What dignity!	[with panache] [dignified]

UBERTO

	[dark, rising chromatically]	
1:28	*(Ah, costei mi va tentando quanto va che me la fa.)*	(Ah, she must be testing me to see how long I can resist.)

SERPINA

1:36	*(Ei mi par che va calando, va calando.) Via, Signore!*	(I think he's weakening, weakening.) Decide then, Sir!	[lightly]

UBERTO

1:42	*Eh, vanne via!*	Get out!

SERPINA			
	1:45	[decisive] *Risolvete!*	Decide!
UBERTO			
	1:47	*Eh, matta sei!*	You must be mad!
SERPINA			
	1:49	*Son per voi gli affetti miei,* *E dovrete sposar me,*	All my feelings are for you. You must marry me.
	1:52	*dovrete, dovrete, dovrete,* *sposar me!*	You must, you must, you must, marry me!
UBERTO			
	1:52	*Oh, che imbroglio, ch'imbroglio,* *ch'imbroglio, egli è per me!*	Oh, what a mess, what a mess, what a mess I've gotten into!

	2:00	[Instrumental interlude, dynamic
		  contrasts, back to tonic key
		  and text of opening. Music is
		  changed, though, and dialogue
		  more broken up.]	

SERPINA			
2	2:07	*Lo conosco a quegli occhietti* *furbi, ladri, malignetti.*	I can see it in your eyes, you cunning, scheming, naughty old man.
UBERTO			
	2:16	[sternly] *Signorina, signorina, v'ingannate.*	Miss, miss, you're wrong.
SERPINA			
	2:22	*No, no, no, no,* *che sebben voi dite "no,"* *pur m'accennano di "si."*	No, no, no, no, you keep saying "no," when you mean to say "yes."
UBERTO			
	2:32	*V'ingannate!*	You're wrong!
SERPINA			
	2:35	*Ma perché, ma perché?* *Non son bella, graziosa, spiritosa?*	But why, but why? Am I not beautiful, graceful, spirited?
UBERTO			
	2:46	*(Ah, costei mi va tentando.)*	(She's testing me.)

SERPINA			
2:51	*(Va calando si, si.)* *Ve'che brio, che brio, che maestà, che* *maestà!*	(He's weakening, yes, yes.) See what panache I have! What panache! What dignity! What dignity!
UBERTO			
3 3:03	[minor key] *(Quanto val, quanto val,* *Quanto val che me fa la.)* *Laralla, laralla, la la la la la la la.*	(She's just seeing how long I can resist.) Laralla, laralla, la la la la la la la.
SERPINA			
3:11	*Via, signore, resolvete!*	Decide then, Sir!
UBERTO			
3:12	*Eh, vanne via. Eh matta sei!*	Get out! You must be mad!
SERPINA			
3:16	*Son per voi gl'affetti mei,*	All my feelings are for you.
UBERTO			
3:16	*Signorina, v'ingannate!*	Miss, you're wrong!
SERPINA			
3:19	*E dovrete si, si!*	You must, yes, yes!
UBERTO			
3:22	*Signorina, no, no!*	Miss, no, no!
SERPINA			
3:24	*E dovrete sposar me!*	You must marry me!
UBERTO			
3:24	*Oh, che imbroglio egli è per me!*	Oh, what a mess I've gotten into!
3:26	*(Quanto va, quanto va, quanto va che me la* *fa!)*	(She's just seeing how long I can resist.)
SERPINA			
3:31	[with long pauses] *Non son bella, graziosa, spiritosa?*	Am I not beautiful, graceful, spirited?
UBERTO			
3:41	*La la la, la la la.*	La la la, la la la.
SERPINA			
3:43	*Ve'che brio, ve che brio!*	What panache I have! What panache!

UBERTO

Oh, che imbroglio, oh, che imbroglio!	Oh, what a mess, oh, what a mess!

SERPINA

3:50

(Va calando, si, si.)	(He's weakening, yes, yes.)
Son per voi, son per voi,	All for you, all for you,
Son per voi gl'affetti miei.	My feelings are all for you.

UBERTO

Signori-, signori-, signorina, matta sei!	Miss … miss …
	Miss, you must be mad!

SERPINA

3:56

E dovrete si, si.	You must, yes, yes.

UBERTO

3:58

Signorina, no, no!	Miss, no, no!

SERPINA

Si, si!	Yes, yes!

UBERTO

No, no!	No, no!

SERPINA

4:03

Si, si dovrete, dovrete, dovrete sposar me,	Yes, yes, you must, you must, you must
sposar me!	marry me, marry me!

UBERTO

Oh, che imbroglio, ch'imbroglio,	Oh, what a mess, what a mess, what a
ch'imbroglio egli è per me, egli è per me!	mess I'm in, I'm in!

SYMPHONY   The most important genre of instrumental music in the Classic era was the symphony. The symphony began life as an instrumental introduction to Italian opera. At the beginning of the eighteenth century, Italian operas were usually preceded by an **overture**—an instrumental introduction in three short movements: fast–slow–fast. The Italian name for this type of opera overture was *sinfonia*. Gradually these instrumental pieces achieved independent status. Soon composers from Italy to Germany to England were writing symphonies with no connection to opera.

Gradually the fast–slow–fast pattern of the Italian *sinfonia* was expanded to a four-movement scheme. The first movement is fast and serious, the second movement slow and lyrical, the third movement graceful and moderate in tempo, and the last movement fast and lively. This pattern of movements became standard for the symphony throughout the Classic period.

The Classic orchestra had three main instrumental groups: strings, woodwinds, and (sometimes) trumpets and drums. The string section consisted of two groups of violins ("first violins" and "second violins,"), as well as violas, cellos, and double basses. The woodwind section had either two flutes or two oboes, plus two horns. Bright, ceremonial symphonies also used trumpets and drums.

In the later Classic period, the orchestra was augmented slightly, particularly in the woodwind section. Composers often used both flutes *and* oboes. Bassoons were employed to fill out the low sounds of the woodwind section, and in the late eighteenth century clarinets also became popular.

A composer could choose the number and types of instruments in a particular work to achieve different effects. If a composer wanted a delicate sound, he or she might write for strings, one flute, and two horns. A fuller, richer sound could be obtained with the strings plus all the woodwind instruments. And for a really festive piece, trumpets and drums were added.

In actual performance, the size of the string section varied according to the financial resources of the sponsor. In rich cities or aristocratic courts, there could be as many as twelve first violinists, twelve second violinists, six viola players, eight cellists, and four double bass players. In smaller orchestras, there were only three or four first violins, three or four second violins, two violas, two cellos, and one double bass.

CHAMBER MUSIC (STRING QUARTET AND SONATA)   As the middle class became more involved in music making at home, composers responded by writing works for a small number of instruments. Because this music is designed to be played at home rather than in public concert halls, it is usually known as **chamber music**. It includes duets, trios, and quintets for various instrumental combinations, but the most important types of chamber music during this period were the string quartet and the sonata.

The string quartet developed around the middle of the eighteenth century. It involves four string instruments: two violins, a viola, and a cello. Many of the finest works of the eighteenth century are written for string quartet. The string quartet provides an ideal balance between high and low instruments. The smooth, high, silvery sounds of the two violins are balanced by the drier, middle range of the viola and the rich, deep tones of the cello. Because all the instruments belong to the same family, they blend perfectly together.

Works for string quartet closely followed the pattern of symphonic works. They usually had four movements: the first fast and serious, the second slow and lyrical, the third graceful, and the fourth lively.

Sonatas could be written either for a keyboard instrument alone or for a keyboard instrument with another instrument such as a violin or a flute. Until about 1775, the predominant keyboard instrument was the harpsichord. By the last part of the eighteenth century, the piano began to replace the harpsichord as the

An eighteenth-century string quartet playing in a middle-class home. Notice the bust of Mozart on the wall.

String Quartet. Color engraving, 18th century, Austrian. Mozart Museum, Prague, Czech Republic. Giraudon/Art Resource, NY.

favorite keyboard instrument. The piano was capable of gradations of volume—that was why it was originally called the piano-forte ("soft-loud")—and it had a fine, delicate sound.

Convention in Classic Music

The eighteenth century was a time of strict social conventions. Dress codes were carefully followed. Well-to-do people wore powdered wigs, brocaded coats, and silver shoe buckles. They followed an elaborate pattern of rules that governed social behavior—when to curtsy, when to bow. Even spoken communication was highly formalized.

So it is not surprising to learn that strict conventions were established for music, too. The instruments used for particular types of works, the number of movements, the approximate length of each movement, even the keys in which a composition might be written—all these were fixed by convention. The most far-reaching convention in Classic music was the *form* in which a composer could write each individual movement of a composition. There were only a few forms used in Classic music, and composers adhered to them most of the time. The most important of these are sonata form, aria form, minuet-and-trio form, and rondo form. We shall look at each of these in turn, but before we do, let us consider the overall importance of convention in Classic music.

Today, nothing seems more important to us than originality. The cult of originality, however, is a recent phenomenon. In the eighteenth century, writers, artists, and composers were respected not for the originality of their work but for its quality. The works of Haydn and Mozart stand out among the works of hundreds of other Classic composers, not because they are original, but because they demonstrate the most skill, the greatest resourcefulness, and the widest range of expression. Haydn and Mozart were the greatest composers of the age because they used convention to better advantage than anyone else.

Forms of Classic Music

SONATA FORM   The most important single-movement form in Classic music is **sonata form**. This form was used for almost all first movements of Classic instrumental music: sonatas, symphonies, string quartets, and many other genres. For that reason, it is sometimes known as "first-movement form." But sonata form became so popular in the Classic era that it was often used for other movements as well.

Sonata form is intellectually demanding, and composers used it for their most serious ideas. That doesn't mean it has to be difficult to listen to. As with any art form, however, it takes practice to become familiar with the ways in which it is organized. Once we understand sonata form, many of the secrets of Classic music are revealed to us.

Sonata form has three sections: the **exposition**, the **development**, and the **recapitulation**. The exposition begins in the tonic key and presents the opening material of the piece. Then it moves to a second, closely related, key and presents new material in that key. The exposition ends with a clear cadence. In Classic sonata-form movements, the exposition is normally played twice.

The development section explores many different keys. It usually moves quickly from key to key and is generally quite turbulent. The development leads dramatically into the recapitulation, usually without an intervening cadence.

The recapitulation brings back all the music of the exposition, but with one crucial change: *The material that was previously presented in the second key is now played in the home key, so that the movement can end in the key in which it began.* Sometimes there is a short additional section added to the end of a sonata-form movement just to round it off. This short section is called the **coda** (literally "tail").

The diagram summarizes these main features of sonata form.

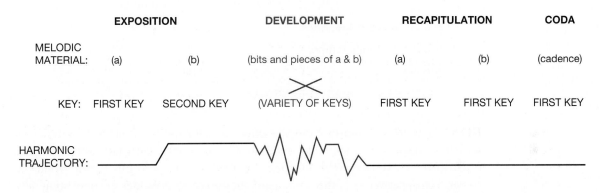

The most important place to listen carefully in a sonata-form movement is right at the beginning. If you remember the sound of the beginning of the exposition, you will be able to recognize the recapitulation when it comes, because it brings back the same music. Also, with practice, you will be able to recognize the development section, partly because it changes key frequently and partly because it contains a great deal of turbulence—as though the material had been thrown into a blender and was being cut up and tossed around.

ARIA FORM   Aria form is simple, and we discussed it in the previous chapter in the context of Baroque opera. Classic composers often used it for the second, slow movement of a sonata, a symphony, or a string quartet. This movement is designed to be lyrical and songlike. Aria form is ABA, with a slow, lyrical opening section (A) that is often in triple meter. This is followed by a contrasting central section in a new key (B). Finally, the opening section (A) is repeated, often decorated or slightly modified. Slow movements are *often* in aria form, but they sometimes use sonata form or theme-and-variations form.

ARIA FORM

A (melody and key)   B (new melody, new key)   A (repeated, often embellished)

MINUET-AND-TRIO FORM   **Minuet-and-trio form** is the standard form for third movements in sonatas, symphonies, and string quartets. The minuet was originally a Baroque court dance in moderate triple meter. In the Classic era, a minuet and trio simply means two minuets played in the pattern Minuet–Trio–Minuet. The trio usually presents some kind of contrast to the minuet—in instrumentation, texture, dynamics, or key.

The minuet *itself* is in two parts, each of which is repeated: AABB. The trio has the same pattern: CCDD. Then the first minuet is played again (often without repeats). The whole scheme of a minuet-and-trio movement looks like this:

Minuet	Trio	Minuet
AABB	CCDD	AABB (or AB)

The most important characteristics of a minuet-and-trio movement are:

1. It is always in 3/4 meter.
2. It has a moderate tempo.
3. It is always in three-part, or *ternary* form (minuet–trio–minuet).
4. It always has some kind of contrast in the trio.

RONDO FORM **Rondo form** was often used for the last (fourth) movement of symphonies, string quartets, and sonatas. Rondos are usually fairly fast, with a lively or catchy tune that keeps on returning or coming round again and again (hence "rondo"). In between appearances of the tune (**main theme**) come **episodes** of contrasting material. Thus, if we designate the main theme as A and the contrasting episodes with other letters, we have:

A B A C A D A

Sometimes composers used the first episode again just before the last appearance of the refrain:

A B A C A B A

This makes a particularly symmetrical kind of rondo.

SUMMARY Let us summarize this overview of the main forms of Classic music. The most common and most serious form is sonata form. First movements are nearly always in sonata form. Second movements are often in aria form: ABA. Minuet-and-trio form is the usual form for third movements. Last movements are often in rondo form.

These are the main forms for the standard four movements of most Classic instrumental music, and you will find listening guides for each of these forms in this chapter. We should recognize that there are variants of this pattern, however. For example, Classic concertos had only three movements: a sonata-form movement, a slow movement, and a rondo. Also, in all genres, sonata form was sometimes used for movements in addition to the first. It is not uncommon for the slow movement of a Classic composition to be in sonata form, and sometimes composers used sonata form for the last movement also. Some compositions reverse the position of the slow movement and the minuet and trio, putting the minuet second and the slow movement third.

FOUR-MOVEMENT STRUCTURE

Movement	Form	Key
I	Sonata	Tonic

II	Aria or Sonata or
	    Theme and Variations
		Dominant or Subdominant
		    or Relative minor

III	Minuet and Trio	Tonic (Trio is sometimes in a different key)
IV	Rondo or Sonata	Tonic

THE CLASSIC MASTERS

The masters of the Classic style were Haydn and Mozart. Both men were extraordinarily prolific, completing many hundreds of superb compositions during their lifetimes. Although the musical language and techniques they used were common throughout Europe at the time, their individual abilities were so remarkable, their grasp of harmony, form, and expression so assured, and their melodic invention so rich that they stand out from their contemporaries.

Haydn in full dress.

Edouard Jean Conrad Hamman, Portrait of Joseph Haydn. Engraving. Bibliothèque Nationale, Paris, France. Giraudon/Art Resource, NY.

Franz Joseph Haydn (1732–1809)

Anyone can see that I'm a good-natured fellow.
—Haydn

Haydn was born in a small village in Austria. There was much music-making at home and in the village, and Haydn displayed an early talent for music. At the age of eight, he was accepted as a choirboy at St. Stephen's Cathedral in Vienna, the biggest city in the Austrian empire. Here he stayed until he was eighteen.

While he was at the cathedral, he had learned to play the harpsichord and the violin, so for the next ten years (about 1750 to 1760), Haydn made a living giving harpsichord lessons and playing in local orchestras. He lived in a small room in an apartment building in Vienna. Luckily for him, one of the grander apartments was occupied by the head of one of the most prominent aristocratic families of the time. Her name was Maria Esterházy, and the Esterházy family was to play a significant role in Haydn's life and career.

In 1761, Haydn was hired as assistant music director to the household of Prince Paul Anton Esterházy. The prince had a sizable retinue of servants, including a small orchestra of about twelve players. Haydn was responsible for composing music on demand, supervising and rehearsing the other musicians, and caring for the instruments.

The music room in the palace of Esterháza.

Prince Paul Anton died in 1762 and was succeeded by his brother Nikolaus. Prince Nikolaus Esterházy was an avid music lover who spent a great deal of money on his court and entertainment. In the countryside, Prince Nikolaus built a magnificent palace that had two large music rooms and two small theaters for opera. He called this palace Esterháza after the family name.

In 1766, Haydn was promoted to music director at Esterháza. He was responsible for directing all the music at the palace. There were usually two full operas as well as two big concerts given each week. Extra concerts were put on for important visitors. Music was performed at meals, and the prince had chamber music played in his own rooms almost every day. Haydn wrote much of this music himself.

Over the course of his lifetime, Haydn wrote about a dozen operas, more than one hundred symphonies, nearly seventy string quartets, more than fifty keyboard sonatas, and a large amount of choral music, songs, and other chamber music. Haydn stayed in the service of the Esterházy family until 1790, when Prince Nikolaus died. The new prince, Nikolaus II, did not like music and disbanded the orchestra. Haydn, now nearly sixty, moved back to Vienna.

By this time, his work was internationally known, and he traveled to London twice. For his visits to London, Haydn wrote his last twelve symphonies, brilliant and fascinating works, which were performed there to wild public acclaim. They are known as the *London* Symphonies.

In his late years, back in Vienna, Haydn wrote mostly string quartets and vocal music. His quartets are varied and masterful, covering the entire range of expression from playfulness to profundity. The vocal works include six Mass settings for chorus and orchestra and two great oratorios, *The Creation* (1798) and *The Seasons* (1801).

Haydn died in 1809 at the age of seventy-seven. His reputation transcended even national disputes. Vienna was under siege by the French army at the time, but Napoleon posted a guard of honor outside Haydn's house to pay homage to the greatest composer of the age.

Haydn's Music

Haydn's operas are full of beautiful music—lyrical, inventive, and moving. His symphonies range from ceremonious public works with trumpets and drums to compositions of great delicacy, charm, and even tragedy. The string quartets explore an enormous range of expression, with a masterful handling of the intimate medium and brilliant writing for the four instruments.

The Haydn Masses are noble, grand structures, combining a conservative choral style appropriate to the traditional texts with his own individual orchestral and symphonic brilliance. And Haydn's two oratorios, *The Creation* and *The Seasons*, display a lively wit, together with the kind of exquisite pictorial writing that never fails to captivate audiences.

We shall study one of the movements from a Haydn symphony from the middle of the composer's career at Esterháza. Haydn was forty years old at the time.

LISTENING GUIDE

FRANZ JOSEPH HAYDN (1732–1809)

Minuet and Trio from Symphony No. 47
 in G Major

Date of composition: 1772
Orchestration: 2 oboes, 2 horns, violins I and
 II, violas, cellos, double bass
Tempo: *Allegretto* ("Moderately fast")
Meter: $\frac{3}{4}$
Key of movement: G Major
Duration: 2:55

Complete CD Collection: 2, Tracks 4–6

 aydn wrote many minuets during his career, and it is amazing how much variety he could put into this very conventional form. This movement is full of dynamic contrasts and juxtapositions of different instruments.

MINUET		
4	0:00	(A) The first section of the minuet. Whole orchestra playing; quick dynamic contrasts. Cadence in the dominant key (D Major).
	0:13	A: Repeat of the first section of the minuet.
	0:26	B: The second section of the minuet, similar in sound to the first. Again full of rapid dynamic changes. Begins in the dominant, returns to the tonic (G Major).
	0:39	B: Repeat.

TRIO		
5	0:53	(C) First section of the trio. Quiet throughout. But the dynamic contrasts are now replaced by contrast of instruments. First horns alone; oboes join in. Then strings alone; and finally oboes with strings. Ends in dominant key.
	1:09	C: Repeat.
	1:26	D: Second section of trio. Oboes and strings, then strings alone. Oboes and horns; then just horns. Ends in tonic key.
	1:42	D: Repeat.

MINUET		
		(The entire minuet is repeated.)
6	1:58	(A) First section.
	2:11	A: Repeat.
	2:24	B: Second section.
	2:37	B: Repeat.

All of Haydn's pieces use Classic forms. Nevertheless, Haydn showed great ingenuity in exploiting the fixed forms of Classic music for his own expressive purposes. One device that he invented was the "false recapitulation." You remember that in sonata form, the opening music of the movement comes back again—after the development section—with the same melody and harmony that it had at the beginning. Haydn sometimes liked to play games with the expectations of his audience by *pretending* to start the recapitulation in the middle of the development section. The music of the opening of the movement is played, leading us to think that the recapitulation has started. But then the harmonies change, the development continues, and we realize we've been tricked. A little while later, the true recapitulation occurs.

Haydn liked to play other kinds of tricks on his listeners. In 1781, he published a set of six string quartets, which have come to be called the "Joke Quartets." The quartets contain serious music and emotionally expressive passages, but there are many witty moments, too: cadences in the "wrong" places, oddly shaped melodies,

LISTENING GUIDE

FRANZ JOSEPH HAYDN (1732–1809)

Fourth Movement from String Quartet, Op. 33, No. 2, in E-flat Major

Tempo: *Presto* ("Very fast")
Meter: $\frac{6}{8}$
Key: E-flat Major
Duration: 3:08

Companion CD, Track 69

This movement is in the form of a rondo. There is a catchy main theme, which constantly returns in the course of the movement. Between appearances of the main theme are passages of contrasting material known as episodes. In this rondo Haydn adopts the following form (A indicates the main theme, and B, C, and D the three episodes):

A B A B A C A B A D A Coda

Haydn has written this movement in the attractive and bouncy meter of $\frac{6}{8}$ and in a fast tempo, which makes the music particularly lively and fun. But the joke comes in the final measures, as the listener has no idea where the ending really is.

A 69	0:00	Main theme.	
	0:06	Repeat.	
B	0:12	First episode.	

A	0:28	Main theme.
B	0:34	Repeat of first episode.
A	0:50	Main theme.
C	0:57	Second episode, many key changes.
A	1:25	Main theme.
B	1:31	First episode again.
A	1:48	Main theme.
D	1:54	Third episode.
	2:13	Pace slows down, anticipation, then:
A	2:23	Main theme again.
CODA	2:30	Final cadence?
	2:32	Sudden change of texture and tempo.
	2:45	Final cadence?
	2:46	Main theme, broken up into four separate phrases.
	2:58	Ending?
	3:01	First phrase of main theme!

and unexpected rhythms. At the end of the second quartet of the set (Opus 33, Number 2), there is a "false ending." The music seems to stop, suddenly moves on, stops again, and then seems to begin again. Then the movement ends. Let's listen to this amusing piece.

This kind of manipulation of audience expectations could occur only in a period in which formal procedures were strict. When there are no rules, breaking the rules is no fun!

As more and more of his compositions become familiar, we realize that Haydn was one of the most versatile and gifted composers of his time.

Wolfgang Amadeus Mozart (1756–1791)

For most listeners, Mozart's music is easier to appreciate than Haydn's. Compared with Haydn, Mozart wears his heart on his sleeve. His music is more colorful, more intense.

Mozart at 33.

Mozart was born into a musical family. His father, Leopold, was a distinguished violinist and composer who held the post of deputy music director at the court of the Prince-Archbishop of Salzburg in Austria. He was also the author of an important book on violin-playing.

He decided to devote his career to promoting the abilities of young Wolfgang. Wolfgang was uniquely, breathtakingly gifted. His father piously referred to him as "this miracle God has caused to be born in Salzburg."

Mozart was born in 1756. By the age of four, he was already displaying amazing musical ability. At six, he had started to compose and was performing brilliantly on the harpsichord. For the next ten years, his father took him to various courts, towns, and principalities around Europe, where he played for noblemen, princes, and even the Empress of Austria, Maria Theresa. Mozart was one of the most famous child prodigies in history.

These constant travels in his formative years had a valuable effect on the young boy. Mozart's principal teacher at this time was his father, but he absorbed other musical influences like a sponge. Wherever he went, he picked up the musical style of the region.

The city of Salzburg, Mozart's birthplace, in the mid eighteenth century.

From all these sources and from his own teeming imagination, Mozart fashioned an individual style. By the time he was eight, Mozart had already had some music published. By ten, he was writing symphonies. At fourteen, he had produced his first full-length opera. By the time he was seventeen, when he and his father returned home to Salzburg to try to find Wolfgang a job, he was a mature and fully formed creative artist.

Finding Mozart a job was not easy. The Prince-Archbishop of Salzburg was an autocratic ruler, and his patience had already been tried by the constant leaves of absence of his deputy music director (Mozart's father). The archbishop agreed to employ Mozart, but only in a junior position. Mozart wrote a fair amount of music in these years, but both he and his father felt that Salzburg was too stifling for him. After a few years, Mozart traveled again to try to find a position elsewhere. This time he traveled with his mother, since his father could not afford to leave his post. He went to Munich, Mannheim, and Paris. But in none of these places was a job forthcoming. Most of Mozart's prospective employers thought he was too young and too talented ("overqualified" is the word we would use today) for a normal position. Indeed, any music director would have been threatened by this brash and brilliant youngster. In Paris, he encountered not only disappointment but also tragedy: his mother died.

Although Mozart was given a promotion upon returning to Salzburg, he was still unsatisfied. In 1780, he accompanied the archbishop on a visit to Vienna. Mozart was outraged when he was forced to eat in the servants' quarters and infuriated when the archbishop refused to let him perform in the houses of local aristocrats. Mozart angrily demanded (and received) his release from the archbishop's employ.

Thus began the freelance career of one of the most brilliant musicians in history. At first Mozart supported himself by giving piano lessons. He also wrote several sonatas for the piano and some piano concertos. Piano music was

Portrait of the Mozart family from about 1780. Mozart plays a duet with his sister, while his father listens, and his mother is remembered in a painting behind them.
Painting, Baroque, 18th Century. Johann Nepomuk Della Croce. *The Mozart Family* (1780–1781). Oil on canvas. 140 × 186 cm. Mozart House, Salzburg, Austria. Erich Lessing/Art Resource.

very popular in Vienna. Mozart had some success with a German comic opera he wrote in 1782. Also in 1782, he married his landlady's daughter, a young soprano named Constanze Weber. His father disapproved strongly of the marriage.

For the next few years, Mozart was highly successful. He undertook a set of string quartets that were designed to emulate those of Haydn, and he dedicated them in a warm and heartfelt style to the older master. We know the two composers met a few times at string quartet parties. Haydn played the violin, Mozart the viola.

In these years, Mozart won great fame—and made quite a lot of money—by means of piano concertos. Between 1784 and 1786, he wrote twelve piano concertos. This was a fine opportunity for him to appear before the Viennese public as both composer and piano soloist. The concertos were very successful, and Mozart was at the height of his career.

Gradually, however, Mozart's popularity began to wane. The Viennese were always eager for some new sensation, and Mozart had been around for a while. In addition, the city was undergoing a recession, and concert dates and composing contracts were hard to come by. Mozart's correspondence from the late 1780s is full of letters requesting loans from friends, and, despite his dislike of authority, he made attempts to find a secure position at the Viennese court.

Mozart did not write many new symphonies during this period, but in the summer of 1788, in the space of about eight weeks, he wrote three symphonies in a row. These last three symphonies, Nos. 39, 40, and 41, are the culmination of his work in the genre. They are very different from each other, but all three are richly orchestrated, enormously inventive, and full of subtle details that repay frequent hearings.

Perhaps the greatest achievement of Mozart's last years is represented by his operas. Mozart had been interested in opera since his boyhood travels to Italy. In the last five years of his life, he completed five great operas. The best known of these are *The Marriage of Figaro* (1786), *Don Giovanni* (1787), and *The Magic Flute* (completed in the year of his death, 1791). These operas are all very different, but in each of them Mozart displays his remarkable understanding of human nature in all its richness. Human ideals and emotions are transformed from the conventions of the opera stage into the deepest expression of real feelings.

In November of 1791, while he was working on a Requiem Mass (Mass for the Dead), Mozart became ill. And on December 5, at the age of thirty-five, with half a lifetime of masterpieces still uncomposed, Wolfgang Amadeus Mozart died.

Mozart's Music

Mozart's music is a remarkable combination of the accessible and the profound: it appeals to experts and amateurs alike. There is also an incredibly wide range of music to

LISTENING GUIDE

WOLFGANG AMADEUS MOZART (1756–1791)

Second Movement from Piano Concerto
  No. 21 in C Major, K. 467

Date of composition: 1785
Orchestration: Solo piano, flute,
  2 oboes, 2 bassoons, 2 horns, and strings
Tempo: *Andante* ("Moderately slow")
Meter: $\frac{4}{4}$
Key of movement: F Major
Duration: 7:46

Complete CD Collection: 2, Tracks 7–9

Mozart wrote this whole piano concerto in the space of twenty-seven days, a period during which he also taught private students, entertained his father, held a string quartet party that included Haydn, and played in about a dozen private and public concerts. One of Mozart's best-known piano concertos, No. 21 follows formal conventions, containing three movements: *Allegro maestoso*, *Andante*, and *Allegro vivace assai*. We will examine the lyrical middle movement. The movement employs wonderfully singable melodies and uses aria form (ABA). Underneath all the melodies throughout the movement we hear the *pizzicato* (plucked) bass and the regular pulsation of triplet (three-in-a-beat) notes. This gives us a wonderful three-layered texture, which you can clearly hear.

SECTION A		
		[divided into three parts]
7	0:00	(1) The gentle opening theme is played by muted violins. The meter is a slow 4/4, but the accompaniment uses triplets.
	0:31	(2) A contrasting phrase is marked by sudden dynamic changes and dramatic downward leaps; woodwinds enter. The mood is one of suspension and weightlessness.

	1:13	(3) The section ends with a pair of balanced phrases on oboe and violins, the second of which is joined by flute and bassoons.
	1:43	The piano enters and repeats the first two sections, (1) and (2), of the preceding material. The underlying triplets are played by the left hand of the piano, the melody by the right. Although this is a repetition of previously heard material, the differences in tone quality render it striking and fresh.
	2:35	Triplet accompaniment moves into B section.

SECTION B

8	2:37	This section is designed as a contrast to the A section, though it contains some material from it. It is more freely structured and introduces some new melodic ideas. It begins in D minor (the relative minor), but it modulates frequently.
	2:44	The piano is still playing, but now faster and more energetically.
	3:15	The "weightless" material that ended part (2) of section A is recalled, leading into idea (3).
	3:41	Now the piano (with violins) states idea (3)—the paired phrases—from section A. A striking moment! Listen also to the rich parts for accompanying woodwinds.
	4:03	Sustained woodwinds, strings, and piano exchange phrases.
	4:51	A passage reminiscent of the "weightless" phrases of (2) leads to the return of section A.

SECTION A'

9	5:24	The return of section A is recognizable, but it is altered by being in a different key. It is also ornamented, much as a singer would ornament the return of the A section in an aria. And some of the ideas come in a slightly different order. (Mozart always made simple things more interesting.)
	7:20	Return to the tonic key. A brief new melody is heard using repeated notes. The triplet accompaniment ends the movement.

choose from—more than 800 compositions, from the lightest little comic pieces to works that explore the great themes of human existence: life and death, love, tragedy, romance, despair and hope.

Mozart wrote in all the main genres of Classic music: opera, symphony, string quartet, and sonata. He wrote solo concertos for a wide variety of instruments: violin, flute, oboe, clarinet, bassoon, and horn. But for his own instrument, the piano, he composed more than twenty concertos, which are among his greatest masterpieces. We shall listen to a slow movement from one of these piano concertos.

Mozart wrote dozens of sonatas, both for solo piano and for combinations of instruments. He also composed many great string quartets. In addition to these works, Mozart wrote several string *quintets*, in which an extra viola is used. This makes the music richer and the counterpoint fuller.

Mozart also greatly enriched the expressive power of opera. In *The Magic Flute*, *Don Giovanni*, and *The Marriage of Figaro*, Mozart transcends convention by portraying people in all their psychological complexity.

There is often an undercurrent of melancholy in Mozart's works. The music often passes briefly into the minor mode, even in major-mode passages, which creates added depth and emotional resonance. It is like the shadow of a small cloud passing over a sunny meadow.

Only a very small number of his works use a minor key as the principal home key. Among these is the Symphony No. 40 in G minor, written in 1788, one of Mozart's greatest works in the symphonic genre.

LISTENING GUIDE

WOLFGANG AMADEUS MOZART (1756–1791)

First Movement from Symphony No. 40 in
  G minor, K. 550

Date of composition: 1788
Orchestration: Flute, 2 oboes, 2 clarinets,
  2 bassoons, 2 horns, and strings
Tempo: *Allegro molto* ("Very fast")
Meter: $\frac{2}{2}$
Key: G minor
Duration: 8:16

Complete CD Collection: 2, Tracks 10–17

In the space of eight weeks during the summer of 1788, Mozart completed three large-scale symphonies. Perhaps he intended them to be published and performed together.

The G-minor Symphony, the middle one of the three, is one of Mozart's best-known works, representing one of his greatest achievements in the symphonic realm. It is marked by perfect balance and control, a wealth of harmonic and instrumental color, and a brilliant use of formal structure.

In the first movement, Mozart takes advantage of the dramatic possibilities of sonata form. The basic structure of sonata form is easy to hear, but we can also see how Mozart *manipulated* the form to surprise and delight his listeners. There are many examples, but the most obvious one is the way he leads us to expect the recapitulation at a certain point, only to pull the rug out from under us.

You should listen first to the piece a few times simply to enjoy the fine expressive writing—the brilliant balance between loud and soft, woodwinds and strings, descending and ascending phrases, and minor and major keys. Notice, too, how Mozart spices up the sound with chromatic passages and surprise notes. Next, listen for the structure, the basic template of sonata form, which is so clearly articulated in this movement. The next couple of times, listen for how Mozart plays with this structure (and with his audience's expectations) for expressive purposes. Finally, try putting all these things together and listen for them all at once.

Don't stop listening after that, however. For you may find, as many of the most experienced listeners do, that you will hear something new in this movement every single time you listen to it. And there are three other movements in this symphony … three other symphonies in the group … dozens of other symphonies by Mozart …

EXPOSITION

[timings for the repeat are in parentheses]

| 10 | 0:00 | Opening theme: violins, quiet, G minor; closed by full orchestra, loud. |
| | (2:02) | |

Allegro molto

| 0:24 | (2:27) | Restatement of opening theme, woodwinds added, beginning modulation to second key. |

| 0:34 | (2:37) | Energetic bridge passage, loud, full orchestra, preparing for second key. (Central to this passage is a strong rising figure, which appears later in the movement.) |

| 0:50 | (2:53) | Cadence in new key (B-flat—the relative major). |

| 11 0:52 | (2:56) | Second theme, also quiet, smooth alternation of strings and woodwinds, quite chromatic. |

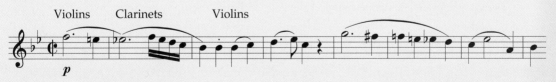

1:10	(3:14)	Odd surprise notes.
1:20	(3:23)	Cadence.
1:27	(3:31)	Spinning-out section (clarinet, bassoon, strings).
1:47	(3:50)	Ending passage, loud, whole orchestra.
2:00	(4:04)	Final cadences of exposition.
12	2:02	(Exact repetition of entire exposition.)

153

13	4:09	Many key changes, by means of first theme being played lower and lower.
	4:23	A "blender" passage, in which the themes are cut up and tossed around; whole orchestra, loud.
14	4:52	Music gets quiet … quieter (we are expecting the recapitulation … but:)
	5:09	Suddenly loud (we've been fooled: no recapitulation here).
	5:19	Another preparation, quiet woodwind descent (watch out: is this real …?)

RECAPITULATION

15	5:24	YES! (But notice how Mozart sneaks it in ever so quietly.) All goes normally here, though there are some changes from the exposition.
	5:57	New material, loud, whole orchestra (sounds like it's left over from the development). It uses the rising figure from the opening bridge passage (shown above at 0:34).
	6:29	Back on track …
16	6:40	Second theme: quiet, winds and strings, this time in tonic key (G minor).
	6:58	Surprise notes.
	7:05	New material.
	7:14	Back on track …
	7:21	Spinning out.
	7:44	Music opens out to:

CODA

17	7:53	Confirming tonic key, floating, quiet.
	8:03	Repeated definitive cadences, loud.
	8:09	Three final chords

Although Mozart's music is richer, more versatile, and more varied than most eighteenth-century music, it does use the same basic conventions as other music of the time. The instruments are the same, the forms are the same, and the primary genres that Mozart cultivated are the same. But Mozart's music speaks deeply to more people, covers a wider range of feeling, and resonates with more human significance than that of almost any other composer before or since. In that sense, Mozart's music is truly "classic."

Listening to...

CLASSIC MUSIC

- In this chapter you can hear all the main movement forms of Classic music: first movement (sonata form)—Mozart's Symphony in G minor; second movement (aria form)—Mozart's Piano Concerto No. 21; third movement (minuet and trio)—Haydn's Minuet and Trio from his Symphony No. 47; fourth movement (rondo form)—Haydn's String Quartet in E-flat Major.

- In all these movements, you can hear the main features of Classic music: accessible and pleasing melodies with symmetrical phrases; simple harmony; and light and rhythmic accompaniment.

- The music is often less serious than the music of the previous era (Pergolesi's *La Serva Padrona*; the rondo from Haydn's string quartet).

- The music you hear is always balanced, attractive, and sometimes extremely beautiful (Mozart's Piano Concerto No. 21).

KEY TERMS

aria form **(p. 141)**
chamber music **(p. 139)**
coda **(p. 141)**
development **(p. 140)**
episode **(p. 142)**

exposition **(p. 140)**
main theme **(p. 142)**
minuet-and-trio form
  (p. 141)
overture **(p. 138)**

recapitulation **(p. 140)**
rondo form **(p. 142)**
sonata form **(p. 140)**

7
Beethoven

CHAPTER OUTLINE

Beethoven's Life	Late Years
Beethoven's Early Life	**Beethoven's Music**
The Heroic Phase	Listening Examples
Personal Crisis and Halt to Productivity	**Listening to Beethoven's Music**

Some composers simply do not fit into pigeonholes or convenient time periods. We have said that the dividing line between the Classic and Romantic eras stands around the year 1800. But there was one composer whose life spanned that boundary by about a quarter century in either direction and whose individuality was so strong that he simply cannot be labeled. That composer was Beethoven.

The shifting nature of the times in which Beethoven lived is represented by the patronage system for composers. Haydn's entire career was funded by a wealthy noble family. Mozart's father and, for a time, Mozart himself were in the employ of the prince. But for the last ten years of his life (1781–1791) Mozart contrived to make a living from a variety of sources: teaching, performing, and putting on concerts of his own music. As the eighteenth century drew to a close, Europe experienced a considerable rise in the number and availability of public concerts. Beethoven started his career at the aristocratic court where his grandfather and his father were employed, but when he moved to Vienna, he began to sell his own music to publishers and to get money from commissions (people paying money for specific pieces). He also put on concerts of his own music and received the profits from ticket sales. Music was becoming more and more the province of the general public, and composers less and less the servants of the rich. Beethoven regarded himself as "naturally" noble and scorned the notion of hereditary aristocracy.

```
           Haydn
1732 ————————————————————————— 1809

        Mozart
    1756 ——————————— 1791

          Beethoven
      1770 ——————————————— 1827
```

Beethoven's early life was lived at a time of revolution: the American Revolution in 1776 and the French Revolution in 1789. At first he admired the brilliant military prowess and heroism of Napoleon (he was thinking of dedicating his Third Symphony to him), but he was disillusioned and outraged when Napoleon had himself crowned Emperor in 1804 (Beethoven scratched out the dedication on the title page of his symphony). Beethoven's beliefs were humanistic, and he was an idealist. He took

Beethoven born in Bonn 1770 — 1770

1780

Beethoven moves to Vienna 1792 — 1790

Postal delivery introduced in Germany 1800
First Symphony 1801
Discovery of impending deafness 1802
Napoleon crowned Emperor 1804 — 1800

Fifth Symphony 1808
French army takes Vienna 1809 — 1810

Congress of Vienna 1814–15

First steamship crosses the Atlantic 1818

Last piano sonatas 1820 — 1820

Ninth Symphony 1824
John Quincy Adams becomes president of the U.S. 1825

Last string quartets 1825–27
Beethoven dies in Vienna 1827 — 1827

The heroic Napoleon Bonaparte, painted in 1800.

as the text of his last great symphony (the Ninth) a poem that speaks of the brotherhood and unity of all mankind.

Beethoven grew up at a time when both Haydn and Mozart were still alive and actively composing. The music he heard and studied was strictly Classic in style. But he died in 1827, well into the nineteenth century, when Romanticism was in full flower. **Romanticism** was an artistic movement that profoundly influenced all of the arts—painting, sculpture, and literature, as well as music—throughout the nineteenth century. Romanticism's focus on the emotions of the individual is the basis for much of Beethoven's music.

Like all great artists who live at a time of change, Beethoven was both a beneficiary of that change and partly responsible for it. He took the forms, procedures, and ideals that he had inherited from the Classic era and developed them beyond their previously accepted limits. He transformed Classic genres—symphony, concerto, sonata, and string quartet—into vehicles of personal expression. He burst through the boundaries of Classic restraint to create works of unprecedented scope and depth. He enlarged the orchestra, changed musical structure, added words to a symphony, and told stories with some of his purely instrumental works—all things that had strong repercussions for a century and more. Finally, he invested music with a personal subjectivity and with the stamp of his own extraordinary personality in such a way that music was never the same again. He was both the child of one era and the founding father of another. That is why Beethoven has a chapter of his own.

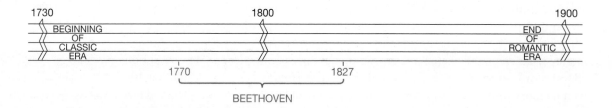

BEETHOVEN'S LIFE

Beethoven is perhaps the most famous musician of all time. Ever since his death in 1827, he has been revered as the principal figure in the history of Western music. His influence on later composers was enormous, to the extent that many actually found his accomplishments intimidating.

Who was this man?

Beethoven's Early Life

Ludwig van Beethoven was born in 1770 into a family of musicians. Both his grandfather and his father were professional musicians at the court of the Elector (the local ruler) in the German town of Bonn. His grandfather was highly respected, but his father became something of a problem at the court because he was an alcoholic. As a teenager, Beethoven was put in charge of the family finances and given a job at the court. He studied organ and composition and helped look after the instruments. At about the same time, he began to write music—mostly songs and chamber works.

In 1790, an important visitor passed through Bonn. This was Haydn, on his way to London for the first of his successful visits. He met the young Beethoven and agreed to take him on as a student when he came back from London. In 1792, Beethoven moved to Vienna to study with the great master. He was twenty-two; Haydn was sixty.

Apparently the lessons did not go well. Haydn was old-fashioned and a little pompous, Beethoven rebellious and headstrong. But Beethoven was a formidable pianist, and he soon found support among the rich patrons of the arts in Vienna. Prince Lichnowsky gave him board and lodging at his palace, in return for which Beethoven was to compose music and play the piano at evening parties … at least that was the arrangement. In fact, Beethoven hated being dependent and often refused to play. But the prince was tolerant; he finally set Beethoven up with his own apartment so that he could work as he pleased.

In the early years, Beethoven wrote mostly keyboard and chamber music pieces. As time went on, however, he decided to start composing in larger musical forms—string quartet, piano concerto, and symphony. By the time Beethoven was thirty-two, he had written—among other works—piano sonatas, a great deal of chamber music, a set of six string quartets, three piano concertos, and two symphonies. The string quartets, concertos, and symphonies owe a stylistic debt to Haydn and Mozart.

But Beethoven's music was already showing considerable individuality. The First Symphony deliberately begins in the wrong key, before turning to the right one. The Third Piano Concerto features a powerful unifying rhythm. And the last movement of one of the early string quartets has a deeply expressive slow introduction entitled *La Malinconia* (*Melancholy*).

Beethoven had every reason to feel melancholic at this time of his life. For it was in 1802 that he discovered the tragic truth that was to haunt him for the rest of his life: He was going deaf. He contemplated suicide but, overcoming his despair, decided that his first responsibility lay with his music. He had to produce the works that were in him.

His disease progressed gradually. It took some years for him to become totally deaf, and there were periods when normal hearing returned. But by 1817, Beethoven could not hear a single note, and his conversations were carried on by means of an ear trumpet and a notebook slung around his neck. His deafness eventually prevented him from performing and conducting, but he continued to compose until the end of his life. He could hear everything inside his head.

Portrait of Beethoven at the age of 49.

Ludwig von Beethoven, portrait by Joseph Karl Stieler, 1820. Beethoven-Haus Bonn.

The Heroic Phase

The middle period of Beethoven's life was marked by a vigorous concentration on work and the sense of triumph over adversity. For these reasons, it is often called the "heroic" phase. "I will seize Fate by the throat," he said. This was also a period of extraordinary

Beethoven at about the time he wrote the Fifth Symphony.

Ludwig von Beethoven, miniature by Christian Horneman, 1802. Beethoven-House Bonn. Collection H.C. Bodmer.

productivity. In the ten years between 1802 and 1812, Beethoven wrote six more symphonies, four concertos, five more string quartets, an entire opera, some orchestral overtures, and several important piano sonatas, as well as other pieces of chamber music.

The music Beethoven wrote during this time is strong and muscular, with contrasting passages of great lyricism. This contrast exists *between* works (Symphonies Nos. 4, 6, and 8, for example, are gentle, whereas Symphonies Nos. 3, 5, and 7 are more powerful) and also *within* works. Some compositions build to aggressive climaxes and then move into moments of purest beauty and radiance. (The first movement of the Fifth Piano Concerto does this.) Like Mozart, Beethoven wrote his piano concertos to display his own virtuosity, but soon his deafness prevented him from playing in public, and he became increasingly introverted and antisocial. He was sometimes seen striding around the countryside without a coat or a hat, ignoring the weather and muttering to himself.

The most striking thing about the compositions from the heroic phase is their length. From the Third Symphony on, Beethoven was writing works much larger in scope than those of his predecessors. The Third Symphony's first movement is as long as many complete symphonies of Haydn and Mozart.

During this phase, Beethoven became famous. His works were regarded as strong and patriotic at a time when his homeland was at war with France. He even wrote some overtly political pieces, such as a *Battle* Symphony—complete with brass fanfares and cannon fire—to celebrate an early victory of the Duke of Wellington over Napoleon. He also became quite wealthy. His music was published and performed more than ever, and his income from these sources as well as from aristocratic and royal patrons was substantial.

Personal Crisis and Halt to Productivity

After the extremely productive years of the heroic phase, Beethoven found himself embroiled in a family crisis, which robbed him of his creativity for several years. In 1815 came the death of Beethoven's brother, who left his widow and Beethoven with joint custody of his son—Beethoven's nephew, Karl. This caused Beethoven great turmoil and distress. Having never married himself, he yearned for a normal family life, with a wife to comfort him and a child of his own. He once said to a friend that such intimacy was "not to be thought of—impossible—a dream. Yet I cannot get it out of my mind."

To be thrust suddenly into a position of paternal responsibility for a child and into close contact with a young woman completely undermined Beethoven's equilibrium. He threw himself into a series of devastating legal battles with his brother's widow to obtain sole custody of Karl. The conflict dragged on for years, sapping Beethoven's energy and destroying his peace of mind (not to mention that of the boy and his poor mother). Ultimately, Beethoven won the legal battles (he had powerful friends), and Karl came to live with him. The relationship was a stormy one, however, because Beethoven was appallingly strict and possessive. At the age of nineteen, Karl pawned his watch, bought two pistols, and tried to kill himself. This action, from which Karl soon recovered, brought some sense back to the situation. Karl was allowed to return to his mother's house, and he escaped from Beethoven's domination by joining the army.

Beethoven's funeral procession in Vienna. There were 20,000 people in attendance at this event.

Late Years

After the most intense period of the battle over Karl, Beethoven only gradually regained his productivity. The most important works of his late years are the last three piano sonatas, the Ninth Symphony, and a series of string quartets. The piano sonatas are remarkable pieces, unusual in form and design, and most moving in their juxtaposition of complexity and simplicity. The Ninth Symphony, finished in 1824, continued Beethoven's tradition of breaking barriers. It is an immense work with a revolutionary last movement that includes a choir and four vocal soloists. This was unheard of in a symphony at this time, although many later composers imitated the idea.

Beethoven's last three years were devoted entirely to string quartets. In this most intimate of genres, he found a medium for his most personal thoughts and ideas. Many people have found Beethoven's late string quartets to be both his greatest and his most difficult music. Yet there are moments of tenderness and great beauty, as well as passages of dissonant harmonies and rhythmic complexity, and some of the most profound music in the Western tradition. Beethoven died on March 26, 1827, at the age of fifty-six, leaving an indelible mark on music and the way it has been experienced by listeners ever since.

BEETHOVEN'S MUSIC

Beethoven's music has always represented the essence of serious music. Nowadays, people who know of only one classical composer know of Beethoven. And his music is played more, written about more, and recorded more than the music of any other composer in the world.

His music is appealing, moving, and forceful. It reaches something inside us that is elemental. It has a unique combination of the simple and the complex, the emotional and the intellectual. We recognize, on hearing it, that it comes from the spiritual side of a man, but also from a man who was entirely, and sometimes painfully, human.

There are some stylistic traits in Beethoven's music that might be regarded as his "fingerprints"—traits that can be instantly recognized and that mark the music as unmistakably his. These include the following: (1) long powerful *crescendos* that seem to carry the music inexorably forward, (2) themes that sound exactly right *both quiet and very loud*, (3) *dramatic* use of Classic structures such as sonata form, and (4) sudden *key changes* that nonetheless fit into a powerful harmonic logic.

The most famous of Beethoven's compositions come from the middle part of his life: the heroic phase. These include Symphonies Nos. 3–8, the middle string quartets, Piano Concertos Nos. 4 and 5, the Violin Concerto, and the opera *Fidelio*. Some of the pieces are actually *about* heroism: The Third Symphony is entitled the *Eroica* (*Heroic*), and the opera *Fidelio* (*The Faithful One*) displays the heroism of a woman who rescues her husband from unjust imprisonment. As a result, much of this music is strong, dramatic, and powerful.

But there is another side to Beethoven: the lyrical side. Some of the middle symphonies are tuneful and smoothly contoured, like the Sixth Symphony, known as the *Pastoral*. And even in the more dramatic pieces, there are often contrasting passages of great tenderness. One of the secrets of Beethoven's style is the way he puts strong and tender passages next to each other within the same work.

Less well known are the compositions from Beethoven's early period. Some are deliberately modeled on the works of his great forebears, Haydn and Mozart; others already show signs of remarkable originality. There are songs, piano pieces, and much chamber music.

Finally, there are the works from the last part of Beethoven's career. These are all very different, and there are fewer of them. They include the Ninth Symphony, the *Missa Solemnis* (*Solemn Mass*), the late piano sonatas, and the last five string quartets. Beethoven's late music is very rich. There is a sense of great depth juxtaposed with an extraordinary, almost heartbreaking, innocence and simplicity. In his last years, Beethoven was no longer concerned with drama and heroism but with pursuing the path of his own creativity, wherever it might lead. Some of the music from this period is demanding and difficult to listen to, but with repeated hearings it can provide listeners with a lifetime of enjoyment and reward.

Listening Examples

To get an idea of the range of Beethoven's achievement, we shall listen to compositions from each of the three main periods of his life. The first is a set of variations on a theme, written by Beethoven in 1790 for solo piano. Next we shall study the first movement of the Fifth Symphony, perhaps the most famous of Beethoven's compositions. It was written in 1807–8, right in the middle of the heroic phase. Finally, we shall listen to one movement from a late piano sonata to see how profound and compelling Beethoven's late music can be.

LISTENING GUIDE

LUDWIG VAN BEETHOVEN (1770–1827)

Six Easy Variations on a Swiss Tune in F Major
  for Piano, WoO 64

Date of composition: 1790
Tempo: *Andante con moto* ("Fairly slow but
  with motion")
Meter: 4/4
Key: F Major
Duration: 2:47

Complete CD Collection: 2, Tracks 18–19

This is one of many sets of variations that Beethoven wrote in his early years. Variations on melodies are an easy way for a composer to learn his or her craft, since the tune and the harmony already exist and all the composer has to do is think of ways to decorate or vary them.

The little Swiss tune that Beethoven uses as the basis for this composition is simple and attractive. Underlying its simplicity, however, is an interesting quirk: It is made up of unusual phrase lengths. This is probably the feature that attracted Beethoven to the theme in the first place. Instead of the usual four-measure phrases, this tune is made up of two three-measure phrases answered by a phrase of five measures.

This phrase structure and the skeleton of the tune and its harmony are carried through all the six variations. Beethoven uses triplets (three notes to a beat), march rhythms, dynamic changes, eighth notes, sixteenth notes, and even a minor key to vary the music. However, if you play the recording of just the theme a few times first, before listening to the variations, you will be able to follow its outline easily throughout the piece.

THEME		
		[Andante con moto—"Fairly slow but with motion"]
18	0:00	The theme is simple and pleasant. Notice how it ends very much as it begins.

VARIATION 1		
	0:23	Beethoven introduces triplets (three notes to a beat) in both the right and the left hands.

VARIATION 2		
	0:40	The melody is mostly unchanged in the right hand, but the left hand has jerky, marchlike accompanying rhythms.

VARIATION 3		
19	1:02	This variation uses the minor key, and Beethoven indicates that it should be played "smoothly and quietly throughout."
	1:28	The last part of this variation is repeated.

1:48   Back to the major and loud again. Octaves in the right hand, triplets in the left.

2:04   The fifth variation is mostly in eighth notes with a little syncopation and some small chromatic decorations.

2:26   Dynamic contrasts, sixteenth-note runs, and trills mark the last variation, which ends with a two-measure coda to round off the piece.

BEETHOVEN'S FIFTH SYMPHONY   Beethoven's Fifth Symphony was written in the middle of his heroic period, when the composer was in his late thirties. It is his most famous piece and probably the most famous symphony ever written. The music is taut and expressive, and unified to an unusual degree. The opening four-note motive, with its short-short-short-LONG rhythm, pervades the whole symphony. There is a cumulative sense of growth from the beginning of the first movement to the end of the last movement, and this conveys a feeling of personal triumph. Underlying this feeling is the motion from C minor to C Major. Symphonies almost always end in the key in which they begin, but Beethoven's Fifth starts out tense and strained in C minor and ends up triumphant and exuberant in C Major. Beethoven also adds several instruments to the orchestra for the last movement, to increase the power and range of the music and add to the sense of triumph. All these things were new to symphonic music at the time and had an enormous influence on later composers. In the Fifth Symphony, Beethoven set the stage for an entirely new view of music. Music was now seen as the expression of personal feelings.

LISTENING GUIDE

LUDWIG VAN BEETHOVEN (1770–1827)

First Movement from Symphony No. 5 in C minor

Date of composition: 1807–8

Orchestration: 2 flutes, 2 oboes, 2 clarinets, 2 horns, 2 trumpets, timpani, strings

Tempo: *Allegro con brio* ("Fast and vigorous")

Meter: $\frac{2}{4}$

Key: C minor

Form: Sonata

Duration: 7:26

Companion CD, Tracks 70–76

he first movement of Beethoven's Fifth Symphony is dense and concentrated. There is not a note or a gesture too many in the whole movement. The movement is in sonata form (see Chapter 6, 140). The exposition begins with a short–short–short–LONG motive that colors almost every measure of the movement.

The second theme is announced by a horn call. The theme itself starts quietly and smoothly, but underneath it, on cellos and basses, the initial rhythmic motive quietly makes itself heard. Quickly another climax builds, and the *exposition* ends with the whole orchestra playing the original motive together.

During the *development* section, the horn call that introduced the second theme is gradually broken down into smaller and smaller elements until only a single chord is echoed quietly between the strings and the woodwinds. Then the *recapitulation* brings back the music of the movement's first part with crashing force. A short *coda* brings the movement to a powerful conclusion.

Throughout the movement, long crescendos (from *pianissimo, pp,* to *fortissimo, ff*) and short passages of quiet music (*piano, p*) serve to increase the intensity and drive. The overall effect is one of great power and compression.

EXPOSITION

70	**0:00**	*First theme*
	(1:25)	Opening motive is played *ff* by the strings and clarinets in octaves and then repeated a step lower.

	0:06	Sudden *p*, strings immediately develop opening motive.
	(1:31)	

	0:14	Crescendo and loud chords lead to a high sustained note in the violins.
	(1:39)	

	0:18	*Transition*
	(1:44)	Opening motive, *ff*, played only once by full orchestra.
		Sudden *p*, further development of the opening motive by strings.
		Strings gradually crescendo and ascend.
		Reiterated timpani notes, sudden stop.

	0:43	Horn-call motive, *ff*.
	(2:08)	

71	**0:46**	*Second theme*
	(2:11)	A contrasting gentle melody, *p*, in the relative major key (E-flat Major), is accompanied by a version of the opening motive in the lower strings.

	0:58 **(2:23)**	Crescendo and ascent lead to another new melody: a jubilant theme, *ff*, in the violins, played twice.
	1:15 **(2:40)**	Woodwinds and horns rapidly descend, twice; then a cadence in E-flat minor, using the rhythm of the basic motive. Pause.
72	**1:25**	(Entire exposition is repeated.)

DEVELOPMENT

73	**2:50**	Opening motive in horns, *ff*, in F minor, echoed by strings. Sudden *p*, basic motive developed by strings and woodwinds. Another gradual ascent and crescendo, leading to forceful repeated chords.
	3:25	Horn-call motive in violins, *ff*, followed by descending line in low strings, twice. Pairs of high chords in woodwinds and brass, *ff*, alternating with lower chords in strings, *ff*. Sudden decrease in volume, alternation between single chords, key changes. Sudden *ff*, horn-call in full orchestra; return to alternation of wind and string chords, *pp*, with key changes. Sudden *ff*, opening motive repeated many times, leading back to recapitulation.

RECAPITULATION

74	**4:08**	*First theme* Opening motive, *ff*, in tonic (C minor), full orchestra. Opening motive developed, strings, *p*, joined by slow-moving melody on one oboe. Oboe unexpectedly interrupts the music with a short, plaintive solo.
	4:39	*Transition* Development of opening motive resumes in strings, *p*. Gradual crescendo, full orchestra, *ff*, repeated timpani notes, sudden stop. Horn-call motive, *ff*, in horns.
75	**5:02**	*Second theme* Contrasting gentle melody, *p*, in C Major (the *major* of the tonic!), played alternately by violins and flutes. (Basic motive accompanies in timpani when flutes play.) Gradual buildup to the return of: Jubilant string theme, *ff*, in violins, played twice. Woodwinds and horns rapidly descend, twice, followed by a cadence using the rhythm of the opening motive. Then, without pause, into:

CODA

76	**5:52**	Forceful repeated chords, *ff*, with pauses. Horn-call motive in lower strings and bassoons, along with flowing violin melody, *ff*, in tonic (C minor). Descending pattern, violins, leads to:
	6:17	A completely new theme in the strings, rising up the minor scale in four-note sequences. Four-note fragments of the new theme are forcefully alternated between woodwinds and strings. A short passage of fast, loud, repeated notes leads into a return of the opening motive, *ff*, full orchestra. Suddenly *pp*; strings and woodwinds develop the motive for a few seconds. A swift and dramatic return to full orchestra, ending with *ff* chords.

BEETHOVEN'S LATE MUSIC   Beethoven's late music presents great challenges to performers and listeners alike. Certainly, the music is technically difficult to play; yet the true challenge comes in the understanding. The performer has to understand the music in order to play it, and the listener must be open to its profound and multiple meanings.

There is great variety in the late works of Beethoven, but they share some characteristics: a combination of inner depth and outward simplicity; new approaches to multi-movement design; and a return to some of the techniques of his youth, such as song form and theme-and-variations form.

To gain some idea of the variety and depth of this music, we shall listen at the end of this chapter to a piano sonata, one of the last three that Beethoven wrote. Remember that of all the instruments, the piano was closest to Beethoven's heart. These last three piano sonatas contain some of the most profound music that Beethoven ever wrote.

LISTENING GUIDE

LUDWIG VAN BEETHOVEN (1770–1827)

Third Movement from Piano Sonata in
E Major, Op. 109

Date of composition: 1820
Tempo: *Andante molto cantabile ed
espressivo* ("Quite slow, very lyrical
and expressive")
Meter: $\frac{3}{4}$
Key: E Major
Duration: 13:34

Complete CD Collection: 2, Tracks 20–27

This is the last movement of one of the last of Beethoven's piano sonatas, written just seven years before his death. It shows the remarkable freedom Beethoven felt in his compositions toward the end of his life. The sonata is completely untraditional in the form of each movement and in the order of its movements. The music itself contains abrupt changes of mood and ideas, as though the great composer was improvising at the keyboard. The whole composition transcends the accepted boundaries for the genre of the piano sonata, both in its architecture and in its emotional depth.

It is unusual for the last movement of a composition to be slow, and this one has, in addition to the detailed Italian tempo marking, a heading in German: *Gesangvoll mit innigster Empfindung* ("Songlike and with the innermost feeling"). Beethoven is using every means at his disposal to invest his music with strong emotion.

Toward the end of his life, Beethoven returned to some of the simple techniques of his youth. This movement is in the form of a theme and variations (the same form as the first piano piece we studied in this chapter). But the spirituality and depth of feeling of this music belong exclusively to the late period of Beethoven's life. The movement lasts more than fifteen minutes, twice the length of the two previous movements put together. The theme has the remarkable combination of simplicity and profound feeling that is characteristic of Beethoven's late music. It is like a song of the soul. The six variations seem to explore the rich inner life of the theme and all its potential.

The theme is originally presented in two sections, both repeated. Each section is eight measures long, divided into two four-measure phrases. Some of the variations follow the scheme of the theme, with two sections, both repeated. But in some of the variations, the "repeats" of the sections are not really repeats but continue the process of evolution and further variation. Technically, these are known as "double variations."

The first variation (again Beethoven marks the music *Molto espressivo*—"Very expressive") explores the lyrical, dreamy side of the theme with wider-ranging music and rich harmonies. In the other variations, the character of the music changes, becoming faster and denser, and the outline of the theme itself becomes progressively more obscured, as its inner essence is revealed. But after the sixth and final variation, the theme returns even more simply than at its very first appearance. This final return of the theme (without repeats) is deeply moving. It sounds radiant and centered, as though it has been purified by the fire and passion of its experiences.

THEME		
		Gesangvoll mit innigster Empfindung ("Songlike and with the innermost feeling"). *Andante molto cantabile ed espressivo* ("Quite slow, very lyrical, and expressive"). [dignified, profound]
20	0:00	First section.
	0:35	Repeat.
	1:10	Second section.
	1:46	Repeat.

VARIATION 1		
		[higher, more decorated, more rhythmic motion]
21	2:13	First section.
	2:43	Repeat.
	3:22	Second section.
	3:52	Repeat.

VARIATION 2		
		[a double variation: lightly delicate, beginning with repeated notes, steady rhythm, and trills, and opening out to syncopated chords]
22	4:25	First section: light and delicate.

	4:49	"Repeat" is varied again. First four-measure phrase: steady rhythm, gradually climbing. Second phrase: alternating syncopated chords.
	5:15	Second section: light and delicate again.
	5:39	"Repeat" continues the variation, also starting with steady phrases and ending with alternating chords.

VARIATION 3

[another double variation: lighthearted in tone; fast, louder, and in duple meter]

23	6:07	First section: staccato eighth notes ascending in right hand, descending sixteenths in left. Switch after four measures.
	6:13	"Repeat" with increasing motion.
	6:19	Second section: still fast, runs continuously into and through the "repeat."

VARIATION 4

[slower than the theme, two-part counterpoint, in $\frac{9}{8}$ meter]

24	6:32	First section: gentle, contemplative.
	7:06	Literal repeat this time.
	7:41	Second section: louder and more determined in the middle.
	8:19	Repeat.

VARIATION 5

[another double variation: complex four-part counterpoint, duple meter]

25	9:02	First section: loud and determined, fast.
	9:13	"Repeat," elaborated.
	9:23	Second section: higher, still loud.
	9:33	Elaborated "repeat."
	9:43	*Extra* repeat, quiet.

VARIATION 6

[This is extraordinary music. Back to $\frac{3}{4}$. Another double variation— really a quadruple one!]

26	9:56	First section. The motion increases from quarter notes to eighths, to triplet eighths, to sixteenths.

	10:30	"Repeat"—ever-increasing motion: thirty-second notes, and finally trills!
	10:58	Second section: cascades of broken chords, rushing passagework, over a deep trilled bass note.
	11:23	In the "repeat," with the trill now *above* the rushing scales, the theme tolls out, syncopated, in the highest reaches of the piano.
	11:46	An added three measures of brilliantly gauged descent (both in pitch and in intensity), leading to:

RETURN OF THEME

[magically peaceful return to theme, even simpler than at first, and without any repeats]

27	12:09	First section.
	12:45	Second section.

This ending, with its return to purified simplicity, has a truly extraordinary quality—peaceful and deeply spiritual.

Listening to...

BEETHOVEN'S MUSIC

- In Beethoven's works you hear greater scope and power and a greater sense of personal expression than in earlier compositions. His symphonies are longer and use more instruments than those of the Classic period. He is freer in his use and transformation of musical forms. In his loud music, Beethoven seems louder and more urgent. In his soft music, he seems to reach for deeper emotion.

- Special characteristics of Beethoven's music include: insistent and driving rhythms; taut and muscular themes; long crescendos and powerful climaxes. But his music also features themes of great beauty and lyricism; passages of extraordinary lightness and delicacy; and a gentleness and spiritual depth that are unprecedented.

- Beethoven made the formal structure of music sound dramatic. Listen to how he does this with sonata form (first movement of the Fifth symphony).

- Beethoven used variation form both at the start of his career to learn how to compose (Six Easy Variations on a Swiss Tune) and towards the end of his life for deep spiritual meaning (Piano Sonata, Op. 109).
- Beethoven laid the groundwork for all our modern ideas of what a composer does and what his or her music can tell us.

KEY TERMS

Romanticism **(p. 158)**

8

The Nineteenth
Century

CHAPTER OUTLINE

THE AGE OF ROMANTICISM

The nineteenth century was a time of great change in Western society. The foundations of modern industry were laid during this period. Far-reaching political and social changes took place. And the arts reflected a new concern with personal feeling. All three of these aspects of the new era—industrialization, changes in the structure of society, and a new artistic spirit—had powerful effects on nineteenth-century music.

The Industrial Revolution

The Industrial Revolution began in England, where a long period of peace and prosperity encouraged economic expansion and innovation. Agriculture was highly efficient, leading to a tripling of the population between 1750 and 1850. Machines were invented for use in mining, iron and steel production, and railways. Communication was revolutionized by

---

1800

1810

First steam locomotive 1814

Napoleon Bonaparte
1769–1821

1820

Franz Schubert 1797–1828

Johann von Goethe
1749–1832
Sir Walter Scott 1771–1832

1830

Fanny Mendelssohn
1805–1847
Felix Mendelssohn
1809–1847
Revolutions in Paris, Vienna,
Berlin, and Milan 1848
First appendectomy
performed 1848
Edgar Allan Poe 1809–1849
Fryderyk Chopin 1810–1849
Population of U.S. reaches 23
million (of whom 14% are
slaves) 1850
William Wordsworth
1770–1850
First appearance of *New York
Times* 1851
Invention of sewing
machine 1851
Joseph Turner 1775–1851
Robert Schumann 1810–1856
Darwin's "Origin of
Species" 1859
Italy unified as a
kingdom 1861

1840

1850

1860

Eugène Delacroix 1798–1863
Louis Pasteur invents
pasteurization 1864
American civil war 1861–65
Alfred Nobel invents
dynamite 1866
Russia sells Alaska
to U.S. 1867
Hector Berlioz 1803–1869

1870

Charles Dickens 1812–1870
Typewriter invented 1873
Telephone invented 1873

Austria, Germany, and Italy
form Triple Alliance 1882
Brooklyn Bridge 1883
Richard Wagner 1813–1883
Karl Marx 1818–1883
Bedrich Smetana 1824–1884
Statue of Liberty 1886
Franz Liszt 1811–1886
Eiffel Tower 1889

1880

Telegraph invented 1891
Herman Melville 1819–1891
Pyotr Ilyich Tchaikovsky
1840–1893
Clara Schumann 1819–1896
Johannes Brahms 1833–1897
First sound recording 1899
Giuseppe Verdi 1813–1901
Mark Twain 1835–1910
Gustav Mahler 1860–1911
Henry James 1843–1916
Giacomo Puccini 1858–1924

1890

1900

A nineteenth-century landscape by John Constable.

John Constable, *Hampstead Heath: Branch Hill Pond*, 1828. Oil on canvas, V&A/Art Resource.

the inauguration of a cheap postal system and then by the American inventions of the telegraph and the telephone.

All these technological advances spread rapidly throughout Western Europe and the United States. And toward the end of the century, the harnessing of electricity marked a new phase in the Industrial Revolution.

Political, Intellectual, and Social Changes

Politically, the most important event for the nineteenth century was the French Revolution, which began in 1789 but whose aftershocks continued to be felt throughout Europe until 1848. Intellectuals and philosophers now began to react strongly against the Enlightenment, whose ideas were believed to have inspired the Revolution.

This reactionary movement was the beginning of Romanticism. Writers, thinkers, and artists reacted against the rationalism and orderliness of the eighteenth century and yearned for a return to emotionalism, complexity, and traditional faith. God and nature were seen as more important than reason and science. Indeed, nature, with all its unpredictability and random profusion, became a central feature of the Romantic ideal. Like many other Romantics, the great English poet of Romanticism William Wordsworth deplored the destruction of the environment by the ravages of industrialization.

The French Revolution and the ensuing Romantic movement had further consequences in the nineteenth century. One of these was the growth of **nationalism**. Peoples throughout Europe began to foster their own national identities and rebel against outside domination. Nationalism remained a potent force on the political landscape throughout the nineteenth century.

Changes in the structure of society were dramatic in this era. The Industrial Revolution created great wealth and an increased standard of living for some, while condemning many others to appalling work conditions in mines and factories.

Large numbers of women and children began to work outside the home. The hours were brutal. In some factories, people worked from dawn until midnight. Women and children were paid half the wages of a man. Children were often used for pulling heavy coal carts through low mining shafts.

A young woman working in a coal mine in the 1840s.

Towns and cities appeared throughout the newly industrialized Europe and United States. Many people left their rural environments for crowded city slums and polluted city air. Living conditions and the dreariness of life in London in the nineteenth century are dramatically described in some of the novels of Charles Dickens.

In spite of the hardships and inequities of the times, the nineteenth century also saw the rise of some of the benefits of modern civilization. Medical advances were dramatic. The prevention of infection by antiseptic measures was begun, and Louis Pasteur saved countless lives by inventing a process for the sterilization of milk (still called pasteurization in his honor).

A biological theory was contained in one of the most revolutionary works of the century: Charles Darwin's *On the Origin of Species* (1859). Darwin argued that species evolved through the process of natural selection and that evolution took place by very gradual change over many generations. Darwin's book seemed to threaten traditional religious beliefs, but it sold out on the first day of its publication.

Glaring social inequities led to a vastly increased social consciousness. The nineteenth century saw the foundation of charitable organizations, the birth of private philanthropy, the establishment of free public schools, and the development of the political ideals of socialism and communism. In England and America, voting rights were extended to include all adult males, not just the rich and powerful.

The New Artistic Spirit

Romanticism was above all an artistic movement. It began in the last two decades of the eighteenth century with the literary works of the two great German writers Goethe (1749–1832) and Schiller (1759–1805).

Goethe was a poet, novelist, and dramatist—and the author of the single most influential literary work of the nineteenth century, his long dramatic poem *Faust*. Goethe's *Faust* summarizes the themes of Romanticism: life, death, faith, sin, individual insight, selflessness, and redemption. Goethe's play served as inspiration to many composers throughout the nineteenth century.

Another element in literary Romanticism was a renewed fascination with the past. Schiller wrote a series of dramas based on historical and legendary figures, including Joan of Arc, Mary Queen of Scots, and William Tell.

The mysterious, the supernatural, and even the macabre fascinated nineteenth-century readers. A favorite American author of the nineteenth century was the ghoulish Edgar Allan Poe (1809–1849). And in 1818, Mary Shelley published the perennially popular story *Frankenstein*.

Romantic poets flung off the strict forms of eighteenth-century classicism and reveled in a new freedom of style. This was the time of the great (mostly English) Romantic poets: Wordsworth, Coleridge, Byron, Shelley, and Keats, as well as the American Longfellow.

The Romantics also developed a love affair with the works of Shakespeare. Shakespeare's works underwent an enormous revival in the nineteenth century, and composers frequently took Shakespearean plays, such as *Romeo and Juliet* or *Othello*, as their inspiration.

In the second half of the century, the technological advances of the Industrial Revolution had a powerful impact on architecture. The new technology produced works of monumental size, the most famous of which are the Brooklyn Bridge (1883), the Statue of Liberty (1886), and the remarkable Eiffel Tower (1889).

In painting, Romantic artists attempted to capture their view of the exotic, the irrational, and the sublime. The French artist Delacroix said that the aim of art was not to depict reality but to "strike the imagination." Nature also inspired the powerful scenes of the great painter William Turner.

Of all the arts, however, music was the most quintessentially Romantic. The German author E. T. A. Hoffmann wrote in 1813 that music was "the most romantic of all the arts, for its only subject is the infinite."

Turbulence, passion, danger, and death are captured in Eugène Delacroix's painting of a lion hunt.

Eugène Delacroix, French (1798–1863), *Lion Hunt*, 1860/61. Oil on canvas, 76.5 × 98.5 cm. Mr. and Mrs. Potter Palmer Collection. © 1993. The Art Institute of Chicago, 1992.404.

Music for All

During the nineteenth century, music became more and more a public concern. From the aristocratic salons of the rich, it moved into the concert halls and parlors of middle-class audiences throughout the United States and Europe. The philanthropic attitude of the times also led to the establishment of free concerts for the "improvement" of the working class. Bandstands were erected in public parks, cheap seats were made available in concert halls, and performing groups traveled to less developed areas such as the American West.

An awe-inspiring, almost Impressionist scene by William Turner.

Turner, Joseph Malord William, English (1775–1851), Slave Ship (Slavers Throwing Overboard the Dead and Dying, Typhoon Coming On), 1840. Oil on canvas, 90.8 × 122.6 cm. (35 11/16 × 48 5/16 in.) unframed. Henry Lillie Pierce Fund, 19.22. Courtesy, Museum of Fine Arts, Boston. Reproduced with permission. © 2000 Museum of Fine Arts, Boston. All rights reserved. Gift of Joseph W., William B., and Edward H. R. Revere.

In addition to public music making, there was an enormous growth in private music making at home. Industrialization had made pianos cheaper and more plentiful. By the last part of the century, most middle-class homes boasted a piano in the parlor. An evening of parlor songs or informal chamber music became commonplace in Victorian times.

The New Sound

If you listen to an orchestral piece from the Romantic era, you will notice that it is very different in *sound* from a piece of music from the Classic era. This, too, is partly a result of social and technological changes. As concerts moved from small halls to larger ones and audiences increased in size, orchestras became bigger, and instruments were adapted so that their sounds would be louder and carry farther. Instruments in the nineteenth century were built for power. They were also built for speed. Nineteenth-century woodwind and brass instruments were equipped with complex key or valve systems whose primary aim was to facilitate fast fingerwork. And new brass instruments were invented during the nineteenth century, such as the tuba and the saxophone.

A cozy scene of nineteenth-century middle-class music making.

Pianos, too, changed enormously during the nineteenth century. The small, delicate, wooden instruments known to Haydn and Mozart were replaced by larger and louder pianos.

Orchestras also increased in size. Whereas a Mozart symphony requires perhaps twenty-five or thirty players, a Romantic symphony needs fifty or sixty people, and some compositions call for an orchestra of more than one hundred players.

Sound is also a matter of how an orchestra is used. Apart from creating huge volume, a large orchestra can be used to produce a very wide range of different sounds. Romantic composers often used their orchestras as Romantic painters used their palettes: to create an almost infinite variety of colors and textures. The technique of manipulating orchestral sounds is known as **orchestration**, and many Romantic composers were brilliant and sensitive orchestrators.

Finally, the sound of a Romantic work depends on a number of other factors, such as dynamics, tempo, melody, harmony, and form, which we shall consider separately.

DYNAMICS   In most Classic music, the range of dynamics does not go beyond *piano* and *forte*. In Romantic music, this range is vastly extended. Dynamics up to triple or even quadruple fortissimo (*fff* and *ffff*) are common, and indications of quietness often go down to triple pianissimo (*ppp*). There is even a famous passage in a Tchaikovsky symphony in which the composer calls for sextuple pianissimo (*pppppp*). Changes of dynamics are much more frequent and less predictable in Romantic music than in music of earlier times.

TEMPO AND EXPRESSION   The range of tempo also increased in Romantic music. Long, languorous, slow movements are common in the nineteenth century, whereas the favorite slow tempo in the eighteenth century had been a graceful, moderate, walking tempo (*andante*). Changes of tempo within a movement are also much

Più moto ed espressivo
dolce ma espr.

(**"*More quickly and expressively*"**)
(*"sweet but expressive"*)

Tempo and expression markings in a nineteenth-century piano piece.

more frequent in the Romantic era. This creates a variety of moods inside a single movement, not just between individual movements of a work. And there is far more flexibility of tempo: A Romantic composition seems to ebb and flow as it goes along.

MELODY   Romantic melodies are very different from Classic ones. In the first place, they are usually much longer. Also, they often have a "surging" or "yearning" quality, which makes them highly emotional. Some of the most famous Romantic melodies are intense and strong, but others are wistful, dreamy, or deeply sad. The primary aim was always expression of feeling. See page 179.

HARMONY   One of the most important weapons in the Romantic search for expression was harmony. More and more unusual chords are used, unexpected combinations appear, and **modulation** (movement among keys) is much more frequent. Chromatic melodies and harmonies also become much more frequent.

FORM   Along with the loosening of harmony came a loosening of form. Romantic pieces tend to blur the outlines of form rather than highlight them. In a Romantic composition it is often harder to "hear" the form than it is in a Classic piece. In part, this is because Romantic works are often much longer, making it more difficult to follow structural devices.

This blurring of formal outlines was deliberate. Romantic composers wanted their music to represent the spontaneous flow of feelings rather than to display a carefully organized structure.

Formal templates are still used, of course. Great art is never without form. In most Romantic pieces, one can still detect arrangements such as sonata form, scherzo and trio, aria form, or rondo. But these are used with great flexibility, and the dividing lines between sections are often deliberately unclear.

Program Music

One of the most important differences between Classic and Romantic music lies in the distinction between "program" and "absolute" music. **Program music** is music that tells some kind of story. It may be a love story, or it could be a different kind of narrative, such as scenes from nature, or a child's reverie. **Absolute music** is music that has no meaning outside the meaning of the music itself and the feelings it produces in its listeners.

A perfect example of Romantic melody—long, emotional, highly expressive.

The nineteenth century did not invent the idea of program music. Vivaldi's *Four Seasons* is a famous example of Baroque program music. But never before had so many composers been so concerned with tying their music to ideas, stories, or events outside the actual notes they were writing.

Massive and Miniature

We have noted before that many Romantic works are longer than their Classic counterparts. And some compositions are very long indeed. Some Romantic symphonies last nearly two hours. A Romantic opera can last four hours or more. And Wagner's cycle of operas, *The Ring of the Nibelungs*, is designed to be performed over four entire evenings!

This love of the massive, or monumental, also determined the size of orchestras, as we have seen. More and more instruments were added to orchestras, and larger numbers of the traditional instruments were used.

In contrast to the massive works of the Romantic era, some compositions went to the opposite extreme, using delicate miniaturization. Most of these were works for solo piano, which could last less than a minute. Some of these piano miniatures were not programmatic and were simply called "Prelude" or "Waltz," but many of them had programmatic titles like "Dreaming," "Why?," and "Poet's Love." The piano miniature was the musical response to the Romantic interest in intimacy and individualism.

Favorite Romantic Genres

Many of the same genres that had been popular in the eighteenth century continued into the nineteenth. Opera and symphony were the most extensive genres, calling as they did for large forces. After Beethoven's revolutionary Ninth Symphony, with its use of solo singers and choir in the last movement, other Romantic composers sometimes used voices in their symphonies.

Voice was the central component of two other Romantic genres: song and the Requiem Mass. These also embody the contrast between intimacy and grandeur. Intimate solo song settings of Romantic poetry accompanied by piano were great favorites of the nineteenth century. And Requiem Mass settings often call for huge musical resources, including enormous orchestras, extra brass groups, solo singers, and large choruses. Their drama, subjectivity, and emotional appeal take the Romantic Requiems very close indeed to the style of Romantic opera.

Another favored orchestral genre was the concerto, which symbolized the highly Romantic notion of the individual against the group. Piano concertos were common, violin concertos even more so. But Romantic composers also chose other instruments to highlight in this way: cello, flute, clarinet, even viola.

Chamber music also was popular in the nineteenth century. After the string quartet, a particular favorite was the combination of piano and strings, as in a piano quintet (piano and string quartet). Composers also enjoyed writing chamber works for larger string groups—quintets, sextets, even octets—to obtain the rich sounds so typical of the Romantic ideal.

Solo piano works were very popular. Many solo piano compositions are programmatic, telling a story or depicting a series of scenes.

The link between program music and literature is particularly evident in a new genre: the **symphonic poem**. The symphonic poem is a relatively short orchestral work in one continuous movement (though it may fall into contrasting sections). Symphonic poems are always programmatic, though the source of the program need not be literary; it may be a painting or a scene from nature.

Favorite Romantic Instruments

The favorite Romantic instruments were probably the piano and the violin. The piano lends itself both to great intimacy and to great drama; the violin has a very wide range and possesses the potential for great lyricism. And yet there were other instruments that captured the Romantic imagination. Both the cello and the French horn—with their rich, expressive tenor range—were heavily favored by nineteenth-century composers.

The Individual and the Crowd

Romantic writers and thinkers were fascinated by the notion of the individual—a single person's thoughts and feelings. This focus on the individual is reflected in the Romantic concentration on dramatic musical genres such as the concerto, which contrasts the individual and the group, and in its love affair with great performing musicians.

During the nineteenth century, some performing musicians became very famous. The great Italian violinist Nicolò Paganini (1782–1840) traveled around the world, displaying his astounding virtuosity. Paganini could perform technical tricks on the violin that nobody else was able to achieve. And he had a flair for the dramatic. He used to cut partway through one or more of the strings on his violin before a performance so that they would snap while he was playing. To the amazement of his audience, he would then complete the piece on the remaining strings. Paganini's technical brilliance was the inspiration for several composers in the nineteenth century, as we shall see.

A daguerreotype (earliest type of photograph) of renowned violinist Paganini, taken shortly before his death in 1840. (The fingers of his left hand have been exaggerated, however.)

Women in Nineteenth-Century Music

The nineteenth century opened doors of opportunity to a wide range of people. Music conservatories began to accept women, and although considerable prejudice remained, some women became famous as performers and composers during the nineteenth century. This is not to say that there was equal opportunity. Most orchestras were still composed entirely of men, and many people thought that it was "unseemly" for women to appear as professional musicians in public. Still, a large number of women played the piano or sang, and many performed in their own living rooms or at the homes of friends.

Among the most important women in the history of nineteenth-century music were Fanny Mendelssohn and Clara Schumann, and we shall look at their lives and contributions to music during the course of this chapter.

Franz Schubert.

EARLY ROMANTICISM

In addition to Beethoven, five great composers were active in the first half of the nineteenth century: Franz Schubert, Hector Berlioz, Felix Mendelssohn, Fryderyk Chopin, and Robert Schumann.

Franz Schubert (1797–1828)

Schubert, the son of a Viennese schoolmaster, lived most of his life in Vienna. It is extraordinary to think that Schubert and Beethoven lived at the same time and in the same city and that they met only once.

The two men could not have been more different. Whereas Beethoven was proud, assertive, and difficult to get along with, Schubert was shy, retiring, and exceedingly modest, with a large number of good friends. Their music, too, is very different: Beethoven's is dramatic and intellectually powerful, Schubert's is gentle, relaxed, and lyrical, with a magical harmonic gift.

Schubert sang as a choirboy when he was young and also played the violin. At choir school he came to know the symphonies of Haydn, Mozart, and Beethoven first-hand. His father wanted Schubert to become a schoolmaster like himself; Schubert tried briefly, but he was a poor teacher and soon gave it up. Schubert then embarked on his quiet career as a composer. He seemed to be a limitless fountain of music. "When I finish one piece," he said, "I begin the next."

Schubert had many friends. Toward the end of his life, however, Schubert's essential loneliness often overcame him, and he despaired of achieving happiness. Some of Schubert's most profound works come from this period of his life.

In his last year, Schubert's productivity increased even further. Perhaps he knew that he did not have much time left. A month before he died, Schubert arranged to take lessons in counterpoint! "Now I see how much I still have to learn," he said. He died of syphilis on November 19, 1828 at the age of thirty-one. According to his last wishes, he was buried near Beethoven. Schubert wrote more than 900 works in his very short life, a level of productivity that surpasses even that of Mozart.

Schubert's Music

"Everything he touched turned to song," said one of his friends about Schubert. Schubert's greatest gift was his genius for capturing the essence of a poem when he set it to music. The melodies he devised for the voice, the harmonies and figuration of the piano part—these turn mediocre poetry into superb song and great poetry into some of the most expressive music ever written. During his life, Schubert composed more than 600 songs. These range from tiny poems on nature to songs of the deepest emotional intensity. In addition to this enormous number of individual songs, Schubert also wrote two great **song cycles**, or series of songs that belong together in a single compositional group. *Die schöne Müllerin* (*The Pretty Miller-Maid*, 1824) tells the story of a love affair that turns from happiness to tragedy. *Winterreise* (*Winter's Journey*, 1827) is a sequence of reflections on nostalgia and old age. Whether expressing the joys of youthful love or the resignation of old age, Schubert's music goes straight to the heart.

Schubert's gift for lyricism influenced everything he wrote, even his instrumental music. He composed a great variety of music for solo piano and some wonderful chamber music. Apart from the innate lyricism of "everything he touched," two of his chamber works are actually based on songs he wrote. Among the larger works are several operas, a number of choral works, and eight symphonies. The best known of Schubert's symphonies are his last two, the so-called *Great* C-Major Symphony (1828) and the *Unfinished* Symphony (Schubert completed only two movements).

From his tiny, moving, earliest songs to the expansiveness and grandeur of his late symphonies, Schubert's music is one of the great legacies of the nineteenth century.

LISTENING GUIDE

FRANZ SCHUBERT (1797–1828)

Song, *Die Forelle* (*The Trout*)

Date of composition: 1817
Voice and piano
Tempo: *Etwas lebhaft* ("Rather lively")
Meter: $\frac{2}{4}$
Key: D-flat Major
Duration: 2:10

Companion CD, Track 77

"The Trout," written to the poem of a German poet, Christian Friedrich Schubart, appeals to today's listeners just as it did to Schubert's contemporaries. Part of the song's charm lies in the composer's remarkable ability to give the melody and its accompaniment an equal share in the musical interpretation of the poem.

The song begins with a piano introduction based on a "rippling" figure that evokes the smooth flow of a stream. This figure dominates the accompaniment.

The first two stanzas are sung to the same music. This makes sense because the scene remains the same: As long as the water in the stream is clear, the fish is safe. In the third stanza, however, when the fisherman grows impatient and maliciously stirs up the water to outwit the trout, the music becomes more agitated and unsettled. After the fish is finally hooked, the smoothing of the water's surface is represented by the return of the gentle "rippling" figure, which gives a sense of artistic unity and makes the song a highly organic work.

The subtlety of expression, the perfect matching of the music to the emotional content, and the gentle pictorial touches all combine to make this song a miniature masterpiece.

77	0:00	Piano introduction based on the rippling figure.	

STANZA 1

[rippling accompaniment continues]

	0:08	*In einem Bächlein helle,*	In a limpid brook
		Da schoss in froher Eil'	In joyous haste
		Die launische Forelle	The whimsical trout
		Vorüber wie ein Pfeil.	Darted about like an arrow.

	0:20	*Ich stand an dem Gestade*	I stood on the bank
		Und sah in süsser Ruh'	In blissful peace, watching
		Des muntern Fischleins Bade	The lively fish swim around
		Im klaren Bächlein zu.	In the clear brook.

[last two lines repeated]

	0:39	Piano interlude	

[same music]

0:45

Ein Fischer mit der Rute	An angler with his rod
Wohl an dem Ufer stand,	Stood on the bank,
Und sah's mit kaltem Blute,	Cold-bloodedly watching
Wie sich das Fischlein wand.	The fish's flicker.

0:57

So lang' dem Wasser Helle,	As long as the water is clear,
So dacht' ich, nicht gebricht,	I thought, and not disturbed,
So fängt er die Forelle	He'll never catch that trout
Mit seiner Angel nicht.	With his rod.

[last two lines repeated]

1:17 | Piano interlude

STANZA 3

[sudden change of rhythm, harmony, and accompanying figures]

1:23

Doch endlich ward dem Diebe	But in the end the thief
Die Zeit zu lang. Er macht	Grew impatient. Cunningly
Das Bächlein tückisch trübe,	He made the brook
	cloudy, [diminished sevenths]
Und eh ich es gedacht,	And in an instant [suspense gaps in piano]

1:37

So zuckte seine Rute,	His rod quivered,
Das Fischlein zappelt dran,	And the fish struggled on it. [crescendo]
Und ich mit regem Blute	And I, my blood boiling, [earlier music returns]
Sah die Betrog'ne an.	Looked at the poor tricked creature.

[last two lines repeated]

1:58 | Piano postlude

Hector Berlioz (1803–1869)

In nineteenth-century France, Romanticism was a vital force, and the works of the French composer Hector Berlioz established music as central to the Romantic ideal. Berlioz began to compose music when he was a teenager.

His father wanted him to become a doctor, so Berlioz entered medical school in Paris. But he became more and more interested in music. He finally quit medical school and enrolled at the Paris Conservatory of Music as a composition student at the age of twenty-three.

During the next few years, he wrote several compositions. He also had some first-time experiences that were to affect him profoundly, such as hearing some of the great

Beethoven symphonies and encountering Shakespeare's plays. He wrote a composition based on *Romeo and Juliet*. He also fell in love with an Irish actress, Harriet Smithson, who was touring with a Shakespearean acting company. All of these experiences had lasting effects on his music.

French audiences found the emotionality of his music too direct. But throughout the rest of Europe, Berlioz was more appreciated. The great Italian virtuoso Paganini sent him 20,000 francs out of the blue, and Wagner described *Romeo and Juliet* as a "revelation." Berlioz was often invited to conduct abroad, and other conductors, especially in Germany, scheduled performances of his music.

In the 1850s, despite his critics at home, Berlioz poured his energies into producing one of his greatest masterpieces, the five-act opera *Les Troyens* (*The Trojans*). Based on Virgil's *Aeneid*, it tells the story of the escape of Aeneas from Troy and his doomed love affair with Dido, the Queen of Carthage.

For the last part of his life, Berlioz was not in good health, and he felt bitter and depressed. Berlioz died in 1869, and his grave may be visited at Montmartre in Paris. In many ways, Hector Berlioz can be seen as the incarnation of the Romantic artist: brilliantly gifted, completely dedicated to his art, yet rejected by society and isolated during his lifetime.

Hector Berlioz.

Berlioz's Music

The most striking aspects of Berlioz's music are its color and atmosphere. He used the orchestra brilliantly, with great sensitivity to the varied qualities of sound available from all of the instruments. Some of his pieces call for enormous resources. His Requiem Mass is written for an orchestra of 140 players, a huge chorus, and four groups of brass and timpani placed at the four corners of the performing space. His *Te Deum* calls for a solo singer, a large orchestra, an organ, two choirs of 100 singers each, and a choir of 600 children!

But even more fascinating than these gigantic effects are quiet places in his works where Berlioz conjures up an unforgettable atmosphere with completely original orchestration. In the Requiem, for example, he uses violas, cellos, bassoons, and English horns in simple, long phrases, for a passage of penitence and introspection. And his *Symphonie fantastique* is full of wonderful atmospheric moments: an echoing song between solo oboe and solo English horn, the quiet rumble of distant thunder on four timpani, and an eerie, menacing march on muted horns and plucked double basses.

Berlioz's best known work is his *Symphonie fantastique* (*Fantastical Symphony*), which is also one of the most famous examples of Romantic program music. Like many other composers of program music, Berlioz felt ambivalent about tying a musical work to a specific verbal narrative. He wanted to explain the ideas behind his music to the audience, but he also felt that the music should be able to stand alone.

LISTENING GUIDE

HECTOR BERLIOZ (1803–1869)

Main Theme and Fourth Movement ("March to the Scaffold") from *Symphonie fantastique* (*Fantastical Symphony*)

Date of composition: 1830

Orchestration: Piccolo, 2 flutes, 2 oboes, 2 clarinets, 4 bassoons, 4 horns, 2 cornets, 2 trumpets, 3 trombones, 2 tubas, 2 timpani, snare drum, bass drum, cymbals, chimes, 2 harps, violins I, violins II, violas, cellos, basses

Tempo: *Allegretto non troppo* (Fairly fast but not too much)

Meter: $\frac{4}{4}$

Key: B-flat Major

Duration: 4:24

Complete CD Collection: 2, Tracks 28–30

The *Symphonie fantastique*, Berlioz said, describes various situations in the life of a young musician: the young man falls desperately in love with a woman at first sight; the symphony depicts his dreams, despairs, and fantasies. Clearly the symphony is autobiographical.

In the first movement we are given a musical theme that represents the beloved. The theme itself is the perfect embodiment of Romantic melody—long, flexible, yearning upward, falling back, hesitating, surging, retiring: it breathes as though alive. It appears in the violins with solo flute, first unaccompanied, then with repeated notes in low strings; striving upward, agitated, then calming.

This melody returns in the other movements. In the fourth movement, the young musician dreams that he has murdered his beloved and has been condemned to death by guillotine. There are two marches, the first low and somber, the second blaring and bright. At the end of the second march, we hear the *melody* returning on the clarinet, ("like a last thought of love," as Berlioz described it), but it is brutally cut off by a massive chord from the orchestra, representing the fall of the guillotine blade.

Berlioz uses a huge orchestra, with a very large brass section and unusual percussion instruments. This movement is frightening ("fifty times more frightening than I expected," said Berlioz in delight) and even gruesome. After the head is cut off, you might even hear it bouncing across the ground!

29	0:00	Timpani, horns, and plucked double basses set the eerie atmosphere. Crescendo.
	0:27	The **first march** is heard, halting and somber, on cellos and double basses. It is made up of a descending melody in the minor.
	0:40	Repeated with commentary from high bassoons.

	0:53	Violins with descending march, but in the major this time, with interruptions and sudden surprises.
	1:18	Pizzicato strings, with bassoons again, back to minor, lead into:
30	1:40	**Second march.** Loud and bright, with brass instruments and drums, major key.
	2:06	Return of opening descending march melody, quiet.
	2:16	Return of second march, loud, whole orchestra.
	2:45	Return of first march, quiet.
	2:53	A wild passage with elements of both marches, including the first one *ascending*, huge crescendos and decrescendos, cymbal crashes.
	3:28	Transition with strings, wild, frenzied; punctuation by brasses and drums.
	4:01	Sudden stop and the wistful "last thought of love" is heard on the plaintive clarinet.
	4:10	This is savagely cut off by the drop of the guillotine blade, and the whole orchestra blares out the conclusion with snare drum rattling.

Felix Mendelssohn (1809–1847)

Mendelssohn is one of the two composers in this chapter (the other being Gustav Mahler) who illustrate the uncomfortable position occupied by Jews in nineteenth-century Europe. His grandfather was the famous Jewish philosopher Moses Mendelssohn. And his parents were members of the cultured middle class of Hamburg. In 1811, the Mendelssohn family was forced to flee from Hamburg to Berlin for political reasons, and when Felix was seven years old, his father had the children baptized as Christians; a few years later, his father converted to Christianity himself. Despite the increasing tolerance of nineteenth-century society, it was still easier to make your way in life if you were not Jewish.

After that, the family enjoyed increasing prosperity and social status. The Mendelssohn home was a focal point for writers, artists, and musicians. Chamber concerts were held every weekend, and under the tutelage of their mother, Felix and his older sister Fanny soon proved to be especially gifted in music.

About Fanny, we shall say more later. Felix was precocious in everything he undertook. At the age of ten, he was reading Latin and studying arithmetic, geometry, history, and geography. He played the piano and the violin, and he started music theory and composition lessons with a distinguished professor of music in Berlin. He began to compose, write poetry, and paint. Several of his early compositions were performed at the Sunday concerts in his parents' home. By the time he was twenty he had written more than one hundred pieces.

Mendelssohn was very interested in music of the past. It was at the age of twenty that, together with a family friend who was a professional actor, he arranged for a

Felix Mendelssohn
about 1829.

performance of one of the great masterpieces of Bach that had not been heard for nearly a century—the *St. Matthew Passion*. The performance, with Mendelssohn conducting, was a landmark in the revival and appreciation of Bach's music in the modern era. "To think," said Mendelssohn, "that it should be an actor and a Jew who give back to the people the greatest of all Christian works."

Mendelssohn was married in 1837, and the couple had five children. In 1843, he was appointed director of the Berlin Cathedral Choir and director of the Berlin Opera, as well as director of the newly opened music conservatory in Leipzig. Despite all these activities, Mendelssohn continued to compose. Among the many works he wrote at this time were an opera, two large oratorios, symphonies, concertos, chamber music, and numerous pieces for solo piano.

In May of 1847, his closest friend and confidante, his sister Fanny, suddenly died. Felix was shattered. His last great work, the String Quartet in F Minor, Op. 80, was composed as a "Requiem for Fanny." He became ill and tired and could no longer conduct. A series of strokes in October led to his death on November 3, 1847, at the age of thirty-eight. Mendelssohn was buried in Berlin, near Fanny's grave.

Mendelssohn's Music

Mendelssohn continued the Classic tradition in his works, while adopting some of the less extreme ideas of Romanticism. He wrote in most of the traditional Classic genres, and the formal outlines of his works are clear and easy to follow. Mendelssohn maintained the greatest respect for the past—especially the music of Bach, Handel, Mozart, and Beethoven—and his music shows the influence of these composers. His style is more transparent and lighter than that of many early Romantic composers. It ranges from lively and brilliantly animated to lyrical and expressive.

Mendelssohn's main orchestral works include five symphonies and several overtures. Many of these are programmatic, though only in a general sense: They do not tell a detailed story but evoke scenes and landscapes. The best known of these are the *Scottish* Symphony (Symphony No. 3), the *Italian* Symphony (Symphony No. 4), and the *Hebrides* Overture, all written after Mendelssohn's travels. The *Hebrides* Overture was inspired by his trip to Scotland and evokes a rocky landscape and the swell of the sea. Like many early Romantics, Mendelssohn read and admired Shakespeare, and another overture often performed today is the Overture to Shakespeare's *A Midsummer Night's Dream*. Listening to this piece, it is hard to believe it was written when the composer was only seventeen.

Mendelssohn also wrote several concertos, mostly for piano but some for violin as well. His Violin Concerto in E minor is certainly the most popular of all his works because of its beauty and lyricism.

Mendelssohn's admiration for Bach and Handel led to his interest in choral writing. After the famous revival of Bach's *St. Matthew Passion*, Mendelssohn studied Handel's oratorios and composed two major oratorios of his own, *Elijah* and *St. Paul*. He also wrote a great deal of other choral music, and his sacred music includes works for Jewish, Catholic, Lutheran, and Anglican services.

His chamber music includes songs, string quartets, sonatas, and piano trios. Perhaps the most popular of these works is the Piano Trio in D minor. In addition, Mendelssohn wrote a large number of miniatures for solo piano; in the typical mold of early Romanticism, he called them *Songs Without Words*. They are gentle, delightful, and lyrical—expressive without being deeply profound. In these ways, they capture the essence of Felix Mendelssohn's music.

Fanny Mendelssohn Hensel (1805–1847)

Fanny was four years older than Felix, and they were very close throughout their lives. Fanny was a talented pianist and a gifted composer, but her career as a composer illustrates the distance women still had to travel for equality of opportunity in the nineteenth century.

Her father strongly disapproved of the idea of her pursuing a career in music. Like many people of his time, he felt that a professional career was unsuitable for a woman. Amateur music making was entirely acceptable—indeed, it was the province of a cultivated young woman—but making a living as a performer or a composer was out of the question. Even her brother Felix agreed with this view.

So Fanny led the conventional life of a well-educated middle-class woman. At twenty-four, she married Wilhelm Hensel, a painter and artist at the court in Berlin. Fanny had a son and ran the family household. She continued to play the piano, and after her mother's death, she took over the organization of the famous Sunday concerts at her parents' home. She often played the piano at the concerts and directed a choral group that performed there. One day, at the age of forty-one, while rehearsing the chorus for a performance of a cantata composed by Felix, she had a stroke. She died that same evening.

Despite discouragement from her father and her brother, Fanny had composed a great deal. She wrote many songs, some cantatas and oratorios, chamber music, and small piano works, which, like Felix, she called *Songs Without Words*. Some of her early songs were published in collections with pieces by her brother, though they carried Felix's name. After the death of her father, she did arrange for publication of one or two works under her own name.

Fanny Mendelssohn about 1830.

All in all, Fanny composed about 400 works, though most of them have never been published. They remain in manuscript in American and European libraries. In the last few years, with increasing focus on the contributions of women to the history of music, more and more of her works are being published and recorded. It is impossible to assess her true contributions or to compare her achievement with that of Felix until her compositions have received the same attention as those of her brother

LISTENING GUIDE

FANNY MENDELSSOHN HENSEL (1805–1847)

Lied from *Songs Without Words*, Op. 8, No. 3

Date of composition: 1840?
Tempo: *Larghetto* ("Fairly slow")
Meter: $\frac{4}{4}$
Key: D Major
Duration: 3:05

Complete CD Collection: 2, Tracks 31–33

The *Lieder ohne Wörte* (*Songs Without Words*) were not published until after Fanny's death. The third of this four-piece set, entitled *Lied* (*Song*), is also marked *Lenau*, the name of a German poet, suggesting that an actual poem may have inspired her to write this song. The tuneful, flowing phrases are indeed highly singable and memorable. The form is a typical one for a song: ABA. Throughout the piece, there is an accompaniment of gentle, repeated chords in the middle range, and slow, isolated bass notes. The atmosphere suggests a reflective inner dialogue.

		A	
31	0:00		Melody repeats a gently curving motive, followed by an ascending leap, as a kind of questioning idea. This is followed by a balanced descending motive. The mood is one of contemplation.
	0:30		Questioning idea in low range, response in higher range.
		B	
32	1:03		Modulating, unstable B section—shorter, faster exchanges of questioning idea, answered by descending arpeggios.
	1:20		Minor version of questioning idea in low range. Crescendo, then decrescendo, leads to:
		A'	
33	1:39		Clear return of the beginning, moving quickly to faster sequential phrases.
	2:15		Closing section using questioning idea, including crescendo and leap to highest note of the piece. Ends with gentle decrescendo.

Fryderyk Chopin (1810–1849)

Chopin was the first of the great piano virtuosos in the Romantic era. Most composers before Chopin played the piano, but Chopin was the first important Romantic composer to achieve fame as a performing pianist, and almost all his compositions are written for solo piano.

Chopin was born in Poland in 1810 to a French father and a Polish mother. His father taught French, and his mother taught piano at a school in Warsaw. Chopin began formal piano lessons at the age of seven, and his first composition was published the same year. At the age of eight, he gave his first public concert, and at the age of fifteen, he was sufficiently accomplished to play before Tsar Alexander I of Russia, who presented him with a diamond ring.

When Chopin was nineteen, he heard the great violinist Paganini play and was inspired to become a touring virtuoso himself. Most of his compositions at this time were designed for his own use. Chopin would improvise for hours at the keyboard and only occasionally write down what he had played. His music was often based on Polish dances such as the polonaise or the mazurka.

In 1830, Chopin completed two piano concertos, which he performed in public concerts, and toward the end of the year he left Poland, unaware that he would never see it again. From a distance, he heard of the Warsaw uprising and the storming of Warsaw by the Russian army. From this time on, the Polish quality of his music deepened, and his compositions became more intense and passionate.

In 1831, at the age of twenty-one, Chopin settled in Paris, the center of European artistic activity. Soon he was caught up in the whirl of Parisian society, and his brilliant and poetic playing made him very much in demand in the city's fashionable salons.

In his late twenties, Chopin was introduced to Aurore Dudevant, a well-known novelist who published under the male pseudonym George Sand. They soon started living together, and the years they spent together were among the most productive of Chopin's life. He was often ill, however, displaying the first signs of the tuberculosis that would later kill him. George Sand looked after him devotedly, though Chopin was a difficult patient, and there is a rather unflattering portrait of him in one of her novels.

The relationship ended in 1847, after which Chopin's health rapidly deteriorated. He composed little, but gave public recitals in London and Paris. It was reported that he was too weak to play louder than *mezzo-forte*. Chopin died in 1849 at the age of thirty-nine. At his request, Mozart's Requiem was played at his funeral.

Portrait of Chopin at the age of twenty-eight by the famous French painter Eugène Delacroix.

Eugène Delacroix (1798–1863), *Portrait of Frederic Chopin* (1810–1860), 1838. Oil on canvas, 45.5 × 38 cm. Louvre, Dpt. des Peintures, France. © Photograph by Erich Lessing. Erich Lessing/Art Resource, NY.

Chopin's Music

The best way to think of Chopin's music is as poetry for the piano. In an English newspaper, he was once called a "musical Wordsworth." Almost all of his works are for solo piano. The two piano concertos are really piano solos with rather sketchy orchestral accompaniment.

Chopin's style is entirely a personal one, as might be expected from one who improvised so freely. Most of his pieces are fairly short, and they fall into several categories. First there are the dances—polonaises, mazurkas, and waltzes. The **waltz** was fast becoming the favorite ballroom dance of the nineteenth century. Chopin managed to create enormous variety of mood with the basic format of this one dance. **Mazurkas** and **polonaises** are both Polish dances, and Chopin invested them with the spirit of Polish nationalism. Mazurkas are in triple meter with a stress on the second or third beat of the bar. Polonaises are stately and proud.

Chopin also wrote in free forms without dance rhythms: preludes, études, nocturnes, and impromptus. The **preludes** follow the pattern established by Bach in his *Well-Tempered Clavier*: There is one in each major and minor key. **Étude** literally means "study piece," and each of Chopin's études concentrates on one facet of musicianship or piano technique. The **nocturnes** are moody, introspective pieces, and the **impromptus** capture the essence of improvisation ("impromptu" means "off the cuff").

The formal structure of these pieces is fundamentally simple, relying on the ABA pattern common to aria or song form. However, Chopin usually varied the return of as on the opening section quite considerably, creating an ABA structure.

In all of these genres, Chopin wrote highly individual pieces, each one with an elegiac or rhapsodic quality, and each one expressive and pianistic—that is, perfectly suited to the special sound and capabilities of the piano. Chopin's works are carefully designed for the instrument of his day. They depend on the new technology of the early nineteenth-century piano, which allowed the rapid repetition of single notes. The sound of the instrument was softer, less brilliant than it is today, and Chopin's melodies and chords exploited this quality. Often, the melodies are highly lyrical and dreamy, and the sustaining pedal allows widely spaced notes to blend together as chords in the left hand. Chopin's left-hand harmony is varied and expressive, and sometimes the main melody can appear in the left hand with the accompaniment above it in the right. There is often much delicate, rapid ornamentation in the right hand, with short free passages or runs or trills that add to the impression of improvisation. Finally, Chopin's written directions often call for a special expressive device called **rubato**. Literally, this Italian word means "robbed." Using this technique, the player slows the music down slightly before catching up a moment later. Carefully applied, rubato can suggest the kind of expressive freedom that must have characterized the playing of Chopin himself.

LISTENING GUIDE

FRYDERYK CHOPIN (1810–1849)

Waltz in D-flat Major, Op. 64, No. 1, for
  Piano Solo (*Minute* Waltz)

Date of composition: 1847
Tempo: *Tempo giusto* ("Exact tempo")
Meter: $\frac{2}{2}$
Duration: 1:47

Companion CD, Track 78

This is the sixth of fourteen waltzes Chopin wrote for the piano. Each one is based on the characteristic "ONE-two-three ONE-two-three" waltz rhythm, but each one is different. The D-flat-Major Waltz is known as the *Minute* Waltz because it is so short, though it actually takes about two minutes to play. Chopin marks it *Molto vivace—leggiero* ("Very fast and lively—light"). The opening theme, in which the melody seems to circle around itself, has been compared to a dog chasing its own tail. The overall scheme is ABCAB, with repetitions of melodic phrases within each section. This gives form to the delicate and swirling music.

	A	
78	0:00	Around and around, right hand only.
	0:04	Waltz rhythm enters in left hand, right-hand melody in eighth notes.

B		
0:12	New melody, rapid key changes, continuing fast eighth notes.
0:22	Repeat of B section.
C		
0:33	Lower melody in A-flat, slower in effect (melody in half and quarter notes).
0:48	Ornamented repeat; slow down.
1:01	Trill, return to:
A		
1:06	Around and around, opening music and melody.
B		
1:19	B section again; repeated.
1:38	Very high descent to closing chords.

Robert Schumann (1810–1856)

Of all the early Romantics, Robert Schumann was the most imbued with a literary imagination. He was born in 1810 in a small German town. His father was a bookseller, so the young boy had unlimited access to the popular Romantic writings of the day.

Schumann read voraciously and began to pour his feelings into poems and novels of his own, before finding a more suitable outlet in music. He played the piano well, though his exuberance outran his discipline. "I was always a fiery performer," he said, "but my technique was full of holes."

After his father died, Schumann went to the University of Leipzig as a law student, but he had no interest in the subject. He drank heavily and spent his money on having a good time. While in Leipzig he met Friedrich Wieck, an eminent piano teacher, and took lessons from him.

A turning point in Schumann's career came (as it did for so many Romantic musicians) upon his first hearing the Italian virtuoso Paganini play a concert. He was entranced by the showmanship and hypnotic intensity of the great violinist and decided to become a piano virtuoso. He gave up his undisciplined life, enrolled as a full-time student of Friedrich Wieck, and took a room in Wieck's house in order to devote himself to constant practice. Unfortunately, Schumann took this to extremes, as he tended to do with everything. He overdid the practicing and permanently damaged his hand.

There was, however, a bright side to this episode: Schumann turned from performing to composing music, and he met Clara, Wieck's daughter, who was to become the love of his life. When Schumann moved in with the Wiecks, Clara was only ten years old. But she was a brilliant pianist, and Wieck had the highest hopes for her. Clara could outplay Schumann, even though he was twice her age.

By the time Clara was fifteen, she was already a great pianist, astounding audiences at home and abroad. But her father suddenly noticed a cloud on the horizon: Clara and Robert were falling in love. This was not at all in Wieck's plans. His daughter had a career ahead of her and didn't need to get involved with a neurotic, obsessive student, ten years her senior, who barely made a living. So he took Clara away on long tours, refused to let the couple meet, and even threatened to shoot Schumann if he tried to see Clara again. During this long period, the two wrote secret letters to each other, and Schumann poured his feelings into his music. He described his F-sharp minor piano sonata as "a single cry of my heart for you," and Clara wrote to him that when she played, she played for him: "I had no other way of showing you what was in my heart."

In the end, the couple had no choice but to go to court to obtain the freedom to marry, and they were finally married in 1840, when Clara was twenty and Robert was thirty. In that year, Schumann turned his attention to compositions for piano and voice. He was on fire with inspiration and composed 140 songs, including three song cycles. Schumann's wedding gift to Clara was a setting of *Du bist wie eine Blume*, a poem comparing his love to the beauty of a flower.

If 1840 was Schumann's "year of song," 1841 was his "year of the symphony." The two settled happily into their home in Leipzig, with a music room each, and Clara wrote: "We enjoy a happiness such as I have never known before." Schumann had recently encountered a symphony by Schubert. He was overwhelmed, and Clara encouraged him to work on a symphony of his own. His Symphony No. 1 (*Spring Symphony*) was sketched out in four days. The first performance was given by the Leipzig Gewandhaus Orchestra with Felix Mendelssohn conducting.

Clara and Robert Schumann.

Photograph of Clara and Robert Schumann, Musée d'Orsay, Paris. Réunion des Musées Nationaux / Art Resource, NY.

Clara went on tour in 1842, and Schumann threw himself into a new passion: chamber music. He studied the string quartets of Haydn, Mozart, and Beethoven intensively. On Clara's return, he wrote three string quartets in five weeks, and by the end of the year had also completed a piano quintet, a piano quartet, and a piano trio.

Around 1845, Schumann began to experience the fits of depression and illness that were to haunt him for the rest of his life. Composition now came only sporadically, and he had occasional nervous breakdowns.

In 1850, Schumann was appointed music director in Düsseldorf, but it soon became clear that his health and mental state were not sufficiently stable to allow him to perform his duties. Newspaper reviews became highly critical, singers refused to attend rehearsals, and Schumann's assistant conductor had to take over concerts at the last minute. Schumann began to suffer from hallucinations.

On a rainy day in February 1854, Schumann left his house in his slippers and walked to the bridge over the Rhine. He stepped over the railing and threw himself into the water.

He was pulled out by some fishermen and carried home. A few days later, he was committed to a mental institution.

With eight children, Clara could not long maintain her household alone. She began touring again, but in 1856 she was summoned back urgently by the doctors. "I had to go to him," she wrote in her diary. "I saw him between 6 and 7 in the evening. He smiled and with great effort put his arms around me. I shall never forget it. All the treasures in the world could not equal this embrace." Two days later Schumann died. He was forty-six.

Schumann's Music

Schumann was a literary Romantic. Much of his music is inspired by literary references, and even when the inspiration is not literary, there is often some other programmatic reference to people or ideas.

His writing for piano, his own instrument, is masterly. The pieces

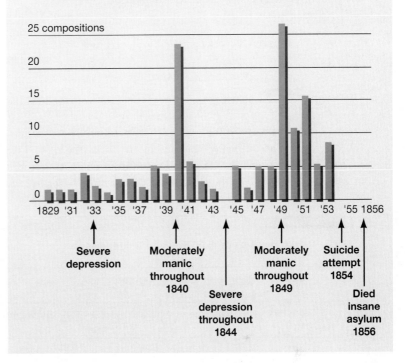

Mapping Madness and Genius

The quantity, if not the quality, of the composer Robert Schumann's output varied strikingly with episodes of depression or mania and the relatively benign periods between. He lived from 1810 to 1856, when he died of self-starvation.

for solo piano range from short works deliberately designed for children to **character pieces** (small programmatic movements) to large sonatas. Many of the character pieces are grouped together into cycles. One such cycle, *Carnaval*, contains musical portraits of Schumann himself, some of his friends, Chopin, Paganini, and the fifteen-year-old Clara Wieck. The piano parts for his songs are also very beautiful, playing an equal role with that of the voice. Many of the songs are also grouped into cycles, the most famous being *Dichterliebe* (*A Poet's Love*) and *Frauen-Liebe und Leben* (*Women's Lives and Loves*).

Schumann wrote only one piano concerto. It is the complete opposite of the typical Romantic concerto. Rather than flashy and brilliant, it is restrained and tender—perhaps because it was written for his beloved Clara to play.

Two of Schumann's four symphonies have programmatic titles. The First Symphony is called the *Spring* Symphony, and the Third Symphony is called the *Rhenish* Symphony. (*Rhenish* means "on the Rhine.") He composed the latter immediately after taking up his appointment in the city of Düsseldorf, on the Rhine River. Like Berlioz's *Symphonie fantastique*, it has five instead of the normal four movements.

Schumann's chamber music is more Classical in form. There are fewer apparent programmatic references, but the music flows with intensity and charm. As with song and symphony, Schumann took hold of Classical genres and invested them with his own particular brand of Romantic imagination.

LISTENING GUIDE

ROBERT SCHUMANN (1810–1856)

Träumerei (Dreaming), from *Kinderszenen*, Op. 15, for Piano

Date of composition: 1838
Meter: $\frac{3}{4}$
Key: F Major
Duration: 3:00

Complete CD Collection: 2, Track 34

This selection comes from Schumann's *Kinderszenen* (*Scenes from Childhood*). It is a simple accompanied melody, in an ABA' structure. The beautiful melody features a fairly wide range, and its ascending contour characterizes all three brief sections. The slow tempo and the reiteration of the theme create a wonderfully "dreamy" atmosphere.

A SECTION

34	0:00	Melody is presented. First phrase:
	0:08	High point of the first phrase.
	0:19	Ending of the first phrase overlaps with the beginning of the second.
	0:27	Melody reaches even higher, to its highest pitch.
	0:38	Cadence.
	0:42	A section repeated.

B SECTION

1:23	Melody is presented, but varied melodically and harmonically.

A' SECTION

2:03	Melody is restated.
2:31	Large, rolled chord under the highest pitch of melody ("signal" that the piece will end soon).
2:45	Ending cadence.

Clara Schumann (1819–1896)

The first part of Clara Schumann's life, from the age of ten to the age of thirty-six, was closely bound up with that of Robert Schumann. There is no doubt that she both loved and admired her husband. He in turn was deeply in love with her and depended heavily on her for emotional support. Robert encouraged her performing career, but in their relationship his composing certainly took precedence over hers.

Her musical career was nonetheless a remarkable one. She benefited from her father's close attention to her musical education. At the age of nine, she first performed in public; two years later, she gave her first complete solo recital.

By the time she married, at the age of twenty, Clara Schumann had an international reputation as a concert pianist. She was renowned for playing everything from memory and for her poetic touch and seriousness of intent. She had also composed a considerable number of works by this time, and several had been published.

During her married life, Clara continued to perform and compose, although we must remember that in fourteen years she had eight children. She submitted all of her compositions to her husband for his criticism, and she clearly regarded him as the greater talent. By the time of his death, she had published twenty or thirty compositions of her own; several others remained unpublished. Her works include character pieces for piano, songs, some chamber music, and a piano concerto, which was completed when she was fifteen years old. Perhaps her best-known work is her Piano Trio in G minor, Op. 17, written in 1846.

After Robert Schumann's death, Clara continued to perform and to teach, though she wrote no more music. She maintained a heavy schedule, doubtless to support her large family. Clara continued to appear in public into her seventies and promoted her husband's music by performing it as much as possible. She also helped prepare a complete edition of his works for publication.

Throughout this latter half of her life, Clara was the friend and confidante of Johannes Brahms, a composer fourteen years her junior. Brahms had been a protégé of Schumann's, and the three musicians had been close. Brahms was especially supportive during the last terrible years of Schumann's illness. Brahms and Clara remained good friends after Schumann's death. He often sent her drafts of his work for her encouragement and criticism. Brahms, however, remained a bachelor, and Clara never remarried. Clara Schumann died on May 20, 1896, at the age of seventy-seven, while her grandson played Robert Schumann's music at the piano.

MID-ROMANTICISM

By the middle of the century, the main aspects of musical Romanticism had become established: Music should represent human emotions to the utmost, and it must tell a story or express an idea that is profound, resonant, or uplifting. A favorite term of the Romantics was "sublime," which means grand, beyond normal experience, awe-inspiring.

During the mid-Romantic period, from the 1850s to the 1870s, the most important musical genres were solo piano works, symphonic program music, and opera. The most important composers were Franz Liszt, Giuseppe Verdi, Richard Wagner, and Pyotr Ilyich Tchaikovsky.

WORKS FOR SOLO PIANO   Solo piano music appealed to the Romantics for its focus on the individual. Audiences could concentrate on both the expression of individual emotions and the technical prowess of a great performer. This was the period during which the idea of the performer-hero first took hold, an idea that is still current today (witness our fascination with stars of both the rock and the classical-music worlds). The great piano performer of the mid-Romantic period was Liszt.

SYMPHONIC PROGRAM MUSIC   Symphonic program music followed two paths during the 1850s and 1860s. The first was that of the programmatic symphony. This path had been made secure by the earlier success of Berlioz's *Symphonie fantastique*. In several movements, usually three to five, the programmatic symphony is a full-length symphony, with each movement depicting an episode in the narrative.

The second path was that of the **symphonic poem**, the successor to such works as Mendelssohn's *Hebrides* Overture. The symphonic poem is a single-movement programmatic work for orchestra. Liszt was the greatest composer of symphonic poems and programmatic symphonies in the mid-Romantic era, though several other composers followed his lead in later decades.

OPERA   During the nineteenth century, there were three national schools of opera: the French, the Italian, and the German. All three had roots going back at least 150 years, and all three had distinct national identities by the time of the mid-Romantic period.

French opera had two very different genres, each with its own style and even its own opera house. The first was **grand opera**, which incorporated lofty subject matter and spectacular staging, including ballet, choruses, and crowd scenes. The second was **opéra comique** (comic opera), with a much smaller cast and orchestra, simpler musical style, and more down-to-earth plots. A technical distinction between grand opera and comic opera was that in grand opera the dialogue was set in accompanied musical recitative, whereas in comic opera the dialogue was spoken.

By the 1850s and 1860s a new, highly popular operatic genre had evolved in France, one that stood between grand opera and comic opera. It was known as **lyric opera**. Lyric opera is melodious, as its name implies; its primary subject matter is tragic love; and its proportions lie somewhere between the spectacular and the skimpy. The greatest lyric opera is *Carmen*, written by Georges Bizet (1838–1875).

Italian opera was dominated by the achievements of one man: Giuseppe Verdi. He was preceded, however, by three important Italian operatic composers: Rossini, Donizetti, and Bellini. Rossini's gifts were best suited to comic operas, and the most famous of these is his *The Barber of Seville* (1816). Donizetti wrote both comic and serious operas, whereas Bellini composed only serious operas. Bellini's best-known opera is *Norma* (1831).

The central figure in German opera was Wagner, who created some of the most significant masterpieces of the nineteenth century, and whose powerful personality made him a major artistic figure of his time. We shall study Wagner's contributions, both positive and negative, to Romantic culture. Wagner was influenced by the operas of Carl Maria von Weber (1786–1826), especially *Der Freischütz* (*The Magic Marksman*, 1821), with its supernatural and heroic subject matter and heavy emphasis on the role of the orchestra.

NATIONALISM   The existence of distinct national styles in Romantic opera was one facet of an important movement in nineteenth-century music. This movement was known as **nationalism**, and it coincided with important political events in Europe.

After the Napoleonic Wars ended in 1814, European countries began to assert their independence and to stress national identity. By the 1870s, both Italy and Germany were unified as independent states. There were rebellions of the Polish people against the ruling Russians, and of the Czechs against the Austrians. Norway gained independence from Sweden, and Finland struggled for independence from Russia.

The nationalist movement was reflected in the arts. In each country, the local language was fostered and people turned to their native folk tales, dances, and songs. Operas were based on national legend or history and were written in the native language. Folk tunes appeared in symphonic music, and the rhythms of folk dances were used in chamber works. Some composers became famous national symbols.

Franz Liszt (1811–1886)

Franz Liszt was born in 1811 in Hungary. His father was an administrator and court musician at the Esterházy palace, where Haydn had spent most of his career. Liszt first learned to play the piano from his father. When the family moved to Vienna, he studied composition from the eminent court composer Salieri, who had previously taught Schubert and Beethoven. At the age of eleven, Liszt gave his first concert, and a year later he played in public again. The great Beethoven was in the audience and, after the concert, kissed the young boy on the forehead.

When Liszt was thirteen, the family moved to Paris, and he began to tour Europe as a piano virtuoso. His incredible technique amazed audiences everywhere, and by his late teens he had become famous as a showman. His striking looks, flamboyant manner, and reputation as a womanizer did not hurt his career a bit.

At the age of twenty, he heard the great violinist Paganini for the first time. Liszt was enormously impressed and vowed to attain the same level of mastery on his own instrument. This he did, and he was soon known as the "Paganini of the piano." Liszt's fingers were unusually long and thin, and he could easily play wide stretches. He soon became the greatest pianist of his age. Some people thought that he was inspired by the devil.

Over the next few years, Liszt developed great friendships with Berlioz and Chopin. He also began living with the Countess Marie d'Agoult, a novelist who published under the name Daniel Stern. She left her husband to live with Liszt, and together they had three children (one of whom, Cosima, later left *her* husband to live with Wagner). They traveled frequently around Europe, and he continued to perform to ever more enthusiastic crowds and to compose prolifically.

A typically Romantic painting of Liszt at the piano. Those listening (from left to right) are the great figures of nineteenth-century music and literature: the poet Alfred de Musset, authors Victor Hugo and George Sand, fabled violinist Paganini and composer Rossini, and author Marie d'Agoult, Liszt's common-law wife. The entire scene is dominated by the almost surreal figure of Ludwig van Beethoven.

Between 1848 and 1858, Liszt completed most of the compositions upon which his fame as a composer now rests. The most important of these are twelve symphonic poems and two programmatic symphonies, as well as a large number of works for solo piano.

In 1861, Liszt suddenly resigned from his position at Weimar and went to Rome to begin religious studies. After four years, he became a member of the church hierarchy and was officially known as an *abbé*. He now undertook several religious compositions, writing psalm settings, Masses, and an oratorio.

Toward the end of his life, Liszt turned again to compositions for solo piano and completed some remarkable pieces that anticipate the shifting harmonies and Impressionism of the early twentieth century. Liszt died in 1886.

With his extraordinary personality, Liszt stood at the center of Romanticism. He was a complex of contradictions: a diabolical figure who sought spiritual solace in the Church, a flamboyant and narcissistic performer who devoted himself to the music of others, a composer whose works range from the flashy and brilliant to the quietly searching.

Liszt's Music

Together with Wagner, Liszt is regarded as one of the most avant-garde composers of the mid-Romantic era. He experimented with unusual harmonies and chords, and in some cases he seemed to ignore the rules of traditional harmony.

Liszt's piano music is quite varied. Much of it is extremely difficult to play. Schumann once said that there were only "ten or twelve people in the world" who had the technical ability to play Liszt's music. Berlioz said that the only person who could play it was Liszt himself. Runs and rippling octaves surround the melody; cascades of notes tumble from top to bottom of the keyboard; often it sounds as though there must be more than one person playing. Liszt's *Transcendental Études* contain some of the most difficult piano music ever written.

One of Liszt's masterpieces is the superb Piano Sonata in B minor, written in one long movement. It has three themes, which are stated at the outset and reappear in different forms throughout the piece. This technique is known as **thematic transformation**. Liszt used it in many of his other compositions.

A number of Liszt's piano pieces are in dance forms, including waltzes, mazurkas, polonaises, and Hungarian dances. Liszt's contribution to the beginning of nationalism in music was a large body of Hungarian music, including the well-known *Hungarian Rhapsodies*.

Liszt influenced several generations of pianists and composers. His phenomenal technique and demanding piano writing expanded the boundaries of what was considered possible on the piano. His symphonic poems inspired other composers to write works in the same form. His Hungarian music contributed to the nationalistic movement. And his novel approach to harmony foreshadowed the great harmonic revolution of the twentieth century.

LISTENING GUIDE

Franz Liszt (1811–1886)

Transcendental Étude No. 10 in F minor

Date of composition: 1839

Tempo: *Allegro agitato molto*
("Fast and very agitated")

Meter: $\frac{2}{4}$

Duration: 4:06

Complete CD Collection: 2, Track 35

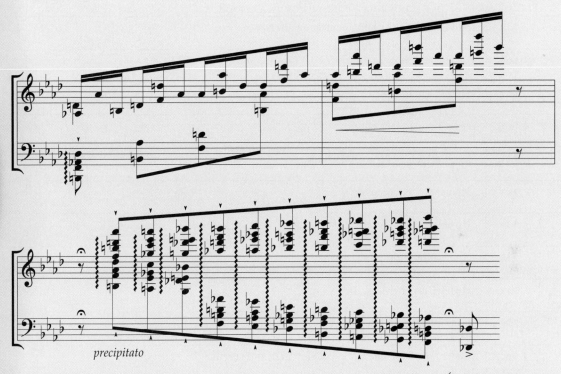

from Liszt, *Transcendental Étude No. 10*

The *Transcendental Études* were first composed in 1826, when Liszt was fifteen years old. But, as with much of Liszt's music, the works were revised and reissued later. Though the music was extremely difficult to perform in its earlier version, Liszt's revisions made it even more demanding. Number 10 in particular was described as being "ten times more difficult than before." Contemporaries of Liszt were amazed by this music and by Liszt's own performances of it.

In this work, Liszt explores every possibility of demanding piano technique, including doubled octave passages, rapid skips, intricate bass tracery, fast runs, massive chords, and widely separated hands. It also has some unusual harmonies and a great sense of *surging*, with occasional slightly quieter passages serving only to heighten the intensity of the remainder. The power and strength of the music are astounding.

35	0:00	Starts quietly with fast descending runs.
	0:07	Crescendo, then quiet.
	0:14	Loud and wild.
	0:23	Descending runs again.
	0:26	Surging melody in octaves in right hand, hectic passagework in left hand.
	0:53	Agitated alternation of short phrases.
	1:07	Heavy chordal melody in bass, fireworks in right hand.
	1:18	Suddenly quiet, surging melody again, crescendo.
	1:32	Descending runs again.
	1:39	Slow down, quieter.
	1:41	Crescendo and speed up.
	1:51	Surging melody again, crescendo.
	2:03	Moment of tenderness.
	2:18	Huge crescendo, massive climax.
	2:58	Alternating short phrases again.
	3:12	Heavy bass chords again.
	3:29	Contrary motion; stop.
	3:33	Coda. Speed up; alternation of very high and very low.
	3:55	Massive ending chords.

Verdi and Wagner

Both Giuseppe Verdi and Richard Wagner were born in 1813. Each transformed the operatic traditions he had received from the past to create new forms, and each became the musical symbol of his own country: Verdi for Italy, Wagner for Germany. In 1842, each composer had his first success. Wagner completed his first major masterpiece in 1850, Verdi in 1851. From then on, both composers turned out one great score after another, working fruitfully into old age. Wagner's last work was written when he was nearly seventy, Verdi's as he approached eighty. Together they made opera the central genre of mid-Romanticism.

Giuseppe Verdi (1813–1901)

In Italy today, Verdi symbolizes opera. Many Italian shopkeepers, vineyard workers, professors, and politicians can sing Verdi arias by heart.

Verdi was born in a small village in northern Italy, where his father ran an inn. As a boy, he played the organ at the village church and conducted the town band in the nearby small town of Busseto. One of the wealthy merchants of Busseto took him into his own home and later sent him to Milan to study music.

Milan was the center of Italian opera and the home of the famous opera house called La Scala. Verdi resolved to become an opera composer. First he went back to Busseto and married his patron's daughter. He was twenty-three, his new wife sixteen. Filled with hope, he returned to Milan and threw himself into composition. But tragedy struck. Within two years, the couple's two babies died; then Verdi's young wife, the girl he had romped with in the hills and fields of the Italian countryside, also died.

Verdi was overcome by depression and decided to compose no more. One night, however, the concert manager at La Scala made him take home a new libretto (opera text) called *Nabucco* (*Nebuchadnezzar*). According to Verdi's own account, the libretto first fell open on the chorus of the Jewish prisoners who mourn their native land by the waters of Babylon. "I was much moved," he said, "because the verses were almost a paraphrase from the Bible, the reading of which had always delighted me." He spent the whole night reading and rereading the libretto, and by the next day he was already working on his new opera. *Nabucco* was produced at La Scala in 1842 and was a great success. It brought Verdi fame throughout Italy, and by the end of the decade his name was known around the world.

Verdi followed *Nabucco* with a string of wonderful operas. During the next eleven years, he wrote fifteen operas, including *Rigoletto* (1851), *Il Trovatore* (1853), and *La Traviata* (1853). By now, Verdi was a wealthy man. He bought a country estate near his home town and lived the life of a country gentleman. He married his second wife, a singer who had starred in his early operas, and their deep and devoted relationship lasted for nearly half a century.

Verdi's pace of composition relaxed, but the depth and richness of his music only increased. In the 1860s and 1870s he wrote three fine operas, including the great *Aida* (1871).

Although he spoke of retirement several times, Verdi was persuaded in his seventies to tackle two Shakespearean projects. The results of this final surge of creativity were two of his greatest masterpieces: the tragedy *Otello* (1887) and the comedy *Falstaff* (1893).

During his life, Verdi became a national symbol. Verdi's name became a rallying cry for the Italian nationalist movement. After the independence of the country in 1870, Verdi was named an honorary member of the new parliament. And when he died, at the age of eighty-eight, Italy declared a national day of mourning.

Giuseppe Verdi.

Verdi's Music

Verdi wrote in genres other than opera. There are several choral works, including a magnificent Requiem. He also wrote several songs and a fine string quartet. But it is on his remarkable operas that his reputation rests. During his long life, he completed twenty-eight full-length operas, among which are some of the best-loved in the world.

What is the secret of Verdi's success? First and foremost, the secret lies in his melodies. His gift for vocal writing has never been exceeded, and singers and listeners alike love his soaring vocal lines. The second special element is rhythm. Verdi specialized in writing stirring rhythms that can set the heart pounding. But finally, the true essence of a Verdi opera is in the human drama. Verdi constantly sought out dramatic situations, full of strong emotional resonance, violent contrasts, and quick action.

As Verdi continued to compose, from the 1840s to the 1880s, his style became more fluid. In place of the set aria-and-recitative style of earlier Italian opera, Verdi created a continuing musical flow through which the drama could unfold naturally. What held this unfolding in place was the orchestra. Throughout a story, Verdi's orchestra binds the voices together, keeps the action moving, and supplies rich and colorful harmonies to underpin moments of climax or poignancy. Verdi also uses the orchestra to sound out musical motives that have symbolic content or to refer to people in the story as the drama progresses. In these ways—his use of the orchestra for continuity and his fashioning of "reference" motives with specific meanings—Verdi approached the style of Wagner, though Wagner employed these techniques in very different ways, as we shall see.

LISTENING GUIDE

GIUSEPPE VERDI (1813–1901)

Otello (Excerpt)

Date of composition: 1887
Duration: 6:17

Complete CD Collection: 2, Tracks 36–39

*O*tello was the last of Verdi's tragic operas. It was inspired by Shakespeare's play *Othello*. Dramatic interest in this work lies not so much in the tragic plot as in the portrayal of human emotions. The story revolves around the evil manipulations of Iago, an ensign in the Venetian army. He is intensely jealous of the promotion of his friend Cassio to a high post. Iago is determined to rectify the situation by deceiving Otello and persuading him that Cassio is having an affair with his wife. The flexible style of the music is perfect for catching the changing feelings of the participants in the drama.

The excerpt begins toward the end of Act II, where Iago cleverly tries to convince his commander (Otello) that his rival (Cassio) has romantic designs on Desdemona (Otello's new bride). The scene builds from the lightly accompanied opening and the representation of sleep-talk to a huge orchestral climax of sworn revenge.

36	0:00	[horn, single note]	
IAGO			
	0:04	*Era la notte, Cassio dormia,*	I watched Cassio the other night
		gli stavo accanto.	as he slept.
		Con interrotte voci tradia	All of a sudden he began to mutter
		l'intimo incanto.	what he was dreaming.
		Le labbra lente, lente movea,	Moving his lips slowly, very slowly,
		nell'abbandono del sogno ardente;	I heard him betray his secret thoughts;
	0:40	*e allor dicea, con flebil suono:*	saying in a passionate voice:
	0:48	*"Desdemona soave!*	"My sweetest Desdemona!
		Il nostro amor s'asconda,	let us be careful,
		cauti vegliamo	cautiously hiding our love,
	1:02	*l'estasi del ciel tutto m'innonda!"*	our heavenly rapture!"
	1:14	[more agitated orchestral accompaniment]	
	1:16	*Seguia più vago l'incubo blando;*	Then he moved toward me
		con molle angoscia l'interna imago	and gently caressing
		quasi baciando,	the person in his dreams,
	1:32	*ei disse poscia: "Il rio destino*	he said this: "Oh accursed fortune
		impreco che al Moro ti donò!"	that gave you to the Moor!"
	1:55	*E allora il sogno*	And after his dream,
		in cieco letargo si mutò.	he went calmly back to sleep.
OTELLO			
37	2:17	*Oh, mostruosa colpa!*	Oh, monstrous deed!
IAGO			
		Io non narrai che un sogno …	No, this was only his dreaming …
OTELLO			
	2:22	*Un sogno che rivela un fatto …*	A dream that reveals the truth …
IAGO			
	2:25	*Un sogno che può dar forma*	A dream that may support other
		di prova ad altro indizio.	evidence.

OTELLO

Equal?

What kind of evidence?

[a little slower; horn note]

IAGO

2:37

Talor vedeste
in mano di Desdemona
un tessuto trapunto a fior
e più sottil d'un velo?

Have you ever seen
in Desdemona's hand
a handkerchief decorated with flowers
and of the finest texture?

OTELLO

2:54

È il fazzoletto ch'io le diedi,
pegno primo d'amor.

That is the handkerchief I gave her,
It was my first gift to her.

IAGO

3:01

Quel fazzoletto ieri certo ne son
lo vidi in man di Cassio.

That same handkerchief I swear
I saw in Cassio's hand.

OTELLO

[agitated; furious]

38   3:13

Ah! mille gli
donasse Iddio!
Una è povera preda al furor mio!
Iago, ho il cuore di gelo.
Lungi da me le pietose larve:
Tutto il mio vano amor,
esalo al cielo—
Guardami, ei sparve!
Nelle sue spire d'angue l'idra m'avvince!

Ah! May God give the slave
a thousand lives!
One is all too little for my revenge!
Iago, my heart is ice.
Rise, Vengeance, from your cave:
my deepest love—
I vow to heaven—
look, it's gone!
I yield to tyrannous hate!

3:49

Ah sangue! sangue! sangue!

Oh blood! blood! blood!

[determined]

3:56

Si pel ciel marmoreo giuro!
Per le attorte folgori,
per la Morte e per l'oscuro mar sterminator.
D'ira e d'impeto tremendo,
presto fia che sfolgori questa man
ch'io levo e stendo!

I swear by yonder marble heaven!
and the eternal stars above,
and the darkest sea below,
Never shall my anger cease
until this hand
has brought about my revenge!

IAGO

4:28

Non v'alzate ancor!
Testimon è il Sol ch'io miro;
che m'irradia e inanima,
l'ampia terra e il vasto spiro,
del Creato inter;
che ad Otello io sacro ardenti,
core, braccio ed anima s'anco
ad opere cruenti

No, wait!
Witness Sun, which illumines us;
Earth, on which we live,
you, ambient air that we breathe,
the Creator's breath;
witness that I eagerly give Othello
my heart, my hands, and my soul
to these bloody deeds.

Plate 9:
An eighteenth-century string quartet playing in a middle-class home. Notice the bust of Mozart on the wall.
SOURCE: String Quartet. Color engraving, 18th century, Austrian. Mozart Museum, Prague, Czech Republica. Giraudon/ Art Resource, NY.

Plate 10:
Portrait of the Mozart family from about 1780. Mozart plays a duet with his sister, while his father listens, and his mother is remembered in a painting behind them.
SOURCE: Painting, Baroque, 18th Century. Johann Nepomuk Della Croce. The Mozart Family (1780 – 1781). Oil on canvas. 140 x 186 cm. Mozart House, Salzburg, Austria. Erich Lessing/ Art Resource.

Plate 11: The heroic Napolean Bonaparte, painted in 1800.

SOURCE: Stiftung Preussische Schloesser und Gaerten Berlin-Brandenburg, Schloss Charlottenburg.

Plate 12: An awe-inspiring, almost Impressionist scene by William Turner.

SOURCE: Turner, Joseph Malord William, English (1775 – 1851), Slave Ship (Slavers Throwing Overboard the Dead and Dying, Typhoon Coming On), 1840. Oil on canvas, 90.8 x 122.6 cm. (35-11/16 x 48-5/16 in.) unframed. Henry Lillie Pierce Fund, 19.22. Courtesy, Museum of Fine Arts, Boston. Reproduced with permission. ©2000 Museum of Fine Arts, Boston. All rights reserved. Gift of Joseph W., William B., and Edward H. R. Revere.

Plate 13:
A typically Romantic painting of Liszt at the piano. Those listening (from left to right) are the great figures of nineteenth-century music and literature: the poet Alfred de Musset, authors Victor Hugo and George Sand, fabled violinist Paganini and composter Rossini, and (seated) author Marie d'Agoult, Liszt's common-law wife. The entire scene is dominated by the almost surreal figure of Ludwig van Beethoven.

Plate 14:
A nightmarish evocation by Kokoschka (1914).

SOURCE: Oskar Kokoschka (1886 – 1980). De Windsbraut, 1914. Oil on canvas, 181 x 220 cm. Basel, Kunstmuseum, Archiv fur Kunst und Geschichte, Berlin. ©1998 Artists Rights Society (ARS), New York/ Pro Litteris, Zurich.

Plate 15:
The postmodern
Dolphin Hotel at
Walt Disney World
Resort, Florida,
completed in 1990.
SOURCE: William Taylor/
Arcaid © Disney
Enterprises, Inc.

Plate 16:
Jazz singer Betty
Carter performing in
Carnegie Hall.

	5:01	*s'armi suo voler!*	Let him command!

OTELLO & IAGO

		[duet, rising to a powerful climax]	
39	5:07	*Si pel ciel marmoreo giuro!* *per le attorte folgori,* *per la Morte e per l'oscuro mar sterminator.*	I swear by yonder marble heaven! and eternal stars above, and the darkest sea below,
	5:25	*D'ira e d'impeto tremendo* *presto fia che sfolgori questa man* *ch'io levo e stendo;* *presto fia che sfolgori questa man,* *presto fia che sfolgori questa man*	Never shall my anger cease until this hand has brought about my revenge; until this hand, until this hand
	5:46	*ch'io levo e stendo.*	has brought about my revenge.
	5:53	*Dio vendicator!*	God of vengeance!
		[unaccompanied]	
	5:59	[loud orchestral postlude; brass and timpani; whole orchestra]	
	6:13	[End of Act II]	

Richard Wagner (1813–1883)

Richard Wagner is a perfect example of the contradictions inherent in genius. His importance as a composer was enormous, and his writings on music, literature, and politics exerted a tremendous influence on artistic and intellectual thought throughout the second half of the nineteenth century. Yet he was an appalling egoist, a home-wrecker, and a virulent and outspoken anti-Semite.

Photographic portrait of Richard Wagner in velvet coat and hat.

Wagner was born in Leipzig. His father died when Wagner was an infant, and when his mother married again, Wagner was educated under the influence of his stepfather, who was a writer and an artist. Wagner studied Shakespeare and Homer and was overwhelmed by hearing Beethoven. At Leipzig University he studied music, but, before completing his degree, left to take a job in a small opera house. For the next six years, Wagner learned about opera from the inside, as a chorus director and a conductor. He married an actress, Minna Planer, and composed his own first operas. From the beginning, Wagner wrote his own librettos and was thus able to achieve remarkable cohesion between the drama and the music.

From the beginning, too, Wagner spent more than he earned. In 1839, he was forced to flee Germany rather than end up in debtor's prison. His passport and Minna's had been revoked, so they crossed the border at night and made a harrowing journey to Paris.

The two were extremely poor, and the Paris Opera would not accept Wagner's latest work, *Rienzi*, for production. He made a living by selling some music—and most of Minna's clothes! He also composed another opera, based on the folk tale of *The Flying Dutchman*.

Discouraged by his reception in Paris, Wagner suddenly received news that both *Rienzi* and *The Flying Dutchman* had been accepted for production in Germany. He was overwhelmed with gratitude and swore never to leave his native land again. The operas were a great success. At the première of *Rienzi* at the Dresden opera house, Wagner "cried and laughed at the same time, and hugged everyone he met." At the age of thirty, Wagner was appointed court conductor in Dresden.

The couple was financially comfortable for the first time, and Wagner was able to compose two more operas: *Tannhäuser* (1845) and *Lohengrin* (1848). In both operas, Wagner continued to base his librettos not on historical drama but on folk legend. *Tannhäuser* is the story of a medieval German troubadour; *Lohengrin* is based on Grimm's fairy tale of the Swan Knight of the Holy Grail.

After joining a failed coup against the monarchy in 1848, Wagner again had to leave the country. And despite his earlier vow, the next twelve years were years of exile. He and Minna settled in Zurich, and from this period date his most important writings: an essay called *The Art Work of the Future* (1849) and a book entitled *Opera and Drama* (1851). In these works, he called for a renewal of the artistic ideals of Greek antiquity, in which poetry, drama, philosophy, and music would be combined into a single work of art: the "complete art work," as Wagner called it. Music and words should be completely interwoven in a retelling of old myths, which could carry the resonance of profound human truth. This new type of opera was known as **music drama**.

Wagner spent the next thirty-five years fulfilling this vision. But before he did so, he revealed a far less attractive side of his personality by publishing a vicious anti-Semitic essay entitled *Jewishness in Music*. He attacked the music of Mendelssohn and other Jewish composers and went on to call for the removal of the entire Jewish community ("this destructive foreign element") from Germany.

Wagner next started composing the poetry and the music for the largest musical project of the entire Romantic period: his cycle of music dramas entitled *The Ring of the Nibelungs*. This was to be a series of four long operas based on medieval German legend, involving gods and goddesses, dwarfs and giants, and human heroes. The central symbol of the cycle is a magic ring made of stolen gold that dooms all who possess it.

Wagner set about this enormous task with no hope of performance. Halfway through, he broke off work to write two other operas unconnected to the Ring cycle: *Tristan and Isolde* (1859) and *The Mastersingers of Nuremberg* (1867). He was in the grip of an unstoppable creative urge. Speaking of these years later in life, he said: "The towering fires of life burned in me with such unutterable heat and brilliance that they almost consumed me."

He had affairs with other women: the wife of a French patron (her husband threatened to put a bullet through Wagner's head), the wife of a wealthy merchant who lent him money (she was the inspiration for *Tristan and Isolde*), and the new wife of a good friend, the conductor and enthusiastic Wagner supporter Hans von Bülow. Cosima von Bülow was the daughter of Franz Liszt, another loyal friend of Wagner's. The affair gradually deepened, and Wagner and Minna separated. But it was not until eight years later that Wagner and Cosima could be married, after overcoming the objections of both Liszt and Hans von Bülow. By then, the couple had already had two daughters and a son. Cosima was thirty-two, Wagner fifty-seven.

During these last eight years, Wagner had despaired of having his new operas produced, but his hopes were suddenly realized beyond his wildest dreams. In 1864 an eighteen-year-old youth ascended the throne of Bavaria as King Ludwig II. Having read Wagner's writings and admired his operas, King Ludwig was an ardent fan of Wagner's. He was also in love with Wagner. "An earthly being cannot match up to a divine spirit," the king wrote to Wagner. "But it can love; it can venerate. You are my first, my only love, and always will be."

For the rest of Wagner's life, the young king met his extravagant financial demands with unparalleled generosity. Wagner's work prospered. He was able to finish the gigantic *Ring* cycle, and he made plans for a new theater in which the four-evening event could be staged. These plans finally came to fruition in a new opera house in Bayreuth (pronounced "BYE-royt"), a small town in Bavaria.

On February 13, 1883, Wagner died of a heart attack. Since Wagner's death, his memory has inspired a cult. Worshippers make the pilgrimage to Bayreuth for the annual Wagner festival. Wagner societies exist in countries around the world. The Bayreuth Festival has been run by members of Wagner's family since his death.

Wagner's Music

Wagner's only important works are for the opera stage. His first two operas, *Rienzi* and *The Flying Dutchman*, are in the tradition of German Romantic opera, with grand scenes and with separate arias, duets, ensembles, and choruses. Already, however, we see Wagner writing his own librettos and concentrating on human beings as symbols of grand ideas. (Verdi, by contrast, concentrated on human beings for the expression of their humanity.) By the time of *Tannhäuser* and *Lohengrin*, Wagner had developed his poetic skill and found fertile ground in ancient legend. His poetry is terse and powerful. In both operas, the individual items (aria, recitative, chorus) are less distinct in musical style, and there is much more musical continuity.

For the works up to *Lohengrin*, we can still use the term "opera"; the later works are music dramas. In the *Ring* cycle (made up of four music dramas: *The Rhinegold*, *The Valkyries*, *Siegfried*, and *The Twilight of the Gods*), Wagner developed his technique of continuity to the fullest. The music is absolutely continuous, and the orchestra carries the main musical content. The voices sing in an **arioso** style (that is, halfway between speechlike recitative and lyrical aria), blending into the instrumental fabric. *Tristan and Isolde* and *The Mastersingers*, which Wagner composed in the middle of *The Ring*, and *Parsifal*, which he composed after it, also display this technique.

The orchestra is central to Wagner's music, and he wrote for a large one. He particularly enjoyed using brass instruments. He even invented a new musical instrument to cover the gap between the horns and the trombones. This instrument is known as a **Wagner tuba**. The orchestra of the *Ring* uses four of them. Their sound is rounder, a little deeper, and more solemn than that of the horns.

Musical continuity in Wagner's music dramas is also achieved through harmonic means. In this, too, Wagner was a revolutionary. Instead of ending each phrase with a cadence, he tends to melt the end of one phrase into the beginning of the next. And whereas most music of the time is clearly in a specific key, Wagner's music is tonally ambiguous. Often it is hard to say which key is being used at any one point. In *Tristan and Isolde*, for example, there seems to be no fixed key or clear-cut cadence until the end of the work! This perfectly suits the sense of unfulfillment and longing that is the subject of the drama.

Finally, Wagner's music depends on a technique that he himself invented (though it might be seen as the logical outcome of earlier musical developments). This technique is the use of **leitmotiv** (pronounced "LIGHT-moteef"). This is a German word that means "leading motive." A leitmotiv is a musical phrase or fragment that carries associations with a person, object, or idea in the drama.

You may remember that Berlioz used a recurrent theme (*idée fixe*) to refer to the beloved in his *Symphonie fantastique*. And other composers used themes associated with particular characters in their operas. Wagner's leitmotiv technique is different. First, leitmotivs can refer to many things other than a person. Leitmotivs in Wagner's music dramas are associated with a spear, longing, fate, and the magic ring itself. Second, Wagner's leitmotivs are flexible, undergoing musical transformation in the course of the drama. Finally, Wagner uses his leitmotivs like threads in a tapestry. They can be combined, interwoven, contrasted, or blended to create an infinity of allusions and meanings.

Wagner revolutionized music by his brilliant writing for orchestra, by making the orchestra the central "character" of his dramas, and by his development of the leitmotiv technique. In addition, Wagner's continuity of musical flow and tonally ambiguous harmonic style laid the foundation for the completely new language of twentieth-century music.

LISTENING GUIDE

RICHARD WAGNER (1813–1883)

Prelude and *Liebestod* from the Music
  Drama *Tristan und Isolde*

Date of composition: 1865
Orchestration: 3 flutes, 2 oboes, English horn,
  2 clarinets, bass clarinet, 3 bassoons,
  4 horns, 3 trumpets, 3 trombones, tuba,
  timpani, harp, violins I and II, violas, cellos,
  double basses; voice
Duration: 18:03

Complete CD Collection: 3, Tracks 1–5

Like most of Wagner's works, *Tristan und Isolde* is based on a medieval legend. Tristan and Isolde are lovers, and the opera is about their passion and final union in death. The Prelude and *Liebestod*, respectively the beginning and the end of the opera, are often excerpted from the work. The Prelude introduces the main leitmotiv of the work, an upward-striving phrase that never quite resolves. This phrase saturates the whole Prelude, giving it a strong sense of urgency and yearning. In addition, there is a rising cello theme, closely based on the opening leitmotiv.

Wagner creates a feeling of constant flowing motion. This feeling is enhanced by the harmony. Although the music remains (barely) anchored to a tonal center, the harmony is so free that it also seems to float and surge loosely above this anchor.

Liebestod ("Love-Death") comes at the very end of the opera. At the moment of reunion with Isolde, Tristan dies; Isolde then also dies, joining him in the transcendence of death. Like the Prelude, *Liebestod* is based primarily on two leitmotivs: the "love-death" music heard when the voice enters, and the motive of "transcendental bliss" first played by the flutes a third of the way through.

Toward the end, the "yearning" leitmotiv from the beginning of the Prelude recurs, but here, for the first time, it ends in harmonic resolution. It is as though only the final chords can resolve the urgent longing established at the outset of the work.

The large orchestra is used for delicate passages as well as for enormous climaxes. And the voice soars in and out and over the orchestral fabric, as though it were an additional thread in the overall texture of the work.

	PRELUDE	
1	0:00	"Yearning" leitmotiv; cellos, woodwinds. Pause.

	0:30	Leitmotiv repeated at slightly higher pitch. Pause.
	0:55	Third statement of leitmotiv at an even higher pitch. Pause.
	1:18	Extension on woodwinds.
	1:32	Reduction of leitmotiv to two notes; strings, winds.
	1:43	Loud deceptive cadence, pizzicato in bass.
2	1:53	Cello theme, clearly based on "yearning" leitmotiv but constantly striving higher. Pizzicato bass accompaniment.

	2:26	Continuation on strings.
	3:20	Surging crescendos.
3	3:37	Development of cello theme on woodwinds.
	4:03	Reduction of cello theme (strings and woodwinds).
	4:28	Surging; strings, horns, woodwinds.
	5:27	Further crescendos; long flowing section.
	6:29	Rising violin passages, getting increasingly intense.

	7:17	Climax and loud intense passage.
	7:48	Orchestral climax, very loud; brass.
	7:58	Orchestra winds down.
4	8:10	Return to "yearning" leitmotiv.
	8:30	Repetitions of leitmotiv at higher pitches.
	9:09	Climax, followed by decrescendo.
	9:26	Fragments.
	9:52	Timpani roll, English horn, "yearning" leitmotiv.
	10:13	Timpani; bass clarinet; "yearning" leitmotiv stripped down; quiet.
	10:31	Double basses only; ending with two pizzicato notes; very quiet.

LIEBESTOD

"Love-death" leitmotiv in voice, continues throughout section.

etc.

5	0:00	*Mild und leise wie er lächelt,*	How quietly and tenderly he smiles,
		[String tremolos; trombones]	
	0:16	*wie das Auge hold er öffnet,* *seht ihr's, Freunde? Seht ihr's nicht?*	How sweetly he opens his eyes! Do you see, my friends? Do you not see?
		[Tremolos continue; horn]	
	0:41	*Immer lichter, wie er leuchtet,*	How brightly he shines,
		[Sudden crescendo, high notes on "leuchtet" ("shines")]	
	0:55	*stern-umstrahlet hoch sich hebt?*	How high he soars, surrounded by stars?
		[Harp; high on "hoch" ("high")]	
	1:10	*Seht ihr's nicht?* *Wie das Herz ihm mutig schwillt,*	Do you not see? How valiantly his heart swells,
		[Loud]	
	1:25	*voll und hehr im Busen ihm quillt?*	Majestic and full, beats in his breast?
	1:41	*Wie den Lippen, sonnig mild,* *süsser Atem sanft entweht?*	How his lips, soft and gentle, Exhale sweet, delightful breath?
		[Horns, woodwinds, "bliss" leitmotiv on flutes (continues throughout section)]	

etc.

2:15	*Freunde! Seht! Fühlt und seht ihr's nicht?*	Friends! Look! Do you not feel it and see it?
2:35	*Höre ich nur diese Weise,* *die so wundervoll und leise,* [Sense of return to opening; surging]	Do I alone hear this melody, Which, so wondrously tender,
2:58	*Wonne klagend, alles sagend,* *mild versöhnend aus ihm tönend,* [Voice takes over "bliss" leitmotiv]	Softly mourning, saying all, Gently forgiving, sounds from him,
3:20	*in mich dringet, auf sich schwinget,* *hold erhallend um mich klinget?* [Speeding up; crescendo]	Penetrates within me, rising up, Sweetly echoes and rings around me?
3:43	*Heller schallend, mich umwallend,* *sind es Wellen sanfter Lüfte?* *Sind es Wogen wonniger Düfte?* [Repeated phrase in orchestra ... rising ever higher]	Sounding yet more clearly, surrounding me, Are they waves of holy breezes? Are they clouds of wondrous fragrance?

4:08	*Wie sie schwellen, mich umrauschen,*
	soll ich atmen, soll ich lauschen?
	Soll ich schlürfen, untertauchen?
	Süss in Düften mich verhauchen?
	In dem wogenden Schwall, in dem
	    tönenden Schall,
	
	[More and more agitated]
		As they swell and roar around me,
		Shall I breathe them in, shall I listen to them?
		Shall I sip them, dive in among them?
		Sweetly expire amidst the fragrance?
		In the surging swell, in the ringing
		    sounds,

4:40	*in des Welt-Atems wehendem All* *ertrinken, versinken* [Huge climax; decrescendo. Dramatic change of harmony]	In the world's breath, encompassing everything, To drown, to sink
5:25	*unbewusst höchste Lust!* [Last word floats ... Slow. Decrescendo. "Bliss" leitmotiv very slowly leads to:]	Unconscious—what utter bliss!
6:09	Return of "yearning" leitmotiv from Prelude	
6:24	Resolution chord	
6:31	Final chords	

The Nationalist Composers

One of the consequences of Romanticism was the growth of nationalism throughout Europe. We have seen how this affected some of the composers we have already discussed. Verdi became a national hero. Wagner became a symbol of German ethnic pride.

But there were other composers whose music responded even more obviously to the nationalist movements in their own countries. They did this in several ways. First, they wrote operas in their own native languages, such as Russian or Czech. Second, they based operas and symphonic poems on national folk stories and on descriptions of nature. Finally, composers often wove their own countries' folk tunes into their compositions to give their music a distinct national identity. There were many countries represented by nationalist composers in the nineteenth century, including France, Spain, and Moravia, but the most important were Russia, Bohemia (now part of the Czech Republic), and Scandinavia.

RUSSIA   The nationalist movement in music was first felt in Russia, where music had been dominated entirely by foreign influence. Starting in the middle of the nineteenth century, Russian composers began to write operas in their own language, on Russian themes, and they often based their librettos on literary works by the great Russian writers of the time. The most important Russian nationalist was Modest Mussorgsky (1839–1881), whose works include the opera *Boris Godunov*, based on a story by the Russian writer Alexander Pushkin; the series of pieces known as *Pictures at an Exhibition*, which describe paintings hanging in a gallery; and the symphonic poem *Night on Bald Mountain*.

BOHEMIA   The two principal Bohemian composers of the nineteenth century were Bedřich Smetana (1824–1884) and Antonin Dvořák (1841–1904). Smetana's most famous work is the symphonic poem *The Moldau*, which describes the flow of a river across the Bohemian countryside. It cleverly combines depictions of nature with feelings of national pride. Dvořák wrote symphonies, concertos, operas, choral works, and chamber music. Chief among these are the Ninth (*New World*) Symphony (which he wrote in America), the Cello Concerto, and his *Slavonic Dances* for orchestra. The *New World* Symphony combines American themes with Bohemian folk melodies. Dvořák hoped it would inspire American composers to become nationalists. "America can have her own music," he said.

LISTENING GUIDE

BEDŘICH SMETANA (1824–1884)

Symphonic Poem, *The Moldau*

Date of composition: 1874
Orchestration: Piccolo, 2 flutes, 2 oboes, 2 bassoons, 4 French horns, 2 trumpets, 3 trombones, tuba, timpani, bass drum, triangle, cymbals, harp, strings
Tempo: *Allegro commodo non agitato* ("Fast but comfortable and not agitated")
Meter: $\frac{6}{8}$
Key: E minor
Duration: 12:46

Complete CD Collection: 3, Tracks 6–15

The Moldau is a majestic tone poem that combines several components of Romanticism: it is descriptive program music, and it expresses an interest in nature and, above all, nationalism. The title of the work refers to a powerful river. This piece is part of a cycle, *Má Vlast* (*My Country*), which depicts six different scenes of Smetana's native Bohemia.

Smetana employs the rich color of a large orchestra: Note the use of harp, tuba, piccolo, bass drum, cymbals, and triangle. With this vivid palette he creates scenes of contrasting atmosphere. Smetana's program describes the river Moldau beginning from two small streams, growing in size, and then flowing through the countryside, in the moonlight, over rapids, and past an ancient castle, finally disappearing into the distance. These distinct scenes are clearly audible. Throughout, the flowing water is suggested by smooth stepwise melodies.

		THE TWO SPRINGS
		[This section acts as an introduction, a brief prelude before we actually reach the river.]
6	0:00	Smooth running line in the two flutes, *p*, representing the two springs. Sparse accompaniment of pizzicato violins and high harp suggests a delicate stream.
	0:40	The lower strings enter on a long-held dominant chord, building a feeling of expectation.

		THE RIVER
	1:00	Sense of arrival as the dominant chord resolves to the tonic, accented by pizzicato lower strings and triangle.
7	1:06	River theme, E minor, a songlike melody, smooth and stepwise, and with longer note values providing a gentle rocking motion. Swirling sixteenth notes act as accompaniment, adding to the depth of the river.

		HUNTING IN THE FOREST
8	2:59	The four horns play in chordal harmony, *f*; accented repeated notes; then an up-and-down melody. Winds and lower strings pick up the leaping melody, violins continue the flowing sixteenth notes. Decrescendo to repeated notes, leading into:

		PEASANT WEDDING
9	4:03	Simple rhythms and motives evoke a country dance, *p*. Short phrases and homophonic texture, G Major. Repeated notes fade into:

		MOONLIGHT: DANCE OF THE WATER NYMPHS (TRANQUILLY)
10	5:39	Still in major key, *pp*; sustained chords.
11	6:06	High melody of even, stately half notes in muted violins. Accompaniment of sixteenth notes and graceful ascending harp arpeggios. Gradual increase in dynamics and level of activity; more instruments and new rhythms added.
	7:46	Crescendo, aggressive sounds, brass enter with staccato chords. Timpani rolls and trumpet fanfares accentuate the growing intensity. Accelerating runs of sixteenth notes lead into:
12	8:38	The return of the river theme. But the waters suddenly turn turbulent.
		THE RAPIDS OF ST. JOHN
13	9:29	Ascending minor scales alternate in the low brass and low strings, *ff*. Jagged, piercing arpeggios in the piccolos. Both outline harsh dissonant chords. Timpani rolls and cymbal crashes of increasing speed suggest violently cresting waves. Gradual shortening of the phrase lengths adds to building intensity and leads to:
14	10:43	An accelerated return of the river theme, now in *major* and loud; the river is more powerful than ever.
		THE ANCIENT CASTLE VYŠEHRAD
15	11:13	Chordal brass melody, harmonized by the full brass sections, *ff* the tempo is stately and broad.
	11:31	Bright cadential chords, in arpeggios like a fanfare; the ending section is triumphal and in major.
	12:02	Final decrescendo, still with the rocking motion of the river theme, as the Moldau disappears in the distance, *pp*. Full orchestra for the strong closing chords, *ff*.

SCANDINAVIA Norway produced the most famous Scandinavian nationalist composer in Edvard Grieg (1843–1907). Grieg specialized in piano miniatures inspired by Norwegian tunes. His well-known orchestral *Peer Gynt* Suite was written for the play of the same name by the Norwegian writer Henrik Ibsen. The leading composer of Finland was Jan Sibelius (1865–1957). He wrote seven superb symphonies and a deeply emotional string quartet, but his most famous work is the symphonic poem *Finlandia* (1899), whose intense national flavor made it an immense success throughout Europe.

Pyotr Ilyich Tchaikovsky (1840–1893)

The Russian composer Pyotr Ilyich Tchaikovsky wrote operas in Russian based on works of Russian literature and also made use of Russian folk songs—but he was not as committed a nationalist as some of his contemporaries. It may be partly for this reason that he achieved an international success.

Tchaikovsky was the son of a mining engineer and a mother of French background, to whom he was very close. He had piano lessons as a child and did some composing, but he turned to music as his main emotional outlet only after his mother died when he was fourteen. Tchaikovsky began to earn a living as a government clerk at the age of nineteen, but when the new St. Petersburg Music Conservatory was founded, he quit his job and entered the Conservatory as a full-time student. A family friend described him as "poor but profoundly happy" at having chosen music as a career. His talents were such that, a year after graduating, he was appointed professor at the music conservatory in Moscow. From that time on, he devoted his life to music.

In Moscow, he met many other composers and publishers and flourished in the lively atmosphere of the cosmopolitan city. He also traveled abroad. He wrote articles and a book on music and composed prolifically.

All this time, however, Tchaikovsky lived with a secret: He was gay. He was tormented by self-hatred and the fear of being exposed. In 1877, at the age of thirty-seven, he suddenly decided to get married. Partly, he may have felt that this step might "cure" him of his nature; partly, he may have thought he needed the cover. The marriage was an instant disaster. Tchaikovsky fled, attempted suicide, and had a nervous breakdown.

After some months of convalescence, Tchaikovsky gradually recovered and turned once more to music. Both his Fourth Symphony and his opera *Eugene Onyegin* date from this time, and both contain powerful reflections of his emotional state.

A strange turn of events helped to provide emotional and financial support for Tchaikovsky. A wealthy widow named Madame von Meck decided to become his patron. She said she would commission some pieces and provide the composer with an annual income. There was only one condition: The two must never meet. This suited Tchaikovsky perfectly, and for the next thirteen years, Madame von Meck and Tchaikovsky carried on an intense personal relationship without ever seeing each other. They shared their innermost thoughts, but only by letter, and they wrote to each other every day.

Tchaikovsky in 1888.

Tchaikovsky was able to resign his teaching post, and he composed a great deal of music during those years. In 1890, Madame von Meck suddenly broke off the relationship and the patronage. No explanation was offered, though her family may have put pressure on her to direct her funds elsewhere. Tchaikovsky was deeply hurt, but by now he had a substantial income from his music, and the Russian czar had provided him with a life pension.

In his last years, Tchaikovsky wrote some of his best-known music, including a ballet entitled *The Nutcracker* and his Sixth Symphony, subtitled *Pathétique*. Tchaikovsky died in 1893, apparently of cholera.

Tchaikovsky's Music

Tchaikovsky's music is highly emotional. It surges with passion and appeals directly to the senses. The range of expression is very great, from the depths of despair to the height of joy. There is sensuousness, delicacy, nobility, tenderness, and fire. *The Nutcracker* is one of the most popular ballet scores in the world, though it is followed closely by *Sleeping Beauty* and *Swan Lake*, both also by Tchaikovsky. The Fourth and Sixth Symphonies are deeply emotional utterances, and his operas, such as *Eugene Onyegin* and *The Queen of Spades*, though less well known, are powerfully dramatic works. Tchaikovsky also wrote three piano concertos as well as a violin concerto that enraptures audiences every time it is played.

Tchaikovsky used an orchestra of moderate size; he never went to the extremes of some other Romantic composers. But he was very interested in orchestral color. There is little in music to match the stirring brass fanfare at the beginning of the Fourth Symphony or the paired clarinets at the beginning of the Sixth. For "The Dance of the Sugar-Plum Fairy" in *The Nutcracker*, Tchaikovsky contrasts the delicate shimmery sound of the celesta with the deep richness of a bass clarinet.

Tchaikovsky was a master of melody. Some of his tunes have become a part of the Western consciousness, featured in famous popular songs or as soundtracks to movies. He sometimes used folk tunes, but most of his melodies came from his own inexhaustible lyrical gift. Tchaikovsky was a Russian composer, as he always insisted, but his music speaks to millions of people who have never even been to Russia.

LISTENING GUIDE

PYOTR ILYICH TCHAIKOVSKY

Scene from Act I of the Ballet *Swan Lake*

Date of composition: 1876
Orchestration: 2 flutes, 2 oboes, 2 clarinets, 2 bassoons, 4 horns, 2 trumpets, 3 trombones, tuba, timpani, harp, strings
Tempo: *Moderato* (Moderate)
Meter: $\frac{4}{4}$
Key: B minor
Duration: 3:12

Complete CD Collection: 3, Track 16

Tchaikovsky's ballet *Swan Lake* contains some wonderful music. This was the composer's first major ballet score, which he completed in 1876. It is full of stirring melodies, gorgeous orchestration, and a masterly sense of atmosphere. The story is derived from a Russian folk tale and, like all ballet stories, is relatively simple: A Prince falls in love with a woman who, like her companions, has been turned into a swan. This scene depicts the swans gliding majestically on a moonlit lake. The principal theme is presented with ever increasing richness and passion.

16	0:00	The strings set the scene (ripples on the moonlit lake?) by playing *tremolo*. This is a technique of moving the bow back and forth rapidly on the strings. We also hear the harp. Both the harp and the tremolo strings are heard throughout this movement.
	0:04	With the harp and strings in the background, a solo oboe plays the gliding swan theme.
	0:30	Continuation of the theme. The music rises and falls. You can still hear the harp.
	1:02	Horns come in loud and proud with the theme, accompanied by strings and the timpani.

1:27	Woodwinds set up a triplet accompaniment.
1:30	Continuation of theme on high strings, accompanied by the woodwinds and pizzicato basses.
1:51	A new extension of the theme is heard.
2:05	Low brass instruments are added, crescendo …
2:18	Now trumpets too! *More* crescendo …
2:25	Just when you think the climax is coming, the strings break into a descending pattern, continued down by the trombones until:
2:32	Wham! *Now* comes the climax. The whole orchestra plays *fff*. (You can hear the timpani rolls underneath). Continued by the mass of strings with punctuation by brass and timpani strokes.
2:45	Woodwinds and violins. Less loud.
2:52	Cellos, basses, and bassoons. Less loud still. Slowing down.
3:00	Final notes. Quieter still. You can still hear the tremolo strings (and see the shimmering of the water in your mind's eye).

LATE ROMANTICISM

Toward the end of the nineteenth century, a new atmosphere reigned in Europe and the United States. Independence and unification brought stability to many countries, and there were moves toward greater democracy, with monarchies being replaced by parliamentary governments. Free compulsory education led to a more educated public. Commerce and industry were central preoccupations, and a more down-to-earth attitude replaced the dreamy fantasyland of high Romanticism.

Johannes Brahms as a young man.

The major composers of late Romanticism were Johannes Brahms, Giacomo Puccini, and Gustav Mahler. Each reflected the new atmosphere in a different way. Brahms found new force in the rigor of Classic and Baroque musical genres and forms. Puccini wrote dramatic realist operas of acute psychological insight. Mahler created a new synthesis of song and symphony.

Johannes Brahms (1833–1897)

Johannes Brahms was born in Hamburg in 1833. His father was an orchestral and band musician; his mother came from a wealthy family and was forty-four when Brahms was born, a fact that may have colored Brahms's later relationship with Clara Schumann, who was fourteen years older than he.

Brahms was a child prodigy. He gave his first piano recital at the age of ten, and an American entrepreneur tried to book him for a concert tour of the United States, but his piano teacher

refused. Brahms spent much of his youth playing the piano at bars and coffee houses; he also wrote pieces for his father's band. A real turning point for Brahms came when he was twenty and he met Robert Schumann. Brahms played some of his own compositions for the great Romantic master in Schumann's study. After a few minutes, Schumann stopped him and went to fetch Clara. "Now you will hear music such as you have never heard before," he said to her. During the time of Schumann's illness, Brahms and Clara Schumann became very close. Their friendship lasted until Clara's death forty-three years later, one year before Brahms's own.

Throughout his life, Brahms compared himself, mostly unfavorably, with other great composers of the past, especially Beethoven. He said that he felt the presence of Beethoven as "the step of a giant over my shoulder." Because Beethoven was associated above all with symphonic music, it took Brahms twenty years to summon the courage to publish his First Symphony.

Brahms settled in Vienna, the imperial capital, where he made a name for himself as a pianist. "He plays so brightly and clearly," wrote a local musician. "I have never met such talent." He also worked as a conductor. Brahms lived a quiet, reserved life, and although he enjoyed the company of many friends, he also needed a great deal of solitude. He usually hid his feelings. Clara Schumann, who knew him better than anyone else, called him "a riddle."

In 1896, after Clara's death, he wrote one of his most beautiful works, the *Four Serious Songs* for piano and voice on texts from the Bible. The fourth song, with a text from Corinthians, describes the immortality of love: "These three things endure: faith, hope, and love; but the greatest of these is love." A month after Clara's funeral, Brahms was diagnosed with cancer. He died on April 3, 1897, at the age of sixty-four. Large crowds attended his funeral, and messages of sadness poured in from all over Europe.

Brahms's Music

Brahms was a Romantic who expressed himself in Classic and sometimes even Baroque forms; within these forms, his music is highly original. Brahms deliberately avoided the innovative genres of modern music, such as the symphonic poem and music drama, preferring instead more traditional forms. He continued to be conscious of the great achievements of the past. The last movement of his First Symphony makes a deliberate reference to Beethoven's Ninth, and the last movement of his Fourth Symphony uses a Baroque form and is based on a theme by Bach. He adored the human voice, and his Romantic songs follow directly in the line of Schubert and Schumann.

His four symphonies are masterpieces—the first and the fourth powerful and intense, the second and the third more lyrical and serene. We shall study a movement from the Fourth Symphony. The Violin Concerto stands with those of Beethoven, Mendelssohn, and Tchaikovsky as one of the great violin concertos of the nineteenth century. Brahms's two piano concertos are also masterpieces. In all his orchestral works, Brahms used an orchestra not much bigger than Beethoven's, avoiding the huge, showy sounds of Wagner and Liszt. One characteristic of Brahms's style is his thick orchestral textures. He liked to "fill in" the sound between treble and bass with many musical lines, and to double melodies in thirds or sixths. He especially favored instruments that play in the middle range, such as clarinet, viola, and French horn.

This warmth of sound may be found in his chamber music as well. Because he was a fine pianist, Brahms wrote several chamber works for piano and strings, but he also composed some excellent string quartets. His love of rich textures is shown in the two string *quintets* and two string *sextets*. Brahms's solo piano music was written mostly for his own performance. The early pieces are strong and showy, but the later ones are much more delicate and extremely profound.

Brahms composed several choral works. The most important of these is the *German Requiem*, for which Brahms chose his own texts from the German Bible. It was not written for a religious service but for concert performance. Nevertheless, the music is sincere and deeply felt. Brahms was a man who did not believe in organized religion, yet he was privately devout and read every day from the Bible he had owned since childhood.

Brahms has been called a conservative composer because of his adherence to models from the past. Yet he was an innovator in many ways. His rhythms are always complex and interesting, with syncopation and offbeat accents and frequent use of mixed duple and triple meters. And he was a master of variation, in which something familiar is constantly undergoing change. Indeed, in Brahms's music there is very little exact repetition or recapitulation: the music seems to grow organically from beginning to end.

LISTENING GUIDE

JOHANNES BRAHMS (1833–1897)

Fourth Movement from Symphony No. 4
    in E minor

Date of composition: 1885
Duration: 10:36
Orchestration: 2 flutes, 2 oboes, 2 clarinets, 2
    bassoons, contrabassoon, 4 French horns, 2
    trumpets, 3 trombones, timpani, full string section
Tempo: *Allegro energico e passionato* ("Fast,
    energetic, and passionate")
Meter: $\frac{3}{4}$
Key: E minor

Complete CD Collection: 3, Tracks 17–22

The fourth movement of Brahms's Symphony No. 4 is based on a regularly recurring eight-measure harmonic progression. This form is known as a *passacaglia*, a variation form that was popular with Baroque composers. Brahms's use of this form shows how he valued the musical past as a source of inspiration.

The repetitive harmonic element gives the movement a clear and accessible form, and the eight-measure patterns can be followed simply by counting. The harmonic progression is not repeated strictly each time but is used instead as a flexible point of departure. The variations range from pure harmonic chord progressions, as in the initial statement, to melodic ideas.

The initial presentation of the theme is bold, strong, and direct. Although this statement is primarily harmonic—a series of chords—it also has a powerful melodic element, a relentless ascending line that dramatically drops an octave just before the end.

In addition to the element of variation, Brahms organizes the work by grouping the thirty variations into three large sections in the form ABA′ with Coda:

A	B	A′	CODA
Theme, and Variations 1–11	Variations 12–15	Variations 16–30	

Within these large groups, Brahms focuses our attention by grouping similar variations together. Variations that share related ideas are bracketed in the timed description that follows.

A SECTION		
		[minor key, 3/4 meter]
17	0:00	Theme. Strong, measure-long chords, ascending melodic line, brass and woodwinds. (Count the eight measures.)
	0:16	*Variation 1* Also chordal, with timpani rolls and string pizzicatos on the second beat of the measures.
	0:30	*Variation 2* Smooth melody with regular rhythmic values and smooth motion. Flutes join clarinets and oboes in a crescendo.
	0:46	*Variation 3* The regular rhythm of the melody is given a staccato articulation; brass is added.
	1:01	*Variation 4* The ascending melody of the theme is used as a bass line in the lower strings, while the violins introduce a new melody, featuring leaping motion and jumpy rhythms.
	1:18	*Variation 5* Violins elaborate this melody with faster rhythms; accompaniment thickens with arpeggios.
	1:33	*Variation 6* Rhythms become even faster and more intense, building to the next variation.
	1:48	*Variation 7* New melodic idea, with the violins strained in their upper register, and a new jumpy rhythm.
18	2:04	*Variation 8* Faster rhythms (sixteenth notes) used in violins, busy energetic feel; violins repeat a single high note while the flute plays a smoother melodic line.
	2:19	*Variation 9* Suddenly loud; even faster rhythms (sixteenth-note triplets), violins swoop from high to low range; decrescendo with violins again on repeated note; descending chromatic scale in the winds.

	2:35	*Variation 10* Calm exchanges of chords between winds and strings.
	2:53	*Variation 11* More chord exchanges, but the violins elaborate theirs with faster, detached notes. Descending and slowing chromatic scale in the flute connects to solo of the next variation.

B SECTION

[Here the new, slower tempo and meter (3/2) result in longer variations, although they still span eight measures. The descending chromatic scale that ended Variation 11 also ends Variations 13, 14, and 15.]

19	3:14	*Variation 12* Flute solo that restlessly ascends, gradually reaching into higher ranges, and then descends. Duple pattern in accompaniment emphasizes the new meter.
	3:57	*Variation 13* Change to brighter E Major. Much calmer mood. Clarinet and oboe alternate simple phrases. Duple pattern in accompaniment continues, supplemented by long rising arpeggios in the strings.
	4:36	*Variation 14* Trombones enter with chordal, hymnlike sound. Short rising arpeggios in the strings are the only accompaniment.
	5:17	*Variation 15* Brass and winds continue rich chordal sound, with fuller string arpeggios, as in Var. 14. Descending line in flute, slows to a halt.

A' SECTION

[The return of the A material is bold and dramatic. The faster tempo has renewed drive and energy after the contemplative B section.]

20	6:03	*Variation 16* Repeat of the original statement of the theme, only joined in measure 4 by searingly high violins descending a scale. Back to E minor and $\frac{3}{4}$ meter.
	6:16	*Variation 17* String tremolos crescendo and decrescendo while winds emphasize beats 2 and 3 of the $\frac{3}{4}$ meter.
	6:27	*Variation 18* String tremolos continue while winds and brass exchange a jumpy figure that builds in a rising melody.
	6:40	*Variation 19* *f*; new staccato articulation as strings and winds alternate bold eighth-note gestures.
	6:53	*Variation 20* Staccato figure builds in intensity, using faster triplet rhythm.
	7:05	*Variation 21* Swift ascending scales in strings, ending with accented notes, alternate with brass unison attacks rising in pitch.

	7:18	*Variation 22* *p*; syncopated quarter notes, creating a two-against-three feeling, are exchanged with staccato triplet figures.
	7:30	*Variation 23* Suddenly *f*; theme in French horns, triplet figures build in strings and winds, ending in eighth notes moving by leaps.
21	7:44	*Variation 24* With its accents on beat 2, this variation recalls Var. 1 but is much more forceful, with heavy accents.
	7:59	*Variation 25* Here the soft melody of Var. 2 returns, now frenzied in intensity through the loud volume and string tremolos. Emphasis on beat 2 continues with brass and timpani repeated notes.
	8:12	*Variation 26* The staccato quarter notes of Var. 3 are smooth and rich here, in the French horns, then moving to the oboes.
	8:25	*Variation 27* Sustained chords in the high winds, with smooth arpeggios rising and falling in the violas and cellos.
	8:40	*Variation 28* Sustained melody in winds becomes more active; faster arpeggios rise to violins and violas.
	8:53	*Variation 29* Rising two-note figures in flutes, accompanied by syncopated string offbeats; ends with stepwise violin melody.
	9:07	*Variation 30* Suddenly *f*; accented quarter notes, with offbeats; slight slowing and ever wider leaps in the violins; four additional measures outside of the theme move us into the Coda.

CODA

22	9:29	Based on melodic outline of theme; increasing tempo; high violin line accompanied by driving arpeggios and tremolos; two-note exchanges between high and low.
	9:51	Trombones with two accented, compressed statements of the theme melody, punctuated by strings.
	9:59	Violins crescendo; winds play theme statements answered by orchestra; strings and winds in a syncopated statement of the theme; vigorous descending arpeggios add weight to the concluding chords.

Giacomo Puccini (1858–1924)

The greatest opera composer of the late nineteenth century was Giacomo Puccini. He grew up in Lucca, a medieval town near the coast of Italy. Puccini came from a family of musicians: His father, grandfather, great-grandfather, and great-great-grandfather were all composers. At the age of fourteen, he became the organist at Lucca, and he surprised the congregation by working the tunes of opera arias into his organ-playing during services. He was in love with opera, and after he saw a performance of Verdi's *Aida* at the age of eighteen, he decided to become an opera composer himself.

Puccini went to Milan, the opera capital of Italy; there he led a typical student life, refining his composing skills, and soaking up opera. After he graduated, he got his first break when he played and sang portions of one of his own works at a private party. An important impresario and the head of the largest publishing firm in Italy were at the party, and they were so impressed they decided to publish the opera and stage it. Puccini spent five years on his next opera, which was not a success.

For both of these early works, Puccini had relied on other people's choice of libretto. Now he decided to choose his own. At thirty-five, he produced the first of his string of immortal Romantic operas: *Manon Lescaut*, based on a French love story. It came in the same year as the last opera of the grand old man of Italian opera, Verdi. Immediately, Puccini was hailed as "the heir of Verdi." He was an overnight success, his fortune was assured, and his name traveled around the world. *Manon Lescaut* was followed by *La Bohème*

Giacomo Puccini

(1896), *Tosca* (1900), and *Madama Butterfly* (1904), three of the most popular operas in the repertory. They are all cast in the new *verismo* (realist) mode of opera. *La Bohème* tells the story of a group of poor students and artists living in Paris; *Tosca* contains scenes of attempted rape, murder, execution, and suicide; and *Madama Butterfly* describes the pathetic death of a devoted Japanese geisha girl. But all three are also full of life, love, and passion.

Puccini's next opera, *La fanciulla del West* (*The Girl of the Golden West*, 1910), was given its premiere at the Metropolitan Opera House in New York. This is Puccini's "American" opera, set in the "Wild West," with saloons, guns, and a manhunt.

Puccini's last opera was *Turandot*, set in China and based on a Chinese folk story. It was not quite finished when Puccini died in 1924. A colleague completed the last two scenes, and the first performance was given in 1926 at the great opera house of La Scala in Milan. Puccini's death was declared a national day of mourning in Italy.

Before he died, Puccini wrote, "When I was born, the Almighty touched me with his little finger and said: 'Write operas—mind you, only operas!' And I have obeyed the supreme command."

Puccini's Music

Puccini's music never fails to stir the strongest emotions. It touches all who listen to it. His senses of timing, drama, and poignancy were perfect, and he was able to set a scene or a mood with just a few phrases of music. His melodies soar, and the vocal lines are buoyed up on waves of orchestral sound. A trademark of his style is the doubling or even tripling of the vocal lines by the orchestra, especially in the strings, so that the voices gain an almost luminous intensity. Puccini also wrote fresh, modern harmonies, with some strong dissonances and unexpected chord progressions, and these serve to heighten the drama. Sometimes he also employed unusual scales, such as the pentatonic scale, to suggest an exotic locale.

The action in Puccini operas is continuous, with short orchestral phrases woven together under the sung dialogue. For the most part, there is little distinction between recitative and aria, although in each of his operas there are some unforgettable arias. We shall listen to one of them: the exquisite, passionate, heartbreaking melody of an aria from *Madama Butterfly*.

LISTENING GUIDE

GIACOMO PUCCINI (1858–1924)

Un bel dì (One Fine Day) from *Madama Butterfly*

Date of composition: 1904
Duration: 4:32

Complete CD Collection: 3, Tracks 23–25

*M*adama Butterfly, one of Puccini's most beloved operas, premiered in 1904, at a time when American naval vessels frequented Japanese seaports. Oriental customs and exotic scenery provide the background for the tragic plot, which involves Benjamin Franklin Pinkerton (an American lieutenant) and Cio-Cio-San ("Butterfly," a young Japanese girl). Pinkerton has rented a house in Japan. Included in the package is his "betrothal" to Cio-Cio-San.

The tragedy consists in the differing perceptions of the relationship. Pinkerton regards it as a casual affair. Butterfly regards it as a marriage. Pinkerton returns to America after the wedding and marries an American woman. When he returns to Japan three years later with his American wife, the deeply loyal Butterfly, in grief and humiliation, kills herself.

Butterfly's aria *Un bel dì* comes near the beginning of Act II, as she tries to convince herself and her servant that her husband will return to her. You will hear gorgeous soaring melodies and exotic Oriental sounds in this superb *da capo* (ABA) aria. Listen to the doubling and sometimes tripling of the vocal line in the orchestra, which gives great richness to Puccini's wonderful lyricism.

A SECTION			
23	0:00	*Un bel dì, vedremo levarsi un fil di fuomo sull' estremo confin del mare.* *E poi la nave appare.* *Poi la nave bianca* *entra nel porto,*	One fine day, we'll notice a thread of smoke rising on the horizon of the sea. And then the ship will appear. Then the white vessel will glide into the harbor,
	0:50	*romba il suo saluto.* *Vedi? E venuto!* *Io non gli scendo incontro,* *Io no …*	thundering forth her cannon. Do you see? He has come! I don't go to meet him, Not I …

B SECTION			
24	1:18	*Mi metto la sul ciglio del colle,* *e aspetto, e aspetto gran tempo,* *e non mi pesa la lunga attesa.* [more activity in the orchestra]	I stay on the brow of the hill, and wait there, wait for a long time, but never weary of the long waiting.
	1:44	*E … uscito dalla folla cittadina* *un uomo, un picciol punto,* [slowing down]	From the crowded city comes a man, a little speck in the distance,
	2:00	*s'avia per la collina.*	climbing the hill.

	2:15	*Chi sarà? chi sarà?*	Who is it? Who is it?
		E come sara giunto,	And when he's reached the summit,
		che dirà? che dirà?	what will he say? What will he say?

[slower, with solo violin]

	2:24	*Chiamerà "Butterfly"*	He will call "Butterfly"
		dalla lontana.	from a distance.
		Io senza dar riposta me	And I, without answering,
		ne starò nascosta,	will keep myself quietly concealed,
		un po' per celia,	a bit to tease him,
		e un po' per non …	and a bit so as not to …

A SECTION

25	2:52	*morire al primo incontro,*	die at our first meeting,
		ed egli alquanto in pena,	and then, a little troubled,
		chiamerà, chiamerà,	he will call, he will call,
		"Piccina mogliettina,	"Dearest, little wife of mine,
		olezzo di verbena!,"	dear little orange blossom!,"
		i nomi che mi dava	the names he used to call
		al suo venire.	when he first came here.

	3:28	*Tutto questo avverrà,*	This will come to pass,
		te lo prometto.	I promise you.

	3:34	*Tienti la tua paura,*	Banish your idle fears,
		io con sicura fede l'aspetto.	I know for certain he will come.

	3:48	[lush orchestral postlude]

	4:19	[final chords]

Gustav Mahler (1860–1911)

Gustav Mahler was the last great Romantic composer. In his work, Romantic song and the Romantic symphony come together in a final (somewhat nostalgic) triumph of late Romanticism. Mahler was born in Bohemia of Jewish parents and made his career in Germany and Austria. His musical talent was evident at an early age, and he gave his first public piano recital at the age of ten. Mahler lived near a military base, and when he was small he loved to listen to the marching bands. Band music and marches of all kinds show up constantly in Mahler's music.

After studying in Vienna, Mahler gradually made a name for himself as a brilliant conductor, specializing in the works of Mozart, Beethoven, and Wagner. Mahler worked so hard that he had little time for composition, but gradually he developed a habit of composing during the summers, when the concert season was over. In this way, he managed to complete his first three symphonies, but people found them hard to understand.

The most important conducting position in Austria at that time was as music director of the Vienna Opera House. Mahler was by now the obvious choice for the job, but the fact that he was Jewish presented a formidable barrier in a city notorious for its anti-Semitism. He therefore had himself baptized as a Catholic and was appointed to the

Gustav Mahler with his daughter Anna.

position in Vienna in 1897. Mahler's tenure there had its problems: He was unpopular with the players because he was so strict, and there was considerable resentment over his appointment, despite his religious conversion. Mahler continued composing, and he completed several large-scale compositions during this time.

In 1902, when he was in his forties, Mahler fell in love with Alma Schindler, a talented young woman of twenty-three. Mahler was as autocratic in his marriage as he was in his work, and the couple had difficulties, but the depth of their relationship was never in doubt.

In 1907, Mahler suffered three profound setbacks. The campaign against him in Vienna finally led to his resignation from his job; his five-year-old daughter died of scarlet fever; and it was discovered that Mahler himself had a heart condition. In 1908, in an attempt to change the circumstances of his life, Mahler accepted two positions in New York: music director of the Metropolitan Opera and conductor of the New York Philharmonic. Mahler was superstitious and afraid to finish his Ninth Symphony, remembering that both Beethoven and Schubert had died after completing nine symphonies. Nonetheless, his Ninth was finished, and Mahler began working on his Tenth. But his worries turned out to be well founded. In 1911, he fell seriously ill. Mahler decided to return to Vienna, where he died at the age of fifty, leaving the Tenth Symphony incomplete.

Mahler's Music

Mahler's music represents the last great achievement of the Romantic ideal. In it, he tried to capture "the whole world": nature, God, love and death, exaltation and despair. To do this, Mahler had to invent new musical genres and forms. Most of his work is closely connected to song. Four of his symphonies use voices as well as instruments, and song melodies find their way into many of his instrumental works. Mahler wrote some important **orchestral song cycles**, in which the typical Romantic song takes on a completely new guise: In place of piano accompaniment, Mahler uses the orchestra, hugely expanding the range of expressive possibilities.

Mahler was a radical innovator in many other ways. His harmony is quite unorthodox, and he often ends a work in a key different from the one in which it began. We have seen that Beethoven was able to begin a symphony in a minor key and end it in the major, but actually changing the tonal center of a work was quite new. Some of Mahler's symphonies are longer than any that had come before, lasting ninety minutes or more.

Mahler was a brilliant and subtle orchestrator. He had an exact idea of the sound he wanted to produce. He used enormous orchestras, and sometimes the effect is shattering; but the main reason he needed so many instruments was to achieve the widest possible range of tone colors. In the Third Symphony, he writes a solo for a very rare instrument: the posthorn, a small horn generally used on mail coaches. In the Second Symphony, he combines an English horn with a bass clarinet—an amazing and evocative sound. He was meticulous about how he wanted his works to be played. Because he was a conductor himself, his scores are covered with exact instructions for almost every phrase of the music.

Most of Mahler's music is programmatic in some way. The slow movement of the Fifth Symphony is a testament of love for his wife, Alma. And the scherzo of the same symphony is a portrait of his children playing. Some of his programs are ambitious in the extreme, including representations of the creation of the world (Symphony No. 3) and the journey from life to death to resurrection (Symphony No. 2).

Throughout his music, there is a tinge of regret, of irony, even of deliberate distortion. A sense of yearning fills the pages of his work: a feeling of the impossible aims, the losses, the tragic undercurrent of human existence.

Mahler's music is full of quotations from Wagner, Brahms, Mendelssohn, and especially Beethoven. It is as though he were looking backward at the entire history of Romantic music. And this is appropriate, for he was its last and one of its greatest manifestations.

LISTENING GUIDE

GUSTAV MAHLER (1860–1911)

Fourth Movement, *Urlicht* (*Primeval Light*) from Symphony No. 2 in C minor (*Resurrection*)

Date of composition: 1888–94
Orchestration: Alto voice; 2 piccolos, 3 flutes, 2 oboes, English horn, 3 clarinets, 2 bassoons, contrabassoon, 4 horns, 3 trumpets, glockenspiel, 2 harps, and strings
Tempo: *Sehr feierlich, aber schlicht* ("Very ceremonial, but straightforward")
Meter: $\frac{4}{4}$
Key of movement: D-flat Major
Duration: 5:13

Companion CD, Track 79

The *Resurrection* Symphony is an enormous work, lasting nearly ninety minutes. It is in five movements, and it traces a spiritual journey from death to resurrection. In its sense of subjectivity and spiritual progression, it is reminiscent of Beethoven's Fifth Symphony. This parallel is made the more obvious by Mahler's choice of the same key, C minor, and by the move in the last movement to triumphant C Major.

The fourth movement marks the beginning of Mahler's lifelong preoccupation with the blending of symphony and song. The movement is actually the setting of a song text, sung by a solo alto voice with the orchestra. It is entitled *Urlicht* (*Primeval Light*). The text's central message is contained in its eighth line: "Ich bin von Gott und will wieder zu Gott" ("I am made by God and will return to God"). Mahler said of this movement: "The stirring voice of simple faith sounds in our ears." The text was probably written by Mahler himself.

The melodic shape of the vocal line often follows an upward curve followed by a slight fall. In addition, Mahler has composed the most remarkable instrumental music for this movement: quiet, stately, and richly orchestrated, with striking changes of key. The music does far more than accompany the words: It gives them new and profound meaning beyond their own power of expression.

O Röschen rot!	O red rose!
Der Mensch liegt in grösster Not!	Humanity lies in deepest need!
Der Mensch liegt in grösster Pein!	Humanity lies in greatest pain!
Je lieber möcht ich im Himmel sein!	I would rather be in Heaven!
Da kam ich auf einen breiten Weg;	Then I came upon a broad path;
Da kam ein Engelein und wollt mich abweisen.	Then came an angel, that tried to turn me away.
Ach nein! Ich liess mich nicht abweisen!	But no! I will not be turned away!
Ich bin von Gott und will wieder zu Gott!	I am made by God and will return to God!
Der liebe Gott wird mir ein Lichten geben,	Dear God will give me a light,
Wird leuchten mir bis in das ewig, selig Leben!	Will light my way to eternal, blessed life!

79	0:00	Begins with words of alto ("*O Röschen rot!*"), accompanied by low strings.
	0:22	Brass chorale: 3 trumpets, 4 horns, bassoons, contrabassoon.
	1:07	"*Der Mensch liegt in grösster Not!*" (strings).
	1:19	Change of key. "*Der Mensch liegt in grösster Pein!*" (strings).
	1:32	Trumpets.
	1:37	"*Je lieber möcht ich im Himmel sein!*" Note upward swoop on "*Himmel*" ("Heaven").
	1:57	Repeat of previous line. Voice with oboe. Note curve of melodic line.
	2:16	Oboe and strings.
	2:49	Tempo marked: "Somewhat faster." Clarinets, harp, and glockenspiel.
	2:55	"*Da kam ich auf einen breiten Weg;*"
	3:02	Solo violin, representing the "ich" ("I") of the poet.
	3:14	Miraculous key change, very quiet: "*Da kam ein Engelein und wollt mich abweisen.*" Fuller orchestration: piccolos, harps, strings.
	3:32	Back to slow tempo: "*Ach nein! Ich liess mich nicht abweisen!*" (tremolo strings, oboes)
	3:43	Higher: Repeat of previous line.
	3:55	Back to D-flat: strings, horns, harp. "*Ich bin von Gott und will wieder zu Gott!*"
	4:03	"*Der liebe Gott, der liebe Gott,*"
	4:10	Very slow: "*wird mir ein Lichten geben,*"
	4:21	"*Wird leuchten mir bis in das ewig, selig Leben!*" Note wondrous curve of melodic line and the muted violins shimmering *above* the voice on "*Leben*" ("Life").
	4:50	Muted strings, harps; dying away.

In late Romantic music like Mahler's you hear an amalgam of song, symphony, and program music. This is music that has direct and strong links back to Beethoven, but that also stands poised at the end of an era. Three years after Mahler's death, in the early twentieth century, Europe was engulfed in the flames of the First World War.

Listening to...

NINETEENTH-CENTURY MUSIC

- In Romantic music you will hear the heights of joy, the depths of despair, the horror of death, the transcendence of love (Berlioz's *Symphonie fantastique*, Wagner's *Tristan und Isolde*). Compositions range from the tiniest miniatures for solo piano (Chopin's "Minute" Waltz, Schumann's *Traümerei*) to works for the largest conglomeration of performing forces ever seen (Berlioz's *Symphonie fantastique*, Mahler's Second Symphony). Instruments themselves are different now: they have become bigger and louder. And new instruments are heard: trombones, tubas, double bassoons, bass clarinets and piccolos, snare drums, bass drums, celeste, bells.

- Music for solo instruments, especially the piano and violin, sounds as though it is designed to show off the skill of great performers (Liszt's *Transcendental Etude*). The range of dynamics in all music is widened, as is the range of expression (Verdi's *Otello*, Puccini's "Un bel dí"). Above all, Romantic music strives to be expressive (Schubert's "The Trout," Mahler's "Urlicht" from the Second Symphony).

- This striving for expression leads to other changes. Melodies are longer and more flowing (Smetana's *The Moldau*). Tempo becomes more fluid, allowing the music to ebb and flow as it goes along (the *theme* from Berlioz's *Symphonie fantastique*). Harmony becomes more adventurous, with more and more unusual chords appearing and with more rapid changes of key (Mahler's Second Symphony). Finally, Romantic composers like to blur the formal outlines of their works; the organizing structure becomes less obvious and heightens the sense of spontaneity and continuity.

- Program music becomes popular: there's some story behind the music (Berlioz's *Symphonie fantastique*). Sometimes the story is one of national pride or heritage (Smetana's *The Moldau*). In late Romantic music, the subject matter can include murder, rape, and suicide, or even the creation of the world and life after death (Mahler's Second Symphony).

KEY TERMS

absolute music (p. 178)	modulation (p. 179)	prelude (p. 191)
arioso (p. 209)	music drama (p. 208)	program music (p. 178)
character piece (p. 195)	nationalism (p. 174)	rubato (p. 192)
étude (p. 192)	nocturne (p. 192)	song cycles (p. 182)
grand opera (p. 198)	opéra comique (p. 198)	symphonic poem (p. 180)
impromptu (p. 192)	orchestration (p. 177)	Wagner tuba (p. 209)
leitmotiv (p. 210)	orchestral song cycle	waltz (p. 191)
lyric opera (p. 198)	(p. 228)	thematic transformation
mazurka (p. 191)	polonaise (p. 191)	(p. 200)

9
The Twentieth Century I:
The Classical Scene

CHAPTER OUTLINE

AN OVERVIEW: HISTORY AND THE ARTS

The twentieth century was a time of extraordinary contrasts. Technology reached dizzying heights of achievement. Radio, telephone, television, satellites, and computers radically altered both personal and worldwide communication. Travel was revolutionized. Medical science conquered many infectious diseases and invented complex surgical procedures for prolonging life.

But the twentieth century also displayed mankind's weaknesses, cruelty, and inhumanity at their worst. Two world wars decimated populations across Europe. World War II brought one of the most appalling instances of organized savagery in human history and introduced a new word, "genocide," into the language. The destructive

1900

First airplane fight 1903

1910

Bolshevik Revolution 1917
Claude Debussy 1862–1918
World War I 1914–1918

Scopes trial 1925
Joseph Stalin gains leadership of Communist Party in Russia 1925
Charles Lindbergh flies nonstop from New York to Paris 1927
Penicillin discovered 1928

1920

Planet Pluto discovered 1930

1930

Adolf Hitler appointed Chancellor of Germany 1933
Alban Berg 1885–1935
George Gershwin 1898–1937
Sigmund Freud 1856–1939
Ellen Taaffe Zwilich 1939

1940

Béla Bartók 1881–1945
Anton Webern 1883–1945
World War II 1939–1945
Long playing records introduced 1948

1950

Arnold Schoenberg 1874–1951
First hydrogen bomb exploded 1952
Charles Ives 1874–1954
Albert Einstein 1879–1955
Polio vaccine developed 1956
Stereo recording invented 1958
Frank Lloyd Wright 1867–1959

1960

Quasars discovered 1963
President Kennedy assassinated 1963
Sir Winston Churchill 1874–1965
T.S. Eliot 1888–1965
First heart transplant 1967
Martin Luther King assassinated 1968
First man on moon 1969

1970

Igor Stravinsky 1862–1971
Ezra Pound 1885–1972
Pablo Picasso 1881–1973
Henri Matisse 1869–1974
President Nixon resigns his office 1974
Dmitri Shostakovich 1906–1975
Benjamin Britten 1913–1976

1980

IBM personal computer introduced 1981
Berlin wall falls 1989
Aaron Copland 1900–1990
Leonard Bernstein 1918–1990

1990

Millennium celebrations around the world 2000

2000

power of military technology was displayed by the explosion of two atomic bombs on civilian populations in Japan. Millions of people were killed under totalitarian regimes in the Soviet Union and China.

Although science made impressive gains in the last century, its limitations became more apparent as the century waned. AIDS swept across the globe, seeming to represent a return to the incurable plagues of the Middle Ages. Short-sighted economic policies and commercial greed caused widespread destruction to the world's biological diversity and environment. And most damning of all, the richest and most wasteful countries of the world were not able to find a way to save millions of people in other countries from starvation. As the twentieth century gave way to the twenty-first, the contrast between its successes and its failures seemed particularly stark.

1900–1939

In 1900, Europe and the United States were in a period of unusual stability, peace, and prosperity. Economic growth was strong, the standard of living was improving rapidly, and scientific breakthroughs contributed to health and comfort.

At this time, the movement known as Modernism began to affect all of the arts. Modernism was a movement of self-conscious innovation. Artists, writers, poets, and painters created works of striking experimentation and revolutionary force. Composers rejected tonality, the harmonic basis of music since the seventeenth century, and adopted radically new harmonic structures. In this period of excitement, experimentation, and optimism, the greatest composers were Debussy, Schoenberg, and Stravinsky.

World War I (1914–18) shattered this sense of optimism. In this long drawn-out conflict—ugly, brutal, and often senseless—forty million people died and twenty million were wounded.

"Flapper" (fashionable young woman) on the cover of a magazine in the 1920s.
Courtesy of the Library of Congress.

The period after the war was one of uncertainty and a gradual decline into new conflict. The Bolshevik revolution in Russia had given rise to the first Communist state, one of the most influential political developments of the whole twentieth century. The economic devastation of Germany led directly to Hitler's rise to power. Fascist governments were established in Italy and Spain.

During the 1920s, the United States experienced a period of prosperity. The war had strongly stimulated America's economy. American products were sold all over the world, and President Calvin Coolidge made his famous statement that "the business of America is business." A break in this upward spiral came with the Great Depression of 1929–33, which caused widespread unemployment and hunger. During the 1930s, President Franklin D. Roosevelt's policies instilled confidence in the nation and led to gradual economic recovery.

In social terms, the period between the wars was one of turmoil and change. Women won the right to vote in 1920. Prohibition created an entire counterculture of bootleg liquor and organized crime. Many intellectuals were attracted by the social ideals of Marxism.

1939–2000

World War II (1939–45) broke out only twenty-one years after the end of the First World War. Thirty million people died; cities and towns in England, continental Europe, and the Far East suffered enormous and widespread damage; irreplaceable works of art and buildings, some of them dating to the Middle Ages, were destroyed. Six million people—Jews, gypsies, gays, the mentally ill and handicapped, political dissidents—were murdered in Nazi concentration camps. The economy of Europe was in shambles, and the political map was highly uncertain. The Soviet Union and the United States emerged as the dominant powers of the postwar period, and Europe was divided by its allegiance to one or the other of these powers. Populations around Europe were uprooted, and many countries were flooded with refugees.

Refugees leaving the city of Konigsberg with their last possessions after shelling by the Russian army in April 1945.

One of the magnets for refugees was the United States. Large numbers of people—including scholars, artists, writers, composers, and performing musicians—came from Europe to America. This influx made the United States the most prominent center of Western culture after the war.

From 1945 to the 1960s, two musical trends asserted themselves. The first was a tendency toward intellectualization. Music became so organized, so mathematical in its structure that many audiences turned away from classical music altogether. It seemed as though composers were writing only for other composers and were no longer interested in communicating to audiences.

The second trend in this period involved radical experimentation, parallel in some ways to the period around 1900. Composers experimented with music in every conceivable way, throwing out all the conventionally accepted norms of music making. Conventional instruments were pushed to new limits, exotic instruments were introduced, and new instruments were invented. Most influential was the use of tape and then synthesizers and computers in the production of musical sounds.

Since the mid 1960s, a new movement was evident in Western culture, a movement called Postmodernism. From the start of Postmodernism, everything was cast into doubt, including the worth and meaning of Western culture itself. Literary works struggled for identity. Paintings juxtaposed the old and the new in startling ways. Postmodern buildings became highly eclectic, combining an exaggerated variety of styles in a single unit. And music made a move away from the intellectualized compositions of the postwar period toward a new accessibility of style. Composers borrowed ideas from other countries or from pop and rock music.

GENERAL CHARACTERISTICS OF TWENTIETH-CENTURY MUSIC

Music of the twentieth century was more experimental and diverse than that of previous eras. Everything was called into question, including the tonal system upon which Western music had been based for centuries. Pieces could be very tiny or immensely long. All types of sound were used, and the distinction between sound and noise was often erased.

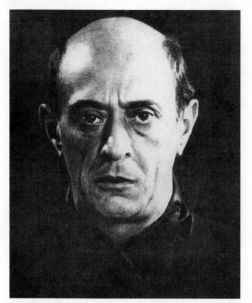

Revolutionary composer
Arnold Schoenberg in a
photograph by Man Ray,
c. 1930.

The Replacement of Tonality

In the early years of the twentieth century, the Viennese composer Arnold Schoenberg invented a new system, which, he said, would free music from "the tyranny of tonality." This new system was the **twelve-tone system**, which treated every pitch as equal in significance to every other. The gravitational pull of a key center was replaced by a sense of complete openness. Rather than **atonality** (non-tonality), Schoenberg preferred the term **pantonality** (all-tonality).

This new system opened the floodgates for a totally new approach to musical composition in the twentieth century. New chord combinations could be used, and consonance and dissonance no longer had the significance of the past. In previous eras, consonance had implied stability, and dissonance instability, but now all kinds of dissonances could be used at any point in a piece. Dissonances could be piled on top of one another to produce new sounds. Composers used chords called **tone clusters**, in which a large number of adjacent pitches are all sounded at once. (On the piano, you can play a tone cluster by pushing down all the keys under your entire forearm.)

Because tonality was based on a standard scale pattern, new scales were used, including the pentatonic scale, the whole-tone scale, and the octatonic scale.

The **pentatonic scale** has only five notes, usually in the following pattern:

Pentatonic Scale

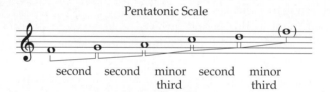

second   second   minor   second   minor
                  third   third

The same pattern of intervals can be reproduced by playing only the black keys on the piano. (You can easily compose your own pentatonic melody this way. Just play around on the black keys. The music will sound evocative and folklike.) Pentatonic scales had been around for a long time in many Asian musics and Western folk musics, but they were new to Western classical music.

The **whole-tone scale** has a whole step between each pitch and the next, and the scale has only six notes:

Whole-tone Scale

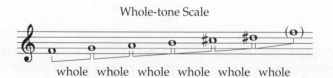

whole whole whole whole whole whole

Because there are no half steps in this scale, the sense of gravitational attraction from one note to another is missing, and tonality is bypassed.

The third new scale developed by composers in the twentieth century was the **octatonic scale**. This has eight pitches *within* the octave, in a pattern of alternating whole and half steps:

Octatonic Scale

whole   half   whole   half   whole   half   whole   half

In addition to using new scales, composers experimented with polytonality and non-triadic harmony. **Polytonality** means the simultaneous sounding of two or more keys at once. Both Igor Stravinsky and the American composer Charles Ives used polytonality. Ives once wrote a piece for two brass bands, each playing in a different key. **Non-triadic harmony** means harmony that is not based on the triad, the standard chord in conventional tonality (see Chapter 1).

Melody

Before the twentieth century, melody was generally smooth, balanced, and predictable. Pitches were usually closely connected, gaps were small, and phrases were balanced. In the twentieth century, melody often became erratic, with wide leaps, irregular rhythms, and unexpected notes. Phrase-lengths changed constantly. It was impossible to anticipate where a melody would go next.

Rhythm

One of the greatest changes in twentieth-century music was in the use of rhythm. Rhythm was the one element of Western music that had remained relatively unexplored. In the twentieth century, composers began to adopt far more complex rhythms in their music. Sometimes they achieved this by constantly changing meters in the course of a composition. For example, instead of remaining in $\frac{4}{4}$ meter, a piece might have a measure in $\frac{3}{4}$ followed by a measure in $\frac{6}{8}$, then a $\frac{2}{4}$ measure and so on. Sometimes composers adopted very unusual meters, such as $\frac{5}{4}$ or $\frac{7}{4}$, which give an unexpected beat to the music. Sometimes rhythms became freer because performers were asked to improvise their parts simultaneously. Finally, the advent of the computer allowed composers to manipulate rhythm in an infinite variety of complex ways.

Tone Color and Sound

One final element that distinguished twentieth-century music from music of earlier eras was a heightened awareness of tone color. Wind players were asked to make squawking, squeaking, or chattering noises on their instruments. String players produced unusual glissandos (slides) on their strings, or banged their instruments with their bows, or plucked the strings so hard that they snapped against the fingerboard. And both string and wind players were called upon to produce **quarter tones**, pitches *between* the half steps.

Instruments that had never or only rarely been used in traditional orchestras—such as saxophones, harps, alto flutes, or high-pitched clarinets—were now featured regularly. The greatest changes occurred in the percussion section. Now, percussion included large and small cymbals, a whole array of drums of different sizes, bells, wooden blocks, whips, rattles, tambourines, gongs, xylophones, vibraphones and chimes.

Monet's painting of Rouen Cathedral is vague, cloudy, and elusive.

Claude Monet (1840–1926), *The Cathedral of Rouen, façade*, circa 1892/94. Oil on canvas, 100.6 × 66 cm. Juliana Cheney Edwards Collection. Museum of Fine Arts, Boston/Archiv für Kunst und Geschichte, Berlin.

Modern technology strongly influenced the sounds of twentieth-century music. At the beginning of the century, new electronic instruments were invented, including the **telharmonium**, an instrument that produces sound by means of electronic generators; the **theremin**, an instrument that can make oscillating streams of sliding sounds, like ghost noises; and the first electronic organ. Later, in the 1940s and 1950s, the advent of magnetic tape brought many new experiments in sound production.

In the latter half of the century, the production and control of musical sounds were revolutionized by the computer and the synthesizer. Much music of the later twentieth century—especially recorded music or film soundtracks—would not have been possible without the synthesizer.

Modernism: The Beginnings of Change

In the Modernist movement, which was centered in Paris, there were many parallels between music and the other arts. To begin this chapter, we will study several Modernist trends—Impressionism, Primitivism, Expressionism—in both their visual and musical aspects. The chief figures of the Modernist movement in music were Debussy, Stravinsky, and Schoenberg. Although they were all striking innovators, each contributed to this movement in his own particular way—Debussy in orchestral color, Stravinsky in rhythm, and Schoenberg in the invention of a new system to replace tonality.

IMPRESSIONISM AND SYMBOLISM

The earliest important movement in Modernist painting was known as Impressionism, in which outlines are vague and details are left to the viewer's imagination. The best-known Impressionist painters were Monet, Sisley, and Pisarro.

Impressionism in music refers to a style of composition in which the shapes are blurred and there is a great deal of harmonic ambiguity, often created by whole-tone, pentatonic, or chromatic scales. Indeed, it was sometimes felt that music, with its natural fluidity, could create an Impressionist atmosphere even more successfully than painting. ·

Claude Debussy (1862–1918)

The composer best known as an Impressionist was Claude Debussy. Debussy was a talented pianist as a child and was accepted as a student at the Paris Conservatory of Music at the age of ten. When he was eighteen, he began to study composition, and when he was twenty-two, he won the prestigious Prix de Rome, the highest award for French composers.

Debussy's most famous orchestral composition is the *Prelude to the Afternoon of a Faun* (1894), which is based on the poem by the French poet Mallarmé. The music is dreamy and suggestive, using a large orchestra primarily for tone color.

Debussy's music was little known until he was about forty. Then he became quite famous and traveled around Europe conducting performances of his work. He loved fine food and fancy clothes and as a result was often short of money. He had two wives and a mistress, though not all at the same time!

Debussy is also well known for his piano music, which is highly varied. There are pieces of pure Impressionism, such as *Gardens in the Rain*, but he also wrote humorous pieces, technical studies, and music for children. His best-known piece for children is *Golliwog's Cake-Walk*. Debussy died of cancer in his native Paris at the age of fifty-six.

Claude Debussy in a portrait by Marcel Baschet, 1884.

LISTENING GUIDE

CLAUDE DEBUSSY (1862–1918)
Prélude à l'après-midi d'un faune

Date of composition: 1894
Orchestration: 3 flutes, 2 oboes, English horn,
  2 clarinets, 2 bassoons, 4 horns, 2 harps,
  antique cymbals, strings
Duration: 11:10

Complete CD Collection: 3, Tracks 26–28

Debussy's *Prelude to the Afternoon of a Faun* is an evocation of moods and natural scenes. It suggests the thoughts and feelings of a mythical creature of the forest, who is half man and half goat (not to be confused with the little, furry, Bambi-like creature, the "fawn"). He is half asleep in the hot sun and his mind dwells on sexual fantasies. He expresses his feelings by playing his panpipes.

Debussy matches the mood of the poem with sensuous, dreamy music that often swells up with emotion. He uses a large orchestra but without trumpets, trombones, or timpani. The only percussion instruments are antique cymbals—very small cymbals that resonate quietly near the end of the piece. Other special orchestral colors are created by harp glissandos and horn calls played with mutes to make them sound far away. Most of the time, the strings play very quietly, and sometimes they use special effects, such as playing with a mute or bowing over the fingerboard, which creates a hushed tone. In this context of a piece that is mostly quiet, the few passages of crescendo sound emotional and surging.

The opening flute melody is sensuous, chromatic, and vague. This melody serves as the basis for much of the piece. It is shaped as a series of curves, gently rising and falling. Debussy deliberately modeled the shape of this melody on medieval plainchant, which he thought could serve as an inspiration for composers in the Modernist era.

The composition falls into three sections in an ABA pattern, though each section merges imperceptibly with the next, and the return of the opening A section is modified. One of Debussy's aims was to break down the clear formal outlines of traditional music.

A SECTION		
		[E Major]
26	0:00	Opening motive, (chromatic motion), dreamy and suggestive.

	0:24	Harp glissando, horns in dialogue.
	0:57	Flute motive again, quietly accompanied by the orchestra.
	1:15	Horns play quick little figures. Oboe elaborates flute motive.
	1:38	Orchestral crescendo, repeated chordal figures.
	1:57	Chordal figures reduce to clarinet.
	2:05	Harp signals a return of the flute motive.
	2:22	Flute accompanied by rising harmonies.
	2:46	Harp plays under flute; flowing movement in orchestra. Cadence.
	3:27	Flute motive migrates to clarinet against ominous, slightly agitated orchestral accompaniment.
	3:35	Chromatic flourishes; dialogue between flute and clarinet.
	3:58	Oboe melody rides on top of the orchestra, beginning another orchestral crescendo.
	4:07	Full, flowing music, decrescendo.
	5:01	Clarinet floats above orchestral accompaniment, transition to new key and new section.

B SECTION		
		[D-flat Major]
27	5:24	New motive (much slower and diatonic).

	5:50	Crescendo.

	6:04	New motive becomes slow-moving melody for strings.
	6:14	Crescendo, decrescendo; music is constantly moving and pulsating.
	6:54	Horn melody in duet with solo violin, harp accompaniment.
	7:23	Flute introduces abbreviated, slower form of the opening motive, at a slightly higher pitch; harp accompaniment continues.

[musical notation] etc.

	7:44	Oboe, faster motion with trill; lively conversation with other woodwinds.
	8:00	Oboe plays slow version of motive.
	8:22	English horn reiterates the oboe motive, with similar comments from the other woodwinds.

A′ SECTION

		[return to E Major]
28	8:40	Flute melody returns, along with E-Major tonality. Diatonic accompaniment against chromatic solos of the woodwinds.
	9:02	Antique cymbals.
	9:54	Ending chords; oboe melody; mixed orchestral colors.
	10:20	Single descending notes from harp. Brief nostalgic reminiscences of motive.
	10:59	Pizzicato (low strings).

PRIMITIVISM

Picasso's revolutionary painting *Les Demoiselles d'Avignon* (1907).

Pablo Picasso, *Le Demoiselles d'Avignon* (June–July 1907). Oil on canvas, 8′ × 7′8″ (243.9 × 233.7 cm). The Museum of Modern Art, New York. Acquired through the Lillie P. Bliss Bequest. Photograph © 1998 The Museum of Modern Art. © 2002 Estate of Pablo Picasso/Artists Rights Society (ARS), New York.

Primitivism is the name given to another movement in painting at the beginning of the twentieth century. Artists were attracted by what they saw as the directness, instinctiveness, and exoticism of nonurban cultures. At this time, writers such as Sigmund Freud were exploring the power of instinct and the unconscious.

Among the painters of Primitivism were Paul Gauguin and Pablo Picasso. Again, the center of this artistic movement was Paris. Paul Gauguin was fascinated by "primitive" cultures and eventually went to the South Sea Islands to live and work among the islanders. Pablo Picasso was one of the greatest painters of the twentieth century, and he changed his style many times during his lifetime. But in the early 1900s, he, too, was interested in Primitivism, and his painting *Les Demoiselles d'Avignon* (*The Young Women of Avignon*) is an example of this style. It is also had a revolutionary impact on the development of modern painting.

Igor Stravinsky in 1925.

Igor Stravinsky (1882–1971)

The musical equivalent of Picasso was Stravinsky. He, too, lived a long life, evolved several distinct styles during his career, and had a lasting impact on twentieth-century culture.

Igor Stravinsky was born in St. Petersburg, Russia. His father was an opera singer, but he insisted that Igor study law at the university instead of music. Stravinsky used to compose on the sly. At the age of twenty-one, he gave up law altogether and began formal music lessons.

In 1910, Stravinsky moved to Paris, at that time the undisputed center of European culture. Stravinsky was asked to produce some works for the Ballets Russes, a famous and influential ballet troupe based in Paris. Stravinsky wrote three of his most important ballet scores as commissions for the Ballets Russes: *The Firebird* (1910), *Petrushka* (1911), and *The Rite of Spring* (1913). All three are inspired by the prevailing style of Primitivism. The primitive atmosphere in Stravinsky's music is enhanced by his use of **polyrhythms** (different meters sounding at the same time), **bitonality** (two different keys sounding at the same time), and **ostinato** (constantly repeated phrases).

The Rite of Spring, a composition of tremendous power and boldness, is one of the most revolutionary works of the twentieth century. It depicts the rituals of ancient pagan tribes, and it caused a riot at its first performance in Paris in 1913. The audience was profoundly shocked by the violent and overtly sexual nature of the choreography on stage as well as by the pounding rhythms and clashing dissonances from the orchestra. Soon thereafter, the work was recognized as a masterpiece.

Stravinsky lived in Switzerland during the First World War, and then returned to Paris in 1920. His most important compositions from this period took a different direction entirely. Smaller and more transparent, they relied on small groups of varied instruments and sometimes were influenced by the new American music—jazz. Stravinsky was attracted to jazz because of its clear, clean textures and lively rhythms.

This led Stravinsky to initiate another new style, Neo-Classicism. Neo-Classical composers in the twentieth century adopted ideas not only from the Classic period, but also from the Baroque era. In place of the big, wild, expressive orchestral sounds of the 1910s (like those in *The Rite of Spring*), the focus now was on small groups, formal balance, and clarity. Although old genres (concerto grosso, symphony) and old forms (sonata form, theme-and-variations, etc.) are adopted, Neo-Classical harmony is modern, and the rhythm is lively and irregular.

In 1939, as Europe headed once again toward the catastrophe of a world war, Stravinsky moved to America. He settled in Los Angeles and was engaged by Hollywood to write film scores. Unfortunately, none of these was ever completed. He did finish a Mass, as well as an opera called *The Rake's Progress* (1951).

After 1951, Stravinsky began to experiment with twelve-tone techniques and again radically changed his musical style. Many of his late compositions use twelve-tone methods of composition. They include an elegy for President John F. Kennedy (completed in 1964) and a Requiem written in anticipation of Stravinsky's own death. Stravinsky died in 1971, near the age of ninety.

Stravinsky's Music

As we have seen, Stravinsky's personal style underwent several changes during his career. He wrote in the splashy, colorful orchestral style of the Russian nationalists, composed music with the force and power of Primitivism, adopted jazz techniques, invented a new musical style known as Neo-Classicism, and turned finally to twelve-tone techniques.

Stravinsky took ideas from the medieval, Baroque, and Classic periods, as well as from contemporary music. He wrote for almost every known musical combination, both instrumental and vocal, choral and orchestral, chamber and stage. His genres included opera, ballet, oratorio, symphony, concerto, chamber music, sonata, piano solo, song, chorus, and Mass. And yet some things remained common to all of Stravinsky's periods and compositional styles. First of all was his interest in rhythm. His rhythms are highly individual—catchy, unexpected, and fascinating. Stravinsky used syncopation with great effect, and often a short rest or silence appears in the midst of a phrase, to throw the rhythm off balance.

Second, Stravinsky had an acute ear for tone color. He used unusual combinations of instruments to get exactly the effect he wanted, and he also used instruments in novel ways. *The Rite of Spring*, for example, begins with a bassoon, which is a low instrument, playing at the very *top* of its range, producing a strange, eerie sound. (This passage is used in Walt Disney's *Fantasia* to suggest the beginning of Creation.)

Finally, Stravinsky's use of harmony was highly original. Much of his music is tonally based, and yet he often used *two* key centers instead of one. Another characteristic harmonic effect is the use of an ostinato (repeated pattern) as an accompaniment. Above this repeated pattern the harmonies shift and waver.

LISTENING GUIDE

IGOR STRAVINSKY (1882–1971)

Le Sacre du Printemps (The Rite of Spring), Opening Section

Date of composition: 1913
Orchestration: Piccolo, 3 flutes, alto flute, 4 oboes, English horn, E-flat clarinet, 3 clarinets, 2 bass clarinets, 4 bassoons, contrabassoon, 8 horns, D trumpet, 4 trumpets, 3 trombones, 2 tubas, 2 timpani, bass drum, side drum, triangle, antique cymbals, strings
Duration: 8:50

Complete CD Collection: 3, Tracks 29–32

Some of Stravinsky's most memorable works were written for the Ballets Russes in Paris before World War I. *Le Sacre du Printemps*, the third of a group of ballets, was finished in 1913. It uses the largest orchestra ever used by Stravinsky and presents bold, daring, and often alarming sounds that shocked the first audiences. Stravinsky's idea was to suggest a succession of tribal rites. The music is brilliantly imaginative, colorful, and striking.

We will listen only to the first several minutes, beginning with a solo bassoon, playing in its eerie highest register:

| 29 | 0:00 | Bassoon playing very high. |

	0:10	Horn enters.
	0:20	Descending woodwinds; clarinet.
	0:44	English horn enters. More bassoon.
	0:58	Woodwinds gather momentum.
	1:12	Trills, fuller texture; small high clarinet.
	1:32	Bubbling bass clarinet.
	1:45	Section comes to a close, trills in violins.
	1:55	Small clarinet, interplay with English horn.
	2:16	Flute response.
	2:24	Oboe.
	2:29	Small clarinet in high register.
	2:47	Muted trumpet.
	2:51	Begin orchestral crescendo.
	3:01	Stop!
	3:02	Bassoon reappears, high-register solo.
	3:10	Clarinet trill, pizzicato strings, chords. Monotonous two-note figure starts and continues through the following:
30	3:34	Pounding, steady orchestral chords, irregular accents.

	3:44	Movement in woodwinds, arpeggios.
	3:53	Trumpet, triplet figures, quick runs on winds.
	4:13	Orchestral pounding returns.
	4:22	Bass melody: bassoons interspersed with orchestra rhythms.

244

	4:32	Trombone, orchestral flashes of color.
	4:53	Big brass chord; timpani; return of two-note figure; orchestral flashes.
	5:17	Horn melody.
	5:21	Flute response.
	5:28	Dialogue between flute and muted trumpet.
	5:36	Flutes enter, accompanied by other woodwinds; two-note figure continues.
31	5:53	Brass chords, parallel motion up and down; much louder now.
	6:09	Agitated strings; piccolo.
	6:17	Woodwind melody.
	6:27	Orchestral crescendo, with short blasts.
	6:53	Loud drum crashes, rhythmic activity increases over static accompaniment.
32	7:03	Brass chords.
	7:29	Triplet rhythms, horn calls, high flutes, dissonant wild trumpet calls, very fast strings punctuated by drum strokes.
	8:17	Clarinets in octaves, melody over flute trills.
	8:42	Pulse slows down to a low-pitched trudge.

EXPRESSIONISM

Expressionism as an artistic movement evolved during a time of growing fascination with the unconscious and people's inner feelings. The center of Expressionism was Vienna. It was here that Sigmund Freud lived and worked, developing his groundbreaking theories on the human psyche. And it was in Vienna that the revolutionary musical world of Schoenberg and his students Berg and Webern was created.

The connections between painting and music at this time were particularly strong. In fact, Schoenberg himself was a talented painter. Both Expressionist painters and Expressionist composers attempted to focus on inner states of being and the evocation of extreme feelings. Today, their concentration on anguish, insanity, fear, hatred, and death may seem obsessive. But the movement was a reaction against what was perceived as the prettiness and superficiality of the Impressionists.

A nightmarish evocation by Kokoschka (1914).

Oskar Kokoschka (1886–1980). Die Windsbraut, 1914. Oil on canvas, 181 × 220 cm. Basel, Kunstmuseum, Archiv für Kunst und Geschichte, Berlin. © 1998 Artists Rights Society (ARS), New York/Pro Litteris, Zurich.

245

Arnold Schoenberg (1874–1951)

The most important Expressionist composer was Arnold Schoenberg. He was also one of the most radically innovative composers of the century, for he evolved a completely new approach to musical harmony.

Schoenberg was born in 1874 in Vienna to a poor Orthodox Jewish family. He took violin lessons as a boy but had no other musical training. He studied the works of Mozart, Haydn, and Beethoven as well as those of Brahms and Mahler, who were still active in Vienna as Schoenberg was growing up.

Schoenberg began composing at about the age of eight. His early works, up to the age of about twenty-five, continued in the Romantic tradition. But soon, Schoenberg started to take a different path.

He gradually came to feel that tonality—the centuries-old harmonic basis of music, with its carefully ordered hierarchy of keys and its feeling of a single, central key for each movement or work—had outlived its usefulness. And he began to develop a completely new system of musical organization. At first he called this system *a*tonality—that is, a system *without* key. In Schoenberg's atonal works, the feeling of key is deliberately avoided. The music uses so many chromatic notes that no tonal center can be heard.

Schoenberg wrote many atonal pieces between 1908 and 1915. Among the most important of these is the song cycle *Pierrot Lunaire* (*Moonstruck Pierrot*), 1912. Schoenberg's atonal music was not well received. Yet he continued to struggle with the idea of writing music without tonality. "I feel that I have a mission," he said.

For the next several years, Schoenberg wrote no music at all. This period coincided with the First World War. After the war and the collapse of the Austro-Hungarian Empire, Schoenberg faced a personal and intellectual crisis in addition to a national and political one. The problem was in the direction his music should take. Atonality freed music from the "straitjacket" of tonality, but it had no organizing principle. How can you *structure* a piece with no keys? So far he had solved the problem in two ways: Either the pieces were very short, or they were held together by a text.

Schoenberg gradually developed a solution to this problem, coming up with an idea that held composers in its grip for much of the remainder of the twentieth century. His idea was the **twelve-tone system**.

The twelve-tone system has a strict unifying principle. The composer uses all the available notes (there are twelve notes in an octave, counting all the half steps). And the notes are used in a strict order (established in advance by the composer).

Schoenberg first used his twelve-tone system in his *Five Piano Pieces* of 1923. From then on, he used the system (more or less strictly) in almost all of his compositions, including large orchestral works and even an opera. The twelve-tone system allowed Schoenberg to write far more extended compositions than had been possible before.

During the time of these developments, Schoenberg was fortunate enough to have two brilliant and like-minded students. They were Alban Berg and Anton Webern, only about ten years younger than he was. The three shared a great many of their ideas and wrote similar kinds of pieces, yet each composer developed his own distinct musical personality.

This was a dangerous period for Jews in Germany. When the Nazis came to power in 1933, Schoenberg was summarily dismissed from his teaching job at the Academy of Arts in Berlin, along with the hundreds of thousands of other Jews around Germany who lost their jobs. As a result, Schoenberg embraced Judaism, from which he had lapsed at the age of eighteen, more firmly than ever. Many of Schoenberg's works are based on Jewish themes. In addition, after the Second World War he wrote a cantata entitled *A Survivor from Warsaw* (1947), which relives the horror of the Warsaw Ghetto, in which more than 400,000 Jews were systematically murdered by the Nazis. The text is based on a personal account by one of the few people who survived.

After Schoenberg was fired from his job in Berlin, he moved to the United States and settled in Los Angeles, where he taught at the University of California and took on private students. This was the period of his large-scale twelve-tone works, but he also wrote two "old-fashioned" tonal pieces for student ensembles.

Schoenberg died in 1951. During his life, his music was not much performed—and even since then, most audiences have found it difficult and inaccessible. But Schoenberg was highly influential in two ways: directly, because he was the teacher of Berg and Webern, and indirectly, because his development of the twelve-tone system affected an entire generation of composers who came after him.

Schoenberg's Music

Schoenberg's music can be divided into three periods: the early Romantic period, the atonal period, and the much longer twelve-tone period.

From 1923 until the end of his life, Schoenberg concentrated on twelve-tone composition. By the middle of the twentieth century, many composers modeled their own musical styles on the work of this remarkable man. And even composers who avoided the twelve-tone system had available to them a vocabulary of sounds that could be called upon occasionally to enrich their overall language.

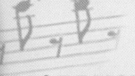

LISTENING GUIDE

ARNOLD SCHOENBERG (1874–1951)

Madonna from *Pierrot Lunaire*

Date of composition: 1912
Orchestration: Voice; flute, bass clarinet, viola, cello, piano
Duration: 1:47

Companion CD, Track 80

choenberg's *Pierrot Lunaire* sets twenty-one poems by Albert Giraud. The songs represent the viewpoint of Pierrot, a deeply troubled clown who seems to have a fascination with the mysterious powers of the moon.

Pierrot Lunaire has been described as an Expressionist art form because it reveals the dark side of human nature and the power of inner emotional expression. It is an atonal composition. In a technique called *Sprechstimme* ("speech-song"), the singer merges singing with speaking. She is accompanied by a small group of instrumentalists.

Madonna seems to be inspired by some of the more graphic elements of Catholic ritual. The lyrics speak of blood, wounds, redness of the eyes, and so on, which are effectively rendered in Schoenberg's setting. Notice particularly the instance of word painting on the word "Rise" (*Steig*) in the second stanza. Here Schoenberg writes the widest interval between two notes in the whole song. Notice also how expressively the words "blood" (*Blut*) and "sorrows" (*Schmerzen*) are presented.

80	0:00	[Flute, clarinet, cello (1 measure)]	

STANZA 1

	0:03	*Steig, o Mutter aller Schmerzen,* *Auf den Altar meiner Verse!*	Rise, O Mother of all Sorrows, On the altar of my verses!
	0:18	*Blut aus deinen magern Bruesten* *Hat den Schwerten Wut vergossen.*	Blood pours forth from your withered Breast where the cruel sword has pierced it.

STANZA 2

	0:32	*Deine ewig frischen Wunden* *Gleichen Augen, rot und offen.*	And your ever-bleeding wounds Seem like eyes, red and open.
	0:42	*Steig, o Mutter aller Schmerzen,* *Auf den Altar meiner Verse!*	Rise, O Mother of all Sorrows, On the altar of my verses!
	0:57	[Instrumental interlude; change in instrumental figures]	
	1:09	*In den abgezehrten Händen* *Hälst du deines Sohnes Leiche,* *Ihn zu zeigen aller Menschheit—*	In your torn and wasted hands Holding your Son's holy body, You reveal Him to all mankind—
	1:42	*Doch der Blick der Menschen meidet*	But the eyes of men are turned away,
	1:23	*Dich, o Mutter aller Schmerzen!*	O Mother of all Sorrows!

[Piano enters, loud and abrupt with cello]

	1:28	[Final chord, piano]	

LISTENING GUIDE

ARNOLD SCHOENBERG (1874–1951)

Theme and Sixth Variation from *Variations for Orchestra*, Op. 31

Date of composition: 1928
Duration: 2:36

Complete CD Collection: 3, Tracks 33–34

The second piece we will study by Schoenberg, *Variations for Orchestra*, Op. 31, employs Schoenberg's twelve-tone method, and features a tone row, the basic building block for twelve-tone music. The row is as follows:

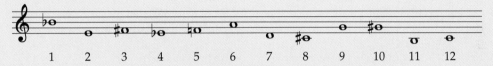

It is used four times to make up the theme. The theme itself is in ternary form (it has three sections), and is made up of unusual and irregular phrases of five and seven measures.

In this composition, Schoenberg uses a large orchestra. But the scoring is very spare, so that the effect is like chamber music in texture. We shall listen to the theme and the sixth variation.

(Read the Listening Guide first, and then while listening.)

THEME		
		[Molto moderato ("Very moderate")]
33	0:00	The first appearance of the tone row (cello melody, first twelve notes) presents the row in its ORIGINAL sequence:

| | 0:12 | The continuation of the cello melody (next twelve notes) presents the row in RETROGRADE INVERSION (backwards and upside-down), beginning on the note E-sharp: |

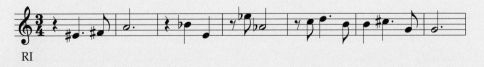

| | 0:30 | The middle section of the theme is played as RETROGRADE ORIGINAL (the row backwards): |

	0:42	Gentle cadence.
	0:43	The melody travels to the violins, which present the row in INVERSION (upside-down), beginning on high G:

I

	1:04	The movement ends very quietly. Conclusion.

VARIATION VI

[Andante ("Quite slow")]
(This variation features several instruments playing the main theme against varying combinations of instruments playing melodic figures derived from the tone row.)

34	0:00	Main theme, clarinets, answered by English horn and flute.
	0:07	Continuation.
	0:18	Main theme inverted, played by solo viola, answered by flute and horn.
	0:26	Melodic fragments, all instruments.
	0:31	Flute, short chromatic figure, followed by solo viola playing descending line in longer notes.
	0:43	Main theme, clarinets.
	0:51	More rhythmic movement, entire orchestra.
	0:55	Muted trumpet chords.
	1:07	Main theme, violins.
	1:16	Faster motion.
	1:28	Motion stops, movement ends.

Schoenberg's Students

The two most famous students of Schoenberg were Alban Berg and Anton Webern. Both men began studying with Schoenberg in their late teens, and both became deeply absorbed in his pursuit of atonality and finally of the twelve-tone system. Despite this close association, however, each composer managed to keep his own individual musical personality, and each one's work is clearly distinguishable.

Alban Berg (1885–1935)

Berg was, like Schoenberg, born in Vienna, and he, too, had no formal training before he began writing music. Berg was nineteen years old and working as a government clerk when he saw Schoenberg's newspaper advertisement for students and signed up for private lessons. He studied with Schoenberg for six years, and the two men became close friends.

During World War I, Berg served three years in the army and worked in the Ministry of War, but he also began composing an opera. *Wozzeck* was completed in 1922 and stands as the first atonal Expressionist opera. It is also one of the great operas of the twentieth century.

Alban Berg (left) and Anton Webern in 1914.

In 1928, Berg began work on his second Expressionist opera, *Lulu*. The entire opera was complete, except for the orchestration of the third act, when Berg died in 1935 of an infected insect bite (this was before the discovery of antibiotics). Berg's widow refused to release his draft for the third act, and the opera was not performed in its entirety until 1979, after she died.

Berg's last completed composition also comes from the year of his death. He broke off work on *Lulu* to write his Violin Concerto as a memorial to Manon Gropius, the eighteen-year-old daughter of Mahler's widow. Berg dedicated the work "to the memory of an angel."

Berg's Music

Of the three colleagues, Berg retained the strongest links with the past. He adopted atonality and twelve-tone technique, but with great flexibility. You can find passages of tonal music in many of his compositions, and he never abandoned the Romantic idea of lyricism. His music is more passionate and emotionally intense than that of the other two composers.

BERG'S WOZZECK   Berg's experience of war is reflected in *Wozzeck*. The opera was begun during World War I but not completed until 1922. The opera tells the story of a poor, working-class soldier (Franz Wozzeck) who is bullied by his superiors, betrayed by the woman he loves (Marie), and beaten up by his rival. Driven to madness, Wozzeck murders Marie and then commits suicide. The drama is intensely emotional, and the music, like much of Berg's work, is both highly expressive and tightly organized. Although the music is atonal, Berg uses tight, closed structures borrowed from the past: sonata form, rondo form, fugue, theme and variations, and many others. We shall listen carefully to the climactic final scenes of *Wozzeck*.

The music that Berg crafted is brilliant, powerful, and enormously inventive. The sounds are atonal, producing new combinations and colors. The palette is very wide, as Berg uses an enormous orchestra. The music is jagged, distorted, careening wildly between extremes: very loud and very soft, very high and very low, singing and talking. Perhaps the greatest extremes come in the vocal line: The singers use *Sprechstimme*, flowing melody, screams, whispers, and folk tunes.

WOZZECK, ACT III, SCENE 4   Wozzeck had earlier stabbed Marie to death near a pond in the woods. He now returns to the pond to hide the knife. He tries to wash the blood off his hands, but it seems to him that the whole pond is turning to blood. He drowns. The captain and the army doctor hear him drowning but leave him to his fate. The music for this scene contains powerful pictorial descriptions: the moon rising, the forest at night, the water welling over Wozzeck's head, the gradual ebbing of life.

ORCHESTRAL INTERLUDE   The orchestral interlude that follows is the longest and most emotional in the whole opera. Berg writes a deeply sympathetic lament for Wozzeck and his tragic existence. The music is purely Romantic; it is even fully in a key (D minor), which gives it a powerful emotional appeal in the stark and jagged context of its atonal surroundings.

WOZZECK, ACT III, SCENE 5   Wozzeck and Marie have had a little boy. He is playing in front of his house with some other children. They run off to see Marie's body, and he follows them naively, not understanding what has happened.

The music for this scene is finely drawn, with continuous running notes, throwing into relief the cruelty/ innocence of the children. The scene does not end, it simply stops, providing no feeling of conclusion to the opera, only a sense of isolation and continuing horror.

LISTENING GUIDE

Alban Berg (1885–1935)
Wozzeck, Act III, Scenes 4 and 5

Date of composition: 1924
Orchestration: Piccolo, 4 flutes, 4 oboes, English horn, 2 E-flat clarinets, 4 clarinets, bass clarinet, 3 bassoons, contrabassoon, 4 horns, 4 trumpets, 4 trombones, bass trombone, tuba, 2 timpani, bass drum, side drum, tam-tams, 2 cymbals, triangle, xylophone, celesta, harp, strings
Duration: 9:45

Complete CD Collection: 4, Tracks 1–3

In these two scenes, Berg's use of instrumental colors and texture is extraordinary. From the high, silvery celesta to the low trombones and tuba, he exploits the richest possible palette of sounds.

[by the pond, scene of the crime]

WOZZECK

1   0:00
Das Messer? Wo ist das Messer: Ich
habs da gelassen. Näher, noch
näher. Mir graut's. Da regt
sich was. Still!
Alles still und tot.

Where is it? Where can the knife
be? Somewhere here, I left it
somewhere. I'm scared. There.
Something moved. Quiet!
All is quiet and dead.

[Celesta]

[trumpets, low trombones]

0:31
Mörder! Mörder!!
Ha! da ruft's?
Nein. Ich selbst.

Murder! Murder!!
Ah, who cried?
No. It was me.

[discovering the corpse]

Marie! Marie! Was hast du für
eine rote Schnur um den Hals?
Hast Dir das rote Halsband
verdient, wie die Ohr-Ringlein,
mit Deiner Sünde?! Was hängen
Dir die schwarzen Haare so wild?!
Mörder! Mörder!! Sie werden nach
mir suchen. Das Messer verrät mich!

Marie! Marie! What is that like a
crimson cord round your neck? And
was that crimson necklace a gift,
like the golden earrings, the
price of sin?! Why is your fine
black hair so wild on your face?!
Murder! Murder!! They'll soon be
coming for me. That knife will betray me.

[slide on strings]

[discovering the knife]

Da, da ist's!

Here it is!

[throwing the knife into the pond]

So! da hinunter!

Down! to the bottom!

[bass tuba, trombones, contrabassoon]

Es taucht ins dunkle Wasser wie
ein Stein.

It sinks through deep dark water
like a stone.

[voice sinking]

[looking up at the moon; harp]

Aber der Mond verrät mich. Der Mond is
    Blutig. [solo violins]
Will den die ganze Welt es ausplaudern?!
    Das Messer, es liegt zu weit vorn, sie
    finden's beim Baden oder wenn sie nach
    Muscheln tauchen.

See how the moon betrays me. The moon is
bloody. Must the whole wide world be shout-
ing it?! That knife is too near the shore.
They will find it when bathing, or when they
are gathering mussels.

253

[wading into the pond]

Ich find's nicht.
Aber ich muss mich waschen. Ich bin
blutig. Da ein fleck und noch einer.

I can't find it now.
I should wash myself. I am
bloody. Here's a spot and here another.

[lamenting]

2:35

Weh! Weh! Ich wasche mich mit Blut.
Das Wasser ist Blut … Blut …

Woe! Woe! I wash myself with blood.
The water is blood … blood …

[slow rising strings, representing the water rising]
[He begins to drown. The Captain and the Doctor enter.]

CAPTAIN

3:21

Halt!

Stop!

DOCTOR

Hören Sie? Dort!

Do you hear? There!

CAPTAIN

Jesus! Was war ein Ton.

Jesus! What a sound.

DOCTOR

Ja, dort!

Yes, over there!

CAPTAIN

Es ist das Wasser im Teich. Das
Wasser ruft. Es ist schon lange
niemand entrunken. Kommen Sie,
Doktor! Es ist nicht gut zu hören.

It is the water. The water is
calling out. No one has drowned
here for a long time. Come,
Doctor! It is not good to hear.

DOCTOR

Das stöhnt, [clarinets, horn]
als stürbe ein Mensch.
Da ertrinkt Jemand!

Groaning like a man dying.

Someone is drowning!

CAPTAIN

Unheimlich! [celesta and harp]
Der Mond rot, und die Nebel grau.
Hören Sie? jetzt wieder das Aechzen.

Eerie!
The moon is red, the mist grey.
Do you hear? Again that sound.

DOCTOR

Stiller, jetzt ganz still.

Quieter now. Now completely quiet.
[silence]

4:29 | *Kommen Sie! Kommen Sie schnell.* | Come! Come quickly.

[timpani, basses; low harp]
[End of scene]

ACT III, SCENE FOUR
ORCHESTRAL INTERLUDE

[D minor]
(This is the only section in the entire opera that has a tonal center.)

2 **4:35** | Low strings and horns; orchestral crescendo.

5:29 | Brass instruments are heard, followed by harp glissando.

5:53 | There begins a series of orchestral crescendos. Trombones; horns.

6:34 | The mood changes. Trumpets prominent.

7:05 | Drumroll. More drumbeats.

7:11 | Trombones.

7:38 | Loud cymbal crash, slow descending dissonant orchestral chords, arriving again at D minor.

8:19 | End of interlude.

SCENE FIVE

(This final scene is probably the most dismal of all. The simple children's melodies heard here are every bit as disturbing as the grotesque sounds of Scene 4.)

3 **8:20** | *Ringel, Ringel, Rosenkranz, Ringelreih'n'* | Ring-a-ring-a-rosie, all fall down!
Ringel, Ringel, Rosenkranz, Rin- | Ring-a-ring-a-rosie, all-

ONE OF THE CHILDREN

8:33 | *Du, Kaethe! Die Marie ...* | You, Kathy! Do you know about Marie?

SECOND CHILD

Was ist? | What is it?

FIRST CHILD

Weisst' es nit? Sie sind schon Alle 'naus. | Don't you know? They've all gone out there.

[solo violin]

THIRD CHILD

[to Marie's son]

Du! Dein Mutter ist tot! | You! Your mother is dead.

[string harmonics]

255

MARIE'S SON		
	[not really paying attention, riding his play-horse]	
	Hopp, hopp. Hopp, hopp.	Hop, hop. Hop, hop.
	Hopp, hopp.	Hop, hop.
	[sticks]	

SECOND CHILD		
	Wo ist sie denn?	Where is she then?

FIRST CHILD		
	Draus liegt sie, am Weg,	Out there, on the path,
	neben dem Teich.	by the water.

THIRD CHILD		
	Kommt, anschaun!	Come! Let's go and look!
	[clarinets]	

MARIE'S SON		
9:13	*Hopp, hopp. Hopp, hopp.*	Hop, hop. Hop, hop.
	Hopp, hopp.	Hop, hop.
	[xylophone]	
	[Discovering he has been left alone, he stops, then follows after the others.]	

9:24	Strange inconclusive finish and end of the opera.
	[flutes, celesta, strings]

Anton Webern (1883–1945)

If Berg represented the link backward from Modernism to the past, Webern may be seen as the link forward. Whereas Berg's music is lush, intense, and emotionally committed, Webern's is spare, abstract, and restrained.

Webern was born in Vienna, like Schoenberg and Berg. He came from a middle-class family and as a teenager was immersed in music; he played the piano and the cello in addition to composing many pieces. While he was at the university, Webern studied musicology and wrote a doctoral dissertation on the music of a Renaissance composer. This close study of counterpoint had a strong influence on his own music. Like Berg, he took private composition lessons with Schoenberg.

Webern's death goes down in history as one of the many thousands of incongruous tragedies caused by war. In 1945, after the war had ended and American forces were occupying Austria, Webern went outside one night to smoke a cigarette and was shot by a jittery American soldier.

Webern's Music

Webern's music is extraordinarily concentrated and delicate. Everything is understated, and there is never an extra note. In this very finely sculpted atmosphere, the silences are as meaningful as the notes. In painting, a close parallel can be found in the *Constellations* series of Joan Miró, in which stars and tiny figures are carefully balanced with empty space to create an overall effect.

Webern had an exact ear for precisely the sounds he wanted to achieve. He wrote detailed instructions all over his scores, indicating exactly how he wanted each tiny phrase to sound. It is a measure of the refinement of his music that although there is a whole spectrum of dynamics in his works, almost all of it lies between medium loud and very, very soft.

Most of Webern's compositions are quite short. Many movements last less than a minute, and some are as short as twenty seconds. Even the biggest works are only ten minutes long.

Webern used a great deal of counterpoint in his music, like the Renaissance master he studied. But in Webern's style, the counterpoint is atonal and, from the 1920s on, twelve-tone. The intervals are often sevenths and ninths, and there are many dissonances, but the texture is so light and transparent that the dissonances sound colorful rather than harsh.

In addition to his finely honed ear for dynamics, Webern possessed a keen awareness of very fine distinctions in instrumental sound. He calls for a great variety of tones and timbres, especially from string instruments, which are asked to play *pizzicato* (plucked), *sul ponticello* (bowed near the bridge), *con sordino* (with a mute), or *tremolo* (very rapid bowing on a single note), as well as combinations of the four. And each one of these instructions may appear over a phrase of just two or three notes.

Webern also had very specific instrumental sounds in mind when writing for orchestra. His music calls for guitars, chimes, cowbells, mandolins, and all kinds of unusual instruments. On the other hand, even a conventional group like a string quartet sounds completely new in the hands of this delicate colorist. We shall listen to one of Webern's very short movements for string quartet.

In Webern's music, with its rarefied atmosphere and extreme concision, every note has meaning, every gesture is significant. The utmost attention is required from the listener. Nothing could be further removed from the soaring passion of Romantic music.

The Migratory Bird (1941) from the *Constellations* series by Joan Miró.

Joan Miró, *The Migratory Bird*, Gouache and oil wash, paper, 18 1/8" × 15" (46.1 × 38.1 cm). From the *Constellations* series. Palma de Mallorca, Private Collection, Pierre Matisse Gallery. © 1998 Artists Rights Society (ARS), New York/ADAGP, Paris.

LISTENING GUIDE

ANTON WEBERN (1883–1945)

Third Movement from *Five Movements for String Quartet*, Op. 5

Date of composition: 1909
Orchestration: 2 violins, viola, cello
Duration: 0:41

Companion CD, Track 81

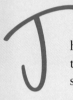

The third movement of Webern's *Five Movements for String Quartet* is so short that even the tiniest gesture becomes significant. Also, Webern uses a wide range of articulations and special string sounds that throw every note into relief. These include:

1. *am steg*, "at the bridge." This produces very scratchy, high-pitched sounds.
2. *pizzicato*, "plucked."
3. *arco*, "bowed."
4. *staccato*, "short, detached notes."
5. *col legno*, "with the wood." The strings are struck with the wood of the bow.

81	0:00	*staccato*, cello, short notes.
	0:01	*am steg*, violins and viola.
	0:03	*pizzicato*, violins and viola.
	0:04	*arco*, violins and viola.
	0:08	*arco staccato*, first violin and cello.
	0:10	*col legno*, violins and viola.
	0:16	*arco*, first violin; *pizzicato*, second violin, viola, cello.
	0:26	*arco*, cello; *pizzicato*, first violin and viola.
	0:30	*arco*, first violin; *arco staccato*, second violin, viola, cello.
	0:35	Loud finish, all instruments *staccato*, with two final *pizzicato* chords.

OTHER COMPOSERS ACTIVE BEFORE WORLD WAR II: BARTÓK, SHOSTAKOVICH, BRITTEN, IVES, COPLAND

We have examined the music of the most influential composers up to the middle of the twentieth century, but there were other important figures in music at this time. Although none of them founded a school or had brilliant and influential students, each one wrote compelling music of profound significance. Among the five composers, four different nationalities are represented.

Béla Bartók (1881–1945)

One of the most independent and original composers of the first half of the century was Béla Bartók. Bartók was born in Hungary. As a student, he entered the Budapest Academy of Music, where he later became professor of piano. He toured extensively as a concert pianist. But he also spent a great deal of time in Eastern Europe, Turkey, and North Africa, listening to, recording, and notating indigenous music, including songs and instrumental pieces. He ultimately published 2,000 tunes he had heard.

In the 1930s, Bartók was able to spend more and more time on his own compositions. In 1940, he immigrated to the United States with his wife, who was also a concert pianist. The couple made a meager living playing concerts, and Bartók worked for the folk music collection at Columbia University. He was virtually unrecognized, however, and he wrote no new music.

In 1943, though very ill, Bartók was given an important commission by the music director of the Boston Symphony Orchestra, Serge Koussevitsky, whose patronage helped support many struggling artists. The composition, known as the Concerto for Orchestra, was first performed in 1944. Bartók began to compose once again and almost finished three more major works before he died on September 26, 1945.

Bartók's Music

Bartók had three simultaneous careers: as an ethnomusicologist (someone who studies indigenous musics), a concert pianist, and a composer. Each of the first two influenced the third. Many of his compositions are colored by the rhythms and melodies of Eastern Europe. And the piano is featured in many of his works.

Partly for his students and partly for his son, Bartók wrote a series of piano pieces that start out very simple and gradually increase in difficulty. The series is called *Mikrokosmos* ("Microcosm"). Other Bartók piano compositions include three highly original piano concertos.

Like Beethoven, Bartók reserved his most profound music for his string quartets. The six quartets span most of his career, the first dating from 1908, when he was twenty-seven, and the last from 1939, just before he left Hungary for the United States. Each quartet is a profound and brilliant example of his art.

The most famous of the works composed in America is the Concerto for Orchestra (1943). The title is a play on words, because concertos usually put the spotlight on a single instrument rather than on a whole orchestra. But the work was written to celebrate the brilliance of all the orchestra's players.

Bartók's musical style is very individual. The fast movements are often very exciting—both wild and passionate. And his slow movements range from pieces of delicate mystery to extremes of lyrical intensity.

In his harmony, too, Bartók was highly original. You have the feeling that a key center is always present, giving the work a gravitational center, but it may be lost or disguised for long passages. Bartók also invented new forms. One of his favorites was the *arch form*. In a five-movement piece, movements one and five correspond, and so do movements two and four. Movement three is considered the apex of the arch. Bartók used this form with great effect in the Concerto for Orchestra and in his Fourth String Quartet, of which we shall hear the last movement.

LISTENING GUIDE

BÉLA BARTÓK (1881–1945)
Fifth Movement (*Allegro molto*) from String
  Quartet No. 4

Date of composition: 1928
Orchestration: 2 violins, viola, cello
Duration: 5:38

Companion CD, Track 82

Bartók's Fourth String Quartet uses an arch form. The quartet has five movements, of which the first and the last are related, as are the second and the fourth; the central slow movement stands at the apex of the work. The last movement, which we shall hear, unleashes an almost barbaric energy. It is propelled by clashing chords, whirling melodies, and asymmetrical rhythms. A rough approximation of sonata form can be heard, with a first theme of great intensity, a second theme that is lighter and more graceful, a condensed and varied recapitulation, and a fast coda. Techniques of counterpoint, such as **canon,** which is just like a **round** in singing, enrich the texture. The movement ends with the same heavy chords that ended the first movement. The dissonances in this quartet are extreme; for example listen to the repeated loud chords that open the movement:

$f\!f$

82	0:00	Violent, highly dissonant chords; cross-rhythms in cello.
	0:08	Rhythmic pattern established.
	0:11	Heavy, brusque **first theme** (low).

0:17	Answer, inverted (high).
0:23	Rhythmic accompaniment continues; varied and expanded statements of first theme; continued loud.
1:18	Cadential chords.
1:22	Quieter transitional passage.
1:38	Return of violent dissonant chords with cross-rhythms.
1:55	Cadential passage; sudden ending; pause.
2:05	*pp* muted arpeggios accompany **second theme**, light and graceful; answered by rhythmic cello phrase.
2:30	(**Development?**) Rhythmic phrase becomes central; soft and loud passages alternate; fragments of both themes combined.
2:41	Pizzicato rising phrases against quiet scattered fragments.
2:52	Crescendo to louder section; *pp*, crescendo again to two loud cadential chords; pause.
3:15	Condensed **recapitulation,** *ff*, first theme combined with violent chords.
3:35	Continuation and expansion, *ff*.
3:47	Loud folklike theme emerges.
3:55	Variant of folk theme in close canon; dissonant cadential chords.
4:09	Suddenly *pp*, close double canon, violins moving up, viola/cello down; gradual crescendo.
4:24	Reemergence of rhythmic phrase, then first theme, broken down and punctuated by dissonant chords.
4:39	Dissonant chords alternate with chords played *col legno* (with the wood of the bow).
4:46	Cello slide and recitative, with brief fragments on other strings.
5:04	Sustained harmonics lead into:
5:06	**Coda;** faster, growing in intensity.
5:14	Rhythmic phrase, *f*, close canon, descending in pitch; sudden stop.
5:25	Fragment and sustained harmonics.
5:31	Heavy closing chords.

Portrait of Shostakovich,
1964.

Dmitri Shostakovich (1906–1975)

Shostakovich was born just before the Russian Revolution and died fourteen years before the collapse of Communism. He lived most of his life under the Soviet system, attempting to find a balance between creative freedom and the demands of a totalitarian state. His plight is movingly described in his memoirs, entitled *Testimony*, smuggled out of the Soviet Union and published in 1979. Because music in the Soviet Union was supposed to represent the policies of the state, Shostakovich often came in for official criticism. Often, he would write a piece and not even publish it. Shostakovich's fear was justified. Under Stalin, twenty million people, including many artists, writers, and musicians, were murdered.

After Stalin's death, Shostakovich wrote his Tenth Symphony, in 1953. This is one of his greatest works. It is highly expressive and personal, with a voice of grieving introspection.

By the time of his death, Shostakovich had composed fifteen symphonies. He also wrote fifteen string quartets, some of which are also intensely personal.

Shostakovich often used a short musical motive in his works to put his signature on them. Bach had done this in the eighteenth century: The letters B-A-C-H are all names of notes in German (B is B-flat, H is B-natural). Shostakovich's signature is based on his monogram "D. Sch." S is E-flat, so D-S-C-H in notes is D, E-flat, C, and B-natural. This musical signature is found in many works, especially the very personal Eighth String Quartet and the Tenth Symphony.

The musical style of Shostakovich is intense, overlaying tonal areas with dense chromaticism or playing off highly dissonant chord structures with passages of great lyricism. Like Bartók, Shostakovich proved that tonality, updated, refreshed, and reinvented for the twentieth century, was still a highly viable means of expression.

Benjamin Britten (1913–1976)

Benjamin Britten was born in a small English country town. He was a child prodigy and began turning out compositions at the age of five. Later, he arranged some of these childhood pieces into the *Simple Symphony* (1934), which is one of his most attractive works. Britten's *The Young Person's Guide to the Orchestra* (1946) is designed to display all the different instruments of a symphony orchestra.

Britten was gay, and his lifelong companion was Peter Pears, a fine tenor singer. During World War II, the couple was invited to America by the poet W. H. Auden, who was also gay and who had formed an artists' community in New York. But after only two years, Britten and Pears returned to England.

Then began the remarkable series of English operas on which Britten concentrated for the next ten years. The first was *Peter Grimes* (1945), then came *Billy Budd* (1951), *Gloriana* (1953), written for the coronation of Queen Elizabeth II, and *The Turn of the Screw* (1954). In most of his vocal works, a central role is designed for Peter Pears.

The most important achievement of Britten's career is the *War Requiem* (1961). Britten's *War Requiem* was written for the dedication of a new cathedral in Coventry, England, which had been constructed to replace the great medieval church destroyed during World War II. For this work, Britten juxtaposes settings of the age-old, timeless Latin Mass for the Dead with settings of English poems by Wilfred Owen, who had been killed a week before the end of the First World War at the age of twenty-four.

Britten's very individual sound is based on many factors: the directness and lack of pretension in the melodic lines, the common use of high tenor voice (this range seems to affect even his instrumental compositions), and an almost constant tension between conflicting tonalities. This can extend sometimes to clear instances of bitonality.

The American Scene

The history of classical music in America reaches back to Colonial times, when the most significant composer was William Billings (1746–1800), a composer of rough-hewn (he called himself a "carver") and highly original settings of psalms and songs for unaccompanied chorus. His publication in 1770 of *The New-England Psalm-Singer* marked the appearance of the very first published collection of American music.

In the nineteenth century, the American tradition was kept alive in the South and the Midwest by means of "shape-note" books, in which pitches are indicated (for people who cannot read music) by simple signs such as small triangles, circles, and squares. One of the best-known of these shape-note hymn collections is *The Sacred Harp*, published in 1844. African-American spirituals were also sung widely throughout the nineteenth century, although the first published collection did not appear until 1867. And in the Midwest, one of the most original American composers, Anthony Heinrich (1781–1861, known as "the Beethoven of Kentucky") wrote elaborate and complex orchestral works that depicted nature on the frontier.

But the rough-and-ready style of American music was soon overwhelmed by the work of more "proper," European-trained composers. One of these was Lowell Mason (1792–1872), who wrote over a thousand hymn settings, some of which may still be found in Protestant hymnals.

Around the beginning of the twentieth century, American music and music making were still strongly influenced by the European tradition. The United States had not participated in the nationalist wave that swept through many other countries from the 1860s to the 1890s. During this period, America was absorbed by its own inner turmoil: the Civil War, the assassination of President Lincoln, and Reconstruction. American composers, mostly trained in Europe, paid little attention to the enormously varied indigenous music around them: African-American spirituals, New England hymn tunes, Native American songs and dances, the music of jazz bands, revival-meeting songs, and Irish-Scottish-English-American folk melodies. And the American public was interested only in imported music: Italian operas, Handel's English oratorios, and above all, German symphonies and chamber music.

Music was, however, becoming better established on the American scene. Conservatories of music were founded, concert halls were built, and music began to be taught as a serious discipline on university campuses. Most composers around the turn of the century began or concentrated their careers in Boston. They included John Paine (1839–1906), who was the first professor of music ever to be appointed in the United States (at Harvard University); Edward MacDowell (1860–1908), a fine pianist as well as a composer; Horatio Parker (1863–1919), a choral composer on mostly religious texts; George Chadwick (1854–1931), a symphonist and American opera composer, who was for more than thirty years director of the newly founded New England

Conservatory of Music in Boston; and Arthur Foote (1853–1937), whose best works are his beautiful solo songs and chamber music.

Boston was also the home of several women composers. They included Helen Hood, Mabel Daniels, Helen Hopekirk, and Margaret Lang, who was born in 1867 and died in 1972 at the age of 104.

Perhaps the best-known woman composer in Boston at the turn of the century was Amy Beach (1867–1944). She began her musical career as a concert pianist but also composed a wealth of important music. Her *Gaelic Symphony* (1896), based on Irish folk tunes, carries the distinction of being the first American symphony by a woman.

Today, although there are some attempts at an American music revival, little of this late nineteenth- and early twentieth-century music receives regular concert performance. Perhaps the inferiority complex regarding music from Europe has still not quite disappeared.

Charles Ives (1874–1954)

The first Modernist composer whose work was distinctively American was Charles Ives, who grew up in a small Connecticut town. He was the son of a bandmaster and music teacher whose approach to music was fun-loving and unconventional. Ives's father used to play tunes in two different keys at once, and he sometimes asked Charles to sing a song while he played the accompaniment in the "wrong" key on the piano. This open-minded and experimental approach stayed with Ives all his life.

Ives went to Yale as an undergraduate and then went into the insurance business, devoting his spare time to music. Over the next ten years, he wrote an enormous quantity of music, while his business prospered, too. Although he lived until 1954, most of his music dates from before the First World War.

Ives's music is a remarkable, unique mixture. He was a radical experimentalist who nonetheless believed in the values of small-town America. Most of his compositions are based on American cultural themes: baseball, Thanksgiving, marching bands, popular songs, the Fourth of July, fireworks, and American literature. Work-

Charles Ives, composer and insurance agent.

ing alone, Ives developed some of the innovations that would not take hold in the broader musical scene until the 1960s. He composed music with wild dissonances. Ives once wrote a letter to his music copyist, who had "corrected" some of the notes in his manuscript: "Please don't correct the wrong notes. The wrong notes are right." He wrote for pianos specially tuned in quarter tones; in his *Concord* Sonata, he called for the pianist to use an elbow to press down notes and, in one place, a wooden board to hold down sixteen notes at once. "Is it the composer's fault that a man has only ten fingers?" he asked. Ives's most famous composition is *The Unanswered Question* (1908), in which two different instrumental groups, sitting separately, play different music at the same time. And in his program piece called *Putnam's Camp*, the music depicts two marching bands passing each other, playing different tunes.

The music of Charles Ives was virtually unknown in its own time. It was only in the 1940s that Ives's work began to be performed, and only many years later that he began to be recognized as a truly original American musical genius.

LISTENING GUIDE

CHARLES IVES (1874–1954)

Second Movement from *Three Places in New England* ("Putnam's Camp, Redding, Conn.")

Date of composition: 1903–11
Orchestration: Flute/piccolo, oboe/English horn, clarinet, bassoon, 2 or more horns, 2 or more trumpets, 2 trombones, tuba, piano; timpani; drums; cymbals; strings
Duration: 5:38

Complete CD Collection: 4, Track 4

"Putnam's Camp" captures a child's impression of a Fourth of July picnic with singing and marching bands. In the middle of the picnic, the boy falls asleep and dreams of songs and marches from the time of the American Revolution. When he awakes, he again hears the noise of the picnic celebration.

Ives's piece is a collage of contrasting sounds and textures. The effect is one of varying successions of vigorous, raucous noise. You will enjoy the extraordinary energy of this work.

4	0:00	*Introduction:* full orchestra with dissonant descending scales, leading to repeated notes; a vigorous marchlike pulse.
	0:10	*Allegro* ("quick-step time"): a bouncy, accessible melody accompanied by a regular thudding bass. Flutes and trumpets can be heard with competing melodies as Ives evokes the atmosphere of a chaotic festive event.
	0:47	After a fanfare by a single trumpet, we hear the clamor of different simultaneous events, with strong melodies in trombones and trumpets, and heavy use of cymbals and snare drum.
	1:00	Thinner texture and softer dynamics lead to parodied quotation of "Rally Round the Flag" and "Yankee Doodle," with:
	1:08	Jagged melody in violins with contrasting piano and percussion, leading to:
	1:50	Softly throbbing cellos and basses, gradually slowing down, illustrating the child gradually falling asleep.
	1:55	Decrescendo, then quiet.
	2:06	*Dream section:* Begins with an ethereal sustained high chord, then continues with a smooth but energetic melody (first flute, then oboe). But the regular pulse (percussion and piano) accompanying this melody accelerates and takes off on its own (the soldiers march off to pipe and drum). Different melodies in the violins, oboes, clarinets, and trumpets, in a number of different meters and keys, combine with a building tension. The conflicting pulse of the piano and snare drum against the slower pulse of the repetitive low strings can be clearly heard. This gradually dies down, and then:

3:10	A bold, new, brass melody emerges and leads to another section of conflicting melodies; simultaneously, "The British Grenadiers," a favorite revolutionary tune, is heard in the flutes.
3:36	A strongly accented and repetitive tune ascends in the brass and starts another dense passage.
3:57	*Awakening:* This comes to an abrupt halt (the boy suddenly awakes), and a lively tune is revealed in the violins (the boy hears children's songs in the background). This builds to another complex passage (combination of different bands, songs, and games). Heavy, low rhythms and several meters combine. Fragments of "The British Grenadiers," and other tunes.
4:47	Repeated notes in trumpets and brass cut in suddenly.
4:54	Another swirl of melodies and rhythms, oscillating notes crescendo, frantic scales, as all the instruments push their dynamic limit, leading to the final jarring chord.

Aaron Copland (1900–1990)

If Ives represents the avant-garde in American music, Aaron Copland represents a more mainstream approach. Copland was born into a Jewish immigrant family in Brooklyn and decided to become a composer at the age of fifteen. When he was twenty, he went to Europe—specifically to Paris, where he studied with Nadia Boulanger.

Boulanger was perhaps the most famous composition teacher of the twentieth century. She was also a composer, pianist, organist, and conductor. She was extremely strict in her teaching, insisting that her students learn all aspects of music. A large number of American composers of the twentieth century studied with Boulanger.

When Copland returned from Paris in 1924, he decided to write works that would be specifically American in style. To do this, he drew on the most recognizably American musical style: jazz. And many of his compositions are infused with the syncopated rhythms and chord combinations of American jazz. One of these is the Clarinet Concerto (1948), which he wrote for the famous jazz clarinetist Benny Goodman.

Another way Copland strove to put America into his music was by the use of purely American cultural topics. His ballet suites *Billy the Kid* (1938) and *Rodeo* (1942) are cowboy stories, and *Appalachian Spring* (1944) depicts a pioneer wedding in rural Pennsylvania.

Appalachian Spring also demonstrates a third technique used by Copland to make his music sound American: quoting from folk songs, hymns, and country tunes. The seventh scene of *Appalachian Spring* is a series of variations on the exquisite Shaker melody "Simple Gifts" (sometimes known by its first line, "'Tis the gift to be simple, 'tis the gift to be free …").

Finally, Copland made his music sound American by a rather more sophisticated technique. He used very widely spaced sonorities—deep basses and high, soaring violins—to evoke the wide-open spaces of the American landscape. In addition, he often used the interval of a fifth in his music, a very open-sounding interval, and his chord changes are slow and static, suggesting the more gradual pace of nature's clock.

Copland wrote books on music, gave lectures, conducted around the world, composed film scores, and was the mentor of such luminaries as Leonard Bernstein. Copland's leading position in American musical life led to his being called "the dean of American music."

Composer, conductor, and author Aaron Copland conducting his own work at Tanglewood, Massachusetts.

LISTENING GUIDE

AARON COPLAND (1900–1990)

Fanfare for the Common Man

Date of composition: 1942
Orchestration: 3 trumpets, 4 horns, 3 trombones, tuba, timpani, bass drum, tam-tam
Duration: 3:36

Companion CD, Track 83

Perhaps today we might find Copland's piece more aptly titled *Fanfare for the Average American.* Certainly Copland did not intend to exclude women. And although Copland's title does not mention any nationality, this piece has become almost a sound icon for the spirit of America. Much of the piece's bold, assertive mood comes from its instrumentation, as it is scored entirely for brass and percussion. The simplicity of its motives—using triads, fifths and octaves—gives an open, spacious quality to the piece.

83	0:00	Somber strokes on the bass drum, timpani, and gong (tam-tam); gradual decrease in volume.
	0:25	Fanfare idea in a steady, deliberate tempo—ascending triad; then the fifth outlining that same triad leads to a high note and a slower, descending arpeggio. Stark, unison trumpets.

0:54	Timpani and bass drum.
0:59	Fanfare idea, louder, now harmonized with one additional contrapuntal line in the French horns.
1:39	Tam-tam, timpani, and bass drum.
1:50	Accented low brass take up the fanfare, imitated by timpani, then by trumpets and French horns. Harmony expands richly to three and more chord tones. Rising fifth and octave intervals in timpani.
2:38	Another series of statements of the fanfare motive begins. This moves to a series of stepwise descents from the highest pitch of the piece.
3:04	A contrasting harmonic area is introduced, but with the same rising fifth–octave motive.
3:27	The work ends with a bold crescendo but an unsettled harmonic feeling, evoking a restless spirit, the spirit of exploration.

BUILDING BRIDGES

Much of Copland's music tries to bridge the gap between "serious" music and listeners. Audiences were increasingly alienated by Modernism, and Copland's more accessible and traditional style helped bring them back to the concert hall. Two other American composers did this in different ways; these composers were George Gershwin and Leonard Bernstein.

George Gershwin (1898–1937)

George Gershwin was primarily a composer of popular songs and a jazz pianist. But he was also attracted to the world of the concert hall, and he wrote four works that reach across the cultural divide between popular and classical music. The first was *Rhapsody in Blue* (1924), a highly attractive and successful mixture of the jazz idiom and concert music, scored for solo piano and orchestra. Next came the jazzy Piano Concerto in F (1925). Both compositions were designed for Gershwin's own brilliant piano playing.

In 1928, Gershwin composed *An American in Paris*, a programmatic symphonic poem. The music is colorful, lively, and drawn from Gershwin's own experience in visiting Paris several times.

The last of Gershwin's works to bridge the gap between popular and classical music is by far the most ambitious. It is a full-length opera, in which Gershwin combines elements of jazz, church meetings, street cries, lullabies, and spirituals. The opera is *Porgy and Bess*, which contains some of Gershwin's best-known tunes, including "It Ain't Necessarily So" and "Summertime." Many people know these songs, but not so many have heard the entire opera, which is one of Gershwin's greatest achievements. *Porgy and Bess* was completed in 1935. A year and a half later, the brilliant young composer was dead, cut off in the midst of his career by a brain tumor at the age of thirty-eight.

Leonard Bernstein (1918–1990)

The person who best represented American music and music making in the second half of the twentieth century was also one of the most famous musicians in the world. His name was Leonard Bernstein, and he continued the tradition, started by Copland and Gershwin, of blending popular and "serious" styles. Like Copland and Gershwin, Bernstein was Jewish. Like them, he was a brilliant pianist and a prodigiously gifted all-round musician. Like Copland, Bernstein lectured and wrote books about music and loved to teach. Like Gershwin, Bernstein enjoyed fast cars, fancy clothes, and all-night parties.

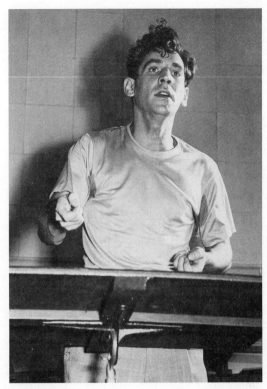

Leonard Bermstein in 1947.
Copyright William P. Gottlieb, Library of congress: Ira and Lenore S. Gershwin Fund.

Bernstein got his start in music at Tanglewood, where he became a protégé of the conductor and music patron Serge Koussevitsky. In 1943, Bernstein caused a sensation when he took over a New York Philharmonic concert as conductor on only a few hours notice. From then on, his career was assured.

Bernstein was enormously versatile, and he had the energy of three men. He used to sleep only two or three hours a night. He could have been a great pianist, a great conductor, or a great composer. Instead, he was all three.

As a pianist, Bernstein enjoyed playing everything from Mozart to Gershwin. As a conductor, Bernstein's career was unparalleled. He was for ten years the permanent conductor of the New York Philharmonic, but he was in demand by orchestras all over the world. His conducting was manically energetic: He would throw his arms around, shake his fists, twist and cavort. Sometimes he would leap into the air to express his excitement. But underneath the showmanship, there was a profound musical intelligence.

As a composer, Bernstein was highly versatile. Like Stravinsky and Copland, he wrote ballet music. Bernstein also wrote musicals, including *On the Town* (1944), *Wonderful Town* (1953), and *Candide* (1956). His most successful musical, and his most famous composition, was *West Side Story*, written in 1957. An updating of Shakespeare's *Romeo and Juliet*, it tells the story of lovers separated by the gulf between rival gangs on Manhattan's West Side. The score is brilliant, combining jazz, snappy dances, and moving lyricism.

In addition to ballets and musicals, Bernstein wrote gentle songs and delicate piano pieces, as well as big choral works, three symphonies, two operas, and a Mass. Multiple reconciliations are attempted in his *Mass*, written in 1971. It is a rock setting of the Catholic Mass with singers and orchestra; it is a concert piece that is designed to be staged; and some of the text is in Hebrew.

Bernstein lived his life to the hilt. It always seemed he didn't want to miss anything. He was bisexual, smoked and drank to excess, and loved to surround himself with people. His charisma was magnetic. He managed to wring seventy-two years out of life, though he never stopped smoking, and suffered from severe emphysema. In the end, he simply dropped dead. In his passionate commitment and his manifold achievements, Leonard Bernstein personified American music for half a century.

LISTENING GUIDE

LEONARD BERNSTEIN (1918–1990)

"Greeting" from *Arias and Barcarolles*

Voice and piano
Date of composition: 1955 (rev. 1988)
Duration: 2:50

Complete CD Collection: 4, Track 5

Bernstein was a larger-than-life personality, but he was also the composer of some of the best-loved songs in the American popular psyche ("Maria," "I Want to Be in America"). The little song "Greeting" is not very well known, but it is extremely beautiful and touching. It was written after the birth of Bernstein's first child.

5	0:00	[Gentle piano introduction]
	0:58	[First verse] When a boy is born, the world is born again, And takes its first breath with him.
	1:25	[Second verse] When a girl is born, the world stops turning round, And keeps a moment's hushed wonder.
	1:53	[Third verse] Every time a child is born, for the space of that brief instant, The world is pure.
	2:17	[Piano postlude]

AFTER THE WAR: MODERNISM, THE SECOND STAGE

Although the careers of many of the composers discussed earlier (e.g., Stravinsky, Shostakovich, Britten, Bernstein) continued well into the second half of the century, the end of World War II marked a real turning point in the development of new music. It was a turning point for the Western world, of course. As societies struggled to recover from the enormous human loss and destruction of the war, economies boomed, and a new optimism reigned. In the 1950s, Americans enjoyed a higher standard of living than ever before, and in Europe, though recovery was much slower, hopes increased for the future. The birthrate multiplied, resulting in what has been called the "baby boom," whose effects (and ripple effects) continue to have an enormous influence on our society.

After the war, and especially in the fortunate Fifties and the radical Sixties, the arts flourished, and music entered the second stage of Modernism. This was a period of radical experimentation, expanding on ideas set forth in the first stage and marked by two opposing tendencies: extreme control and complete freedom. The controls were established by a technique known as total serialism, in which mathematical models determined every aspect of a composition. The outer fringes of the "freedom movement" allowed performers to play what they liked when they liked.

The Radical Sixties: New Sounds, Freedom, and Chance

In the 1960s, the United States and Europe underwent profound change. The "baby boomers" grew to adulthood, and experimentation was in the air. It was a time of unprecedented freedom in the areas of sex, drugs, and individual lifestyles, and this sense of radical experimentation was reflected in the music. This was the era in which popular music began to overwhelm the music of "serious" composers. And yet it was certainly in "serious" music that the most interesting musical experiments were being made.

NEW SOUNDS   Many of these experiments revolved around new sounds. The synthesizer, the tape recorder, and the computer made available to composers both new sounds and the ability to manipulate sounds in completely new ways. New sounds were also produced by an inventive and imaginative use of normal musical instruments: squeaks, whines, and flutters from wind instruments, bonks and slides from string instruments. Modification of the piano became popular at this time, with nuts and bolts or other objects lying on top of the strings to create new sounds. And some of the more radical composers wrote fascinating pieces for large groups of instruments playing in quite novel ways.

One of the most interesting composers working with sound textures in the 1960s was the Polish composer Krzysztof Penderecki (b. 1933, last name pronounced Pender*etz*ki). His *St. Luke Passion* for solo singers, chorus, and orchestra, written in 1965, pays homage to Bach, but the sounds are very new. Penderecki has the chorus shout, whisper, and moan; the solo singing is wild and dramatic; and the orchestra uses massive sound blocks, with special instrumental effects.

Penderecki's most famous composition dates from 1960. It is written for a string orchestra composed of twenty-four violins, ten violas, ten cellos, and eight double basses, and it is entitled *Threnody* (which means a homage to the dead) *for the Victims of Hiroshima*. This is an incredibly powerful piece—lamenting, angry, and intense. Sometimes it seems even to assault the listener. Huge sound blocks are used, and the players produce a wide assortment of noises by knocking on the bodies of their instruments or by scraping the strings hard. Often the effects are strikingly similar to those produced by electronic means. Once you hear this piece, you will never forget it.

LISTENING GUIDE

KRZYSZTOF PENDERECKI (B. 1933)

Threnody for the Victims of Hiroshima

Date of composition: 1960
Orchestration: 24 violins, 10 violas, 10 cellos,
    8 double basses
Duration: 9:44

Complete CD Collection: 4, Track 6

Penderecki's *Threnody* is a work of great power. The piece falls into six identifiable sections with an introduction, reaching a peak of intensity in section IV and finally fading, after a roar of sound, to nothingness at the end of section VI.

6	0:00	High sustained pitches; at first two, then joined by others to produce a piercing effect.
	0:18	Sound spreads and softens, some of the pitches waver and oscillate.
I		
	0:38	Sudden drop in volume, sound still high and sustained, but with some wavering.
	0:49	Pizzicato and thumping on instruments; these percussive effects build in intensity and gradually (1:19) are replaced by high, brief squeaks and short runs and flourishes; these also build in rhythmic activity and intensity; some lower grunts are added (1:34); crescendo.
	2:10	Suddenly calm and sustained. Unison pitch that spreads into a cluster and returns to a unison,
	2:42	then fades; a faint distant pitch emerges, then another one, in a lower range; overlapping successions of single pitches enter, spread into a cluster, return to a unison and fade.
II		
	2:53	A high pitch enters; it crescendos gradually while lower pitches continue to enter beneath it.
	3:02	High pitch spreads to cluster and returns to near-unison.
	3:13	Sudden break; low, unfocused tone cluster.
	3:27	Pause, then loud tone clusters enter at various pitch levels, and are sustained.

FREEDOM AND CHANCE The kind of music composed in the *Threnody* requires very careful control on the part of the composer. At the same time as these ideas were being explored, a completely opposite tendency was prevalent in music. This was a move *away from* control, in the direction of freedom for the performers, even to the point of leaving some musical matters to chance. Some scores have several pages of music for each of the performers, allowing them to choose which page they want to play and when. Others simply give general instructions: "As high as you can," or "Any sound repeated five times." And

III		
	4:03	Instruments drop out, and sense of spreading is created as low instruments fall in pitch while high ones slide higher; decrescendo; sound seems to "disappear" at the outer edges of perception.
	4:15	Beginning softly, instruments enter with short accented notes, gradually increasing in volume and becoming more sustained; builds to an intense level, then
IV		
	4:44	violins drop out, leaving lower instruments exposed; they glissando (slide), first downward in a cluster, then arrive at a unison (4:55), and decrescendo, the sound again gradually disappears. Long pause.
	5:45	Diffuse texture of plucking, thumps, extreme highs and low tremolos and glassy single pitches;
	5:56	calmer, fewer events;
	6:10	more activity, faster rhythms;
	6:56	sounds press higher,
	7:14	upward fast glissandos and quick thumping are added,
	7:26	occurring in an intense succession.
V		
	7:36	High clusters are sustained, string basses make grunting sounds, intensity builds, clusters oscillate with vibrato; crescendo,
	8:02	then sound ebbs, sustained pitches take over with a dense, focused, sustained cluster, then fade away,
	8:10	revealing a lower, busy oscillating sound.
	8:21	Higher clusters reenter, and are joined by more low- and high-range clusters, active with various speeds of tremolos.
	8:39	Suddenly gentle, but still active and intense.
VI		
	8:52	Entrance of a dense, broad wall of sound, thick and heavy. A very long decrescendo, finally fading into nothingness.

some scores simply give rough drawings or sketches on the page, abandoning musical notation altogether.

The idea of leaving musical events to chance was the main focus of a musical revolutionary named John Cage (1912–1992). Cage was born in Los Angeles, the son of an inventor. At the age of twenty-two, he studied with Schoenberg—who told him he had no ear for music and would never make a composer. But Cage decided that music was too narrowly defined. "*Everything* we do is music," he said.

Cage invented the idea of the "prepared piano," with nuts and bolts and plastic spoons inside the lid. He asked performers to throw dice and toss coins to determine which parts of a composition would be played. He wrote a piece called *Imaginary Landscape No. 4* (1951) for twelve radios, all playing on different stations. Once, when invited to give a lecture, he read for hours from various scraps of newspaper. "If my work is accepted," he once said, "I must move on to the point where it isn't."

Cage deliberately erased conventional boundaries. His most famous composition was written in 1952 and is entitled *4' 33''*. In it, the performer is instructed to sit at the piano for four minutes and thirty-three seconds and do *nothing*. The audience grows restless and finally starts listening to sounds inside and outside the hall—sounds of rustling, coughing, the buzz of the lights, police sirens—sounds that are not music. Or are they?

Cage was a leading member of the postwar avant-garde. He infuriated many critics, performers, and scholars, who thought he was destroying music, but his influence was vast, ranging from the painter Robert Motherwell to the rock group the Grateful Dead. "One need not fear," he once said, "about the future of music."

POSTMODERNISM

During the latter part of the twentieth century, artists began to question the continued viability of the Modernist movement. It had been unusually productive and long-lived: The feeling of innovation and experimentation had lasted from 1900 to the mid 1960s. Now some of its achievements were thrown into doubt. The meaning of art itself was no longer certain. Was a can of paint dropped on the floor "art?"

During the century, people had become increasingly alienated from modern classical music. Young people turned to rock and other forms of popular music.

From the mid 1960s through today, a new movement has taken hold in music and the other arts. This new movement is known as Postmodernism. **Postmodernism** is a style that juxtaposes many varied elements, especially familiar ones, in new and interesting ways.

Postmodernism has many facets. The most significant aspect of the movement is a deliberate return to the past. In music, the return to the past was exemplified by a return to the language of tonality, so resoundingly rejected for so many years. It was suggested that the main characteristics of tonal music—a key center, repetition, and return—correspond to basic impulses in the human brain and are therefore fundamental to human nature.

The postmodern Walt Disney World Dolphin Hotel at Walt Disney World Resort, Florida, completed in 1990.
William Taylor/Arcaid © Disney Enterprises, Inc.

Other facets of Postmodernism are a tendency to quote directly from earlier composers and to borrow from the music of other cultures. Compositions contain snippets or long extracts from older musical works. These references are juxtaposed in new and startling ways, and the old is embedded in a context of the new, throwing new light upon both of them. There is also a deliberate attempt to incorporate styles from other parts of the world, as the world becomes a smaller place.

Finally, Postmodernism deliberately reaches out across the traditional barrier between classical and popular music. Classical music of the late twentieth and early twenty-first centuries has moved closer to rock and even rap. The dividing line between operas and musicals (such as those of Andrew Lloyd Webber) is narrowing sharply. And performing groups deliberately mix genres: A string quartet plays arrangements of Jimi Hendrix; chamber groups include electric guitars, amplification, and video in their performances; performance artists play the violin, sing, and paint their bodies on stage.

What is common to these ideas is a deliberate mixing of styles. The late twentieth century began the idea that we should be open to all influences, past and present, local and foreign, popular and refined. In this new mixture all barriers will come down, the past will be absorbed into the present, and all art will become one, in a global unity. Is this the way of the future?

We'll see.

Postmodern Music

One of the ways in which Postmodernism first began to manifest itself in music was by quotation. In one composition entitled *Nach Bach* (*After Bach*, 1967), the American composer George Rochberg suspends little fragments of Bach's harpsichord music in a surrounding context of dissonance and abrupt silences. Luciano Berio's *Sinfonia* (1969) has a movement-length quotation from Mahler's Second Symphony, overlaid with readings of modern poetry, shouts, and tiny fragments of quotations from many *other* composers. And Lukas Foss's *Renaissance Concerto* (1986) is based on the music of Orfeo's lament from Monteverdi's *Orfeo*.

LISTENING GUIDE

LUKAS FOSS (b. 1922)

Third Movement (*Recitative*—after *Monteverdi*) from *Renaissance Concerto* for Flute and Orchestra

Date of composition: 1986
Orchestration: Solo flute and strings (plus "distant" small group of strings and flute)
Tempo: *Lento* ("Slow")
Meter: $\frac{4}{4}$
Duration: 5:15

Complete CD Collection: 4, Track 7

e have mentioned how much Postmodern music tends to rely on quotation or reference. *The Renaissance Concerto* of Lukas Foss is based on several themes and snippets from earlier eras. Despite the title, most of them are from the Baroque era. Perhaps Foss meant his piece to suggest "renaissance" in its generic meaning of "rebirth," for his concerto reinterprets and brings to life many works from the past. Foss calls this approach a "handshake across the centuries."

The third movement of this concerto is based on the lament of Orfeo for Euridice from Monteverdi's great opera *Orfeo*, of 1607. Foss recaptures the atmosphere of that music in several ways. First, many repeated pitches in the solo flute evoke Monteverdi's recitative style. Notice how many of the flute's phrases (such as the one at 0:40) seem speechlike in their shape and rhythm. Second, the opening phrase, with its distinctive falling interval of a diminished fourth, is taken directly from the opening of Monteverdi's lament. And finally, the mournful, haunting quality of the music and the curious echoing effect of the "distant" flute and strings suggest a timeless other world—the other world that Orpheus vows to visit to rescue Euridice from death.

7	0:00	Diminished fourth, first chordally in strings, then melodically in flute, imitated in strings. Fade.
	0:27	Stepwise rising idea, beginning with sliding half step that returns in final section.
	0:40	Even, repeated notes on flute, then descent.
	0:54	Falling diminished fourth returns in strings, then flute.
	1:12	Accented repeated notes on flute; quieter.
	1:25	Fast declamatory pitches on flute over high sustained string tone; flute moves higher, reaching highest pitch.
	1:48	Texture thins, flute descends slowly.
	2:07	Flute alone descends in slow arpeggio.
	2:45	Faster ascending idea on flute, imitated on strings.
	3:05	Flute: short phrases with two repeated notes, echoed in "distant" flute and strings; quieter.
	3:45	Slow slide up half step, reiterated higher and louder; "distant" flute echoes clearly.

Flute

	4:25	Slide pushes up to a high dissonant chord; then the tension is released as the accompaniment thins and the flute unwinds with a relaxed swirl of descending notes; movement ends with a low, hollow fifth in the strings.

The return to tonality was another striking feature of Postmodern music. David del Tredici (b. 1937) is best known for a series of extended compositions based on the stories *Alice in Wonderland* and *Through the Looking Glass.* The music is wonderfully inventive and captures the tone of Lewis Carroll's quirky prose with a modern aesthetic.

Tonality is mingled with Modernism in the work of the English composer Oliver Knussen (b. 1952). Knussen's setting of Maurice Sendak's children's story *Where the Wild Things Are* (1983) can be performed both as an opera and as a concert piece.

Multimedia Postmodernist work is perhaps best represented by the performance artist Laurie Anderson (b. 1947). A trained violinist, Anderson is also actress, singer, poet, and storyteller.

The meditative, spun-out quality of music from the East has been a major contributor to New Age music, which is also neotonal, but with a minimal sense of drive and resolution; it is floating, gentle, calm, and without form. A newer category of New Age music is known as Space Music. Formed mostly on synthesizers, it evokes the openness, vastness, and formlessness of outer space.

The merging of popular and "serious" music is perhaps the most interesting trend in Postmodern music. Starting in the 1960s but continuing strongly into the 1970s and 1980s, a new type of music was born, which was labeled **minimalism**. Like many other musical style terms, this one came from the art world. Artists reduced their paintings to the bare minimum, with flat surfaces, thin lines, simple shapes, and primary colors.

Minimalist music borrows from rock music the idea of harmonic simplicity and repetitive rhythm. It uses very limited materials and remains at an almost constant tempo and dynamic. The result is music that is hypnotizing in its sameness, inducing an almost trancelike state in the listener. It changes the listener's perception of the passage of time. Many examples of minimalist music involve very slow shifts over a long period of time. Perhaps because of its links to rock, minimalism brought classical music back into favor again and attracted large audiences. The central principle of minimalist music is that under the seeming changelessness there *is* change.

Fusion

Perhaps the most important aspect of the Postmodern era is the narrowing of gaps between all types of music. The jazz trumpeter Miles Davis and others created a mixture of jazz and rock that was called **fusion**. There are many different kinds of fusion today, created by artists as diverse as Keith Jarrett, Malcolm McLaren, Yo-Yo Ma, and Eric Clapton.

One of the most fertile meeting places of the several worlds of music has been the musical theater. The works of Andrew Lloyd Webber among others combine the style of the Broadway musical with the continuous musical settings and extended scenes of opera, the heavy beat and synthesizer-enhanced sound of rock, the sentimental lyricism of pop, and elaborate, high-tech, Postmodern stage effects.

In the modern era, as one contemporary composer and cultural commentator has written: "Multi-track, multi-layer experience becomes the norm: Ravi Shankar, John Cage, the Beatles, Gregorian chant, electronic music, Renaissance madrigals and motets, Bob Dylan, German *Lieder*; soul, J. S. Bach, jazz, Ives, Balinese gamelan, Boulez, African drumming, Mahler, *gagaku*, Frank Zappa, Tchaikovsky, … all become part of the common shared experience."

INCLUSION

It is a commonplace of historiography (the writing of history) that the present is too close to see with any perspective. Who are the great composers of today? Will their works last? We don't know the answers to these questions.

One thing *is* clear, however. In the late twentieth century, women and minorities gradually began taking their rightful place in American music making. In every chapter of this book, we have considered the role of women in the history of music. On the whole, with significant exceptions, it has been a history of exclusion or marginalization. One striking element of our present time has been the unraveling of this pattern and the gradual acceptance of women as full partners in the world of music. Although there are one or two orchestras in Europe that (believe it or not) still do not hire women, most European and North American orchestras contain large numbers of female musicians. There is an increasing number of conductors who are women, and some of the foremost composers of our age are women.

Representation for African-American musicians in the world of classical music still lags behind. There are a few black players in orchestras, some black conductors, and very few well-known composers.

To try to represent this picture of growing inclusiveness, we have chosen to end this chapter with the work of four contemporary American composers—three women, one African American. These works do not claim to speak for their composers' gender or race. They are not typical of any stylistic trends. They simply show that the differences between male and female or black and white in music disappear in the individuality that human beings share. The music of a gay composer or a black composer or a woman or an Australian aborigine or a Japanese master of the shakuhachi speaks to us because it is the communication of one human being to others. All we have to do is listen.

The first work we shall listen to is *Sound Patterns* by Pauline Oliveros. Born in Houston in 1932, Oliveros has written numerous compositions, served as composer-in-residence at several colleges, and toured the country in performances of contemporary music. In 1992, she won a fellowship from the National Endowment for the Arts. She is the founder of a group of women musicians and has worked frequently with actors, dancers, and filmmakers.

Composer Ellen Taaffe Zwilich.

Composer Olly Wilson.

LISTENING GUIDE

PAULINE OLIVEROS (b. 1932)

Sound Patterns

Date of composition: 1964
Orchestration: Mixed chorus
Duration: 4:01

Complete CD Collection: 4, Track 8

*S*ound Patterns is written for a mixed chorus (sopranos, altos, tenors, and basses). It involves no text. Rather, the composer calls for a huge range of nonverbal sounds from the singers, including clicking, trilling, hissing, sliding, screeching, whooping, popping, *ow*-ing, and *zz*-ing. The music mixes men and women, loud and soft, group and separate textures, high and low, all in a kaleidoscope of sound. The first few measures of music are shown here:

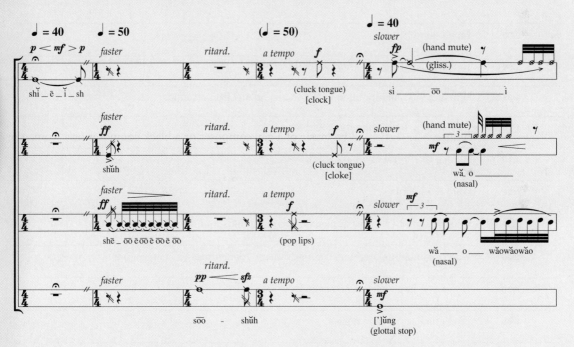

The work is so fascinating in its variety and so continuous that a timed Listening Guide would serve only as a distraction. Listen and enjoy!

Olly Wilson is an African-American composer who was born in St. Louis, Missouri, in 1937. He has degrees in music from Washington University in St. Louis, the University of Illinois, and the University of Iowa, and he is currently professor of music at the University of California at Berkeley. Wilson has won numerous prizes, grants, and fellowships, including a Guggenheim Fellowship that allowed him to spend a year studying music in Africa. He has published a book on black music in America. In 1995, Olly Wilson was elected to the American Academy of Arts and Letters. Wilson has specialized in electronic music, much of which was created in the Electronic Music Studio at Berkeley.

LISTENING GUIDE

OLLY WILSON (b. 1937)

Sometimes

Date of composition: 1976
Orchestration: Tenor and taped electronic sounds
Duration: 6:02

Companion CD, Track 84

Sometimes is based on the spiritual "Sometimes I Feel Like a Motherless Child." It is written for tenor and tape, and it calls for extraordinarily demanding singing. The tape uses both electronic sounds and manipulated snippets of the tenor's voice. Throughout the work, of which we shall hear an extract, the spiritual lends its powerful presence (even when it is absent).

84	0:00	Tape noises.
	0:09	Taped whispering: "motherless child."
	0:35	More activity; manipulated taped voice and electronic sounds; echoes.
	1:00	Tape noises, both screeching and low.
	1:10	Sounds like those of a bass guitar.
	1:28	Loud bass. Pause.
	1:39	Whistle sounds, feedback, clonks, ringing sounds, chimes, blips, etc. Pause.
	2:30	Voice and manipulated taped voice; noises. "Sometimes …"; crescendo.
	3:23	"I feel …" Tape noises; crescendo.
	3:43	"Sometimes …" Tape noises.
	4:08	Very high singing, "Sometimes …"; much more activity, crescendo.
	4:33	Voice over bass tape noises.
	4:38	"I feel like a motherless child."
	4:56	"True believer …" Whistles, blips, feedback.
	5:17	Voice and distorted taped voice ("Sometimes I feel …").
	5:44	Extremely high singing.
	5:58	Pause.

Joan Tower was born in New York in 1938 but was raised in South America. After returning to New York and earning degrees at Bennington College and Columbia University, Tower founded a contemporary music ensemble in which she played the piano. She has won several composition prizes and served as composer-in-residence to the Saint Louis Symphony. In 1990, she was the first woman to win the prestigious Grawemeyer Award for Music Composition, and in 1998, she won a Distinguished American Composers award. She lives in upstate New York and is professor of music at Bard College.

Composer Joan Tower.

LISTENING GUIDE

JOAN TOWER (b. 1938)

Wings

Date of composition: 1981
Orchestration: Solo clarinet
Duration: 6:01

Complete CD Collection: 4, Track 9

Tower has written that the image behind *Wings* is that of a falcon, at times gliding high along the air currents and at other times "going into elaborate flight patterns that loop around, diving downwards, gaining tremendous speeds." *Wings* lasts more than ten minutes; we shall hear a little more than half of the work.

9	0:00	Clarinet begins from no sound to a very quiet single tone.
	0:19	Change of pitch. More activity, though still quiet.
	0:53	Crescendo. Long tones mixed with faster notes.
	1:25	New melodic and rhythmic fragment.
	1:45	Excited. Trill.
	1:51	Jumpy, loud. Jumping high to low.
	2:11	Very fast. High trills.

2:37	Low notes, running passages, high/low. Slowing down, quieter.
2:56	Even notes, tranquil. Very quiet. Pause.
3:35	Climbing even notes. Pause.
3:55	Quiet; climbing even notes, from very low to high.
4:21	Low, quiet passage. Pause.
4:45	Single note, long crescendo.
5:01	Two octaves higher.
5:07	Gradually increasing activity, getting faster and higher.
5:33	Quiet, "echolike."
5:40	Frenetic; gradually calming down.
5:55	Section ends on a single tone. Crescendo to pause.

Ellen Taaffe Zwilich was born in Florida in 1939 and studied with Elliott Carter and Roger Sessions at the Juilliard School of Music. Her music demonstrates a concern with linking the present with the past. Her Symphony No. 1, composed in 1983, won a Pulitzer Prize in music. She was the first woman to win this award. In 1996, she was appointed the first composer-in-residence at Carnegie Hall. Ellen Zwilich describes composition as " … an obsession. It is profoundly thrilling to me."

LISTENING GUIDE

ELLEN TAAFFE ZWILICH (b. 1939)

Third Movement (*Rondo*) from Symphony No. 1

Date of composition: 1983

Orchestration: Piccolo, 2 flutes, oboe, English horn, clarinet, bass clarinet, bassoon, contrabassoon, 4 horns, 2 trumpets, 2 trombones, tuba, piano, harp, strings, and percussion, including timpani, cymbals, tambourine, bass drum (small and large), orchestral bells, vibraphone, tubular bells, snare drum, and suspended cymbals

Duration: 4:01

Complete CD Collection: 4, Track 10

The third movement is a rapid, energetic rondo, but the main thematic material, instead of being identical on each recurrence, is varied every time it returns. The main thematic idea is that of fast eighth notes, occurring in different ways: in the timpani as repeated pitches (A_1), as forceful rising arpeggios (A_2), and as an oscillation between two pitches (A_3). These are contrasted with a slower set of four eighth notes that rise in a jagged ascent (A_4), creating a four-against-six cross-rhythm with the driving faster eighths.

	A	
10	**0:00**	Theme group A_1–A_4, featuring the strings and frequent punctuation by percussion.

	B	
	1:07	The chime strikes a sudden change. Sustained passage with high glassy harmonics in the violins.

	A	
	1:32	Underlying timpani reintroduce the driving material.

	B	
	1:47	The sustained idea returns, with chimes and an ascending violin line. This leads to:

	C	
	2:16	A lyrical new melody in the oboe, with a soothing accompaniment including harp.

A	
2:37	The restless, driving A material enters again, softly in the violins, and then building in dynamics and intensity. Brass and percussion add heavy accents.

A	
3:26	The rising arpeggio idea (A_2) predominates, pushing the violins up to a high strained register.

B + A	
3:37	Sustained idea, now dissonant and harsh rather than soothing, is interrupted by timpani (A_1), leading to the final, driving, accented chords.

CONCLUSION

In the late twentieth century, classical music was in a lively but anxious state. Exciting concerts of new music were still being given, and the fusion of styles, as well as the inclusion of formerly excluded voices, made the music more interesting and of wider appeal. However a large proportion of classical-music concerts even today are devoted to music of earlier centuries. Many older people grew up in the fifties and sixties, when new classical music was difficult and unappealing. These people look backwards for their musical, emotional, and spiritual satisfaction.

Today, we are fortunate that the music of the past is so easily available to us. But new classical music is becoming a rarefied taste. It is not just that older people are afraid of it; young people are more attracted to music that is undemanding and gives easier and quicker gratification. This is a pity, for all worthwhile things take effort. Try listening carefully to the fascinating East/West music of Tan Dun, who won an Oscar in 2001 for the score to the film "Crouching Tiger, Hidden Dragon." Or take a few minutes and go to your music library and listen to a luminous new piece by John Corigliano or the brilliant and profound music of Osvaldo Golijov or Augusta Read Thomas. These people do not appear on Pepsi ads or on huge posters in your record store. But they have something very important to say. To you.

 Listening to...

MUSIC OF THE TWENTIETH CENTURY

- Stylistically, the music of the twentieth century can be divided into three periods: early (Modernism), middle (Serialism; twelve-tone music), and late (Postmodernism).
- The greatest representatives of musical Modernism are Debussy, Stravinsky, and Schoenberg.

- Debussy's music sounds suggestive, unfocused, impressionistic (*Prelude to the Afternoon of a Faun*). His use of the orchestra is highly coloristic, and he manages to evoke cloudy skies, turbulent seas, and rainy gardens, both in his orchestral music and in his music for solo piano.

- Stravinsky was such an original composer that he influenced the music of most of the century. You can hear big, powerful orchestral pieces in primitive style (*The Rite of Spring*), or jazz sounds and rhythms in other works.

- Perhaps the biggest revolution of Modernism was that stirred up by Schoenberg. He replaced the centuries-old system of tonality, first with atonality (Schoenberg's "Madonna"; Berg's *Wozzeck*), and then with a new system based on all twelve pitches (Schoenberg's *Variations for Orchestra*). This twelve-tone system (or Serialism) became the basis of composition for many composers of the mid-twentieth century. It is rigid and intellectually coherent, but people looking for pleasant melodies find Schoenberg difficult.

- Soon other, more popular musical styles were asserting themselves. Folk idioms (Bartok's *String Quartet No. 4*), music of the common people (Ives's *Three Places in New England*; Copland's *Fanfare for the Common Man*), and the sounds of jazz and Broadway (Gershwin's *Porgy and Bess*; Bernstein's "Greeting") infiltrated much classical music; and popular and classical music came closer together.

- This merging of styles culminated in the Postmodern movement (Foss's *Renaissance Concerto*). This movement draws on an eclectic variety of influences: rock, Baroque, Africa, the Middle East, politics, electronics, and new sounds (Pauline Oliveros' *Sound Patterns*; Olly Wilson's *Sometimes*; Joan Tower's *Wings*; Ellen Zwilich's *Symphony No. 1*). You can hear almost anything in today's classical music.

KEY TERMS

atonality **(p. 236)**
bitonality **(p. 242)**
fusion **(p. 277)**
minimalism **(p. 277)**
non-triadic harmony **(p. 237)**
octatonic scale **(p. 236)**

ostinato **(p. 242)**
pantonality **(p. 236)**
pentatonic scale **(p. 236)**
polyrhythm **(p. 242)**
polytonality **(p. 237)**
Postmodernism **(p. 274)**
quarter tone **(p. 237)**

telharmonium **(p. 238)**
theramin **(p. 238)**
tone cluster **(p. 236)**
twelve-tone system **(p. 236)**
whole-tone scale **(p. 236)**

10

The Twentieth Century II: Jazz, an American Original

1900
1910
1920
1930
1940
1950
1960
1970
1980
1990
2000

CHAPTER OUTLINE

What is jazz? Most of us recognize it when we hear it, but it's not so easy to list the essential ingredients of jazz. First of all is the rhythm. Jazz usually has a steady rhythm that continues from the very beginning of a piece to the end. That rhythm is often underscored by a strong beat. The most characteristic part of jazz rhythm is syncopation: the accentuation of "offbeats." The combination of these rhythmic elements contributes to what is known as "swing." Swing is the *feeling* generated by the steady rhythm and accented offbeats of the music and by the lively, spirited playing of jazz performers. Swing is what makes you want to move to the music.

Another primary ingredient of jazz is the use of "blue notes." **Blue notes** are notes that are played or sung lower or flatter than the pitches in a conventional Western scale. Common blue notes in jazz are the third, fifth, and seventh notes of a scale. These blue notes contribute to the expressive nature of much jazz performance.

Third, there are instruments central to jazz that are rarely used in concert music. Foremost among these is the saxophone, which comes in many sizes, from the small soprano sax to the enormous contrabass. Most common in jazz are the alto and tenor instruments. Jazz often features conventional instruments playing in unusual ways. Trumpets playing "wah-wah" with a mute, trombones making slides, clarinets squealing in the high register—these are sounds commonly heard in jazz. Jazz singers also deliberately make use of "bent" or "scooped" notes. A special kind of singing in which the vocalist improvises with wordless syllables ("doo-be-doo dah," etc.) is known as "scat" singing.

The saxophone family (from left to right): bass, baritone, two tenors, two altos, and soprano.

Finally, most people would say that improvisation is a necessary element in jazz. Certainly in many forms of jazz, improvisation plays a central role in the creation of the music, and some of the best jazz performers have been spontaneous and inventive improvisers. But there are many kinds of jazz that contain little or no improvisation (big band arrangements, for example). Perhaps the best approach is to say that improvisation is a typical, but not an absolutely necessary ingredient of jazz.

However, when jazz performers do compose, this means that they are not only performers but *composers* as well.

THE HISTORY OF JAZZ

Origins

Both the place and the time of the emergence of jazz can be fixed with some certainty. The place was New Orleans, the time was the 1890s.

In the late nineteenth century, New Orleans was one of the most culturally diverse and thriving cities in the United States. Its people were of African, French, Spanish, English, and Portuguese origin. There were first-, second-, and third-generation Europeans; African Americans who were former slaves or descendants of former slaves; Haitians; Creoles; and a constant influx of new immigrants from Europe, the Caribbean, and other parts of the United States. Being a flourishing port, New Orleans also drew in sailors and visitors from all over the world.

The city had one of the liveliest musical cultures in America. There was opera and chamber music. European ballroom dances were heard side by side with sailors' songs and hornpipes. Street sellers advertised their produce with musical cries. Work songs and "field hollers" mingled with the piano music of elegant salons. The bars, gambling joints, dance halls, and brothels were filled with smoke, liquor, and music.

Band Music

Everywhere in New Orleans there were bands: marching bands, dance bands, concert bands, and society orchestra bands. Bands played at weddings, funerals, parades, and political rallies, or just for the joy of it. Some of the musicians were classically trained; most could not read a note. But almost everybody played. Bands often held competitions to see which one could play the best. And the sound of a band in the street was an excuse for children (and adults) from all of the neighborhoods to come and join the fun.

The standard instruments in late nineteenth-century American bands were the trumpet (or cornet), clarinet, trombone, banjo, drums, and tuba. This instrumentation provided the proper balance among melody instruments, harmony instruments, bass, and percussion. All of these instruments were, of course, portable. Only later, when band music moved indoors, did the instrumentation include piano and string bass.

Band music was the first of the three major musical influences on early jazz. The other two were ragtime and the blues.

Ragtime

Ragtime was a type of piano music (sometimes played on other instruments) that also became popular in the 1890s. It was originally played mostly by African-American pianists in saloons and dance halls in the South and the Midwest. "Ragging" meant taking a popular or classical melody and playing it in a syncopated style. Later the style caught on, developing a form of its own, and ragtime was played by both black and white musicians to audiences all over the country.

Ragtime music is usually in duple meter and has the feel and tempo of a march. The left hand plays a steady, regular beat while the right hand plays a lively melody in syncopated rhythm. A ragtime composition usually consists of a series of related sections with a repetition pattern, most often AA BB A CC DD or something similar.

The most famous composer and performer of ragtime was the African American Scott Joplin (1868–1917), whose father was a slave. Scott Joplin himself received a formal music education and composed classical music as well as a large number of piano rags. Joplin's first job was as a pianist in the Maple Leaf saloon in Sedalia, Missouri. His most famous piece, the *Maple Leaf Rag*, was published in 1899 and sold so well that Joplin moved to St. Louis to concentrate on composition. In 1909, he settled in New York and composed a full-length opera, *Treemonisha*, which he attempted to have professionally produced, but without success. Joplin died in 1917, completely unrecognized by the musical establishment.

LISTENING GUIDE

SCOTT JOPLIN (1868–1917)

Maple Leaf Rag,
   for Piano Solo

Date of composition: 1899
Tempo: *Tempo di marcia* ("March tempo")
Meter: $\frac{2}{4}$
Key: A-flat Major
Duration: 3:12

Complete CD Collection: 4,
   Track 11

Scott Joplin

Scott Joplin's *Maple Leaf Rag* sold hundreds of thousands of copies after it was published in 1899. It is typical of much ragtime music written around the turn of the century. A steady left-hand accompaniment keeps the march beat going throughout the piece while the right hand plays a lively, syncopated melody against this steady beat. The sections are repeated in the usual pattern: AA BB A CC DD. Each section is 16 measures long. In this recording, we hear a piano roll (mechanical recording) made by Joplin himself in 1916.

	A	
11	0:00	Strong, steady chords in left hand; syncopated rhythm in right hand; short arpeggiated phrases.

	A	
	0:21	Repeat.

B	
0:42	Melody begins higher and moves down; *staccato* articulation.

B	
1:03	Repeat.

A	
1:24	Opening section is played only once here.

C	
1:45	Change of key to D-flat Major (IV); rhythmic change in right hand; left-hand leaps.

C	
2:06	Repeat.

D	
2:28	Return to original key; strong final cadence.

D	
2:48	Repeat.

The Blues

The third principal influence on jazz is the blues. The blues is a form, a sound, and a spirit, all at the same time. It began as a type of vocal music that crystallized in the 1890s from many elements. Among these were African-American spirituals, work songs, and street cries. The blues began as unaccompanied song but soon came to include banjo or guitar accompaniment. The common themes of early blues are sadness in love, betrayal, abandonment, and sometimes humor.

There is great variety in sung blues, but if there is a "standard" form, it is this: a series of three-line stanzas, in each of which the first two lines are the same:

> *I followed her to the station, with a suitcase in my hand.*
> *I followed her to the station, with a suitcase in my hand.*
> *Well, it's hard to tell, it's hard to tell, when all your love's in vain.*
>
> *When the train rolled up to the station, I looked her in the eye.*
> *When the train rolled up to the station, I looked her in the eye.*
> *Well, I was lonesome, I felt so lonesome, and I could not help but cry.*
> (From Robert Johnson, "Love in Vain")

As we saw in Chapter 1, this pattern, known as **12-bar blues**, uses a simple chord progression with only tonic (I), subdominant (IV), and dominant (V) chords. The overall pattern of 12-bar blues looks like this:

	Measure 1	**Measure 2**	**Measure 3**	**Measure 4**
Line 1	I	I	I	I
Line 2	IV	IV	I	I
Line 3	V	V (or IV)	I	I

Every stanza of the song follows the same pattern. The singer may occasionally vary the accompaniment a little by introducing other chords or extra beats, but the basic pattern stays the same. Also, the singer has ample opportunity for varying the melodic line according to the expression of the text and his or her own personal feeling. The best blues singers use the rigid structure of blues for the most subtle variations in pitch (blue notes) and rhythm. Slight shadings of the pitch, little ornaments, and especially deliberate "misplacement" and constant manipulation of the rhythm are part and parcel of blues singing. The effect is of a flexible and personal vocal style against a square and simple background.

The structure of the blues, with its special combination of flexibility and rigidity, began to be widely used by instrumentalists in the 1920s and has strongly influenced other types of popular music and jazz ever since.

Our example of blues singing is by Bessie Smith (1894–1937), known as the "Empress of the Blues." Bessie Smith grew up in Tennessee and from an early age helped support the family by singing on street corners. After false starts as a dancer and a vaudevillian, she devoted herself full-time to singing blues.

Smith had a hit in 1923 with her very first recording. Audiences were astonished by the mature, tragic quality of her voice and by her sensitive, personal style. On her way to a singing session in 1937, her car crashed into the side of the road, and by the next day Bessie Smith was dead.

LISTENING GUIDE

BESSIE SMITH (1894–1937)
Florida-Bound Blues

Date of performance: 1925
Duration: 3:13

Complete CD Collection: 4, Track 12

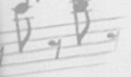
Bessie Smith

Bessie Smith often recorded with a small ensemble, but many of her performances were for piano and voice alone. This recording features pianist Clarence Williams, who was also active as a songwriter, music publisher, and record producer.

Florida-Bound Blues is a standard 12-bar blues with words and melody in an AAB pattern. Listen, though, for subtle changes in the words and melody between the first two lines of each stanza. In the first stanza, for example, "North" and "South" are sung as short notes in the first line but extended in the second line.

Among Smith's many vocal trademarks found in this recording are the addition of an extra note towards the end of a phrase, an occasional "slide," and a sudden drop in pitch at the end of a line, producing a more intimate spoken sound.

12	0:00	Piano introduction	Piano immediately puts listener off balance before settling into a solid key and rhythm.
	0:11	*Goodbye North, Hello South,* *Goodbye North, Hello South.* *It's so cold up here that the words freeze in your mouth.*	Strict rhythm in piano is offset by Bessie's extra beat in the first line. Compare the heavily blued note on "words" to the centered pitch on "freeze."
	0:46	*I'm goin' to Florida where I can have my fun,* *I'm goin' to Florida, where I can have my fun.* *Where I can lay out in the green grass and look up at the sun.*	Piano introduces a smooth, more melodic response to vocal. Listen for the added chromatic note on "fun." Note the piano "roll" filling in the space after "grass."
	1:22	*Hey, hey redcap, help me with this load.* *Redcap porter, help me with this load (step aside).* *Oh, that steamboat, Mr. Captain, let me get on board.*	Listen for the deliberate variety and humor in these two lines. Each of the repeated notes is approached from below, creating a pulse in the line.
	1:58	*I got a letter from my daddy, he bought me a sweet piece of land.* *I got a letter from my daddy, he bought me a small piece of ground.* *You can't blame me for leavin', Lord, I mean I'm Florida bound.*	Heavily blued notes on "from my daddy" ("daddy" means "lover"). Bessie varies this line by not taking a breath in the middle, making the ending breathless.
	2:35	*My papa told me, my mama told me too.* *My papa told me, my mama told me too:* *Don't let them bell-bottom britches make a fool outa you.*	A new ending for the melody of the first two lines. Vocal line moves up on "fool," highlighting the punchline at the end.

DIXIELAND

Dixieland jazz (sometimes known as New Orleans jazz) flourished in the city of New Orleans, especially in the red-light district called Storyville. Small bands played in the brothels and saloons, and a standard form of "combo" arose: a "front line" of trumpet, clarinet, and trombone, and a "rhythm section" of drums, banjo, piano, and bass. Every instrument in a Dixieland band has a specific function. The main melody is played by the trumpet, while the clarinet weaves a high countermelody around it. The trombone plays a simpler, lower tune in harmony. In the rhythm section, the drums keep the beat, the piano and banjo play chords, and the bass plays the bass line (usually on plucked strings).

The sound of Dixieland jazz is of many lines interweaving in a complex but organized way. The effect is of collective improvisation but with every instrument having a carefully defined role. The most common musical forms are 12-bar blues and **32-bar AABA form** (as we saw in Chapter 1, this is the standard form of thousands of pop songs throughout the twentieth century).

The 32-bar AABA form has four eight-measure sections:

A eight measures

A eight measures

B eight measures

A eight measures

The first statement of the tune takes up the first 32 measures. Then the band plays variants of the tune or improvises on its basic chord progressions, while keeping to the 32-measure format. Each statement of the tune or the variation on it is known as a "chorus." In Dixieland jazz, a piece usually begins with the whole band playing the first chorus and then features choruses of (accompanied) solo and collective improvisation. Sometimes everybody stops playing for two or four measures except for a single soloist. This is known as a "break."

Some of the most famous musicians and bandleaders of early jazz were Jelly Roll Morton (piano), Louis Armstrong (trumpet), Joe "King" Oliver (trumpet), Bix Beiderbecke (trumpet), Sidney Bechet (clarinet and soprano saxophone), and Jack Teagarden (trombone).

The most important figure in jazz from the 1920s was Louis Armstrong (1901–1971). After he left New Orleans, Armstrong settled in Chicago, where, with his composer and pianist wife, Lil Hardin, he made a series of groundbreaking recordings. His brilliant trumpet playing and enormously inventive improvisations paved the way for a new focus in jazz on solo playing. Armstrong's career spanned more than fifty years in American music, and in later years, when asked to speak about his life, he would simply point to his trumpet and say: "That's my living; that's my life."

Armstrong's Chicago music brought jazz from the dense polyphony of New Orleans, with many simultaneous lines, to the era of solo playing. The performance we will hear is a Hot Five recording—trumpet, clarinet, and trombone for the musical lines, and piano (Lil Hardin), guitar, and banjo for rhythm and fill-in harmony.

Hotter Than That is a remarkable performance on many levels. It might be seen as a primer on early jazz: It contains passages of the earlier polyphonic New Orleans style as well as the flashy solos that became popular in the 1920s, and it displays breaks, stop-time, and call-and-response, all standard parts of the vocabulary of early ensemble jazz. Beyond that, it is one of the first truly great jazz recordings, showing Armstrong at his exuberant best on both trumpet and vocals.

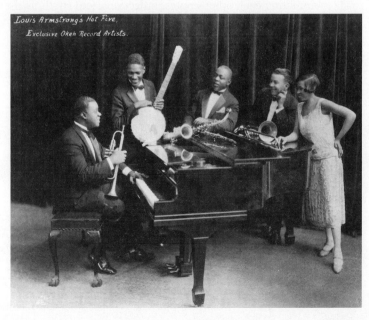

Louis Armstrong's Hot Five, Chicago, 1925 (from left to right): Armstrong, Johnny St. Cyr, Johnny Dodds, Kid Ory, Lil Hardin.

Frank Driggs Collection/Archive Photos.

LISTENING GUIDE

LOUIS ARMSTRONG (1900–1971)

Hotter Than That

Date of performance: 1927
Instruments: Trumpet, clarinet, trombone, piano,
  banjo, guitar
Duration: 3:00

Complete CD Collection: 4, Track 13

Hotter Than That is built around a 32-measure tune written by pianist Lil Hardin. The performers improvise all their melodic lines over each chorus of this tune. The end of each 16-measure section is played as a break: everyone drops out except the soloist, who leads the song into the next half of the chorus or into the next chorus itself. The basic structure of the performance is shown here:

Intro:	full ensemble (8 bars)
Chorus 1:	trumpet solo with rhythm section (32 bars)
Chorus 2:	clarinet solo with rhythm section (32 bars)
Chorus 3:	vocal with guitar (32 bars)
New material:	vocal and guitar duet (16 bars)
Chorus 4:	trombone solo with rhythm section (16 bars)
	full ensemble (16 bars)
Coda:	trumpet and guitar

In the third chorus, Armstrong sings instead of playing, scatting through the entire 32 bars. Pay special attention to the similarity between his trumpet playing and his singing: he uses the same clean attack, the same "shake" at the end of a long note, the same "rips" up to a high note, and the same arpeggiated style of melody. He also builds a string of 24 equal syncopated notes, intensifying the swing in the rhythm.

After the scat chorus, Armstrong and guitarist Lonnie Johnson play a call-and-response chorus, imitating each other's notes, inflections, and rhythms. In this section, as in the whole song, every note drives the song forward, producing a work of great energy and unity.

INTRO		
13	0:00	Full ensemble, New Orleans-style polyphony. Listen for the individual instruments.
CHORUS 1		
	0:08	Trumpet solo. Listen for Armstrong's confident rhythm and occasional "burbles."
	0:24	Break: background drops out, Armstrong "rips" to a high note.
	0:26	Armstrong improvises on arpeggios. "Shake" on long notes.
	0:42	Break: clarinet jumps in on trumpet line, prepares for solo.
CHORUS 2		
	0:44	Clarinet solo. Same tempo, but not as much rhythmic variety.

1:00		Break: Clarinet dives into a long blued note.
1:02		Clarinet solo continues.
1:17		Break: Armstrong jumps in, preparing the scat chorus.

CHORUS 3

1:20		Scat chorus. Listen for variety of sound: jagged lines vs. smooth lines, notes hit perfectly vs. notes slid.
1:35		Break: "rip" to high note.
1:39		Scat in syncopation with guitar.
1:53		Break: whining scat, preparing for:

NEW MATERIAL

1:55		Scat/guitar dialogue. Call-and-response.
2:08		"Rip" to high note in voice, imitated in guitar.
2:13		Piano transition to:

CHORUS 4

2:17		Trombone solo, ending with chromatic climb to:
2:32		Break: Armstrong on an energetic climbing sequence into:
2:35		New Orleans–style polyphony by full ensemble, Armstrong on top.
2:43		Multiple breaks ("stop-time").

CODA

2:47		Full group, followed by:
2:49		Guitar/trumpet interchange

SWING

In the 1930s and early 1940s, the most popular jazz style was **Swing**. The Swing Era takes its name from the fact that much of the music of the time was dance music. Because swing was usually played by large bands with as many as fifteen or twenty musicians, the Swing Era is also called the Big Band Era. This period also saw the growth of much solo playing, such as that of tenor saxophonists Coleman Hawkins and Lester Young, trumpeter Roy Eldridge, and pianists Fats Waller and Art Tatum.

The most important changes from Dixieland jazz to the big bands were the larger number of performers, the use of saxophones in the band, and the use of written (composed or "arranged") music. For the first time, jazz was mostly written out, rather

The Duke Ellington Orchestra, 1949.

Benny Goodman in 1938, with manic drummer Gene Krupa.

than mostly improvised. Swing music became extraordinarily popular during these years, and huge ballrooms would be filled with enthusiastic crowds dancing to the music. Some of the great swing bands of the time were those of Fletcher Henderson, Count Basie, Duke Ellington, and Benny Goodman.

The instruments of the big bands were divided into three groups: the saxophones, the brass section, and the rhythm section. The saxophone group included alto and tenor saxophones, and saxophone players ("reedmen") who could usually also play clarinet. The brass section included both trumpets and trombones. The rhythm section included guitar, piano, bass, and drums. In addition, the bandleader (usually a pianist, a clarinetist, or a trumpeter) would often be featured as a soloist.

The sound of the big bands of the Swing Era was smooth and polished. This was partly because of the prominence of the smooth-sounding saxophones, and partly because the music was almost all written down. The polyphonic complexity of collective improvisation had given way to an interest in a big homophonic sound, lively presentation, and polish.

One of the most important and influential composers in the history of jazz was Duke Ellington (1899–1974). He is said to have been responsible for as many as 1,000 jazz compositions. Ellington was a man of many talents: a master songwriter, an innovative composer and arranger, an imaginative and capable pianist, and an extraordinary bandleader.

Ellington was the first to make full use of the rich palette of colors available to the jazz orchestra. Similarly, Ellington's harmony was years ahead of that of his contemporaries.

The bandleader who did the most to popularize swing was Benny Goodman (1909–1986). Known as the "King of Swing," clarinetist Goodman led a band that was heard by millions across America on a weekly radio show, and he achieved the unprecedented in 1938 by bringing his band to Carnegie Hall in New York City, the traditional home of classical music. Goodman was also the first to break through what was then known as the "color barrier" by hiring black musicians such as pianist Teddy Wilson and vibraphonist Lionel Hampton to play among white musicians. This was an important step in what was still an officially segregated country.

Another influential aspect of Goodman's work was his formation of small groups—sometimes a trio or a quartet, most often a sextet. Goodman's sextet and his other small groups paved the way for the virtuoso solo playing and small combos of bebop.

LISTENING GUIDE

DUKE ELLINGTON (1899–1974)

It Don't Mean A Thing (If It Ain't Got That Swing)

Date of performance: 1932
Orchestration: Voice, 3 trumpets,
2 trombones, 3 saxophones, piano, banjo,
  bass, drums
Duration: 3:09

Companion CD, Track 85

The title of *It Don't Mean A Thing (If It Ain't Got That Swing)* became a motto for an era—and has survived as a catch phrase in the jazz world up through today. The song is an exceptionally lively and infectious number that displays numerous hallmarks of the Ellington sound at the beginning of the swing era: the unique interplay between vocals (Ivie Anderson) and orchestra, the growling wah-wah brass contrasted with the sultry saxophones, the driving slap of the bass, the sensational solos, and the wide palette of instrumental timbres used throughout.

85	0:00	Introductory vamp between the singer's scat improvisation and the driving bass and drum.
	0:11	Joe "Tricky Sam" Nanton plays a muted trombone solo atop a subdued chorus of saxophones and muted trumpets that blare out in brief response to each phrase of Nanton's solo. This solo elaborates on the entire tune *before* the band's initial statement.
	0:46	Entry of the first chorus. Blue note on "ain't." Note the call-and-response interplay between singer and orchestra.
	0:54	Second chorus.
	1:03	Transitional section of contrasting character.
	1:13	Restatement of first chorus.
	1:22	Entry of Johnny Hodges' saxophone solo. Notice the orchestral timbres behind Hodges. Notice also the prearranged responses to the solo.
	2:43	Scat improvisation by Anderson.
	2:52	Return to first chorus and fadeout by muted trumpets on the motive from their response.

RECENT FORMS

Bebop

In the early 1940s, a reaction to the glossy, organized sound of some of the big bands set in. Some jazz musicians began to experiment again with smaller combos and with a type of music that was more for listening than for dancing. This style is known as bebop or bop. The name probably derives from some of the nonverbal syllables used in scat

Charlie Parker and Dizzy Gillespie in 1950, with John Coltrane (tenor saxophone) and Tommy Potter (bass).

singing ("Doo-wah doo-wah, be-bop a loo-wah"). And the most frequent phrase ending in bebop solos is, ♫, which fits the word "bebop" perfectly. There is also a composition by Dizzy Gillespie that is called *Bebop*.

The pioneers of bebop were Charlie "Bird" Parker (alto saxophone), Dizzy Gillespie (trumpet), and Thelonious Monk (piano). In turn, these three players influenced other musicians, including Stan Getz, Miles Davis, Sarah Vaughan, and John Coltrane. In fact, it would be difficult to find a jazz musician who has not been influenced by Parker, Gillespie, and Monk.

Bebop is a very different kind of music from swing. It is harder, irregular, and less predictable. It is played by a small group (for example, saxophone and trumpet with piano, bass, and drums). The tempo is generally faster, and there is far more solo improvisation. The chord progressions and rhythmic patterns are complex and varied. Bop is generally considered the beginning of modern jazz.

With its fast pace and its emphasis on solo improvisation, bebop depended on the inventiveness, quick thinking, virtuosity, and creativity of individual musicians. The improvisations of Charlie Parker, Dizzy Gillespie, and Thelonious Monk were quick and unpredictable, full of fiery fast notes, lengthy pauses, and sudden changes of direction. Although bop was still based on popular songs (AABA form) or on the 12-bar blues pattern, the simple harmonies were enriched with new and more dissonant chords, and the accompanying rhythms were more complex.

Bebop musicians sometimes wrote new tunes themselves, but more often they improvised around well-known songs of the day. Beboppers avoided improvising on the melody; their solos were built strictly on the chord patterns and often made no reference to the tune. As a result, their music could sound quite different from the original song.

A distinct culture surrounded bebop. It was a music of rebellion. And for such controversial music, bebop is based on a remarkably conventional structure. Normally, it begins with a 32-bar tune, which is played by the melody instruments in unison (one "chorus") accompanied by the rhythm section. Then each soloist improvises for as many choruses as he or she wants. Then there is a final chorus in unison again.

The great genius of bebop was Charlie Parker (1920–1955), a brilliant, self-destructive saxophonist who died at the age of thirty-four from alcoholism and drug addiction. His improvisations changed the way a generation thought about jazz. His playing was profound, dizzying, subtle, and complex; his phrasing unconventional and inspired; his tone edgy and intense. Parker absorbed music of all kinds, including Stravinsky and Bartók. And he was both loyal and inspiring: Dizzy Gillespie called him "the other half of my heartbeat."

We shall listen to a remarkable performance by Parker, entitled *Confirmation*, which he recorded in 1953. Charlie Parker's *Confirmation* is based on the chord changes of Gershwin's *I Got Rhythm*, known familiarly as "rhythm changes." *Confirmation* is a 32-bar AABA form. But these aspects of the piece, though they are important, pale in comparison with the extraordinary creativity and brilliance of the saxophonist.

LISTENING GUIDE

THE CHARLIE PARKER QUARTET

Confirmation

Date of performance: July 30, 1953
Personnel: Charlie Parker, alto saxophone;
  Al Haig, piano; Percy Heath, bass;
  Max Roach, drums.
Duration: 2:58

Complete CD Collection: 4, Track 14

*C*onfirmation is one of the most stunning of Parker's many extraordinary performances. The studio tapes show that the piece was recorded straight through, with no splicing, no alternative takes, and no errors. It is important to remember that although the first chorus has been worked out beforehand, all the rest of what Parker plays is made up on the spot. All the running notes, the rhythmic figures, the cascades of musical gestures—all these are created in the very moment of performance. Not only that, but each time Parker plays the A section—every single time—he varies it considerably. It is hard to imagine that anyone could display such rich and instantaneous creativity.

Charlie Parker's alto saxophone is accompanied by piano, bass, and drums. These create a harmonic foundation and keep a consistent beat, against which Parker's ingenuity, flexibility, and expressive flights can shine. Toward the end of the piece, each of the other players gets a few measures to improvise on his own: first the pianist, then the bass player, and then the drummer. Parker wraps everything up with everyone playing together again.

INTRODUCTION

14   0:00   A brief 4-measure introduction by the piano.

CHORUS 1

0:05   The tune is a typical bebop composition: angular, irregular, and offbeat. The B section (0:25–0:34) is not as highly differentiated in this piece as it is in some bebop compositions, though its harmonies are different.

CHORUS 2

0:44   Parker really starts to fly on this chorus (hence his nickname, "Bird"). He also plays in the lower register of the saxophone to give variety to his solo.

CHORUS 3

1:22   The third chorus is unified by rapid, descending chromatic phrases. Parker plays right across the "seams" of the AABA form to make long, compelling musical statements of his own.

PIANO SOLO (AA)

2:00   Al Haig takes 16 measures for his solo, which is quite musical for a normal human being, but which sounds pretty tame after listening to Charlie Parker!

BASS SOLO (B)

2:16 | Percy Heath gets to play some different rhythms for 8 measures with some hints of the tune.

DRUM SOLO (A)

2:28 | Amazingly, Max Roach manages to suggest the melody on his 8 measures. (Try humming it along with him.)

FINAL HALF-CHORUS (BA)

2:35 | Parker repeats the B and A sections as a final half-chorus, playing with intensity, but closer to the original melody. Percy Heath (who was said to be overwhelmed by Parker's playing on this recording date) gets in the last word!

Cool Jazz

Cool jazz was really a subcategory of bop. It continued to use small combos, and the forms and harmonic styles were similar. Cool-jazz pieces also were based on popular tunes or blues patterns. The departures from bop can be noted immediately in the overall sound. The playing is more subdued and less frenetic. Pieces tend to be longer, and they feature a larger variety of instruments, sometimes including the baritone saxophone, with its deep, full sound, and even some classical instruments, such as the French horn and the flute.

Some groups specializing in cool jazz became quite popular in the 1950s. The most popular group of all (certainly one of the longest lasting) was the Modern Jazz Quartet, which featured Milt Jackson on vibraphone. The vibraphone (an instrument like a xylophone, with metal bars and an electronically enhanced, sustained, fluctuating tone) is the perfect instrument for projecting the "coolth" of cool jazz.

Free Jazz

In the 1960s, another revolution led to the development of what is known as free jazz. The most influential musician of this period was Ornette Coleman, alto saxophonist, trumpeter, violinist, and composer. Several pieces have been named for him, and an album of his, made in 1960 and entitled *Free Jazz*, gave its name to the whole period.

Free jazz is abstract and can be dense and difficult to follow. The idea was to allow musicians to improvise (together) completely freely, without predetermined chord progressions or even regular rhythmic patterns or melodies. Drumming is energetic, full of color and activity, without a steady and constant pattern of beats. Solo improvisations are full of extremes: very high notes, squawks and squeals, long-held tones, fragmented phrases, and sudden silences.

The Modern Jazz Quartet.

Free jazz in its purest form was not popular. Totally free collective improvisation must necessarily have many moments of complete chaos. Free-jazz composers responded to this problem by writing compositions that would begin and end with a set theme or melody, allowing room for free improvisation in between. Obviously, in these cases the melody provides a common basis for the intervening improvisations and eliminates the randomness of complete freedom.

Fusion

Fusion is the name given to the musical style of the 1970s and 1980s that combined elements of jazz and rock music. Rock and jazz have some elements in common: the blues and popular ballads. But they developed along separate lines. Rock is largely vocal music and is based on simple and accessible forms and harmonies. Jazz is mostly instrumental music, and some forms of jazz are quite complex, ignoring popular appeal.

Miles Davis.

Fusion was the first jazz style to achieve wide popularity since the mass appeal of swing in the 1930s and 1940s. Its most influential proponent was Miles Davis, who made two records in the late Sixties that established the fusion style for the 1970s and 1980s: *In a Silent Way* and *Bitches Brew*.

The primary characteristics of fusion are the adoption of electric instruments (electric piano, synthesizer, and electric bass guitar) in place of their traditional ancestors; a large percussion section (including several non-European instruments such as hand drums, bells, gongs, shakers, and scrapers); and simplicity of form and harmony. Fusion is often based on straightforward chord progressions and highly repetitive rhythmic patterns. Over this accessible and almost hypnotic foundation, however, fusion presents a kaleidoscopic variety of sounds.

The most popular fusion group of this era was Weather Report, founded by musicians who had worked with Miles Davis on *In a Silent Way* and *Bitches Brew*. Other important groups were founded by Herbie Hancock and Chick Corea.

The Current Scene

The 1990s witnessed a big jazz revival and the coexistence of many different jazz styles. Many colleges and universities began adding jazz courses to the curriculum. Women were more active than ever in jazz. Jazz is also fast becoming an international language. It has large audiences and great performers in Japan, as well as in Western Europe (especially Scandinavia), Latin America, the Caribbean, Africa, and Eastern Europe.

In the 1990s, many of the jazz legends passed away, among them Miles Davis (1991), Dizzy Gillespie (1993), and Ella Fitzgerald (1996), but a new generation of talented young players has established itself on the mainstream jazz scene. As an alternative to mainstream jazz, various blends of jazz with pop, rap, and classical idioms continue to take place, and new musical horizons are being explored by such diverse avant-garde artists as John Zorn and Steve Coleman. A special kind of blend has been called "acid jazz" (a particularly unhelpful name). Acid jazz functions primarily as dance music. A bluesy, complex, repetitive but rhythmic style of jazz called funk or

Wynton Marsalis in concert, Lincoln Center, New York City, 1991.

groove music has also become popular. Its best-known exponents include guitarist John Scofield, saxophonist Maceo Parker, and the organ-bass-drums trio Medeski, Martin, and Wood. Some of the most innovative jazz now comes from outside the United States. A Swedish group known as E. S. T. (the Esbjörn Svensson Trio) is currently making some of the most interesting new music.

In addition to the highly eclectic mixture of up-to-date jazz styles available today, a new movement has manifested itself, which might be called a "return to the past." This movement treats jazz as a great musical repertory, as important in its way as written, "serious" classical music. Performers attempt to "capture" great jazz styles of past eras in clean, modern performances, enhanced by the new virtuoso instrumental techniques of young performers.

The prime exponent of this approach has been Wynton Marsalis, a superb classical trumpeter, a fine jazz improviser, and a musician with a great respect for the past. His clean, sophisticated, modern technique, allied with his reverence for the jazz greats of earlier eras, has made him the most popular jazz artist in modern times. In 1997, Marsalis became the first jazz musician ever to be awarded the esteemed Pulitzer Prize.

His compositions are often focused on the history of black people in America. One of Marsalis's works, *Harriet Tubman*, is named after the runaway slave who helped hundreds of other slaves escape before the end of the Civil War in 1865.

LISTENING GUIDE

WYNTON MARSALIS

Harriet Tubman

Date of performance: 1991
Personnel: Wynton Marsalis, trumpet; Marcus Roberts, piano; Joe Henderson, tenor sax; Bob Hurst, bass; Jeff Watts, drums
Duration: 7:43

Complete CD Collection: 4, Track 15

arsalis describes the piece thus:

"*Harriet Tubman* makes homage to a woman who acted as a personal agent against the slavery that so severely limited the spiritual potential of our nation and was detrimental to the fulfillment of our democracy. She and the Underground Railroad represent the same thing that the blues does, that optimism at the core of the human will which motivates us to heroic action and tells us: NO MATTER HOW BAD, everything is going to be all right.

   This blues begins in the bass with a motif that speaks of the late-night mystery. Its muted bell-like quality uses bass harmonics for an allusion to the African thumb piano [mbira]. The drums come in with another meter to enhance the African underpinnings. Siren horns and a bass vamp signal the beginning of a journey on the Underground Railway, then the sound of the blues and the wash of swing identify this as a uniquely American expression. The piece ends as it begins, in the bass, reminding us that even though the journey has ended, there is still much more to do...."

The underlying structure of this piece is the traditional harmonic pattern of 12-bar blues, although Marsalis adds a flexible lilt by having each measure contain six beats instead of the traditional four.

15	0:00	Introduction: Light, percussive use of harmonics and a syncopated rhythmic pattern on the bass suggest the *mbira*. (The African *mbira* is discussed and can be heard in Chapter 2.)
	0:11	Short rhythmic pattern on percussion; then short scalar pattern on piano.
	0:31	Entrance of sustained trumpet and saxophone, leading to faster or more jagged melodies.
	1:22	Arrival at sustained notes, with pause in underlying rhythm, establishes the end of the section.
	1:34	Marsalis (trumpet) takes the solo on the first chorus. Starts with leaps to a high note. More conventional accompaniment, with a regular walking bass and light cymbal strokes giving a regular pulse; harmonies filled out by the piano.
	2:18	Faster melodic fragments and scales lead to:
	2:42	Arrival of full ascending arpeggios reaching the same high note, rich chords in piano.
	3:20	Tenor saxophone—picks up arpeggio figure last stated by trumpet, moves to fast three-note ideas. Emphasis on quick flourishes.
	4:25	Regular ascending notes, but slightly off the beat as laid down by steady piano, then elaborated with virtuosic flourishes.
	5:01	The piano takes its solo, still providing accompaniment with the left hand. It begins with short melodic fragments, then moves to a wide-sweeping longer line.
	5:16	Back to short, nervous gestures that work in a narrow range, then cascade down.
	5:33	Short gestures are repeated insistently in right hand, while harmonies move around them.

5:51	Repeated series of three notes with octave leap; the piano continues to alternate between very restricted gestures and freer ones.
6:42	Return of initial theme (sustained notes in trumpet and sax), and emphasis on off-beat rhythms.
7:14	Trumpet and sax quieter with held notes, bass returns to its original pattern of harmonics; fade out.

Listening to...

JAZZ

- Important forerunners of jazz were band music, ragtime (Scott Joplin, *Maple Leaf Rag*), and the blues (Bessie Smith, *Florida-Bound Blues*).

- Each kind of jazz has its own special qualities to listen for.

- In Dixieland (New Orleans) jazz, listen for the collective sound of several instruments improvising simultaneously, though you will notice that their roles are clearly defined, so that the trumpet is playing the main tune, the clarinet is soaring above, and the trombone playing longer notes below (Louis Armstrong, "Hotter Than That"). All the while the rhythm section is laying down a steady swinging pulse.

- Jazz of the 1920s began to feature great soloists, and you will hear none better than the amazing Louis Armstrong. Listen for his golden sound, the naturalness and ease of his playing, and the warmth of his personality shining through the music.

- If you can dance, or even if you can't, the music of the swing bands of the 1930s is a delight. It sounds polished, catchy, and lively. This did not stop one of the greatest band composers, Duke Ellington, from using his band to highlight his own remarkably original and sophisticated compositions (*It Don't Mean a Thing [If It Ain't Got That Swing]*).

- The music of the bebop style is more sophisticated. You have to listen hard and follow the individual expression, instrumental virtuosity, and challenging improvisation of a genius like alto saxophonist Charlie Parker or the taciturn, oblique trumpeter Miles Davis to see how the smaller combos can be a framework for complex, profound statements (Charlie Parker, *Confirmation*).

- A jazz movement of the 1980s and 1990s brought a return to classic jazz with modern elements (Wynton Marsalis, *Harriet Tubman*).

- Blends of jazz with a large assortment of other elements—including Latin sounds and rhythms, synthesized mood music, rap, and funk—can now be heard all over the airwaves, in nightclubs, and on recordings. There is also some jazz so watered-down ("smooth jazz") that it approaches background music. Some of the main, serious achievements of the second century in the history of jazz seem to be coming from outside the United States.

KEY TERMS

bebop or bop **(p. 297)**   swing **(p. 294)**   12-bar blues **(p. 290)**
blue note **(p. 287)**   32-bar AABA form **(p. 293)**

11
The Twentieth Century III: Popular Music

Popular music is one of the most widespread phenomena of contemporary Western culture. Throughout the world, American popular music is a symbol of the twentieth-century success story. The music represents Western commercial and popular culture with the same force as such powerful icons as Coca-Cola, Microsoft, and Cadillac.

Popular music also connotes youth. Young people buy the largest share of recordings, and most performers are under thirty. The vast spread and commercial success of popular music are the result of a society with time on its hands and money to spend.

By definition, popular music is designed to appeal to the widest possible audience. No formal training is required to appreciate it, and it is usually vocal, because everybody can sing (more or less). Its subject matter—usually love or sex—is attractive to all, and the style and structure of the music are simple and repetitive.

The three most important elements in popular music are the words, the rhythm, and the melody. (The harmony is usually kept very simple.) Different types of popular music tend to stress one or another of the three factors over the other two. For example, the most notable characteristic of rock music is the driving rhythm. In country music, the words are foremost: they generally tell a story. In pop ballads, it is the smooth melody that creates a special atmosphere.

BEGINNINGS: 1850–1950

How did the phenomenon of popular music begin? Where did it come from?

American popular music has a long history, reaching back to the mid nineteenth century. The first important popular songwriter was Stephen Foster (1826–1864). During his lifetime, Foster wrote some of the most enduring songs of the American tradition, including *Oh! Susanna*, *Camptown Races*, and *Old Folks at Home*.

1850
1860
Stephen Foster 1826–1864
1870
1880
1890
1900
Richard Rodgers 1902–1979
1910
Frank Sinatra 1915–19
1920
Charles K. Harris 1865–1930
1930
George Gershwin 1898–1937
1940
Bob Dylan b. 1941
1950
"Rock Around the Clock" 1954
Worldwide spread of pop and rock 1960s
Assassination of President Kennedy 1963
The Rolling Stones founded 1963
1960
Woodstock Music Festival 1969
The Beatles 1959–1970
Jimi Hendrix 1942–1970
1970
Vietnam War 1957–1975
Elvis Presley 1935–1977
Heavy metal 1980s
Start of MTV 1981
1980
Beginning of rap music 1985
Grunge, new punk, electronica 1990s
1990
Boy bands and teen queens 2000–
2000

Stephen Foster.
Stephen Collins Foster, 1826– 1864.
Watercolor by Walter L. White cf
from Ambrotype, Foster Hall Collection. Source ID# 120.

Old Folks at Home is typical of the early popular song in three ways. First, it has a catchy melody. In fact, its first line is so catchy ("Way down upon the Swanee River") that most people think it is the song's title. Second, the words are sentimental. And third, the harmony is extremely simple, using only three chords throughout.

```
G                    G    C
Way down upon the Swanee River,
G      D
Far, far away,
G                         G    C
There's where my heart is turnin' ever,
G          D        G
There's where the old folks stay.
G               G    C
All up and down the whole creation
G      D
Sadly I roam,
G              G  C
Still longing for the old plantation,
G          D          G
And for the old folks at home.
```

With the success achieved by Stephen Foster and other songwriters, music publishers began to realize the commercial potential of popular music. Charles K. Harris (1865–1930), a songwriter who set up his own publishing company, landed a major hit with the publication in 1892 of his song *After the Ball*. Within a few years, the song had sold an unprecedented two million copies. Remember that in those days all home entertainment was "homemade"—provided by a willing voice, a piano, and copies of songs in sheet music.

One of the most concentrated periods in the history of American popular song came in the 1920s, 1930s, and 1940s. This was the era of great songwriters such as Cole Porter, Irving Berlin, Richard Rodgers, Jerome Kern, and George Gershwin, and of popular singers such as Al Jolson, Bing Crosby, and Frank Sinatra. It was also the era of new technologies that revolutionized popular music. Sound movies, radio, and the phonograph all hit their stride in the 1920s, and all three supported and fostered popular songs.

In the 1930s, George Gershwin (1898–1937) wrote the music and his brother Ira wrote the lyrics for many songs that have become American classics. They include *'S Wonderful, I Got Rhythm*, and *Love Walked In*, as well as the great songs from the opera *Porgy and Bess*, especially the enduringly popular *Summertime*.

Richard Rodgers (1902–1979) was one of the most successful songwriters of the 1930s and 1940s, writing the music for many of the era's famous shows, including *Oklahoma!, Carousel*, and *South Pacific*, as well as many

The *Summertime* scene from a 1987 production of George Gershwin's *Porgy and Bess*.

songs not associated with shows. Among his hits were *Oh, What a Beautiful Morning*, *Some Enchanted Evening*, and *Blue Moon*.

(Note: It is extremely difficult to obtain permission to distribute copies of popular music. On the other hand, the records themselves are widely available. Please borrow recordings of the songs in this chapter from friends or from your library.)

LISTENING GUIDE

FRANK SINATRA (performer)   Date of composition: 1934

Blue Moon

Music by Richard Rodgers, words by Lorenz Hart

This ballad follows the character of most songs from the 30s and 40s in that it is slow, lyrical, and sentimental. Sinatra's singing style beautifully conforms to the character of the song. It is relaxed, casual, and somehow intimate. He sounds very comfortable, almost as if he were talking.

The structure of the song is simple. It is cast in AABA form, with eight measures for each section. In this song, the pattern is easy to follow, because all three A sections begin with the words "Blue moon …" As with many songs of the era, the B section ("And then there suddenly appeared …") uses more colorful chords than the A section, which emphasizes the contrast.

0:00	[Instrumental introduction]
A	
0:16	Blue moon! You saw me standing alone, Without a dream in my heart, Without a love of my own.
A	
0:33	Blue moon! You knew just what I was there for. You heard me saying a prayer for Someone I really could care for.
B	
0:49	And then there suddenly appeared before me The only one my arms will ever hold. I heard somebody whisper "Please adore me." And when I looked, the moon had turned to gold!

A		
1:06		Blue moon! Now I'm no longer alone. Without a dream in my heart, Without a love of my own.

A		
1:23		[Saxophone solo]

B		
1:56		And then there suddenly appeared before me The only one my arms will ever hold. I heard somebody whisper "Please adore me." And when I looked, the moon had turned to gold!

A		
2:13		Blue moon! Now I'm no longer alone, Without a dream in my heart, Without a love of my own—

A		
2:30		[repeat] Blue moon! Now I'm no longer alone, Without a dream in my heart, Without a love of my own.

There are hundreds of other composers whose names are largely forgotten, but whose music lives on in songs such as *Take Me Out to the Ball Game, Happy Birthday to You,* and *When Irish Eyes are Smiling.* All these familiar songs, numerous as they are, constitute only a brief list compared with the thousands that once swept the country, but have since been forgotten. Stylistically, most of these songs conform to the model of the sentimental ballad: lyrical melodies, simple harmonies, repetitive rhythm, and a recurring refrain (chorus).

Some of the Most Successful Popular Songs before 1950

Title	Date	Composer
Old Folks at Home	1851	Stephen Foster
When Johnny Comes Marching Home Again	1863	Louis Lambert
After the Ball	1892	Charles K. Harris
The Birthday Song	1893	Patty Hill and Mildred Hill
Bill Bailey, Won't You Please Come Home	1902	Hughie Cannon
Oh, You Beautiful Doll	1911	Seymour Brown/Nat D. Ayer
Swanee	1919	George Gershwin/Irving Caesar
Avalon	1920	Al Jolson/Vincent Rose

Tea for Two	1924	Irving Caesar/Vincent Youmans
Sweet Georgia Brown	1925	Ben Bernie/Maceo Pinkard/Kenneth Casey
Ain't Misbehavin'	1929	Fats Waller
I Got Rhythm	1930	George and Ira Gershwin
On the Sunny Side of the Street	1930	Jimmy McHugh/Dorothy Fields
Smoke Gets in Your Eyes	1933	Jerome Kern
Blue Moon	1934	Richard Rodgers/Lorenz Hart
Begin the Beguine	1935	Cole Porter
Summertime	1935	George Gershwin/DuBose Heyward
Over the Rainbow	1939	Harold Arlen
White Christmas	1942	Irving Berlin
Some Enchanted Evening	1949	Richard Rodgers/Oscar Hammerstein
Rudolph the Red-Nosed Reindeer	1949	Johnny Marks

THE FORTUNATE FIFTIES

The post-World War II period in the United States was a time of unprecedented economic prosperity. There was an economic boom, and relief at the ending of the war and a new optimism for the future led to what has been called the "baby boom." Many Americans also had more leisure time and higher incomes than ever before.

This idyllic life was represented in the new television shows of the 1950s that pictured the perfect family, complete with working father, beautifully groomed mother, two or three kids, and a dog. By the late 1950s, the babies of the "baby boom" were becoming teenagers, enjoying the fruits of the new prosperity. Teenagers bought an average of two new records a month, but there were many who bought twelve or more.

Technology fueled the teenage buying spree. Long-playing (LP) records swept the country in the 1950s, replacing the old 78s. These new discs contained much more music and reproduced sounds with far greater accuracy. Most teenagers had access to a small record player or portable radio. By the mid-1950s, teenagers could take their radios to the park, to a picnic, or to the beach. The swamping of America with popular song had begun.

Scene from the popular 1950s television show *Father Knows Best.*

Portable record player from the 1950s.

Rock-and-Roll: The Beginnings

The early influences on rock-and-roll were many and varied. First and most important was the mixture of slow blues singing with a harder, more rhythmic accompaniment that became known as **rhythm and blues**. Early R & B artists mostly were black. Rhythm and blues often expanded the personal, one-man-with-a-guitar tradition of country blues into a group of musicians. Also vital to the early growth of rock-and-roll were the hard-driving instrumental sounds of Little Richard and Chuck Berry. Little Richard pounded the piano and screamed his lyrics like a wild man. Chuck Berry played a clean, hard guitar and wrote fast songs with an irresistible beat. A list of his hits includes some of the early classics of rock-and-roll: *Roll Over Beethoven*, *Rock and Roll Music*, and *Johnny B. Goode*. As one Chicago bluesman said: "You're playing rhythm and blues. You step the stuff up, and you're playing rock-and-roll."

Another early influence on rock-and-roll was country music. Before the term "rock-and-roll" was widely used, the early sound of Elvis Presley and others was known as "rockabilly" ("rock" + "hillbilly"). It combined the drive of rhythm and blues with music from the rural South known as Country and Western, with its fiddle playing, guitar picking, and warm harmonies. Rockabilly stars who scored big hits at this time were Jerry Lee Lewis (*Great Balls of Fire* and *Whole Lotta Shakin' Goin' On*), Johnny Cash (*I Walk the Line*), and Carl Perkins (*Blue Suede Shoes*). All were white, poor, and from the rural South. Another rockabilly star from this time was the unlikely looking Buddy Holly, skinny and bespectacled. Buddy Holly was on the threshold of an important career when he died in a plane crash at the age of twenty-two.

Elvis Presley

Despite strings of hits, none of these singing stars came close to the phenomenon of Elvis Presley. Presley came from a poor background in Mississippi. Born in 1935, he moved with his family to Memphis when he was thirteen. Elvis worked in a factory and drove a truck until he turned to music, singing with a small group. At the age of eighteen, he went to the local recording studio, where anyone could make a record for four dollars, and recorded a song as a present for his mother. Six months and two or three recordings later, his records suddenly began to attract attention on radio stations. Elvis took his group around the South. And on his very first tour, in the summer of 1955, the hysteria started. A country singer described the scene:

> The cat came out in red pants and a green coat and a pink shirt and socks, and he had this sneer on his face and he stood behind the mike for five minutes, I'll bet, before he made a move. Then he hit his guitar a lick, and he broke two strings. So there he was, these two strings dangling, and he hadn't done anything yet, and these high school girls were screaming and fainting and running up to the stage, and then he started to move his hips real slow like he had a thing for his guitar. That was Elvis Presley when he was about nineteen, playing Kilgore, Texas.

By 1957, Elvis mania was sweeping the country. And the new technology fueled the fire. Presley appeared on television; a new radio format, the Top Forty, aired Presley hits almost constantly; and Elvis appeared in his first movie.

After this period, Presley began to retreat to the sound of the more mainstream sentimental ballad that had been the staple of popular music for decades. This smoother, more acceptable Elvis appealed to an even wider audience and sold even more records. The commercial success of Elvis the singer led to the creation of an entire industry. There were Elvis pajamas, an Elvis pillow, and a glow-in-the-dark Elvis poster, as well as bobby socks, blouses, skirts, shoes, and lipstick. By the end of 1957, the Elvis business had grossed fifty-five million dollars.

This poor-boy-made-good couldn't spend money fast enough. He bought a mansion in Memphis, called Graceland, for himself and his parents. He also bought a fleet of Cadillacs, an airplane, and hundreds of television sets. And yet his very fame eventually made his life miserable.

Elvis became depressed and sometimes violent. He retreated into drugs and alcohol. Gradually, the charismatic teenage sex idol turned into an overweight, drugged parody of himself, singing ballads in Las Vegas hotels, squeezed into a sequined costume. He died in 1977 at the age of forty-two, a victim of the commercial world of popular music.

Elvis Presley in concert, 1956.

LISTENING GUIDE

ELVIS PRESLEY   Date of performance: 1956

Blue Suede Shoes

Words and music by Carl Perkins

Like a number of Presley's early hits, *Blue Suede Shoes* was written and first recorded by another artist, in this case Carl Perkins. Presley's recordings of these songs were often the principal catalyst for their immense popularity, and they became immediately associated with his name. His studio recording of *Blue Suede Shoes* didn't match the phenomenal success of some of his early No. 1 hits (*Heartbreak Hotel, Hound Dog, Don't Be Cruel*), but it did make it to No. 20 on the pop charts in 1956. There is also a recording of a mid-1950s live performance, which captures the atmosphere and intensity of the early Elvis phenomenon. The performance is swinging, rough, and exciting.

The song is essentially a basic 12-bar blues progression with a rockabilly backbeat.

0:00	[Brief guitar riff as an introduction]
0:02	Well it's one for the money, two for the show, three to get ready, now go cat go,
0:06	But don't you step on my blue suede shoes. Well you can do anything but lay off of my blue suede shoes.
0:16	You can knock me down, step in my face, slander my name all over the place. Do anything that you wanna do, but uh-uh honey lay off of my shoes.
0:26	Now don't you step on my blue suede shoes. Well you can do anything but lay off of my blue suede shoes.
0:37	Well it's blue, blue, my blue suede shoes, my baby, blue, blue, blue suede shoes, yeah, Blue, blue, my blue suede shoes, baby, blue, blue, blue suede shoes— Well you can do anything, but lay off of my blue suede shoes.
0:52	You can knock me down, step in my face, slander my name all over the place. Do anything that you wanna do, but uh-uh honey lay off of my shoes.
1:02	Now don't you step on my blue suede shoes. Well you can do anything but lay off of my blue suede shoes.
1:13	Well it's blue, blue, my blue suede shoes, my baby, [etc.]

The live performance omits the third verse, which Presley included on his studio recording:

You can burn my house, steal my car, drink my liquor from an old fruit jar,
Do anything that you wanna do, but uh-uh honey lay off of my shoes.
Now don't you step on my blue suede shoes.
Well you can do anything, but lay off of my blue suede shoes.

Rebellion

In his early years, Elvis Presley symbolized something very important for American youth. He was the symbol of freedom, of rebellion. The spirit of rebellion was in the air. James Dean and Marlon Brando projected restlessness and moody defiance in their movies. And J. D. Salinger's novel *Catcher in the Rye*, about a student at odds with society, was extremely popular with high-school students throughout the 1950s and 1960s.

This wild and rebellious spirit was captured by a song that did more to popularize the term "rock-and-roll" than any other. *Rock Around the Clock*, sung by Bill Haley and the Comets, became a major hit when it was used in the opening and closing sequences of *Blackboard Jungle*, a movie of teenage violence and rejection.

Rock-and-roll also fed into the dance craze that gripped America's young people in the '50s. Dancing was a physical outlet for repressed energy, and teenagers went wild with dancing. School dances, "sock hops," picnics, and parties were soon filled with rock-and-roll music, and with teenagers jiving, stomping, and swinging.

Rock-and-roll represented a dramatic change from the smooth musical style that had dominated popular music for the previous hundred years. It was rough, raucous, loud, electric, and intense. And then, of course, there was the beat. Most of the early rock-and-roll songs were fast. And there was a pounding accent on the first beat of every measure. Both the sound and the lyrics were often frankly sexual.

Local police departments banned rock-and-roll dances. Speeches were made in the House of Representatives. Religious leaders sermonized against rock-and-roll. A distinguished psychiatrist called rock-and-roll "a communicable disease," and a composer described it as "acoustical pollution."

High-school dance in the 1950s.

Early Rock-and-Roll: Structure and Style

Many early rock-and-roll songs are based on the 12-bar blues pattern. The harmony is limited and repetitive—insistent rather than complex. This puts more focus on the rhythm. It, too, is insistent, with a strong accent on the first beat of every measure and secondary accents on the second and fourth beats.

Early rock-and-roll bands usually featured a limited number of instruments: piano, bass, and drums, occasionally with an electric guitar or saxophone. Almost all songs from this time last about three minutes, because they were designed to fit on one side of a 45-rpm record.

The lyrics of early rock-and-roll concentrated on the few subjects guaranteed to appeal to teenagers: love, sex, and dancing. As rock-and-roll transformed the landscape of American popular music, some room was still left for the 32-measure, AABA-form slow ballad that was popular in the first half of the century. Sentimental songs always have an audience. There was a brief rash of sentimental songs that displayed a morbid fascination with death: *Teen Angel* (Mark Dinning, 1959) and *Tell Laura I Love Her* (Roy Peterson, 1960) both describe tragic deaths of young people, one killed by a train and the other in a car crash. But the main subject of slow songs was romance. And teenagers were quite happy to have a few ballads played at their parties for slow dancing.

Early Rock-and-Roll: Black and White

An important social element of rock-and-roll was the racial integration that it helped to accomplish. The Supreme Court ruled in 1954 that equal access must be granted to all students in the nation's public schools. Rock-and-roll was itself a melding of black and white music: the blues plus Country and Western. Audiences at concerts began to be more mixed, and teenagers from different ethnic backgrounds bought many of the same records and listened to the same radio shows.

Elements of prejudice continued to exist, however, and to prevent racism from cutting into their profits, record companies often hired white singers to "cover"—that is, copy—popular hits by black singers. The covers were smoother, less raucous, and more acceptable to adults. As a result, black singers were often denied the success that was their due. A black singer recalls: "With me there had to be a copy. They wouldn't buy me, but they would buy a white copy of me … I don't even like to talk about it."

THE TURBULENT SIXTIES

The 1960s were a decade of profound social upheaval. The period began with optimism and excitement, as the young and charismatic John F. Kennedy was elected president of the United States. Idealistic civil rights workers, both black and white, struggled to end discrimination. The Rev. Dr. Martin Luther King, Jr. fought with unprecedented success (and immense dignity) to end segregation and racism in America without the use of violence.

Soon, however, the idealism and optimism were shattered. President Kennedy was assassinated in 1963. The passage of the Civil Rights Act in 1965 was regarded by many new militant black groups as "too little, too late." Riots broke out in many cities in the summers of 1965–68. And in 1968, both Martin Luther King, Jr. and Robert Kennedy, the president's brother, were gunned down. But the most divisive force in American society in the 1960s was the Vietnam War.

The American presence in Vietnam had begun in the 1950s. And by the time the war ended with a Communist victory in 1975, 600,000 North Vietnamese, 200,000 South Vietnamese, and 57,000 Americans were dead; 155,000 were wounded.

The Vietnam War was one of the focal points for student uprisings throughout the 1960s and early 1970s. Many young people "dropped out" of society, living in communes, wearing deliberately outrageous clothes, and taking drugs.

The alienation of almost an entire generation of young people, the baby boomers, was reinforced by the events of the early 1970s. In 1973, the vice president of the United States, Spiro Agnew, resigned amid charges of corruption and bribery. In 1974, as a result of the Watergate scandal, President Richard Nixon resigned in disgrace.

"Hippies" in the 1960s.

Throughout this era, it was popular music that bound members of the younger generation together. The main performers of the 1960s were the Beatles, Bob Dylan, and Jimi Hendrix.

The Beatles

The Beatles represented the first wave in what has been called the British Invasion of America. During the 1960s, England became a world center of pop and rock music. There were few jobs, as England still suffered economically from the aftereffects of World War II. "Music was a way out," explained the Beatles' drummer, Ringo Starr. "We all picked up guitars and drums and filled our time with music."

All four members of the Beatles grew up in working-class backgrounds in Liverpool, an industrial city in the north of England. The group was founded in 1959. By 1962, they had completely conquered England and much of the rest of Europe. Two years later, they embarked on their first tour of the United States. In 1964, in the course of one week, the Beatles appeared on *The Ed Sullivan Show*, played two concerts at Carnegie Hall, and appeared before 8,000 fans at the Washington Coliseum. In 1965, they toured the United States again, including a concert at New York's Shea Stadium before 55,000 screaming teenagers. The nationwide tour grossed more than fifty-six million dollars.

The most important musical influences on the Beatles were rhythm and blues and American rockabilly. With the advent of the Beatles in the early 1960s, the character of popular music changed in fundamental ways. First, rock music became an international phenomenon. Second, every rock group developed its own identifiable sound and its own specific look. In the early days, for example, the Beatles all wore the same clothes and had matching haircuts.

Many other rock groups surfaced in the 1960s, the most famous of which was the five-member group that called themselves The Rolling Stones. They were deliberately rougher and more hard-edged. Their manager described them as "the opposite of those nice little chaps, the Beatles."

The Beatles in concert, 1963.

The Beatles' career as a group may be divided into two periods: the public and the private. The public period is represented by the first half of the decade, when they toured and made records of songs they could sing on stage. The private period, the second half of the Sixties, was devoted exclusively to recording, using the technology of the studio in novel ways that could not be reproduced in a live performance. These technologically advanced records had an enormous influence on recording techniques for the whole of the later history of rock music.

We shall examine two Beatles songs from the 1960s. The first one, *It Won't Be Long*, comes from what we have called the public period in the Beatles' career. The second, *Strawberry Fields Forever*, is from their private (studio) period. (See Listening Guide, pp. 318–319)

With the release in 1967 of their album *Sgt. Pepper's Lonely Hearts Club Band*, the record album took on a new dimension in artistic production. Rather than bringing together a collection of previously released hits and perhaps a few new songs, the new "concept album" was a completely integrated entity, with songs that were connected, either literally or thematically. Every aspect of *Sgt. Pepper* received special attention, including elaborate jacket and sleeve design with printed lyrics.

As a group, the Beatles lasted until 1970, when they broke up with some bitterness and acrimony. All four then began individual careers, with varying degrees of success. But the individual achievements of the four men never matched the extraordinary synergy they experienced as a group. From 1963 to 1970, the group known as the Beatles released thirteen record albums, from the early, energetic, tight-harmony *Please Please Me* to the strange and questing *Rubber Soul* to the amazingly varied *Sgt. Pepper* and, finally, *Abbey Road*. In only seven years, they changed the entire course of popular music.

The Beatles on Abbey Road, London, 1969.

LISTENING GUIDE

THE BEATLES

It Won't Be Long

Music and words by John Lennon
and Paul McCartney

Date of recording: 1964

An example of the Beatles' early, public sound is *It Won't Be Long*. Notice here the prominence of the electric bass and the background vocals. Other features that are trademarks of the Beatles' early style are the "yeah, yeah, yeah" exclamations and the constant interchange between lead and background vocals. The Beatles tended to use more interesting chord progressions and more complex harmonies than other groups. In *It Won't Be Long*, we can hear an unusual chord progression (major tonic to lowered submediant—I-♭VI—and back again) on the words of the two-line verses:

E (I)   C (♭VI)   E (I)
Every night when everybody has fun

E (I)   C (♭VI)   E (I)
Here am I sitting all on my own.

Colorful harmonies like this give added richness and depth to the song. Notice, too, how the repeated guitar riff is derived from the vocal line on "Every night …," "Here am I …," etc., and listen to the chromatic descent of the background vocals on "Since you left me …"

0:00	It won't be long yeah (yeah), yeah (yeah), yeah (yeah) It won't be long yeah (yeah), yeah (yeah), yeah (yeah) It won't be long yeah (yeah), 'til I belong to you.
0:16	Every night when everybody has fun, Here am I sitting all on my own.
0:27	It won't be long, etc.
0:42	Since you left me, I'm so alone, Now you're comin', you're comin' on home. I'll be good like I know I should, You're comin' home—you're comin' home.
0:57	Every night, the tears come down from my eyes; Every day, I've done nothing but cry.
1:09	It won't be long, etc.
1:23	Since you left me, etc.
1:38	So, every day we'll be happy, I know. Now I know that you won't leave me no mo'.
1:50	It won't be long, etc.

LISTENING GUIDE

THE BEATLES   Date of recording: 1967

Strawberry Fields Forever

Words and music by John Lennon
  and Paul McCartney

The Beatles' studio period can be represented by *Strawberry Fields Forever*, a song that originally appeared on a single with *Penny Lane* on the other side. In this song, notice the instrumental exploration (including orchestral instruments, flute sounds, and an Indian harp), the cymbals recorded backwards, and the really interesting chord progression. Notice also the somewhat mysterious and elusive nature of the words. It was at this time that the Beatles began to move away from the conventional lyrics of the standard pop song.

The electronically produced studio sound makes this song a production rather than a performance. Even today, with the rapid advances in technology that have occurred since 1967, it would be difficult to render a live performance of it.

A
Let me take you down 'cause I'm going to
Emin   **F♯**
Strawberry Fields, nothing is real
       D   **F♯**
And nothing to get hung about.
D   **A**
Strawberry Fields forever.

Bob Dylan in concert, 1978.

Bob Dylan

Apart from the many groups that sprang up in the 1960s, two individuals had a powerful influence on pop and rock music during that turbulent decade. They were Bob Dylan and Jimi Hendrix.

Bob Dylan's brand of intense **protest song** caught the imagination and fired the spirits of millions of young people in the rebellious, activist Sixties. He sang about the threat of nuclear war, about civil rights and racism, and about the military-industrial complex. "There's other things in this world besides love and sex that're important," Dylan said.

The protest song was not new. American slaves used to sing songs of protest under the guise of ballads or lullabies. And from the 1920s to the 1950s, the tradition of the protest song was continued by Woody Guthrie and Pete Seeger, who composed, sang, and accompanied their own songs on the guitar. But during the 1960s, Bob Dylan captivated the popular music world with his intensity and commitment. He seemed to personify a generation constantly in search of answers to new and profound questions. The protest songs—especially those with an antiwar sentiment, such as

Masters of War and *Blowin' in the Wind* (1963)—strongly caught the 1960s mood of bitterness and alienation. Dylan's snarling, nasal delivery and his rough guitar and harmonica playing gave bite and impetus to the music. Dylan is a restless and creative spirit, and no sooner had he made a major hit with one style than he was exploring something new and different. He was always ahead of his fans, shifting from folk ballads to protest songs to electrified rock to country.

Bob Dylan has changed his focus many times since those early days, and each time his followers have complained. Since the 1960s, he has sung Christian anthems, Jewish ballads, raucous rock, and deeply moving love songs. Many of his songs, both from the Sixties and later, are so original they defy classification. One of these is the brilliant, bitter, mournful *Sad-eyed Lady of the Lowlands* (1966). Other examples among many include the exquisite *Sara* (1975), a testament of love for his wife, and the intense, slow, lustful *Blood in My Eyes* (1993). Bob Dylan continues to compose, perform, protest, release records, and experiment with expressing his mind and heart in music.

LISTENING GUIDE

BOB DYLAN   Date of recording: 1966

Sad-eyed Lady of the Lowlands

Words and music by Bob Dylan

*S*ad-eyed Lady of the Lowlands is an epic ballad more than ten minutes long. Like much of Dylan's music, the essence of this song is in its superb poetry and its charismatic vocal delivery. The accompaniment of Dylan's guitar and his backup group at the time, the Band, is fairly static. However, notice Dylan's subtle shifts in accent and his colorful emotive changes through each of the verses and each chorus. Dylan transcends the simple framework of his song to create a performance that is more a powerful musical-poetic reading than a song.

0:00	[Instrumental introduction with harmonica solo]

VERSE 1

0:17

        D   F#min   Bmin   A
With your mercury mouth in the missionary times,
        D   F#min   Bmin   A
And your eyes like smoke and your prayers like rhymes,
      G   F#min   Emin   D
And your silver cross, and your voice like chimes,
      D   Emin   A
Oh, who among them do they think could bury you?

		D	F#min	Bmin		A	

0:51
               D   **F#min**   **Bmin**   **A**
With your pockets well protected at last,
               D   **F#min**   **Bmin**   **A**
And your streetcar visions which you place on the grass,
               G   **F#min**   **Emin**   **D**
And your flesh like silk, and your face like glass,
        D   **Emin**   **A**
Who among them do they think could carry you?

CHORUS

1:23
       Emin   **G**   **D** **A**
Sad-eyed lady of the lowlands,
               Emin   **G**   **D**   **A**
Where the sad-eyed prophet says that no man comes,

1:46
        D   **F#min** **Bmin** **A**   **G** **F#min** **Emin**
My warehouse eyes, my Arabian drums,
Emin   **A**
Should I leave them by your gate,
   Emin   **D**
Or, sad-eyed lady, should I wait?

VERSE 2

2:11
With your sheets like metal and your belt like lace,
And your deck of cards missing the jack and the ace,
And your basement clothes and your hollow face,
Who among them can think he could outguess you?

2:45
With your silhouette when the sunlight dims
Into your eyes where the moonlight swims,
And your match-book songs and your gypsy hymns,
Who among them would try to impress you?

CHORUS

3:20
Sad-eyed lady ....

VERSE 3

4:06
The kings of Tyrus with their convict list
Are waiting in line for their geranium kiss,
And you wouldn't know it would happen like this,
But who among them really wants just to kiss you?

4:41
With your childhood flames on your midnight rug,
And your Spanish manners and your mother's drugs,
And your cowboy mouth and your curfew plugs,
Who among them do you think could resist you?

CHORUS

5:13
Sad-eyed lady ....

321

VERSE 4	
6:01	Oh, the farmers and the businessmen, they all did decide To show you the dead angels that they used to hide. But why did they pick you to sympathize with their side? Oh, how could they ever mistake you?
6:35	They wished you'd accepted the blame for the farm, But with the sea at your feet and the phony false alarm, And with the child of a hoodlum wrapped up in your arms, How could they ever, ever persuade you?
CHORUS	
7:09	Sad-eyed lady ...
VERSE 5	
7:55	With your sheet-metal memory of Cannery Row, And your magazine-husband who one day just had to go, And your gentleness now, which you just can't help but show, Who among them do you think would employ you?
8:29	Now you stand with your thief, you're on his parole, With your holy medallion which your fingertips fold, And your saintlike face and your ghostlike soul, Oh, who among them do you think could destroy you?
CHORUS	
9:03	Sad-eyed lady ....
9:46	[harmonica solo; fade out]

Jimi Hendrix playing his "Strat."

Jimi Hendrix

In the 1960s, Jimi Hendrix was a unique figure. He was part black and part Native American, and he played the electric guitar like a man possessed. Accompanied only by bass and drums, Hendrix sang and played high-intensity versions of other people's songs (including his own protest: a wildly distorted, lamenting, dragged-out *Star-Spangled Banner*). But he also sang and played many highly original songs of his own, including *Purple Haze* (1967), *Foxy Lady* (1967), and the remarkable *Voodoo Chile* (1968).

The guitar playing of Jimi Hendrix was loud, sometimes angry, and always brilliantly inventive. He used electronic devices such as the wah-wah pedal and the fuzz box as well as effects such as feedback to create a dizzying array of sounds, and his virtuosity on his instrument was unparalleled. He played the Fender Stratocaster, the choice of many early rockers. Hendrix's playing was an inspiration for the sounds later explored by many heavy-metal guitar soloists, though very few guitarists can match his brilliance even today. He used his guitar to express musical ideas of startling originality, intensity, and complexity.

Additional Notes to the Sixties

The amount and variety of popular music during the 1960s could take up a book by itself; here we must be content with just a few notes on some of the other musical trends of the era. Each of these was a significant force at the time and also had important consequences for the later development of popular music.

The Supremes.

MOTOWN   Motown was the creation of Berry Gordy, a producer and songwriter who built one of America's most successful music empires. Named after the great city of the automotive industry ("Motortown" = Detroit), the company created an assembly line of successful black groups, including the Supremes, the Temptations, the Miracles, the Four Tops, and the Jackson 5.

The Motown sound was distinctive—polished, smooth, heavily orchestrated, with a danceable beat and the call-and-response quality of gospel singing. Motown was responsible for launching the solo careers of Diana Ross, Stevie Wonder, and Michael Jackson.

SURFING SONGS   Another element in the sounds of the Sixties was the music of the surfer groups. Surfing became a California craze in the early 1960s, partly as a result of the movie *Gidget* (1959), which depicted a beach romance.

Surfing songs featured a high, bright sound with close harmonies and bouncy rhythms. Formed in 1961, the kings of the surfing song were The Beach Boys, who carried their tanned, clean-cut image and distinctive multivoiced harmony around the nation with such hits as *Surfer Girl, California Girls, Fun, Fun, Fun,* and the national anthem of the surfing craze, *Surfin' U.S.A.*

FOLK   The history of folk song goes back to the early seventeenth century in America, and of course much farther back than that in Europe. The subject matter touched on the fundamental themes of rural human existence: love, death, nature, parting, work. Folk songs often tell a story.

In the 1960s, folk music experienced an enormous upsurge of interest among young people. The Kingston Trio had scored a major hit with their recording of the traditional folk ballad *Tom Dooley* in 1958. For the next ten years, The Kingston Trio remained one of the favorite groups in America. They sang folk songs in smooth harmonies accompanied by acoustic guitars. Other successful folk groups included The Limeliters and the perennially popular Peter, Paul, and Mary, who combined traditional songs (*Lemon Tree*) with twentieth-century American classics (Pete Seeger's *If I Had a Hammer*), as well as new songs written by themselves (the wonderfully evocative *Puff, the Magic Dragon*).

COUNTRY   Country music dates back to the 1920s, when a brand of folk music—featuring steel guitar, violin ("fiddle"), and quick rhythms—began to take on its own style. This style became known as Country and Western when, in the 1940s, songs became popular that featured the American West.

Country music gained widespread appeal in the 1940s and 1950s with such singing stars as Hank Williams and Eddy Arnold. Their songs were delivered in a nasal twang, with an occasional sob or "catch" in the voice, and accompanied by a relaxed beat.

In the 1960s, country music began to cross over into the pop charts. Country music is accessible and easy to understand. Many of its stories contain old-fashioned moralistic points of view or religious convictions rooted in rural society. The songs often have repeated sections or refrains, and the words are clear and prominent. Accompanying instruments include steel guitar (sometimes a "Hawaiian" guitar that *slides* between notes), fiddle, banjo, and "honky-tonk" piano. A typical country bass line bounces from the tonic to the dominant and back again.

THE BRITISH BLUES REVIVAL   At the height of the Beatles' popularity, an additional musical current was evident in England. This was the British blues revival. British groups such as the Yardbirds attempted to revive old blues styles and translate them into the rock idiom. Eric Clapton was the first of a trio of brilliant guitarists who were associated with the Yardbirds. Clapton, Jeff Beck, and Jimmy Page had a lasting impact, not only on the new interpretation of the blues, but also on guitar virtuosity.

Clapton's guitar-playing abilities and his musicianship caused him to be respected and imitated in all branches of popular music. His work contributed to the extremely high profile of the electric guitar, which became a universal symbol of rock music. Eric Clapton continues to be a driving force in rock and popular music.

THE 1970s AND 1980s: VARIETY, LEGACY, AND CHANGE

The story of popular music in the 1970s and 1980s is one of great diversity. The rebellious baby-boom generation, whose rallying cry used to be "Never trust anyone over thirty," were now in their forties. During this time, popular music spread into the mainstream. Rock music became the staple sound of radio stations all over the country. It could be heard in bus stations, supermarkets, and elevators.

Diversity was the hallmark of pop and rock. *Acid rock* was an outgrowth of the drug culture, "acid" being a term for the drug LSD. One of the most successful acid-rock groups was The Grateful Dead. Acid rock was extremely loud; it also featured songs of considerable length, with extended guitar solos. Acid rock evolved into *heavy metal*, a loud, thickly textured rock style with a deeply pounding beat, based primarily on the sounds of guitars and drums, often heavily distorted and employing "power chords." Power chords use the lowest, open strings of the guitar, often punched at tremendous volume. Heavy-metal bands included Led Zeppelin, Black Sabbath, Metallica, and Aerosmith.

The 1970s brought a resurgence of interest in solo performers: Carole King, Joni Mitchell, Roberta Flack, Judy Collins, Carly Simon, and Linda Ronstadt were the most prominent female singers; James Taylor, Stevie Wonder, Paul Simon, and Elton John became the most popular male singers. Often their sound was in deliberate contrast to the ear-splitting levels of acid rock, with more relaxed, introspective singing, accompanied by acoustic guitars, background strings, or sometimes just a single piano.

Many songs in this era successfully blended the traditional country style with rock elements to produce the blend known as *country rock*. One of the biggest stars of country rock was Willie Nelson, who produced an extraordinary string of hits starting in the mid 1970s and continuing into the 1990s. Nelson spoke of his music as appealing to "both rednecks and hippies."

A new fad of the 1970s, discos, originating in Europe, ushered in a special musical style and brought back the popularity of dancing. The disco sound was light, crisp, and intense, with fast drumming, high vocals, and a solid, thumping bass.

Some '70s phenomena seemed to suggest that the originality and interest had gone out of pop music. Gigantic, and in some cases grotesque, stage shows accompanied rock tours. This focus on the visual element set the stage for the music videos of the 1980s.

In the 1970s, more rock stars made more money than ever before. But if the musicians were making money, it was nothing compared with the profits of the record industry. In 1950, total record sales in the United States amounted to $189 million; by the late 1970s, that total had increased to $4 billion. Popular music was no longer the province of the counterculture; it was the product of corporate America.

In the 1980s, an antiestablishment trend once more reasserted itself. This was a deliberately shocking style of rock known as *punk*. Punk rock featured performers with outrageous costumes and nasty names. Lyrics were offensive, often violent. The titles of some songs from this time include *Slip It In*, *Killing an Arab*, and *Suicide Madness*.

A technological phenomenon of the 1980s revolutionized the way young people experienced popular music. Music Television, or MTV, a cable channel broadcasting nonstop music videos, was begun in 1981. Technology also influenced the sound of rock groups themselves. Synthesizers allowed the realistic duplication of sounds, which could be combined, modified, and manipulated in the most sophisticated ways.

MTV helped to create the solo careers of Michael Jackson and Madonna. Jackson's biggest success came during the 1980s, when his solo album *Thriller* (1982)

Michael Jackson in concert, 1988.

LISTENING GUIDE

MICHAEL JACKSON   Date of recording: 1982

Billie Jean

Words and music by Michael Jackson

Michael Jackson's album *Thriller* contains ten songs, nine of which reached the Top Ten as singles! Perhaps the most typical of Jackson's style is *Billie Jean*. The music is fast and glossy, with a high, artificial, synthesized sound and a persistent disco beat. Jackson's voice is high, slick, and breathless.

Madonna.

sold more than forty million copies worldwide. Madonna's dance training, combined with an overt sexuality, made her videos widely popular.

One final technological innovation of the 1980s that had an enormous impact on the spread (and the profits) of popular music was the invention of the compact disc. It was introduced in 1983, and quickly gained popularity. Gradually, CDs and the newly popular cassettes began to replace vinyl LPs. Many consumers not only bought new recordings as they came out on CD but also bought CDs to replace all their favorite old albums. It was a bonanza for the record industry. A CD costs less than $1 to manufacture and sells for between $12 and $20. The profits were enormous. In 1987, CBS made more than $200 million in profits. In 1989, Time Warner announced profits of nearly $500 million.

LISTENING GUIDE

MADONNA   Date of recording: 1984

Material Girl

Words and music by Peter Brown
   and Robert Rans

*M*aterial Girl was one of the principal hit singles from Madonna's phenomenally successful album *Like a Virgin*. The video to the song introduced one of Madonna's many well-known images: a blonde bombshell who is being fawned over by a large chorus of male suitors (who form a robotic chorus later in the song). The song is a fairly straightforward dance-club pop number. It is based on several recurrent melodic lines, or riffs, and has a persistent rhythmic beat and catchy lyrics.

0:00	[dance-pop introduction with synthesized keyboards and bass, electric guitar, and drums; guitar has main riff.]
VERSE	
0:28	Some boys kiss me, some boys hug me. I think they're okay. If they don't give me proper credit I just walk away.
0:42	They can beg and they can plead, but they can't see the light, that's right. 'Cause the boy with the cold hard cash is always Mr. Right.

| 0:56 | "Cause we are living in a material world and I am a material girl. You know that we are living in a material world and I am a material girl. |

| 1:09 | [Guitar break of main riff with echoes of squealing pleasure sounds by Madonna.] |

VERSE

| 1:16 | Some boys romance, some boys slow dance. That's all right with me. If they can't raise my interest then I have to let them be. |

| 1:30 | Some boys try and some boys lie, but I don't let them play. (No way.) Only boys who save their pennies make my rainy day. |

CHORUS

| 1:43 | 'Cause they are living in a material world and I am a material girl. You know that we are living in a material world and I am a material girl. |

| 1:58 | Living in a material world and I am a material girl. You know that we are living in a material world and I am a material girl. |

| 2:10 | [Guitar break of main riff with echoes of Madonna squealing.] |

| 2:24 | Living in a material world. (Material.) Living in a material world. Living in a material world. (Material.) Living in a material world. |

VERSE

| 2:38 | Boys may come and boys may go and that's all right, you see. Experience has made me rich and now they're after me. |

CHORUS

| 2:51 | 'Cause everybody's living in a material world and I am a material girl. You know that we are living in a material world and I am a material girl. |

| 3:06 | Living in a material world and I am a material girl. You know that we are living in a material world and I am a material girl. |

| 3:24 | A material, a material, a material, a material world. |

| 3:32 | [Echoes and fades; a false ending, which returns to the main song. Robotic men's chorus.]

Living in a material world. (Material.)
Living in a material world.
Living in a material world. (Material.)
Living in a material world.

[Fade out.] |

THE NINETIES: RAP, RAGE, AND REACTION

The main musical phenomenon of the nineties was **rap**. Rap is usually half-spoken, rather than sung, with a strong and complex rhythm, backed by bass, synthesizer, and percussion. Rap traded on ideas of violence, aggression, and resentment.

Some rap records provoked serious controversy. The song *Cop Killer* by the rap artist Ice-T spoke of the delights of slitting a policeman's throat and watching his family mourn. Police organizations around the country called for a boycott of Time Warner, Ice-T's record company, and the Vice President of the United States publicly joined the call. The result: the record surged strongly in the charts.

There were other ugly elements in rap music. Some rap songs displayed overt racism against Asians; some were offensively homophobic. But a common trait was prejudice against women. Many rap songs referred to women as "bitches" or "ho's" (whores), and some even advocated deliberate violence and brutality against women.

The public militancy of rap was partly boosted by commercial considerations. Record companies soon discovered that aggression and a militant image sold a lot of records. Bill Stephney, one of the founders of the group Public Enemy, said that he had deliberately polished the group's militant image: "In many respects, that was done on purpose … to curry favor with a white audience by showing rebellion."

Rap features a repetitive, heavy bass (often produced electronically) with a hard, high drumbeat (made on a drum machine). Rapid splicing, overdubbing, and heavy engineering produce a glossy, unvarying sound that is often hypnotizing in its sameness.

As rap settled into the mainstream, it tended to fall into two categories. The first, "gangsta rap," continued the angry image. The second, sometimes called pop rap, spoke more of unity than of violence, often featured female singers, and tended to incorporate more melodic interest. Rap even became the medium for gospel and Christian music.

THE CURRENT SCENE

After the turn of the millennium, the commercial element of popular music was its most prominent feature. Record companies became more sophisticated than ever at marketing their products, giving the maximum exposure to a star or a group at just the right

The rapper Eminem.

time. Successful debut albums are followed by singles that whet fans' appetites for the inevitable blockbuster. Teenagers in the United States now number over thirty million, and a strong economy gives them massive buying power. In the year 2000, American teenagers were able to spend over $150 billion.

In that same year, record companies created three popular-music phenomena. Britney Spears sold 1.3 million copies of her new album, the white rapper Eminem 1.7 million copies, and the pop group 'N Sync an amazing 2.4 million copies—all in the first *week* of sales.

'N Sync and Britney Spears record for the same company and depend on the same upbeat pop sound, pretty looks, and smooth moves for their appeal. Nowadays the pop world seems to be full of "boy bands" and "teen queens." Eminem, however, is a different proposition: he's ironic, clever, parodistic, and often vicious.

As the twenty-first century gets underway, a serious question arises. Will the accessibility and enormous profitability of popular music swamp more delicate and profound kinds of music? Nowadays jazz and classical music each represent less than five percent of record sales. Will young people grow up appreciating the diversity, complexity, and richness of older musical traditions? And, around the world, will the musical traditions of other cultures survive the overwhelming popularity and commercial pressures of Western pop and rock? In twenty or thirty years, we'll know the answers to these questions.

Bringing it up to Date

In 2001, the National Endowment for the Arts and the Recording Industry of America published a list of the top 365 "Songs of the Century." The top ten were:

1. "Somewhere Over the Rainbow"
2. "White Christmas"
3. "This Land Is Your Land"
4. "Respect"
5. "American Pie"
6. "Boogie Woogie Bugle Boy"
7. All of *West Side Story*
8. "Take Me Out to the Ball Game"
9. "You've Lost That Lovin' Feelin' "
10. "The Entertainer"

Listening to...

POPULAR MUSIC

- The most important requirement of popular music is that it must appeal to a large number of people. This obviously affects musical style: popular music must have (1) an attractive melody (Frank Sinatra, *Blue Moon*) or (2) catchy rhythms (Elvis Presley, *Blue Suede Shoes*; Michael Jackson, *Billie Jean*) or (3) interesting words, (The Beatles, *Strawberry Fields*) or some combination of all three (Bob Dylan, *Sad-Eyed Lady of the Lowlands*).

- By far the largest proportion of popular music is vocal. Perhaps that is because we can (more or less) reproduce the sounds ourselves as we go though the day (The Beatles, *It Won't Be Long*; Madonna, *Material Girl*).

- The principal topic of popular music is love or sex (*Blue Moon, It Won't Be Long, Billie Jean*).

- The most important driving force in popular music is strictly a commercial one. The music depends on a massive machinery of corporate interests, which spends millions of dollars in advertising and generates billions of dollars in profits. Popular music equals money. Are you listening to your favorites because you chose them yourself, or because you were convinced by advertising?

KEY TERMS

protest song **(p. 319)**   rap **(p. 328)**   rhythm and blues **(p. 312)**

GLOSSARY

$\mathcal{G}$LOSSARY AND MUSICAL EXAMPLE LOCATOR

(Fuller discussions of these terms may be found on the pages indicated.)

absolute music   Music that is not programmatic, i.e. that has no reference outside the music itself.

aria   Lyrical section of opera for solo singer and orchestra, usually in ABA form. (See p. 22) (Musical example: George Frideric Handel, Giulio Cesare, p. 122)

arioso   A style of vocal music halfway between aria and recitative.

arpeggio   The notes of a chord played consecutively up or down rather than simultaneously.

atonality   The lack of a key system or tonal center in music. (See p. 236) (Musical example: Arnold Schoenberg, *Madonna* from *Pierrot Lunaire*, p. 247.)

authentic cadence   A chord progression moving from the dominant of the home key (V) to the tonic (I).

bar (Synonymous with "measure".)   Short unit of time in music. Each bar usually takes up the same amount of time as every other.

bar lines   Lines drawn in the written music to separate bars.

beat   Recurring pattern of accents in music.

bebop or bop   Form of jazz that developed in the 1940s for small combos, with difficult, more improvisatory music. (See p. 297.) (Musical example: Charlie Parker, *Confirmation*, p. 299.)

binary form   A form with two sections, each of which is repeated, as in the pattern AABB. (See p. 22.) (Musical example: Franz Joseph Haydn, Minuet and Trio from Symphony No. 47 in G-major p. 145.)

bitonality   Two different keys sounding simultaneously. (See p. 242.) (Musical example: Charles Ives, "Putnam's Camp" from *Three Places in New England*, p. 264.)

blue note   Flattened or "bent" note played or sung in jazz. (See p. 287.) (Musical examples: Bessie Smith, *Florida-Bound Blues*, p. 291, and Duke Ellington, *It Don't Mean a Thing (If It Ain't Got That Swing)*, p. 297.)

cadence   Closing group of sounds.

canzona   Renaissance instrumental work, often involving counterpoint. (See p. 90.) (Musical example: Giovanni Gabrieli, *Canzona Duodecimi Toni*, p. 90.)

chamber music   Music for a small group of musicians.

character piece   Short programmatic piece usually for solo piano. (See p. 195.) (Musical example: Robert Schumann, *Träumerei (Dreaming)* from *Kinderszenen*, Op. 15, p. 196.)

chorale   A Protestant hymn sung in unison by the entire congregation in even rhythm. Often harmonized for use by church choir. (See p. 98.) (Musical example: Johann Sebastian Bach, *St. Matthew Passion*, p. 117.)

chord   The simultaneous sounding of two or more notes.

chord progression   Movement from one chord to another.

chromatic   The sounding of unexpected sharps and flats in composition.

chromatic scale   A scale made up entirely of half steps.

coda   The closing portion of a movement.

concerto   Instrumental work, usually in three movements, highlighting contrast. Baroque concertos were usually written in the pattern fast-slow-fast, featuring ritornello form. A *concerto grosso* featured a small group of instruments contrasted with the whole group. A *solo concerto* featured a single instrument contrasted with the whole group. (See p. 97.) (Musical examples: Antonio Vivaldi, *La Primavera* ("Spring") from *The Four Seasons*, p. 109, and Johann Sebastian Bach, *Brandenburg* Concerto No. 2 in F Major, p. 000.) Classic and Romantic concertos tended to be solo concertos, retaining the fast-slowfast pattern, and combining ritornello form with Classic forms, such as sonata form or aria form. (See pp. 107.)

concerto grosso   A concerto for (orchestra and) more than one solo instrument.

consonant   Sounds that mesh pleasantly with each other.

continuo   See **basso continuo**.

counterpoint   The simultaneous sounding of independent musical lines.

crescendo   Getting louder.

dance suite   A multi-movement composition for instruments, with each of the movements based on the rhythms and affect of a particular dance, and with all the movements usually in the same key.

decrescendo   Getting softer.

development   The central main section of a sonata-form movement, in which many keys are introduced, often in a somewhat turbulent or contrapuntal context.

diminuendo   Getting softer.

dissonant   Sounds that mesh harshly together.

dominant   The chord built on the fifth note of a scale.

duple   A meter that is divisible by two.

dynamics   Loudness and softness.

episode   The musical material that occurs between statements of a main theme.

exposition   The opening section of a sonata-form movement, in which the two main keys of the movement are juxtaposed together with the thematic material that represents them.

étude   Solo instrumental piece focusing on a particular aspect of technique. (See p. 191.)

form   The overall structure of a piece of music.

fusion   Music combining elements of both jazz and rock. (See p. 301.)

gamelan   Indonesian musical ensemble involving mostly metal percussion. (See pp. 56.) (Musical example: *Gangsaran-Bima Kurda-Gangsaran*, p. 57.)

glissando   Sliding from one note to another.

grand opera   Spectacular type of nineteenth-century French opera, with elaborate stage sets, ballet, and crowd scenes. (See p. 198.)

ground bass   A phrase in the bass that is repeated over and over again. (See p. 102.) (Musical example: Henry Purcell, Dido's Lament from *Dido and Aeneas*, p. 103.)

half cadence   A cadence that ends on the dominant chord (V).

half step   The smallest common interval between adjacent notes.

harmony   The overall sound and tonal pattern of the chords in a piece of music.

homophony   Music that moves mostly in chords.

imitation   A form of polyphony in which all the musical lines present the same musical phrase, one after the other.

impromptu   Instrumental piece, usually for piano, that gives the impression of being improvised. (See p. 191.)

improvisation   Composing music during the act of playing or singing.

interval   The distance between two notes.

keynote   The principal note of a scale or melody.

leitmotiv   Musical phrase or fragment with associations to a character, object, or idea. (See p. 209.) (Musical example: Richard Wagner, Prelude and *Liebestod* from *Tristan und Isolde*, p. 210.)

liturgical music   Music for a religious ceremony. (See p. 65.)

lute   A plucked instrument with a rounded back, short neck, and frets. (See p. 72.) (Musical example: Guillaume de Machaut, *Doulz Viaire Gracieus*, p. 71.)

lyric opera   Type of French opera midway between grand opéra and opéra comique, usually featuring plots of tragic love. (See p. 198.)

madrigal   Secular vocal work, often in Italian, for a small group of singers. (See pp. 88–89.) (Musical example: Thomas Morley, Two English Madrigals, See p. 89.)

major scale   Seven notes arranged in the following pattern of intervals: whole step, whole step, half step, whole step, whole step, whole step, half step.

mass setting   A setting to music of the words from the Catholic Mass (usually just the Ordinary of the Mass: Kyrie, Gloria, Credo, Sanctus, Agnus Dei).

mbira   African instrument made of a small wooden box or gourd with thin metal strips attached. (See p. 52.)

measure   *See* bar.

melody   Notes arranged in a coherent sequence.

melodic motion   The arrangement of the notes in a melody.

meter   A recurring pattern of strong and weak beats.

minimalism   Musical style of the 1960s to the 1990s involving very limited materials, constant repetition, and very gradual change. (See p. 277.)

minor scale   Seven notes arranged in the following pattern of intervals: whole step, half step, whole step, whole step, half step, whole step, whole step.

minuet-and-trio form   Often used for third movements of Classic instrumental works. Both minuet and trio are in two parts, each of which is repeated. The minuet is played twice, once before and once after the trio. (See p. 141.) (Musical example: Franz Joseph Haydn, Minuet and Trio from Symphony No. 47 in G-Major Minor, p. 145.)

mode   System of melodic organization used in music of the Middle Ages and early Renaissance. There are four main medieval modes, designating pieces ending on D, E, F, and G, respectively. (See p. 65.) (Musical example: Kyrie, p. 83.)

modulation   The process of changing from one key to another.

monody   Type of early Baroque music for solo voice and **basso continuo** with vocal line imitating the rhythms of speech. (See p. 99.) (Musical example: Claudio Monteverdi, extracts from *Orfeo*, p. 99.)

monophony   Music sung or played in unison.

motet   (Renaissance) A vocal setting of a Latin text, usually sacred. (See p. 81.) (Musical example: Giovanni Pierluigi da Palestrina, Exsultate Deo, p. 86.)

movement   Large, separate section of a musical work.

music drama   Term coined by Wagner to refer to his operas, which involve ancient myth, resonant poetry, and rich, dramatic music. (See p. 209.) (Musical example: Richard Wagner, Prelude and *Liebestod* from *Tristan and Isolde*, p. 210.)

nationalism   A nineteenth-century movement that stressed national identity. In music, this led to the creation of works in native languages, using national myths and legends, and incorporating local rhythms, themes, and melodies. (See p. 174.) (Musical example: Bedřich Smetana, The Moldau, p. 214.)

nocturne   Moody, introspective piece, usually for solo piano. (See p. 191.)

noh   Ancient Japanese theatrical genre, with highly stylized acting. (See p. 54.)

non–triadic harmony   Harmony based not on thirds, but on other intervals.

octatonic scale   Scale with eight notes within the octave, separated by a series of alternating whole and half steps. (See p. 236.)

octave   The distance between one note and the next higher or lower note of the same name.

opéra comique   Small-scale French nineteenth-century opera, with humorous or romantic plots. (See p. 198.)

oral tradition   The practice of passing music (or other aspects of culture) orally from one generation to another. (See pp. 45.)

oratorio   An unstaged dramatic sacred work, featuring solo singers (including a narrator), choir, and orchestra, and usually based on a biblical story. (See p. 98.)

orchestral song cycle   Song cycle in which the voice is accompanied by an orchestra instead of a piano. (See p. 228.)

Ordinary of the Mass   The collective name for those five sections of the Catholic Mass (Kyrie, Gloria, Credo, Sanctus, Agnus Dei) that occur in every Mass. (See p. 81.)

ostinato   Constantly repeated musical phrase. (See p. 242.) (Musical example: Igor Stravinsky, *Le Sacre du Printemps (The Rite of Spring)*, p. 243.)

overlapping cadences   In imitative music, a technique whereby some voices create a cadence while others continue.

paired imitation   Music in which two voices engage in imitation as a pair, followed later by another pairing of different voices.

overture   A short orchestral work, usually designed to precede the performance of an opera

pantonality   Term referring to the simultaneous existence of all keys in music. (See p. 236.)

Passion   Similar to the oratorio. An unstaged dramatic sacred work, featuring solo singers (including a narrator), choir, and orchestra, and based on one of the Gospel accounts of the last days of Jesus. (See p. 117.) (Musical example: Johann Sebastian Bach, St. *Matthew Passion*, p. 117.)

pentatonic scale   A scale with five notes; the most common form has the following intervals: whole step, whole step, minor third, whole step. (See p. 16.)

percussion   Instruments that are hit or shaken to produce their sound.

phrase   The smallest coherent unit of a melody.

pitch   The exact highness or lowness of a note.

pizzicato   Plucking a string to produce a note.

plagal cadence   Chord sequence that ends with the subdominant harmony (IV) moving to the tonic (I).

plainchant   Monophonic liturgical vocal music of the Middle Ages. (See p. 65.) (Musical example: Kyrie, p. 83.)

point of imitation   Section of music presenting a short phrase imitated among the voices. (See p. 83.) (Musical example: Josquin Desprez, Kyrie from the *Pange Lingua* Mass, p. 83.)

polyphony   Music with more than one line sounding at the same time. (See p. 18.) (Musical example: Perotinus, *Viderunt Omnes*, p. 69.)

polyrhythm   Different meters sounding simultaneously.

polytonality   The existence in music of two or more keys at the same time.

Postmodernism   A cultural movement of the last part of the twentieth century, involving a juxtaposition of past and present, popular and refined, Western and nonWestern styles. (See p. 274.)

prelude (toccata)   Free, improvisatory work or movement, usually for organ. (See p. 113.) (Musical example: Johann Sebastian Bach, Prelude and Fugue in E minor, p. 113.)

program music   Instrumental music that tells a story or describes a picture or a scene. (See pp. 109, 178.) (Musical example: Antonio Vivaldi, La Primavera ("Spring") from *The Four Seasons*, p. 109.)

protest song   A song devoted to a social cause, such as the fight against injustice, antiwar sentiment, etc. (See p. 319.)

quarter note   A note that usually takes a single beat in a measure.

quarter tone Pitches separated by a quarter of a step rather than a half or a whole step. (See p. 237.)

rap Popular music style of the 1980s and 1990s with fast, spoken lyrics and a strong, and often complex beat. (See p. 328.)

recitative Music for solo voice and simple accompaniment, designed to reflect the irregularity and naturalness of speech. (See p. 99.) (Musical example: Claudio Monteverdi, extracts from *Orfeo*, p. 99.)

refrain Recurring text in a poem or song.

recapitulation The third main section of a sonata-form movement, in which the material of the exposition returns (sometimes slightly altered) and with the second-key material of the exposition transposed into the tonic key.

register Area of a voice or instrument's range.

rest A unit of silence.

rhythm A pattern of short and long notes.

rhythm and blues An early forerunner of rock-and-roll, featuring blues singing with a hard, electrified, rhythmic accompaniment.

ritornello An orchestral passage in a concerto that returns several times, in the same or in different keys. (See p. 100.) (Musical example: Antonio Vivaldi, *La Primavera* ("*Spring*") from *The Four Seasons*, p. 109.)

rondeau A medieval poetic form (often set to music) with a refrain that occurs in full at the beginning and end of each verse and in part in the middle.

rondo form Often used for last movements of Classic instrumental works. A theme constantly returns, alternating with constrasting passages (episodes). (See p. 142.) (Musical example: Franz Joseph Haydn, String Quartet, Op. 33, No. 2, in E-flat Major, p. 146.)

round The same melody sung or played by two or more voices at staggered intervals.

rubato Slight stretching of the time in performance.

scale A fixed series of notes.

secular song Music that is nonreligious (See p. 88)

shakuhaehi Japanese end-blown bamboo flute. (See p. 54.) (Musical example: Koku-Reibo, p. 55.)

shape The pattern made by the rising and falling of a melody.

sitar A long-necked, resonant, plucked string instrument from India.

solo sonata An instrumental work for a single instrument accompanied by basso continuo.

solo concerto A concerto for (orchestra and) one solo instrument.

sonata Baroque: A work for a small group of instruments. Sonatas include solo sonatas (one instrument

and basso continuo) and trio sonatas (two instruments and basso continuo). Also divided by style into *sonata da camera* ("chamber sonata"), whose movements are based on dance rhythms, and *sonata da chiesa* ("church sonata"), whose movements are more serious in character. (See p. 104). Classic and Romantic: Work for solo piano or piano and another instrument in three or four movements. (Musical examples: Arcangelo Corelli, Trio Sonata, Op. 3, No. 7, p. 105, and Ludwig van Beethoven, Piano Sonata in E Major, Op. 109, p. 167)

sonata form Organizing structure for a musical work or movement. It has three main parts: an *exposition*, in which the main themes are presented and the primary key moves from tonic to dominant; a *development* in which many keys are explored and the themes are often presented in fragments; and a *recapitulation*, in which the music of the exposition returns, usually staying in the tonic key throughout. (See p. 22.) (Musical examples: Wolfgang Amadeus Mozart, Symphony No. 40 in G minor, K. 550, p. 152, and Ludwig van Beethoven, Symphony No. 5 in C minor, p. 163.)

song cycles Series of songs linked together. (See p. 182.)

song texture Music produced by a single voice or instrument with chordal accompaniment.

sound Any noise or music.

string quartet Work, usually in four movements, for two violins, viola, and cello. (See p. 25.) (Musical examples: Franz Joseph Haydn, String Quartet, Op. 33, No. 2, in E-flat Major, p. 146, and Béla Bartók, String Quartet No. 4, p. 259.)

strophic Song in which all stanzas are sung to the same music. (See p. 82.) (Musical example: Franz Schubert, *Die Forelle* p. 183.)

subdominant A chord built on the fourth note of a scale.

swing (1) The feeling generated by the regular rhythm and the syncopated accents of jazz. (2) Dance music played by jazz bands in the 1930s and early 1940s. (See p. 294.) (Musical example: Duke Ellington, *It Don't Mean a Thing (If It Ain't Got That Swing)*, p. 297.)

symphonic poem Programmatic orchestral work in one movement. (See p. 180.) (Musical example: Bedřich Smetana, The Moldau, p. 214.)

syncopation A note played in anticipation of (before) a beat.

telharmonium An instrument that produces sound by means of electronic generators.

tempo The speed at which a piece of music is performed.

ternary form Overall structure of a piece in the pattern ABA.

texture The way in which different lines of music are combined.

thematic transformation Technique of changing or varying a theme in its different appearances throughout a work. (See p. 198.)

theremin An instrument that can make oscillating sliding sounds, like ghost noises.

theme-and-variations form Form of a work or a movement in which successive statements of a melody are altered or embellished each time. (See p. 22.) (Musical examples: Ludwig van Beethoven, *Six Easy Variations on a Swiss Tune*, p. 163, and Ludwig van Beethoven, Piano Sonata, Op. 109, p. 167.)

timbre The quality of a sound.

time signature Numerical indication of the number and type of beats in a measure.

32-bar AABA form Format involving four eight-measure phrases, the first two and the last being the same. This form is very common in popular songs and jazz. (See p. 23.) (Musical example: The Charlie Parker Quartet, *Confirmation* p. 299.)

tone cluster A large dissonant group of notes played together.

tone color The distinctive sound of an instrument or voice. (See p. 237.)

tonic The home key in which a piece of music is written.

triad A chord made up of three notes.

trio sonata An instrumental work for two instruments accompanied by basso continuo.

triple A meter that is divisible by three.

troubadour Poet-musician of medieval southern France. (See p. 70.)

twelve-tone system Twentieth-century compositional technique in which the composer treats all twelve pitches as equal and uses them in a highly organized way. (See p. 236.) (Musical example: Arnold Schoenberg, Theme and Sixth Variation, *Variations for Orchestra*, Op. 31, p. 249.)

12–bar blues A pattern of verse and harmony, rhyming AAB and using the I chord for the first four measures, IV for measures 5 and 6, I for measures 7 and 8, and V, IV, I, I for the last four measures.

unison Two or more notes sounding together on the same pitch.

vibrato A slight wavering of pitch.

Wagner tuba Brass instrument with a range between French horn and trombone. (See p. 209.)

whole step An interval made up of two half steps.

whole-tone scale A scale with six notes, each separated from the next by a whole step. (See p. 236.)

woodwind Instruments in the orchestra whose sound is created by blowing across a hole (flute) or by blowing through bamboo strips or reeds (clarinet, oboe, bassoon).

word-painting The technique of depicting the *meaning* of words through music. (See p. 88.) (Musical example: Thomas Morley, Two English Madrigals p. 89.)

CREDITS

MUSIC

5 "Happy Birthday to You," by Mildred J. Hill and Patty S. Hill. © 1935 (renewed) Summy-Birchard Music, a division of Summy-Birchard, Inc. All Rights Reserved. Used by permission. Warner Bros. Publications U.S., Inc. Miami, FL 30014.

242 THE RITE OF SPRING (Igor Stravinsky) © Copyright 1912, 1921 by Hawkes & Son (London), Ltd. Copyright renewed by permission of Boosey & Hawkes, Inc.

31, 249–250 Used by permission of Belmont Music Publishers, Pacific Palisades, CA 90272.

259 String Quartet No. 4 (Bela Bartok) copyright © 1929 for the USA by Boosey & Hawkes, Inc. Copyright renewed. Reprinted by permission.

278–279 © TONOS Musikverlags GmbH, Damstadt. Reproduced by kind permission.

282–283 THIRD MOVEMENT (FROM SYMPHONY NO. 1) by Ellen Taafe Zwilch. Copyright © 1983 by Associated Music Publishers, Inc. (BMI). International Copyright Secured. All rights reserved. Reprinted by permission.

252–256 Berg Wozzeck © 1931 by Universal Edition A.G., Vienna. English translation © 1952 by Alfred A. Kalmus, London W. 1 © renewed. All rights reserved. Used by permission of European Music Distributors LLC, sole US and Canadian agent for Universal Edition A.G. Vienna.

309–310 "Blue Moon" by Lorenz Hart and Richard Rogers, © 1934 (renewed) Metro-Goldwyn-Mayer, Inc. All rights reserved. Used by permission. Warner Brothers Publications U.S., Inc. Miami, FL 33014.

313–314 "Blue Suede Shoes," words and music by Carl Lee Perkins. Copyright 1955 by Carl Perkins Music, Inc. Copyright renewed. All rights administered by Unichappell Music, Inc. International Copyright secured. All rights reserved.

318 "It Won't Be Long," words and music by John Lennon and Paul McCartney. Copyright 1963, 1964 Northern Songs Ltd. Copyright renewed. All rights controlled and administered by EMI Blackwood Music Inc. under license from ATV Music (Maclen Music). All rights reserved.

319 "Strawberry Fields Forever," words and music by John Lennon and Paul McCartney. Copyright 1967 Northern Songs Ltd. Copyright renewed. All rights controlled and administered by EMI Blackwood Music Inc. under license from ATV Music (Maclen Music). All rights reserved.

320–322 SAD-EYED LADY OF THE LOWLANDS, words and music by Bob Dylan. Copyright © 1966; Renewed 1994 by Dwarf Music. International Copyright Secured. All rights reserved. Reprinted by permission of Music Sales Corporation (ASCAP).

326–327 "Material Girl" by Peter Brown and Robert Rans. © 1984 Candy Castle Music. All rights administered by Warner-Tamerland Publishing Corp. All rights reserved. Used by permission. Warner Bros. Publications U.S. Inc., Miami, FL 33014.

PHOTOS: CHAPTER 1

CO: Mary Kate Denny, PhotoEdit.

24 (top): Stephen Morley, Retna Ltd. USA. (bottom) UPI, Corbis / Bettman.

25 (top): Volkman Kurt Wentzel, National Geographic Image Collection. (bottom) Richard Hamilton Smith, Corbis/Bettman.

26 Jon Blumb.

28 Jon Blumb.

29 Index Stock Imagery, Inc.

30 John Bacchus, Pearson Education Corporate Digital Archive.

31 (top): Todd Powell, Index Stock Imagery, Inc. (bottom) Tony Freeman, PhotoEdit.

32 Dave King, Dorling Kindersley Media Library.

33 (top): Giraudon, Art Resource, N.Y. (bottom) Michael Newman, PhotoEdit.

36 Peter Menzel, Stock Boston.

37 (left): Walter H. Scott. (right) Walther H. Scott.

38 (top): John Abbott Photography. (bottom) Lynn Goldsmith, Corbis/Bettmann.

CHAPTER 2

CO: Steve Cole, Getty Images, Inc.–PhotoDisc.

46 (top left): Jack Vartoogian. (top right) eStock Photography LLC. (bottom) Jason Laure, The Image Works.

47 (top): Jay Blakesberg, Retna Ltd. USA. (bottom) John Lei, Stock Boston.

49 Steve Vidler, eStock Photography LLC.

50 (top): Jack Vartoogian. (bottom) Jagdish Agarwal, Dinodia Picture Agency.

51 (top): Jack Vartoogian. (bottom) Paolo Koch, Photo Researchers, Inc.

52 (top left): Jeremy Yudkin. (top right) Sarah Errington, The Hutchison Library. (bottom) Jose Azel, Woodfin Camp & Associates.

53 Lester Sloan.

54 Jack Vartoogian.

55 Jack Vartoogian.

56 Steve Vidler, eStock Photography LLC.

59 (bottom): Marc & Evelyne Bernheim, Woodfin Camp & Associates.

60 Shanachie Entertainment.

CHAPTER 3

CO: Lebrecht Music Collection/NL

63 The British Library/Topham-HIP/The Image Works

64 (top): The Art Archive/Bodleian Library Oxford/ The Bodleian Library/Picture Desk/Shelf mark Douce 195 fol 47. (bottom) Photography by Jean Bernard in "L'Univers de Chartres." Copyright Bordas, Paris 1988.

65 AKG London LTD.

66 Art Resource, NY.
68 Chad Ehlers, Getty Images Inc. – Stone Allstock.
70 Courtesy of the Library of Congress.

CHAPTER 4

CO: Thomas–Photos, Thomas–Photos, Oxford.
78 (top): Peter Hvizdak/The Image Works. (lower left): Getty Images Inc.–Hulton Archive Photos; (lower right): Courtesy of the Library of Congress.
79 (top): Siegfried Layda/Getty Images Inc.–Stone Allstock. (bottom): the Art Archive/Musee des Beaux Arts Nantes/Dagli Orti/Picture Desk.
80 Bayerishce Staatsbibliothek Munich, Musikabteilung, 2 Mus. Pr. 106/4.
84 Bildarchiv der Oesterreichischen Nationalbibliothek.
87 Thomas – Photos Oxford.

CHAPTER 5

CO: Eugene Delacroix (1798–1863). Portrait of Frederic Chopin (1810–1860), 1838. Oil on canvas, 45.5 × 38 cm. Louvre, Dept. de Peintures, France. © Photograph by Erich Lessing. Erich Lessing/Art Resource, NY
95 Hyacinth Rigaud (1659–1743). Louis XIV, King of France (1638–1715). Portrait in royal costume (the head was painted on a separate canvas and later added). Oil on canvas, 227 × 194 cm. Louvre, Dpt. Des Peintures, Paris, France. © Photograph by Erich Lessing. Erich Lessing/Art Resource, NY.
96 (top): View of the Chateau Versailles in 1668. Chateaux de Versailles et de Trianon, Versailles, France. Reunion des Musees Nationaux/Art Resources, NY.
96 (bottom): Rembrandt Harmensz van Rign (1606–1669). Rembrandt, self-portrait at old age. Oil on canvas. National Gallery, London, Great Britain. © Photograph by Erich Lessing. Erich Lessing/Art Resource, NY.
98 Musik/Konzert: "Hofkonzert beim Furstbischof von Luttich auf Schloss Seraing." (Mit Violoncello der Furstbischof Kardinal Johann Theodor von Bayern). Ausschnitt. Gemalde, 1753, von Paul Joseph Delcloche (1716–1759). 186 × 240,5 cm. Concerto with Harpsichord in middle of orchestra. Munchen, Baerisches Nationalmuseum.
102 Henry Purcell (1659–1695). Oil on canvas, 1695, by or after J. Closterman. The Granger Collection.
106 Pierre Rameau, "Le Maitre a danser," Paris, 1725. Courtesy of the Library of Congress.
107 Two heads; hope and fear, from Charles Le Brun's "conference sur l'Expression," 1698. Musee du Louvre, Paris. Reunion des Musees Nationaux/Art Resource, NY.
108 The Granger Collection.
111 (top): Stadtgeschichtlic hes Museum Leipzig.
111 (bottom): AKG London Ltd.
112 Bildarchiv Foto Marburg/Art Resource, NY.
120 Copyright: Dean & Chapter of Westminster, London.

CHAPTER 6

CO: Corbis/Bettman.
129 The Granger Collection.
130 (left): Corbis Bettman.
130 (right): The Granger Collection.
131 (top): Photographie Giraudon/Art Resource.
131 (bottom): Giraudon/Art Resource, NY.
132 Pietro Longhi (1702–1785). The House Concert. Around 1760. Oil on canvas, 50 × 62 cm. Pinacoteca di Brera, Milan Italy. © Photograph by Erich Lessing. Erich Lessing/Art Resource, NY.

139 String Quartet. Color engraving, 18th century, Austrian. Mozart Museum, Prague, Czech Republic. Giraudon/Art Resource, NY.
143 Edouard Jean Conrad Hamman, Portrait of Joseph Haydn. Engraving. Biblioteque Nationale, Paris, France. Giroudon / Art Resource, NY.
144 Erich Lessing, AKG London, Ltd.
148 (top): The Granger Collection.
148 (bottom): AKG London Ltd.
149 Painting, Barouque, 18th century. Della Croce, Johann Nepomuk (18th), "the Mozart Family: (1780–1781). Oil on canvas. 140 × 186 cm. Mozart House, Salzburg, Austria. Erich Lessing/Art Resource.

CHAPTER 7

CO: Damien Lovegrove/Science Photo Library. Photo Researcher Inc.
158 Stiftung Preussische Schloesser und Gaerten Berlin – Brandenburg, Schloss Charlottenburg.
159 Ludwig van Beethoven, portrait by Joseph Karl Stieler, 1820. Beethoven – Haus Bonn.
160 Ludwig van Beethoven, miniature by Christian Horneman, 1802. Beethoven–Haus Bonn, collection H.C. Bodmer. The Granger Collection.
161 The Granger Collection.

CHAPTER 8

CO: Richard Hutchings, Photo Reseachers, Inc.
174 (top): John Constable (1776–1837), "Hamstead Heath: Branch Hill Pond," 1828. Oil on canvas. V&A/Art Resource.
174 (bottom): The Illustrated London News.
176 (top): Eugene Delacroix, French, 1798–1863, "Lioon Hunt," 1860/61. Oil on canvas, 76.5 × 98.5 cm. Mr. And Mrs. Potter Palmer Collection. Copyright 1993 The Art Institute of Chicago, 1922.404.
176 (bottom): Joseph Mallord William Turner, English (1775–1851), "Slave Ship (Slavers throwing Overboard the Dead and Dying, Typhoon Comoin On)," 1840. Oil on canvas, 90.8 × 122.6 cm. (35 3/4 × 43 1/4 in.). Museum of Fine Arts, Boston. Henry Lillie Pierce Fund, 99.22. © 2003 Museum of Fine Arts, Boston.
177 AKG London.
181 (top): Getty Images, Inc.–Stone Allstock.
181 (bottom): Bildarchiv der Oesterreichischen Nationalbibliothek
185 Getty Images, Inc. – Stone Allstock.
188 Staatsbibliothek zu Berlin, Stiftung peruischer Kulturvesitz
189 AKG London, Ltd
191 Eugene Delacroix (1798 – 1863). Portrait of Frederic Chopin (1810–1860), 1838. Oil on canvas, 45.5 × 38 cm. Louvre, Dept des Peintures, France. © Photograph by Erich Lessing. Erich Lessing/Art Resource, NY.
194 Photograph of Clara & Robert Schumann, Musée d'Orsay, Paris. Reunion des Musées Nationaux/Art Resource, NY.
199 Staatliche Musseen zu Berlin, Stuftung Preussischer Kulturbesitz, Nationalgalerie.
203 Brown Brothers.
207 Corbis/Bettmann.
217 Getty Images, Inc.–Liaison
219 Getty Images, Inc.–Hulton Archive Photos
225 Getty Images Inc.–Hulton Archive Photos
228 Bildarchiv Oesterreichischen Nationalbibliothek.

CHAPTER 9

CO: Dan Nelken, Dan Nelken Studio, Inc.

234 Library of Congress

235 Arkadi Shaykhet, Bildarchiv Preubischer Kulturbesitz.

236 Man Ray, AKG London, Ltd.

238 Claude Monet (1840–1926), "The Cathedral of Rouen, Façade," circa 1892/94. Oil on canvas, 100.6 × 66 cm. Juliana Cheney Edwards Collection, Museum of Fine Arts, Boston/Archiv fur Kunst und Geschichte, Berlin.

239 Lauros – Giraudon; Art Resource, NY.

241 Picasso, Pablo. "Les Demoiselles d'Avignon". Paris (June – July 1907). Oil on canvas, 8′ × 7′8″ (243.9 ×233.7 cm). digital Image © The Museum of Modern Art / Licensed by SCALA/Art Resource, NY. Acquired through the Lillie P. Bliss Bequest. (333.1939). © 2004 Estate of Pablo Picasso/Artists Rights Society (ARS), New York/Pro Litteris, Zurich.

242 AKG London Ltd.

245 Oskar Kokoschka (1886–1980), "Die Windsbraut (The Tempest)," 1914. Oil on canvas, 181 × 220 cm. Basel, Kunstmuseum/Archiv fur Kunst und Geschichte, Berlin. © 2004 Artists Rights Society (ARS), New York/Pro Litteris, Zurich.

251 © Universal Edition

257 Joan Miro, "The Migratory Bird," from the Constellation series. Palma de Mallorca, May 26, 1941. Gouache and oil wash on paper, 18 1/8 × 15″ (46.1 × 38.1 cm). Private Collection. Pierre Matisse Gallery. © 2004 Successio Miro/Artists Rights Society (ARS), New York/ADAGP, Paris.

262 Bildarchiv Preussischer Kulturbesitz.

264 Courtesy of the Library of Congress.

267 Walter H. Scott.,

269 Copyright William P. Gottlieb. Library of congress: Ira and Lenore S. Gershwin Fund.

274 Copyright William Taylor/Arcaid © Disney Enterprises, Inc.

278 (left): Steve j. Sherman

278 (right): Eliot Khuner, Eliot Khuner Photography.

281 Steve J. Sherman

CHAPTER 10

CO: Mel Lindstrom, Photo Researchers, Inc.

287 Popperfoto

289 The New York Public Library for the Performing Arts/ Art Resource.

291 Corbis/Bettmann

293 Frank Driggs Collection/Archive Photos.

296 (top): Corbis/Bettmann.

296 (bottom): Corbis/Bettmann

298 Corbis/Bettmann

300 David Gahr

301 © Bettmann/Corbis

302 Jack Vartoogian.

CHAPTER 11

CO: Tony Garcia, Getty Images Inc.–Stone Allstock

308 (top): Stephen Collins Foster, 1826–1864. Watercolor by Walter L. White, cf from Ambrotype, Foster Hall Collection, Center for American Music, University of Pittsburgh. Source ID #120.

308 (bottom): Jim Caldwell, Houston Grand Opera.

311 (left): Corbis/Bettmann

311 (right): Corbis/Bettmann

313 Corbis/Bettmann

315 Getty Images Inc.–Hulton Archive Photos

316 Ken Heyman, Black Star

317 (top): Frank Driggs Collection.

317 (bottom): John Launois, Black Star

319 Michael Putland, Retna Ltd. USA

322 Joel Axelrad, Retna Ltd USA

323 UPI/Corbis/Bettmann

325 (top): Hollis, Retna Ltd. USA

325 (bottom): Ian McKell, Retna Ltd. USA

328 Patrick Ford, Retna Ltd. USA

INSERTS:

Plate 1 Richard Hamilton Smith; Corbis/Bettmann

Plate 2 Lynn Goldsmith; Corbis/Bettmann

Plate 3 Steve Vidler, eStock Photography, LLC.

Plate 4 The Pierpont Morgan Library/Art Resource, NY

Plate 5 Bronzino Agnolo (Agniolo di Cosimo) (1503–1572), "Maria de Medici", Painting, Renaissance, 16th Century. Oil on poplar wood. Kunsthistorisches Museum, Gemaeldegalerie, Vienna Austria. Art Resource.

Plate 6 Thomas – Photos, Thomas–Photos Oxford.

Plate 7 Reunion de Musees Nationaux / Art Resource, NY

Plate 8 "Court concert at Prince Bishop of Luettich at Seraing Palace". (with violoncello of Prince Bishop Cardinal Johann Theodor of Bavaria). Painting, 1753, by Paul Joseph Delcloche (1716–1759). Oil on canvas, 186×240.5 cm. Munich, Bayerisches Nationalmuseum. Photo: AKG London.

Plate 9 String Quartet. Color Engraving, 18th century, Austrian. Mozart Museum, Prague, Czech Republic. Giraudon/Art Resource, NY.

Plate 10 Painting, Baroque, 18th Century, Austrian. Mozart Museum, Prague, Czech Republic. Giraudon/Art Resource, NY

Plate 11 Stiftung Preussische Schloesser und Gaerten Berlin–Brandenburg, Schloss Charlottenburg.

Plate 12 Jospeh Mallord William Turner, English (1775–1851), "Slave Ship (Slavers Throwing Overboard the Dead and Dying, Typhoon Coming On)," 1840. Oil on Canvas, 90.8 × 122.6 cm. (35 3/4 × 48 1/4 in). Museum of Fine Arts, Boston. Henry Lillie Pierce Fund, 99.22. © 2003 Museum of Fine Arts, Boston.

Plate 13 Staatliche Musseen zu Berlin, Stiftung Preussischer Kulturbesitz, Nationalgalerie.

Plate 14 Oskar Kokoschka (1886–1980) "Die Windsbraut (The Tempest)," 1914. Oil on canvas, 181 × 220 cm. Basl Kunstmuseum/Archiv fur Kunst und Geschichte, Berlin. © 2004 Artists Rights Society (ARS), New York/Pro Litteris, Zurich.

Plate 15 William Taylor/Arcaid © Disney Enterprises Inc.

INDEX

12-bar blues form, 22, 290–291
32-bar AABA form, 23
  of Dixieland jazz, 293
ABA form, 22
Abbey Road (Beatles), 317
Absolute music, 178
Accompaniment, in Classic music,
  132–133
Acid jazz, 301–302
Acid rock, 325
Active listening, 3
Adagio, 13
Aerosmith, 324
African drumming, 58–61
African music, 58–61
  North African, 58
  sub-Saharan, 58–59
  texture, in, 50
After the Ball (Harris), 308
Aida (Verdi), 203
Alberti bass, in Classic music, 133
Alice in Wonderland (del Trediei), 277
Allegretto, 36
Allegro, 13
Allegro, 36
Allemande, 106
Alphorn, 52
Alto, 24
America, 4–5
An American in Paris (Gershwin), 268
American scene, in music, 263–264
Andante, 13, 36
Antithesis, in Renaissance
  music, 88–90
Appalachian Spring (Copland), 266
Aquinas, Thomas, *Pange Lingua*, 82
Arch form, 260
  in Classic music, 141
Aria, in opera, 102
  ABA form, 107
  Dido's Lament, *102–104*
  in late Baroque music, 107
Arias and Barcarolle (Bernstein), *270*
Arioso style of singing, 209
Armstrong, Louis, 292–295
  Hotter Than That, 293, *294–295*
Arnold, Eddy, 324
Arpeggio, 17
The Art Work of the Future
  (Wagner), 208
Atonality, in Twentieth-Century
  music, 236
Authentic cadence, 18, 20

Bach, Johann Sebastian, 111–119
Brandenburg Concertos, 115, *115–117*
  life of, 111–112
  music of, 112–119
  orchestral, 114–117
  organ music of, 112, 113–114
  Prelude and Fugue in E minor, *113–114*
  St. Matthew Passion (Bach), *117–119*
  vocal church music of, 117–119
Balance and proportion, in Classic music,
  132
Balanced phrases, in Classic music,
  132–133
Band music, in jazz, 288
Bar lines, 12
The Barber of Seville (Rossini), 198
Baritone, 24
Baroque era
  bass line in, 98
  basso continuo, 98
  cantata, 97
  chorale in, 98
  concerto, 97–98
  dance suite, 97–98
  dances, 106
    allemande, 106
    bouré, 106
    courante, 106
    gavotte, 106
    gigue, 106
    minuet, 106
    sarabande, 106
  early Baroque music. *See* Early Baroque
    music.
  in France, 106
  late Baroque music. *See* Late Baroque
    music, 98, 107–126
  life in, 95–97
  music in, 95–127
    characteristics of, 97–98
  opera, 97
  oratorio, 98
  Passion, 98
  sonata, 97–98
Bartók, Béla, 259–260
  arch form, 260
  Concerto for Orchestra, 259
  Fifth Movement from String Quartet
    No. 4, *259–260*
  Mikrokosmos, 259
  string quartets, 259
Basie, Count, 296
Bass clarinet, 28–29

Bass drum, 32
Bass, 24
Basso continuo, in Baroque music, 98
Bassoon, 28–29
Battle Symphony (Beethoven), 160
Beach Boys, 323
  California Girls, 323
  Fun, Fun, Fun, 323
  Surfer Girl, 323
  Surfin' U.S.A., 323
Beach, Amy, 264
  Gaelic Symphony, 264
Beat, 11, 14
Beatles, 316–319
  Abbey Road, 317
  It Won't Be Long, 317, *318*
  Please, Please Me, 317
  private period, 317
  public period, 317
  Rubber Sole, 317
  Sgt. Pepper's Lonely Hearts Club Band, 317
  Strawberry Fields Forever, 317, *319*
Bebop, 297–300
Bechet, Sidney, 293
Beck, Jeff, 324
Beethoven, Ludwig van, 157–171
  Battle Symphony, 160
  Eroica, 162
  Fidelio, *162*
  Fifth Symphony, 162–163
  First Movement from Symphony No. 5,
    165–167
  Haydn and, 159
  life of, 158–161
    heroic phase, 159–160
  La Malinconia (Melancholy), 159
  Missa Solemnis, 162
  music of, 161–171
    "fingerprints," 162
    contrast in, 160
    heroic phase, 159–160
  and patronage system, 157
  piano concertos, 160
  and Romanticism, 158
  Six Easy Variations on a Swiss Tune,
    163–164
  Third Movement from Piano Sonata in
    E Major, 167–170
Beiderbecke, Bix, 293
Berg, Alban, 246, 251–256
  Lulu, 251
  music of, 251–256
  Wozzeck, 251, *252–256*

339